The Second Worl

Counterfire

Series Editor: Neil Faulkner

Counterfire is a socialist organisation which campaigns against capitalism, war, and injustice. It organises nationally, locally, and through its website and print publications, operating as part of broader mass movements, for a society based on democracy, equality, and human need.

Counterfire stands in the revolutionary Marxist tradition, believing that radical change can come only through the mass action of ordinary people. To find out more, visit www.counterfire.org

This series aims to present radical perspectives on history, society, and current affairs to a general audience of trade unionists, students, and other activists. The best measure of its success will be the degree to which it inspires readers to be active in the struggle to change the world.

Also available:

A Marxist History of the World:
From Neanderthals to Neoliberals
Neil Faulkner

How a Century of War Changed the Lives of Women
Lindsey German

Stitched Up:
The Anti-Capitalist Book of Fashion
Tansy E. Hoskins

The Second World War

A Marxist History

Chris Bambery

PLUTO PRESS

First published 2014 by Pluto Press
345 Archway Road, London N6 5AA

www.plutobooks.com

Copyright © Chris Bambery 2014

The right of Chris Bambery to be identified as the author of this work has been asserted by him in accordance with the Copyright, Designs and Patents Act 1988.

British Library Cataloguing in Publication Data
A catalogue record for this book is available from the British Library

ISBN   978 0 7453 3302 1   Hardback
ISBN   978 0 7453 3301 4   Paperback
ISBN   978 1 8496 4921 6   PDF eBook
ISBN   978 1 8496 4922 3   Kindle eBook
ISBN   978 1 8496 4923 0   EPUB eBook

Library of Congress Cataloging in Publication Data applied for

This book is printed on paper suitable for recycling and made from fully managed and sustained forest sources. Logging, pulping and manufacturing processes are expected to conform to the environmental standards of the country of origin.

10   9   8   7   6   5   4   3   2   1

Typeset from disk by Stanford DTP Services, Northampton, England
Text design by Melanie Patrick

To
Sheila Atkinson, Auxiliary Territorial Service,
and Charles Bambery, Royal Navy:
They fought a war in which their enemy was fascism.

Contents

Acknowledgements	viii
Introduction	1
1 Competing Empires at a Time of Economic Crisis	5
2 The Allied Powers	12
3 The Axis Powers	35
4 The Countdown to War	61
5 The Early War	81
6 Russia: The Crucible of Victory	115
7 The End of the Third Reich	141
8 Resistance in Europe	169
9 Asia and the Pacific	193
10 The East is Red	214
11 The Post-War World	225
Conclusion	239
Timeline	249
Notes	256
Index	285

Acknowledgements

I would like to thank the following people for their help in the writing and editing of this book: Alex Anievas for his comments and corrections, the late and much missed Tom Behan, Ian Birchall for his comments, Sebastian Budgen for first suggesting I write it, Neil Faulkner for editing an earlier draft, Lindsey German for her encouragement, and Barbara Rampoli for her support. My comrades of the International Socialist Group (Scotland) deserve thanks for their support and vitality. Thanks to David Castle, my excellent editor, and everyone at Pluto Press.

Apologies to Carmela Ozzi and Malcolm and Leonardo Ozzi Bambery who have had to put up with me writing in the kitchen, listening to opera and preventing them playing games on the computer.

Whenever I have done meetings and lectures on the Second World War I have always recommended my three favourite books on the subject, so here goes. To understand what the British ruling class was fighting for and to grasp their ineffectiveness at waging war, read Evelyn Waugh's *Sword of Honour* trilogy. For the reality of Russia's war and of Stalingrad, Vasily Grossman's *Life and Fate*. And for the sheer scale of the Yugoslav partisan war, Milovan Djilas's memoir, *Wartime*.

Chris Bambery
November 2013

Introduction

The Second World War casts a long shadow. It dominates the various history channels on offer, along with the rise of the Nazis which preceded it. Popular films about the war still command vast audiences and are repeated endlessly on the small screen. Its ghost has also been present in the wars which have scarred our planet in recent years. The 'war against terror' following the attacks of 11 September 2001 was cast as a continuance of democracy's struggle against a new totalitarian threat which echoed that of the Nazis, while opponents of the wars in Iraq and Afghanistan were regularly portrayed as 'appeasers'. As the US radio talk-show host and Fox News Channel political analyst, Tammy Bruce, argued in September 2002:

> Now, in 2002, it is our responsibility to stop Saddam Hussein and yet the whining grandchildren of Chamberlain, now strewn throughout Europe and the world, have felt compelled to demand we not attack Iraq ... no one, especially in Europe, has the moral standing to tell us what to do when faced with war and evil. They lost that right when they accepted hundreds of thousands of American deaths to save their soil from the monsters they refused to stop early on.[1]

Iraq in 2003 stood mid-table in the league of global power, with an economy wrecked by a decade of international sanctions. In comparison, when the Second World War began, Germany was the primary military power in the world. Its economy was the second biggest. Attempts to compare Saddam Hussein with Hitler simply demean the latter's crimes, above all the Holocaust. Saddam was a brutal mass murderer but his crimes do not stand comparison with Hitler's.[2]

At the time of the first Gulf War in 1990–91 we were already being told that Saddam Hussein was another Hitler, and that anything short of military force, for example economic sanctions, would be 'giving way' to dictators. The *Sun* pilloried 'spineless appeasers' who believe 'a combination of sanctions and sweet reason will be enough', while the *Daily Express* ridiculed 'the appeasers and the give-sanctions-a-chance-brigade' (both from 16 January 1991). The same arguments were deployed again in the build up to the attacks by NATO on Serbia in 1995 and 1999.[3]

This attempt to paint critics of the US's and UK's wars as spiritual heirs of the British prime minister, Neville Chamberlain, who so desperately tried to buy off Hitler in order to avert war, dates back at least to 1982 when Britain went to war with Argentina over the Falkland Islands, or Malvinas. When the House of Commons debated the decision to go to war the leader of the opposition Labour Party was Michael Foot. Four decades earlier Foot had railed against appeasement and contributed to *The Guilty Men*, a bestselling pamphlet which appeared in the summer of 1940, blaming Chamberlain and his supporters for the expected German invasion. Describing himself as an 'inveterate peacemaker' Foot urged the government 'to prove by deeds' that the Falklands had not been betrayed. After he sat down the Tory MP Edward du Cann responded, 'The leader of the opposition spoke for us all. He did the nation a service.'[4]

Du Cann was consciously echoing the cry of Leo Amery in September 1939. As Chamberlain prevaricated over declaring war on Hitler, despite Germany's invasion of Poland, the acting Labour leader, Arthur Greenwood, rose to reply. Greenwood began by saying he would speak for the Labour Party; Amery, a right-wing Tory and champion of imperialism, shouted out 'Speak for England!' This is held up as one of those great Westminster moments.[5]

When US and British political leaders allege today that anti-war leftists and liberals are the heirs to those who curried favour with Hitler, they ignore the simple fact that the appeasers of the 1930s were largely on the right and included virtually the entire British Conservative Party, senior members of the royal family, and the pro-Tory press. These were not rogue elements in British ruling circles. They represented majority opinion. The near revolutionary events which engulfed France in 1934–36, and the full-scale revolution at the commencement of the Spanish Civil War, had reinforced their view that Communism was the main enemy. In London, Berlin, Paris, Moscow, Washington and Tokyo there were real fears before and during the war that social conflict could break through to challenge the ruling order.

In his history of the twentieth century, Eric Hobsbawm argues that the Second World War in the west can be best understood,

> not through the contest of states, but as an international ideological civil war ... And, as it turned out, the crucial lines in this civil war were not drawn between capitalism and communist social revolution, but between ideological families ... between what the 19th century would have called 'progress' and 'reaction' – only that these terms were no longer quite apposite.[6]

From the start it was clear to millions of people that this was not simply a war against Nazism but a war in which their own ruling classes were divided. Nowhere was this truer than in France. The election in May 1936 of a Popular Front government under the Socialist Léon Blum, with communist support, and the subsequent strike wave with its factory occupations, terrified the French ruling class. The fall of France in May and June 1940 can only be understood against this background.

Hobsbawm is half right. There was a huge popular struggle against fascism which developed across much of Europe in the final three years of the war, and because the ruling classes in the occupied countries in large part collaborated with the Nazis this took on aspects of a civil war. But his argument overlooks the fact that the Second World War was also a continuation of the 1914–18 conflict – a struggle to re-divide the world between the world's great powers. This was the dominant feature of the war because it was why the rulers of the warring states were conducting it.

This book seeks to argue that the Second World War was indeed an imperialist war, while acknowledging that the issues involved are more complex. Across the globe vast numbers of people wanted to resist fascism, and whatever their suspicions of their own ruling classes they were prepared to follow their lead in the fight against Hitler. Both my parents volunteered to serve in Britain's armed forces. That left its mark. My mother caught rheumatic fever and was left permanently ill, which resulted in an early death. My father, who had served in the navy, became deaf as a result of hours and days spent using radar and submarine detection equipment. In neither case was the damage equal to that visited on millions of people, who saw their whole family wiped out, experienced the atomic bomb or had their home destroyed. Yet despite the harm inflicted on them, both my parents regarded the Second World War as a necessary war, if not a 'good war' – one that needed to be fought in order to stop Hitler and the Nazis. Millions who took part regarded it as a fight that had to be waged. The newsreels from Belsen and the death camps following Germany's surrender only confirmed it.

How the 1939–45 war is seen contrasts with attitudes towards the First World War, which is now widely viewed as an indiscriminate slaughter which settled little. Both my grandfathers took part in that war. One simply never spoke about what he had experienced. The other wished no one in his family would have to go through such things again.

While the Second World War is seen as a necessary war, fought to stop fascism, there are nevertheless evident contradictions. My father visited much of the globe during his naval service. When he described his experiences in East Africa during the liquidation of Italian colonial rule – or later, in India and Sri Lanka during the closing stages of the war against Japan – he was clearly aware that Britain was not fighting for democracy but to maintain its Empire, based on a vicious racism towards its subject peoples. He recalled that Winston Churchill had unleashed troops on Welsh miners at Tonypandy in 1910 and had been viciously anti-union during the 1926 general strike. Churchill was, he told me, 'a bastard', adding, 'but we needed a bastard to fight Hitler'.

In attempting to understand the greatest conflict in human history thus far, we are entering an ideological battlefield. That battle began even before Hitler's troops crossed into Poland, ushering in a European war which would go global within three years. The ideological war has continued to rage, with ebbs and flows, ever since.

This book offers a Marxist explanation of why the Second World War happened, how it was fought, and what its outcome was. It starts by explaining why I believe it was a war fought primarily for global hegemony, but also why it differed from its 1914–18 predecessor, because popular opposition to fascism drove ordinary people to fight, and later to resist. It then examines each of the powers involved, starting with the Allied camp. In particular, it argues the Allies were a band of warring brothers. This then allows us to examine the countdown to war and how dominant the policy of appeasing Hitler was within Western ruling circles.

From the moment the Third Reich was at war it was moving towards genocide, the beginnings of which were apparent in 1939 with the conquest of Poland. In looking at the early war we also see why class division undermined France's ability to fight Hitler, and how Britain survived the collapse of its ally but was in no position to defeat Germany alone.

Hitler's decision to invade Russia seemed to have secured the key victory he desired in late 1941, but Stalin's regime survived and in 1942–43 the Russians would decisively turn the tables on the Third Reich. The war in Russia would be key to the defeat of Hitler. The events contributing to that defeat are charted in the next chapter, which also examines the return of British forces to Europe alongside the Americans. This was an alliance in which American power and wealth would see it establish a clear dominance. Meanwhile, as Germany faced defeat, the Nazis carried out the greatest crime in human history, the Holocaust.

The German occupation of much of Europe bred a resistance that, I will argue, had a revolutionary dynamic, but one which was deflected because the left, and in the main the Communist Parties, helped contain it.

We then turn to the spread of the war into the Pacific and the failure of Japan to capitalise on its initial successes, while the Americans were able to fight a war on two fronts, and eventually secure victory in the Pacific. Less well known is the popular resistance which developed to Japanese imperialism and to the possibility of a return to colonial rule. It was during the war that the Communists would begin their march to power in China.

Despite Churchill's determination to protect and maintain the British Empire, it was a task beyond him. As the book moves towards a conclusion we look at the reasons for the passing of Empire. Finally, we consider how the war shaped today's world, and how peace did not, tragically, bring an end to war and occupation.

CHAPTER ONE

Competing Empires at a Time of Economic Crisis

The Great Depression Fuels Great Power Rivalries

The Second World War might well have happened without Adolf Hitler coming to power. But it would have been a much more limited conflict, and a more conventional one.

In 1929 a sudden and sharp collapse on the New York stock exchange marked the start of the greatest economic crisis in the history of capitalism thus far. The Great Depression bred economic collapse, social polarisation and political instability including war. All within short order. It also heralded a retreat from the old economic liberalism, associated in particular with the British policy of free trade. Politicians moved to protectionism across the globe, which led to a collapse in world trade but also heightened competition over the control of markets and raw materials, competition which quickly took a military shape.

The First World War had ended with a re-partitioning of the world in which Britain and France gained most territory. While the British Empire was bigger than ever, the British ruling class was painfully aware that it had been ousted as the world's financial power by the US. At its height in the mid nineteenth century, Britain had adopted a policy of free trade because that benefited its exports when it was the pre-eminent industrial power. Its rivals, the US and Germany, did not follow suit. Rather, they employed protective measures to defend their domestic markets and emerging industries. Other states would follow their lead.

After 1918 Britain had attempted to maintain sterling as the chief international trading currency by valuing it against gold. But it could maintain neither the gold standard nor free trade as the general rule across the capitalist system. Following the immediate post-war recession at the beginning of the 1920s, the second half of the decade did see a relative stabilisation, before Europe was thrust into depression in 1929. The recovery of the mid 1920s was based on countries importing US goods and borrowing US money. The US had tariffs to prevent those countries to which it sold goods balancing their account by exporting goods to America. Instead they were forced to take out US loans to cover the shortfall. The victors in the First World War had taken out American loans to cover the debts they had incurred, while the losers had taken them to help pay off reparations imposed on them by the post-war treaties agreed at Versailles. The Wall Street Crash in 1929 ended this financial roundabout and the banking crisis spread to Europe heralding an economic slump.

Between 1929 and 1932 the volume of world trade fell by one quarter. Five years later, the 1929 peak had still not been recovered.[1] Much of the decline stemmed from the collapse of incomes, but a substantial portion was a consequence of the rush to trade protection. When the British government defaulted on loan repayments to America, Washington retaliated by enforcing trade restrictions on British imports.

Meanwhile the expansion of US agriculture had led to over-production and a high level of indebtedness from farmers who had borrowed to expand. Pressure had been building from US agriculture for import restrictions even prior to the Wall Street Crash. Herbert Hoover, the Republican candidate, won the 1928 presidential election promising agricultural protection. Subsequently in June 1930, the US erected tariffs on over 20,000 imported goods. Over the next three years, average US tariffs would rise to 54 per cent, compared with 39 per cent in 1928. In short order Britain, France and then Germany introduced similar tariffs over the next two years.

Having erected a complex barrier of import controls to protect its home market, Washington now demanded that the UK and other European countries repay their debts in dollars (which could only be earned by exporting to the US). In October 1932 Britain, Canada, Australia and other dominions created a system whereby British tariffs were lowered for all those trading in pounds. The new Sterling Bloc accounted for a third of world trade. By attempting to stop foreign imports into the new bloc, London was throwing down a gauntlet to its rivals. If they wanted a greater market share they would have to re-order the world.

The US and France followed Britain in attempting to create their own protected trade areas, together with a degree of state direction of the economy. Germany, Japan and Italy did not control overseas territories and looked to military expansion to secure markets and raw materials. For the German economy this global shift to protectionism was a catastrophe. Britain, France, the US and the USSR all had ample supplies of raw materials within their economic zones. Germany did not. Nearly half of Britain's trade was with its dominions and colonies and a third of French exports went to its colonies; Germany had none.

Germany's economic revival had been based on exports, but now they were excluded from key markets, and key raw materials had to be bought with dollars, sterling or francs. In terms of foreign trade Germany had been in third place behind the US and UK in 1928, when its foreign trade was worth $58 billion. By 1935 it was worth $20.8 billion. Financially it was in a weak position holding just 1 per cent of the global gold and financial reserves in 1938, compared to the US holding of 54 per cent and the British and French holdings of 11 per cent each.[2] German governments before Hitler came to power had already resorted to export subsidies and trading via barter or using German Marks, which could only be redeemed in Germany. Before Hitler took power, sections of Germany's ruling circles began to argue that its export problems and lack of raw materials could only be solved by domination of Eastern and South Eastern Europe. They found ready allies in the military command.

Hjalmar Schacht had resigned as president of the Reichsbank in protest at Germany continuing to pay war reparations as determined by the Treaty of Versailles. He went further, arguing that a German trade zone could encompass not just Central and Eastern Europe, but the Middle East, Latin America and the Far East. Although he never joined the Nazi Party, Schacht made the acquaintance of Hitler and facilitated contacts for him amongst bankers in 1932. On 28 November that year, *Time* magazine reported a dinner at the steel tycoon Fritz Thyssen's house:

> At Herr Thyssen's residence ... Leader Hitler and Oberst Göring ate dinner ... Germans soon noticed the surprising fact that several news agencies of Biggest Business, such as 'Deutsche Allgemeine Zeitung' and 'Rheinisch-Westfälische' had abruptly switched from hostility to support of Adolf Hitler.

Noting that these newspapers were closely connected to big business circles, *Time* added: 'For the first time in his blatant, meteoric career Adolf Hitler was "getting warm". Stocks on the Berlin exchange, which eased when the von Papen Cabinet resigned, firmed again and began to rise.'[3]

By January 1933 when Hitler took power, there were 6 million unemployed in Germany. Hitler's initial economic programme was similar to US President Franklin D. Roosevelt's New Deal which was being implemented at around the same time. Public spending on the motorways and railways (both of military importance) increased, subsidies were given to housing, firms were forced into cartels, industry was offered cheap loans and tax exemption while wages were pegged at the same level as at the bottom of the slump. Industrial production rose from 53.8 per cent of the 1929 figure to 79.8 per cent in 1934.[4] Yet unemployment remained at three times the 1929 figure and inflation began to mount.

The major capitalist corporations remained largely intact but they were increasingly subordinated to an arms drive, something they themselves supported. Hitler had at first, in 1933–34, introduced relatively mild measures, some inherited from his predecessors, aimed at creating work. From 1935 onwards these gave way to an arms economy, the 'preparedness economy'. By 1936 Germany's economic output equalled the 1929 figure. Three years later it had grown by a further 30 per cent. Such expansion rested on the cuts in labour costs imposed even before Hitler took power.

In 1938–39 the German economy fell into a grave economic crisis. A huge budgetary deficit existed – public expenditure was 55 million Reichsmarks in 1938–39, but tax and custom receipts were only 18 million. Much of the Third Reich's economic policy was based on 'autarky' – economic self-sufficiency. The Nazis limited exports in order to curb earlier trade deficits. But there was a limit to how far they could go down that road. Rearmament fuelled the need to import raw materials, but the only way Germany could find the necessary materials in a world dominated by protectionism was by physically expanding the borders of the Third Reich. As the British Marxist historian, Tim Mason, argues: 'The only "solution" open to this regime of structural tensions and crises produced by dictatorship and rearmament was more dictatorship and more rearmament, then expansion, then war and terror, then plunder and enslavement.'[5]

Similar pressures were affecting Britain, the United States and Japan. All were locked into a system of trade protection in which the only solution to their economic problems was a re-partition of the world. Russia was a partial exception given its vast territory and raw materials, but even Stalin could not disengage the Russian economy from the competition between states.

State control reached its zenith in the one country that had experienced a successful working-class revolution – Russia. The old ruling class had been destroyed, but amid an economic blockade, foreign invasion and civil war, workers' democracy had been eroded because the working class had been decimated. Instead the state bureaucrats took charge of the economy. They associated with Stalin, the general secretary of the Communist Party, which they joined to benefit their career. Stalin's focus was not on international revolution but on industrialisation. Having removed his opponents from the leadership of both the state and the Communist Party in 1928–29, he presided over a brutal policy of 'top-down', state-led industrialisation at the expense of the working class and peasantry.

In Japan one faction of the ruling class, associated with the army command, regarded China as its natural market and supplier of materials. In the wake of the Wall Street Crash they embarked on the attempted colonisation of Manchuria. But that brought them into conflict with Washington, which was determined to create an 'open door' to China for US goods. A minority faction in the Japanese elite, including the naval command, wanted to expand southwards to gain control of oil (the US controlled Japanese supplies), rubber and other materials from the colonial powers (Britain, France and Holland), and to take the Philippines, which were effectively under US control.

The US looked not just to the Pacific region. It had major investments in Europe and already eyed control of Middle Eastern oil. Germany and Japan would, in the course of the late 1930s, be perceived by Washington as the immediate dangers, but the dismantling of the British sterling bloc and Empire were also key strategic goals.

The Great Depression would only end with the war, as the great powers put the need to arm before the need to make profits in the short term. Both political and corporate leaders understood, increasingly, that there was a battle for survival going on which centred on the ability of each state to control a slice of the global economy, to guarantee the supply of raw materials and to weaken the ability of rival powers to do the same.

In this light, we can see the Second World War as a conflict between rival imperialisms; a conflict as much between the Allies as between them and the Axis. The exiled Russian revolutionary Leon Trotsky understood this when in 1934 he wrote:

> US capitalism is up against the same problems that pushed Germany in 1914 on the path of war. The world is divided? It must be re-divided. For Germany

it was a question of 'organising Europe'. The United States must 'organise' the world. History is bringing humanity face to face with the volcanic eruption of American imperialism.[6]

The conflict would see America finally eclipse Britain as the major imperial power and would lay the basis for the economic and political arrangements that dominated the following half century. Cordell Hull, Roosevelt's secretary of state, explained in a public address in July 1942 that:

> Leadership toward a new system of international relationships in trade and other economic affairs will devolve very largely upon the United States because of our great economic strength. We should assume this leadership, and the responsibility that goes with it, primarily for reasons of pure national self-interest.[7]

Why the Second World War Was Different

The Second World War was a product of an economic recession which bred heightened imperialist tensions. But Hitler's advent to power ensured it was a war quite different from its predecessor two decades before – it became a racial, genocidal war, which threatened the rights and liberties of the working classes and much of the peasantry.

The two decades between 11 November 1918 and the declaration of war on Germany by Britain and France on 3 September 1939 are often described as a breathing space. In relation to Europe a better description might be a period of civil war, while in Asia and Africa it was a time of nationalist rebellion and a renewed imperialist drive.

The First World War had dribbled away into a series of vicious border wars. Unofficial German forces fought Poland and the Baltic states; clashes erupted between irregular Italian forces and the new state of Yugoslavia; Greece was encouraged by the Lloyd George government in London (which wanted to control the Dardanelles) into a disastrous invasion of Turkey which would end with Turkish victory and the withdrawal of British forces from Istanbul, as well as the mass expulsion of Greeks from Turkey and Turks from Greece. France and Britain urged Poland into attacking Russia (the counter-attack carried the Red Army to the gates of Warsaw before it was contained). Fascism triumphed in Italy in 1922 and Central and Eastern Europe was littered with nationalist and anti-Semitic dictatorships. Shortly after the October Revolution in Russia the attempt by the working class to seize power in neighbouring Finland was defeated, and followed by terrible massacres.

The 1930s began with fascism winning control in Germany. In 1934 a right-wing government defeated the working class of Vienna. It seemed that fascism was set to win in France at the beginning of the same year. A fascist assault on the National Assembly was defeated by a general strike, and the French fascist movement floundered. The election of a Popular Front government two years later, with an accompanying wave of factory occupations, meant that a key section of the ruling class began to see German occupation as a price worth paying if it delivered them from the apparent threat of Communist revolution.

The year 1936 also saw a military uprising in Spain against a freshly elected Popular Front government. Workers' uprisings defeated the rebels in Madrid, Barcelona, Bilbao and other cities. A three-year civil war followed, with German and Italian military intervention on the side of General Franco, the rebel military leader, and Stalin providing arms and expertise to the republican government. The Spanish Civil War pitted left against right and haunted the years in the immediate build up to the Second World War, with politicians in European capitals fearing the war might escalate beyond their control. Franco's eventual victory emboldened the fascist powers and their supporters elsewhere.

As the great powers moved towards a world war aimed at re-structuring the global order, millions of people wanted to resist fascism by whatever means. The victory of Hitler in Germany – a country which was home to both the largest Social Democratic party and the largest trade union movement in the world, together with the largest Communist Party outside Russia – was a huge shock to the working-class movement globally. There was a widespread feeling that this could not be allowed to happen again. In 1934 workers took up arms in Asturias in northern Spain and in Vienna in Austria, against right-wing governments which seemed to be the precursors of full-scale fascism. Both went down to defeat, but the slogan 'Better to Fight in Vienna than Die in Berlin' carried a powerful echo.

The left could only lick its wounds while facing up to the challenge of defining and explaining the new vitriolic enemy it faced: fascism.

After Stalin gained control of Russia in 1928–29, the international Communist movement adopted a characterisation of the Nazis as simply tools of finance capital. Later this position was used to justify a policy of seeking alliances with 'progressive' capitalists. More recently it has become common in academic writing to take this formulation as exhausting the Marxist analysis of Hitler's and Mussolini's movements. Having duly demolished this crude argument, it then becomes possible to dismiss anything Marxists have to say about fascism. But the Nazis were never some tool of capitalism. Marxist writers such as Trotsky, Antonio Gramsci and many others saw fascism as being different from other forms of capitalist reaction because it created a mass movement, which meant it was not simply controlled by the ruling class. If the latter decided they would support the rise of Hitler or Mussolini they had to pay a price, and the fascist leaders themselves had to take into account the mass support they'd brought to life, even when in power they no longer had much need for it.

Hitler was brought to power in the world's second largest industrial state by the German ruling class. They initially regarded him with suspicion. Big business funding did not start flowing towards the Nazis until the close of 1932. It required an immense social and economic crisis and real fear among the ruling classes to drive them into viewing fascism as a source of salvation. The ruling class may have disliked political power being exercised by a former house painter, but they discovered they shared certain aims with Hitler. Because of that they were prepared to accept his anti-Semitism and racism. German capitalism stood by the Führer right up until his suicide in the burning ruins of Berlin.

Many, at the time and subsequently, have pictured Hitler as simply pursuing conventional German strategic concerns, gaining control of Central and Eastern Europe. That was part of the story, but for Hitler this was only a stepping stone on the way to European and then global dominance, the destruction of the Soviet Union and world Jewry, the enslavement of 'lesser breeds', and out of all this the creation of a new German warrior race. Hitler was clear about this in 1941:

> The struggle for hegemony in the world will be decided for Europe by possession of the Russian space. Any idea of world politics is ridiculous [for Germany] as long as it does not dominate the continent ... If we are masters of Europe, then we shall have the dominant position in the world.[8]

Earlier, in the winter of 1940, Hitler had explained to his generals:

> Britain's hopes lie in Russia and the United States. If Russia drops out of the picture, America, too, is lost for Britain, because the elimination of Russia would greatly increase Japan's power in the Far East. Decision: Russia's destruction must be made a part of this struggle – the sooner Russia is crushed the better.[9]

The Third Reich was engaged in an imperialist war – an imperialist war that unleashed a horror which will, one can only hope, remain unsurpassed.

CHAPTER TWO

The Allied Powers

Britain: The Lion in Winter

In examining each of the major combatant states in the Second World War, Britain must be our starting point simply because it had the most to lose and the least to gain from any new re-division of the world.

Since the end of the First World War there had been an acute awareness of Britain's weakness. In December 1938 the cabinet discussed the desperate need to avoid a three-front war with Germany, Italy and Japan. Foreign secretary Halifax concluded, 'We ought to make every possible effort to get on good terms with Germany.'[1] Britain's prime concern was to maintain its position as a world power. At the beginning of the 1930s the First Sea Lord, Admiral Chatfield, stated: 'We have got most of the world already, or the best parts of it, and we only want to keep what we have got and prevent others taking it away from us.'[2]

Yet Britain had long since ceased to be the 'workshop of the world', the position it had held in the nineteenth century. In 1880 Britain accounted for 23 per cent of the world's manufacturing output, double the US's share and three times more than Germany. By 1900 it had been overtaken by the US. By 1913 the US share of world manufacturing was 32 per cent, Germany's 13 per cent and the UK's 12 per cent.[3] Between 1860 and 1914 some 60 per cent of world trade was invoiced and settled in sterling. But its dominance was slipping.[4] There was a growing realisation that Britain was being squeezed out of its position as the number one world power by its rival across the Atlantic. This led many on both sides of the ocean to believe war between the two powers was inevitable. Despite mutual hostility, however, both would ultimately view Germany as the greater menace.

Writing after the First World War, when he was head of the Red Army, Leon Trotsky described Britain's traditional policy thus:

> What is the military doctrine of Britain? ... the recognition of the urgent need for naval hegemony; a negative attitude towards a regular land army and towards military conscription; or, still more precisely, the recognition of Britain's need to possess a fleet stronger than the combined fleets of any two other countries and, flowing from this, Britain's being enabled to maintain a small army on a volunteer basis. Combined with this was the maintenance of such an order in Europe as would not allow a single land power to obtain a decisive preponderance on the continent.[5]

Britain's decision in 1914 to commit massive land forces in continental Europe marked a break with this policy. France alone was not capable of defeating Germany in a land war. Britain was forced to raise a conscript army to fight initially on the Western Front, and then against Turkey; by the end of the war it had armies in Italy, the Balkans, and the Middle East, and was intervening against the revolutionary new order in Russia. Britain's naval forces were so stretched that it had to rely on its Japanese ally to capture German possessions in the Far East and eventually asked that Japanese ships be used to patrol the Mediterranean.

The First World War saw Britain's position as the world's largest creditor reversed, so it ended the conflict as the world's largest debtor (the US, pre-war Britain's largest debtor, became Britain's largest creditor). The City of London lost its place as the capital of capital and the pound its position as the world's currency. Britain provided loans and munitions to its allies, France, Russia, Italy and the smaller powers, but in turn had to rely on American loans and munitions.

In order to contain and finally defeat the German forces on the Western Front, Britain and France would require American ground troops. On the seas, by 1918 the US navy was comparable in strength to the combined fleets of France, Italy and Japan. It was planning to build a force greater than the Royal Navy. Lloyd George's government accepted this was an arms race Britain could not win. At the Washington Naval Conference of 1921–22 the US forced acceptance of the Treaty of Washington. As the American historian, James Levy, points out:

> The major naval powers – Britain, the United States, Japan, France, and Italy... agreed to a ten-year building 'holiday' (in which no battleships would be laid down) ... Great Britain and the United States would have parity in battleship tonnage, Japan 60 per cent of that figure, France and Italy proportionately less. The treaty prevented an arms race, but at a major cost to the United Kingdom: Britannia now had to share the waves, not rule them.[6]

In accepting this, the British alliance with Japan fractured because Tokyo did not want to accept such a limitation.

The peace treaties which followed the First World War expanded the British Empire to its furthest limits, with gains in the Middle East and Africa. But the pink on the map of the world marking Britain's imperial possessions masked the fact that Britain was fading economically; and that in colonies like Ireland, India, Iraq and Egypt it faced a rising tide of national liberation movements. British governments and military chiefs knew that they could not fight a war simultaneously in Europe and Asia – something that began to look more and more likely by the 1930s.

Appeasement Flows From Weakness

The divisions within the British ruling class that would become apparent in the late 1930s had their roots in the question of how Britain was to maintain its global position. One faction, including future prime ministers Stanley Baldwin and Neville Chamberlain, wanted to consolidate abroad and concentrate on reviving the British economy by cutting wages and public spending. The other grouping, represented ultimately by Winston Churchill, wanted an aggressive imperial policy.

In 1922 Baldwin, Chamberlain and their Tory allies organised a backbench rebellion, pushing through a vote among Conservative MPs to break from the wartime coalition government led by the Liberal, Lloyd George. At the subsequent election the Tories took office free from any coalition partners.[7] Baldwin and his supporters would dominate the inter-war Tory Party. In terms of the Empire they were prepared to make some concessions to nationalist opponents if it preserved British rule. Baldwin's 'softness' towards nationalist demands in Egypt and then India estranged Tory die-hards, who had initially supported him when he became party leader in 1923.

There were also divisions over what attitude to take towards the growing power of America. Wall Street had replaced the City of London as the leading lender of capital — although Britain's capital exports regained their lead by the mid 1920s (by 1930 they were 43.8 per cent of the global total compared to the US's 35.3 per cent[8]). But this could not mask the fact that the US was replacing Britain as the world's leading financial and industrial nation. Britain lagged behind in the new dynamic industries of car manufacturing, electricity, chemicals and oil. By the 1930s its share of world manufacturing was well below Germany's and a third of America's. Britain was attempting to control a quarter of the world with just 10 per cent of global manufacturing. The country was wracked by high unemployment throughout the 1920s, with the jobless total leaping from 2 per cent to 18 per cent between 1920 and 1921 and never falling below 10 per cent for the rest of the decade. Its economic plight flowed from low levels of investment — a historical problem with British capitalism from the end of the nineteenth century until today. This meant productivity was lower than its rivals. One way Britain tried to offset that was through increasing reliance on its relative financial power — the City of London was still a key global player alongside Wall Street, and Britain remained the biggest global investor, in the United States itself for instance.

Britain was also dominated by clashes between labour and capital, culminating in the 1926 general strike, as Baldwin's Tory government and employers tried to offset the high exchange rate of sterling and low productivity by forcing down wages. In 1929 a Labour government headed by Ramsay Macdonald was elected; by the summer of 1931 it was falling apart as the Great Depression unfolded. Unemployment had reached 21 per cent (it was 25 per cent in the US and 34 per cent in Germany). Industrial production fell by 20 per cent from June to December 1931. The Bank of England had debts that were £250 million greater than its assets. Because sterling was exchangeable for gold there was a rush to exchange it. On 31 July 1931 the budget deficit for the year hit £120 million, nearly double its 1928 level. The government required US loans to meet its spending commitments and to obtain these it was required to implement austerity measures.

MacDonald and his supporters presented a package of cuts, including a reduction in unemployment benefit. They had a narrow majority in cabinet but the minority threatened resignation. The government collapsed. MacDonald broke with the Labour Party to form a coalition National Government with Baldwin's Tories and the Liberals, in order to enforce the cuts. Neville Chamberlain became Chancellor of the Exchequer while Baldwin held the real power in the government as Lord President.[9] Despite a $200 million loan from JP Morgan in New York, and a similar amount from the French national bank, sterling could not continue to be exchangeable for gold. On 21 September that ended, and sterling was devalued by 30 per cent.

The devaluation affected all those who used sterling as the means of international trade as well as those who held British pounds. Treasury undersecretary Sir Frederick Phillips admitted: 'No country ever administered a more severe shock to international trade than we did when we both 1) depreciated the £; 2) almost simultaneously turned from free trade to protection.'[10]

Meanwhile the US had erected a complex barrier of import controls to protect its home market while at the same time demanding that the UK and other European countries repay their debts in dollars (which could only be earned by exporting to the US). Britain responded. Between 1932 and 1935, 17 trade agreements were created, including ones with the Scandinavian countries and Argentina, creating a sterling trade bloc within which there was free trade. Between 1932 and 1935 British exports to the Empire and the Dominions increased from one third to two fifths of its total exports. Imperial imports into Britain increased even more dramatically.[11]

When in 1933 Britain failed to meet its full scheduled debt repayment to the US, Congress declared this a default and blocked any further credits. Washington acted to exclude Britain from ownership of any US or Latin American oilfields and cast greedy eyes at British-controlled Middle Eastern fields. Eventually the two governments agreed a deal whereby the Americans were allowed access to a quarter of the oilfields in Iraq and Turkey, but there was no agreement on Iran. The US controlled half of Kuwaiti oil and was increasingly dominant in Saudi Arabia.

At home the National Government cut spending by £70 million and raised taxes by £75 million. Even the champions of appeasing Hitler and Mussolini realised, however, that Britain needed to wield enough military might to force the dictators to negotiate, and that Britain's military budget in the early 1930s lagged behind Germany's. As a proportion of national wealth, defence expenditure rose from 3 per cent in the early 1930s to 18 per cent in 1939. This increase took place while Britain also had to cope with the highest per capita debt in the world. Rearmament required higher taxes, and turning over industrial capacity to arms manufacturing reduced exports, leading to a growing balance of payments deficit.[12]

Britain now had to pay up front for any American orders. It had depended on US imports to fight the First World War and its need would be greater in any such future conflict. Its financial reserves simply could not meet the costs of a lengthy war. In April 1939 the British Treasury warned, 'If we were under the impression that we were as well able as in 1914 to conduct a long war we were burying our heads in the sand.' Three months later they added, 'Unless, when the time comes, the United States are prepared either to lend or to give us money as required, the prospects for a long war are exceedingly grim.'[13] By February 1940 the Treasury prophesied that Britain's resources might just last for two or three years with care.[14] Britain simply could not plan on fighting a war both in Europe and the Far East.

Back in 1925 the Chancellor of the Exchequer, Winston Churchill, had assured the cabinet, 'I do not believe Japan has any idea of attacking the British Empire, or that there is any danger of her doing so for at least a generation to come.'[15] Six years later Japan seized Manchuria and began its expansion into China. In 1932 the Chiefs of Staff told the Committee of Imperial Defence that not only were the Far East colonies vulnerable, so too were 'the coastline of India and the Dominions and our vast trade and shipping'.[16]

By the late 1930s, the British ruling class knew they were trapped between the devil and the deep blue sea – Hitler and Roosevelt. R.A.B. (Rab) Butler, a junior foreign minister and leading appeaser, wrote a month before war broke out, 'In my political life I have always been convinced that we can no more count on America than Brazil.'[17]

This goes some way to explaining the depths of the commitment to appeasement among the Tories in the late 1930s. Neville Chamberlain noted of his predecessor as prime minister, Stanley Baldwin, that, 'SB says he loathes the Americans so much he hates meeting them.'[18] Chamberlain himself nursed a deep dislike of the US and of President Roosevelt in particular.

Following Japan's attack in Manchuria in September 1931, the US had proposed a joint US-British refusal to recognise the puppet government Japan had installed there. London refused. Chamberlain began pressing for rejection of attempts to develop closer links with Washington, arguing for renewing the alliance with Japan. It was argued that Britain had made concession after concession in order to win Washington's friendship to no avail, with Chamberlain pointing to Lloyd George's acceptance of negotiations over Irish independence in 1921 and the ending of the treaty of friendship with Japan a year later.[19]

Later, in January 1940, Chamberlain wrote to his sister, 'Heaven knows I don't want the Americans to fight for us; we should have to pay too dearly for that if they have any right to be in on the peace terms.'[20]

Domestic Friends of Fascism

The idea that the British state was fighting fascism during the Second World War ignores the warm relationship that existed between the fascist dictators and sections of the British ruling class, dating back to October 1922 when Benito Mussolini and his Blackshirts came to power in Italy. In June 1924 the *Daily Mail* hailed Mussolini as 'the Saviour of Italy' and declared, 'We in England have confidence in Signor Mussolini; so have the Italians.'[21] The paper's owner, Lord Rothermere, journeyed to Italy to meet Mussolini that summer, proclaiming in the *Mail* that, 'In saving Italy he stopped the inroads of Bolshevism which would have left Europe in ruins ... in my judgement he saved the whole Western world.'[22] Rothermere would write to Mussolini thanking him 'for his great services to civilisation and humanity'. Later, in 1928, he would boast, 'I am proud that the *Daily Mail* was the first newspaper in England ... to give the public a right estimate of the soundness and durability of [Mussolini's] work.'[23]

Top politicians were not to be outdone in enthusiasm for Il Duce: 'In December 1924 Sir Austen Chamberlain, then foreign secretary, referred to him when on a visit to Rome as "a wonderful man ... working for the greatness of his country".'[24] In 1927 Winston Churchill visited Rome stating: 'If I were an Italian I would don the Fascist Black Shirt.' 'I could not help being charmed,' he said at a press conference reported by *The Times*,

> like so many other people have been, by Signor Mussolini's gentle and simple bearing and by his calm and detached pose in spite of so many burdens and dangers ... If I had been an Italian I would have been wholeheartedly with you from start to finish in your triumphant struggle against the bestial appetites and passions of Leninism.[25]

Churchill's cousin, Lord Londonderry, visited Rome in January 1933. He judged Mussolini 'a great success', with Italy 'making great progress in every direction'.[26]

Mussolini was seen as a nationalist and an anti-communist. Italy had been, since its formation in 1861, an ally of Britain. No one in Whitehall, or in Paris or Washington either, seemed to take his threats to create a new Roman Empire in the Mediterranean and Africa very seriously, even though they clearly implied a challenge to Britain's imperial interests, because they did not think Italy could afford to confront Britain and France. The same attitude was applied to Hitler among ruling circles in Paris and London. Britain tore up the post-war settlement when it unilaterally signed a naval agreement with Nazi Germany in 1935, allowing it to build up its fleet to 35 per cent of the Royal Navy's strength. The dominant view in British ruling circles was that Germany should be encouraged to satisfy its expansionist ambitions to the east.

In 1935 Field Marshal Sir John Dill, then head of Military Operations and Intelligence, asked openly, 'Could we not let Germany expand eastwards at Russia's expense?'[27] Baldwin was of the opinion that, 'If there was any fighting in Europe to be done, I should like to see the Bolshies and the Nazis doing it.'[28] The policy of appeasement rested on reliance on Germany as an antidote to Communism. A German diplomat reported that he had been told by Chamberlain's closest adviser, Sir Horace Wilson, that

> Britain and Germany were in fact the two countries in which the greatest order reigned and which were the best governed ... It would be the height of folly if these two leading white races were to exterminate each other in war. Bolshevism would be the only gainer...[29]

Hitler entertained the British media magnates, Lord Rothermere and Lord Beaverbrook, plus the former premier, David Lloyd George. Göring's guests included the Tory MP and socialite 'Chips' Channon. Among those the German ambassador Ribbentrop met in London in 1936 were Lord Lothian, the Liberal peer who would become British ambassador in Washington, former deputy secretary to the cabinet Thomas Jones, and Geoffrey Dawson, editor of *The Times*.

A key appeaser was Lord Londonderry, a former leader of the Northern Ireland Senate and aircraft minister in the MacDonald coalition government. After being sacked from that job, Londonderry toured Germany in early 1936, visiting Hitler and striking up a friendship with Göring. Back home Ribbentrop (who would become Hitler's foreign minister in 1938), was a guest at his Northern Ireland stately home and at his County Durham seat. During 1936 Londonderry corresponded with his cousin, Winston Churchill, arguing that Hitler represented no threat to British interests: 'I feel that if the Nazi regime in Germany is destroyed, Germany will go Communist and we shall find a lining of Communism between France, Germany and Russia.'[30] In January 1938 Londonderry signed a message of support published in the *Berliner Tageblatt* on the anniversary of the Nazi 'revolution'.[31]

Londonderry was a doyen of the Anglo-German Fellowship (this had replaced the older Anglo-German Association whose Jewish members had quit in 1934). Among its members were a director of the Bank of England, F.C. Tiarks, and the chair of Midland Bank, Lord Magowan, assorted aristocrats including the former Conservative minister, Lord Mount Temple, and Lord Lothian, whom we shall meet again. Corporate members included Unilever, Firth-Vickers Stainless Steels, and financial companies Schroders, Lazard and the Midland Bank.

In April 1939 a British delegation headed by General J.F.C. Fuller and Lord Brocket travelled to Germany to celebrate Hitler's fiftieth birthday, being rewarded with a meeting with the Führer after a military parade. The Duke of Windsor (formerly King Edward VIII) and his wife were openly pro-Nazi. Robert Bruce Lockhart, a journalist and spy, described a conversation he had with the Duke in 1933, when the latter was still the Prince of Wales. The Duke, who 'was quite pro-Hitler, said it was no business of ours to interfere in Germany's internal affairs, either re Jews or re anything else, and added that dictators were very popular these days and we might want one in England before long'.[32] After his abdication he toured Germany giving Nazi salutes and taking tea with Hitler. When Paris fell to the German army in 1940 he quit his home there, at first for the Riviera and then for Franco's Spain. There a plot was hatched by his old friend the German foreign minister, Ribbentrop, with Hitler's and Franco's knowledge, to lure him to Berlin. It took much manoeuvring to get the Windsors back to Britain, from where Churchill sent them to preside over the Bahamas, under the watchful eyes and ears of the FBI. In April 1941 the Duke was reported as stating that, 'It would be very ill-advised of America to enter the war against Germany as Europe is finished anyway.' He then told the editor of the US magazine *Liberty* that, 'It would be a tragic thing for the world if Hitler was overthrown.'[33] The Duke of Windsor was on the pro-Nazi fringe of the British ruling class; the dominant tendency was for appeasing Hitler.

Edward had been replaced as king by his brother, who took the throne as George VI. Wartime propaganda painted the king and his wife as symbols of Britain's resistance. Yet the Queen Mother, as she would become on the death of her husband, George VI, was a keen appeaser. On 5 March 2000 the *Independent on Sunday* reported that Oxford University's Bodleian Library had held back a box of the Queen Mother's papers and correspondence from those they had released to the public:

> The papers, part of a collection of letters belonging to the first Viscount Monckton of Brenchley, a close friend of Edward VIII, dwell on the relationship between the Queen Mother and the pro-appeasement foreign secretary Lord Halifax. The letters are said to show her hostility towards Churchill and her desire that the deeply unpopular Halifax be Prime Minister instead.
>
> The letters, which include private correspondence between the Queen Mother and Halifax himself, suggest the battle to preserve the monarchy was a concern which weighed above all others. As leader, Halifax was likely to have sued for peace with Hitler on the understanding that he allowed the monarchy to continue under a Nazi occupation.[34]

The British ruling class was split. The dominant group by far was the appeasers. To their right was a pro-fascist fringe which would have welcomed Britain's inclusion into the Third Reich and even its occupation by Germany. Opposing Chamberlain was a small group of disparate Tory MPs who became identified with Winston Churchill and would eventually, despite all their instincts, ally with the Labour opposition.

Winston Churchill is the historic figure most identified with resisting Nazism. What Churchill grasped early on was that the Führer was aiming at German hegemony in Europe and that that was a direct threat to British imperialism, which had always manoeuvred between the various European powers to stop any one becoming too dominant. Unlike Chamberlain, Churchill was prepared to ally Britain with the US against Germany. The overwhelming message propagated by historians and politicians, on the right and the left, is that this was a war against fascism and for democracy. But fighting fascism was never the main concern of Churchill. He was opposed to Germany from the mid 1930s onwards because he recognised that it threatened Britain's position in Europe and the world. He had no problem with the Italian fascist dictator, Mussolini.

Churchill was sidelined by Baldwin and Chamberlain until 1939, excluded from office in the National Government. He represented die-hard support for unbridled British imperialism. Churchill was critical of Hitler's persecution of the Jews, although not of the Communists and Social Democrats, but as the historian Clive Ponting points out, 'Churchill's rooted objection to a reviving Germany was a conventional one – the threat it might pose to British interests in the way Imperial Germany had before the First World War.'[35] So in September

1937 he could write: 'One may dislike Hitler's system and yet admire his patriotic achievement. If our country was defeated, I hope we should find a champion as indomitable to restore our courage and lead us back to our place among nations.'[36]

In hindsight it seems strange that the majority opinion inside the British ruling class could have been so sanguine about the threat Hitler posed. The answer is that their anti-communism and fear of revolution in the mid 1930s blinded them to the principal threat to their imperial standing.

Churchill was not opposed to Japanese expansion in the Far East. In February 1933, as Japan advanced further into Manchuria, he told the Anti-Socialist and Anti-Communist Union, 'I do not think the League of Nations would be well advised to have a quarrel with Japan ... I hope we shall try in England to understand a little the position of Japan, as an ancient state, with the highest sense of national honour and patriotism.' The next month he backed Japanese aggression, telling his constituents, 'It is in the interests of the whole world that law and order should be established in Northern China.'[37]

He took a similar attitude two years later to Mussolini's attack on Ethiopia, telling the House of Commons three weeks after it began, 'No one can keep up the pretence that Abyssinia is a fit, worthy and equal member of a league of civilised nations.' Addressing the Anti-Socialist and Anti-Communist Union once more, he told the audience that the Italian dictator was 'the greatest lawgiver among living men'.[38]

In October 1937, the military adviser assisting him on the writing of a biography of his ancestor, the Duke of Marlborough, noted that, 'Winston says that at heart he is for Franco.' Earlier he had described the besieged Spanish Republicans as, 'A poverty stricken and backward proletariat demand[ing] the overthrow of Church, State and property and the inauguration of a Communist regime.' In contrast he spoke approvingly of 'the patriotic, religious and bourgeois forces, under the leadership of the army ... marching to re-establish order by setting up a military dictatorship'.[39]

How Could Britain Fight a Global War?

Britain entered the Second World War in a dire position. It could not defend its territories which stretched across the globe. It faced two powers but only had the economic and industrial resources to confront one of them. The Baldwin and Chamberlain governments knew all this. If war broke out, victory was only possible if America and possibly the USSR entered the war. The price of this would be to further reduce Britain's position as a world power. The British ruling class chose a twin-track approach of offering concessions to Germany, Italy and Japan while trying to create an effective military deterrent. This bridged a division among the appeasers which emerged by late 1938 between those who now realised Hitler's expansion threatened Britain and those still desperate for an agreement with the Nazi leader.

Britain, because of its relative economic weakness, had no choice but to commit maximum effort to arms production. Once it began re-arming it quickly caught up with the Third Reich and by 1942 its military budget was double that of its enemy. But because of their perception of their own weakness, British military planners and politicians believed a new European war would be a long war of attrition in which the British army could never match the enemy on land and, consequently, sea and air power (particularly heavy bombing) would be decisive.

British politicians and military chiefs seized on the belief of Hugh Trenchard – the first Chief of the Air Staff of the Royal Air Force, who held this position until 1936 – that the best way to defend the UK would be to attack the enemy's bases, cities and factories. Trenchard endorsed the importance of targeting morale, stating that it outweighed the physical by a factor of 20:1.

Up until 1938 the British government and RAF command had concentrated on building up a heavy bomber force capable of carrying the war to Germany or Italy. That year ministers overcome opposition from the RAF to begin building a fighter force capable of defending the UK from enemy attack. Chamberlain could argue that the bombers were useful as a stick with which to threaten Hitler during talks (he believed an aerial bombing campaign would devastate a country) while the fighter force did not threaten Germany.[40]

But Germany was not the only enemy Britain faced. Anthony Eden would become linked to Churchill as an opponent of appeasement, but his gripe with Baldwin was over the failure to stand up to Italy. Eden and others regarded British control of the Mediterranean, the key link to the Empire and Middle East oil, as the major point which must be defended. There was one other advantage to this strategy – Italy was a potential enemy that could be defeated.

In April 1939 it was finally decided to equip 32 divisions to be sent across the Channel in the event of war in Europe. To pay for this Britain imposed a forced loan on India, raising £1,138 million. Britain was now committed to building up its ground, sea and air forces to match those of Germany and Japan, though from the beginning there was considerable doubt in the Treasury and the Bank of England as to how all this could be afforded.[41]

The best hopes Britain could have were that it could impose an economic blockade on Germany as it had in 1914–18, that the French army could hold the Germans, and that somehow Britain would muddle through financially. As we shall see, the first of these two hopes would be shattered, the first by Hitler's pact with Stalin in August 1939, the second by the collapse of France in May and June 1940. In simple terms Britain could not pay for a new global war. When it found the financial and material support it required the cost would be high: the dismantling of the Empire, the very thing Winston Churchill held so dear.

France: On The Brink of Civil War

France, like her neighbour across the Channel, had come out of the First World War with more territory than it could comfortably control. The French government's primary aim, like London's, was to hang on to what she had as younger and more vigorous rivals threatened its possessions.

France's economy was sluggish in the 1920s, and the 1930s also saw far greater class polarisation than in Britain. As the historian Julian Jackson points out:

> The Depression reached France later than elsewhere, but lasted longer, in 1939 industrial production was still below its 1929 levels ... The social consequences of the Depression in France were different from those in other industrialised countries ... Owing to falling prices, real wages of those in work increased. Workers suffered instead from employers' attempts to rationalise work practices ... The worst affected by the Depression were peasants, small businessmen, and artisans. Thus the Depression created the conditions for extreme social polarisation: it hit the conservative electorate and stoked working class resentment.[42]

Sections of the upper and middle classes began looking to authoritarian solutions. Fascism in France was far more divided than in Italy or Germany but it was no less prevalent.

On the evening of 6 February 1934, with the government facing a vote of confidence, the far right attempted to turn a street demonstration over a financial scandal implicating government ministers into a *coup d'état*. The rival fascist leagues held two demonstrations. The biggest on the north side of the Seine was blocked from reaching the Chamber of Deputies, but Colonel de La Rocque, the head of the paramilitary Croix de Feu, led a column of 2,000 along the Left Bank to Parliament with only a flimsy police barricade barring their way. The Colonel then dispersed his men.

The demonstration brought down the government, which could not secure its vote of confidence, bringing to office a right-wing administration led by Gaston Doumergue with Marshal Pétain as minister of war. But it also provoked France's unions into calling an effective one day strike and demonstrations (the enthusiastic rank and file response overcame the divisions which had allowed fascism to triumph in Germany without resistance).

Alastair Horne describes 6 February 1934 as 'marking the beginning of what approximated to civil war in France'.[43] The left engaged in street confrontations with the right, and workers, gaining in confidence, increasingly struck and sat in at their factories. In the meantime a right-wing government signed a pact with the USSR, but this was seen more as a way to pressure Hitler towards a rapprochement rather than an effective military alliance.

With increased social tension and with the 1935 local elections showing advances for the left, some 6.3 billion francs left the country to be invested in the United States or Britain. France had to devalue the franc. From then until 1940 successive French governments relied on borrowing money from the City of London. The Croix de Feu continued to organise parades and paramilitary mobilisations, with de La Rocque warning that 'H Hour' was near at hand when its members would have to act to limit parliamentary power and to counter the Communists. Membership of the Croix de Feu had grown to 300,000 by the end of 1935. Julian Jackson suggests that its membership 'seems to have drawn on the urban lower middle class, but also some managers and salaried engineers'.[44]

As a social force, however, French fascism was about to be eclipsed. In May 1936 a Popular Front of Republicans, Socialists and Communists, all pledged to resist fascism, was elected to office, led by the Socialist Party leader, Léon Blum, who was a Jew. The workers celebrated by downing tools and occupying factories, offices, shops and even theatres. The occupations were ended with a compromise whereby workers got pay increases, shorter hours and paid holidays, but as the strike wave receded the employers wanted revenge. Substantial sections of the ruling class and the intellectual right had been terrified by the whiff of revolution and began to despair of the ability of the French fascist movements to break the left. General Spears, later Britain's liaison officer to the 1939–40 French government, recalled of his bourgeois friends in Paris: 'These people hated the *Front Populaire* and all it stood for.'[45]

'It would be difficult to exaggerate', stressed the French historian, Marc Bloch,

> the sense of shock felt by the comfortable classes, even by men who had a reputation for liberal-mindedness, at the coming of the Popular Front in 1936 ... Dangerously, the French conservatives, in their alarm, persisted in regarding the enemy within as infinitely more menacing than the menace without. 'Rather Hitler than Blum' became their motto.[46]

The failure of native fascism to challenge for power meant a virulent group of fascist intellectuals emerged, grouped round the journal *Je suis partout* (I am everywhere), who were exasperated with the caution of the different leagues, and who looked to Hitler as the saviour from without.

Je suis partout's circulation never exceeded 100,000, but two right-wing mass dailies that had a similar tone, *Le Gringoire* and *Candide*, had a circulation of 640,000 and 460,000 in May 1936. One of their contributors, Robert Brassilach, who would be executed for treason in 1945, wrote: 'When Blum and Cot [air minister in the Popular Front government] have been shot ... by a national government no tears will be shed over these two excrements, but champagne will be drunk by French families.'[47]

On the left a realignment was taking place. In the course of 1936 the Communist Party grew from 90,000 to 288,000, surpassing the Socialists. Its strength was in the new working-class areas on the periphery of Paris, in previously unorganised workplaces like the Renault car plants, and among Jewish and Polish workers.

'Thank God for the French army', Winston Churchill had shouted out in the House of Commons in March 1933, shortly after Hitler took power. He was bemoaning Britain's lack of military preparedness to deal with what he rightly judged to be its greatest enemy. By August 1939 the British were basing their plans for any fresh war with Germany on the ability of the French army to at least hold their German opponents in check, while the Royal Navy controlled the seas, the RAF began a bombing campaign against German cities, and they had time to mobilise and train the forces required to fight a land war in Europe.

In truth, France was a house divided. At the outbreak of war the government was led by the Radical, Édouard Daladier, who was committed to fighting Hitler, but his determination was not shared by his generals, the officer corps or much of big business, who regarded the working class and the communists as the main enemy. For their part, the workers and peasants were sullen in mood and unenthusiastic about a government that they saw as having betrayed the promises of the Popular Front, which the Radicals had belonged to, and as persecuting the left. The stage was set for a disaster. It was not long in coming.

As the 1930s drew to a close parliamentary democracy seemed secure in France. Beneath the surface, however, the working class was alienated from the ruling order and big business and finance doubted the ability of the government to deal with any new bout of unrest. Events were to prove that parliamentary democracy was far from secure.

USSR – Bulwark Against Bolshevism

In a magnificent sweep through Russian history Leon Trotsky described Russia's position in regard to the more advanced states to its west:

> Russia stood not only geographically, but also socially and historically, between Europe and Asia. She was marked off from the European West, but also from the Asiatic East, approaching at different periods and in different features now one, now the other. The East gave her the Tartar yoke, which entered as an important element into the structure of the Russian state. The West was a still more threatening foe – but at the same time a teacher. Russia was unable to settle in the forms of the East because she was continually having to adapt herself to military and economic pressure from the West.[48]

Trotsky argued that Russia was developing unevenly with the West but also in combination with it:

> The laws of history have nothing in common with a pedantic schematism. Unevenness, the most general law of the historic process, reveals itself most sharply and complexly in the destiny of the backward countries. Under the whip of external necessity their backward culture is compelled to make leaps. From the universal law of unevenness thus derives another law which, for the lack of a better name, we may call the law of *combined development* – by which we mean a drawing together of the different stages of the journey, a combining of the separate steps, an amalgam of archaic with more contemporary forms. Without this law, to be taken of course, in its whole material content, it is impossible to understand the history of Russia, and indeed of any country of the second, third or tenth cultural class.[49]

The October Revolution of 1917 was carried through on the basis that it would be the first break in a chain which extended west into Germany and the more developed states. Attacked, besieged and blockaded, it awaited the salvation of successful revolution in Western Europe. The revolutions occurred but were defeated.

The working class which made the October Revolution was decimated by war and economic collapse. Control was increasingly in the hands of state and party bureaucrats who had little time for the hope of international revolution. Lenin died fighting them. Trotsky was driven into exile by them. The figure who came to represent their self-interest was the Communist Party general secretary, Josef Stalin. Stalin's regime turned its back on the world revolution that the Bolsheviks of 1917 had looked to. As the historian E.H. Carr argues: 'It was no longer thought of as the primary condition of the survival of the Soviet regime. "Socialism in one country" had taken its place ... Neither Stalin nor any of the leaders expected such a contingency in any foreseeable future, or even wanted it.'[50]

Addressing industrial managers in February 1931 to demand rapid industrialisation, Stalin waved 'the whip of external necessity' in much the same way as had Peter the Great:

> To slacken the tempo would mean falling behind. And those who fall behind get beaten. But we do not want to be beaten. No, we refuse to be beaten! One feature of the history of old Russia was the continual beatings she suffered because of her backwardness. She was beaten by the Mongol khans. She was beaten by the Turkish beys. She was beaten by the Swedish feudal lords. She was beaten by the Polish and Lithuanian gentry. She was beaten by the British and French capitalists. She was beaten by the Japanese barons. All beat her because of her backwardness, military backwardness, cultural backwardness, political backwardness, industrial backwardness, agricultural backwardness. They beat her because to do so was profitable and could be done with impunity.[51]

Stalin warned: 'We are fifty or a hundred years behind the advanced countries. We must make good this distance in ten years. Either we do so or we shall go under.'[52]

Revolution in Europe (or anywhere else for that matter) was now a threat to Stalin because it might revive the revolutionary ghost of Bolshevism. Because of that he would urge the Spanish and French Communist Parties to contain working-class insurgency in 1936. He also saw it as threatening a possible alliance with Britain and France against Hitler. In 1928–29 Stalin liquidated what remained of workers' democracy, reduced the soviets to rubber stamps, and removed the rights given to women, gay people and national minorities. Peasants were forced off their land into state-run collective farms, and mass famine followed. The Gulag system of forced-labour camps was established to which hundreds of thousands would be consigned. Within six years Stalin would liquidate the vast majority of old Bolsheviks. It was a bloody counter-revolution.

In the 1930s the Russian dictator sought to safeguard economic development by avoiding war. To his west and east stood powers that were virulently anti-communist and that had all intervened militarily against the Bolshevik revolutionary government in 1918 and 1919. Despite the turn away from international revolution, the USSR was still vilified by Western leaders. Firstly, the majority of politicians, generals, media magnates and corporate chiefs believed Stalin's stance was a guise, and that he would revert to revolutionary politics. Secondly, virtually all of them believed Soviet Russia was highly unstable and that Stalin might be replaced by someone committed to revolution. Thirdly, the sight of red flags on the streets of Paris, Madrid and even London and New York overcame any assurances from Moscow that Stalin had ruled out revolution beyond Russia's borders. Finally, London, Berlin and, to a lesser extent, Paris, were suspicious of Russian ambitions, whether promoted by a tsar or by Stalin.[53]

The most class-conscious section of the Western working class still believed, in the main, that Russia represented a socialist alternative. The Western leaders understood that, whatever Stalin's intentions, any advance of Soviet power would act to inspire them, and they were unsure how far Stalin could rein them in. Forced industrialisation, with a timetable set by a five-year plan, was connected to Stalin's aim of strengthening his armed forces, as the military historian Richard Overy explains:

> The significant figure was the proportion of national output devoted to the defence sector ... in 1932 it was already 9 per cent, more than double the figure at the outset of the [five-year] plans; by 1940 it was 19 per cent ... Arms were bought at the expense of living standards.[54]

Industrialisation was accompanied by a war on 'class enemies' – namely Stalin's rivals in the Bolshevik Party – which would weaken Russia militarily. The assassination of the party's Leningrad chief, Sergei Kirov, in 1934 (probably on Stalin's orders) unleashed a wave of terror within the Communist Party. Thousands were jailed, interrogated and tortured. The NKVD secret police were executing 200 party members a day in Leningrad (St Petersburg). Of the 1,966 delegates at the 1934 national Communist Party Congress 1,108 would eventually be shot.[55]

Show trials began at which prominent party figures confessed to incredible crimes after torture or extortion, leading to 'purges' of other members of the party and the military. In June 1937 eight marshals and generals were chosen to pass judgement on eight of their fellow marshals and generals – including the Soviet Chief of Staff, Mikhail Tukhachevsky. The night before the trial began the secret police forced confessions from the defendants against their judges! After a secret trial lasting a day the eight defendants were taken out to be shot. Tukhachevsky died expressing loyalty to Stalin. Out of 85 senior officers on the USSR's military council, 71 were killed by 1941. Out of 837 army and navy commanders, ranging from colonels to marshals, 720 were executed or sacked. Thirty thousand officers, out of a total of 75,000 to 80,000, were imprisoned or executed. The Red Army command was devastated.[56]

Stalin now moved his own creatures into high command. In August 1937 one of Stalin's cronies, Lev Mekhlis, the editor of the party organ *Pravda*, was appointed head of the Red Army's Main Political Directorate. Up until 1941 he kept the Red Army command under a reign of terror, insisting political officers should play a key military role. This had disastrous results in the summer of 1941 when they could not cope with modern warfare.

In recounting this bestial chapter it might seem like simple insanity, but Stalin was determined to extinguish the revolutionary tradition of 1917 because it threatened his dictatorship, and the terror mirrored the breakneck competition with which he drove industrialisation.

The Red Army had pioneered many of the methods the Germans went on to employ in their victories in the first three years of the Second World War. In 1926 Tukhachevsky ordered a total review of Soviet military doctrine. The result, *The Future War*, published two years later, laid out a strategy of a grand offensive employing thousands of tanks, armoured vehicles and aircraft to secure a lightning strike. At the time of publication the Red Army did not have the means to achieve this, but that changed by the early 1930s. In 1932 the Red Army formed its first two mechanised corps – three years before the first German Panzer divisions were born. As David M. Glantz and Jonathan House point out, 'in the mid-1930s, the Soviet Union led the world in production, planning and fielding of mechanised forces'.[57] Amid the military purges came a report on the use of tanks in the Spanish Civil War which challenged Tukhachevsky's theory that armoured formations, backed by artillery and aircraft, could pierce enemy defences and achieve deep penetration. The Russian tanks operating in Spain were too lightly armoured, their crews had difficulty communicating with the Spanish supporting troops, and when in advance they began to outrun them they were picked off by enemy artillery. A special commission convened in 1939 led to the Red Army pulling back from independent armoured corps and reduced tanks to being infantry support weapons.[58]

Stalin's military purges only increased the confidence of Germany and Japan, who were envisaging war with Russia. Germany was at the centre of Russian foreign policy. It was the strongest military power in Europe by the mid 1930s and bordered Russia, therefore it was Stalin's primary concern. But it, like Russia, had been a loser when the map of Europe was redrawn at the end of the First World War. Moscow was aware that there were two contending strands in the foreign policy of the Weimar Republic. One, associated with Gustav Stresemann, who served as chancellor and foreign minister during the 1920s, centred on building economic co-operation with France and the United States. Stresemann died in 1929, but that year the centre-left coalition government headed by the German Social Democrats approved the US-brokered Young Plan, which reduced Germany's reparations and approved the withdrawal of occupation troops from the Rhineland five years early. Moscow saw the Young Plan as a 'military pact against the Soviet Union' and celebrated when the centre-left government fell in the wake of the Wall Street Crash.[59]

The other strand in German foreign policy was prepared to use Russia as a balance against Britain and France. The German military had benefited from the Treaty of Rapallo signed in 1922, whereby each state renounced territorial claims against the other. A secret provision allowed the German army to have training facilities in Russia, in breach of Versailles, in return for them providing training and technology to the Red Army.[60] The creation of a new right-wing government under Heinrich Brüning in March 1930 was welcomed in Moscow, where there was little concern at the sudden leap in support for the Nazis at the polls. *Pravda* even pointed out that the Nazis' success created 'not a few difficulties for French imperialism'.[61] Brüning's successors, Franz von Papen and Kurt von Schleicher, maintained the Treaty of Rapallo approach. Von Schleicher latter assured Moscow that his attitude towards German Communists did not colour his attitude to the Soviet Union.

At first Stalin was sanguine about Hitler's rise to power because he saw him as opposing the post-war carve up of Europe. Moscow viewed Britain as the major threat at this time, with some justification as Baldwin and Chamberlain were notoriously anti-communist. If Hitler broke with the settlement agreed at Versailles in 1919 this would bring him into conflict with Britain and France and thus reaffirm the friendly relations between Weimar Germany and Russia agreed at Rapallo in 1922. In November 1931 Stalin asked a German Communist whether in the event of the Nazis coming to power they might 'concern themselves so exclusively with the west that we can build socialism in peace'.[62]

Two months after the Nazi takeover, in March 1933, the Russian foreign minister Litvinov passed through Berlin, seizing the chance to meet with his German counterpart. Litvinov reported that he was passed an assurance that, 'Hitler knows how to distinguish between communism and our state.'[63] At the end of that month Hitler agreed to extend the Soviet-German treaty of 1926 re-affirming the Rapallo agreement. But in October 1933 Hitler quit the League of Nations and began re-arming Germany, and then in 1934 signed a non-aggression pact with Poland which was clearly aimed at Russia. Stalin had to reconsider his position.

In September 1934 the Soviet Union joined the League of Nations, denounced years before by Lenin as a 'thieves' den'. For the next four years Stalin attempted to create an alliance with Britain and France, but to no avail. The British right-wing governments of Baldwin and Chamberlain were strongly anti-communist and refused to accept Stalin's private assurances that he had no interest in aiding revolutions in Europe or anywhere else. Even when Moscow ordered the Communist Parties in Western Europe to drop overtly class confrontationist policies and promote the unity of all anti-fascists in support of democracy it was to no avail. As the British and French governments continued their policy of appeasement, even after Hitler broke promise after promise, Stalin began to shift his attention towards reaching an accord with Hitler.

Meanwhile, to the east, the Russians faced Japanese occupation forces along the Manchuria-Outer Mongolia border. The Japanese army had already crossed the border in force near Vladivostok, but withdrew after clashes with the Red Army. Russian troops launched frontal attacks demonstrating poor co-ordination between armour and infantry. They suffered heavy losses, encouraging the Japanese to test them again further east.

Faced with a second attack, the Russian commander, Georgi Zhukov, a talented follower of Tukhachevsky, switched to a different military strategy

– one which would eventually pay rich dividends. He used tanks and aircraft to advance around the Japanese flanks and trap them. The invaders suffered 61,000 killed, wounded or captured. Russian losses were 7,974 dead and 15,251 wounded. This success led the Japanese to decide against a full-scale war with Russia, secured Russian's far eastern borders, and ensured Zhukov's rise within the Red Army. Zhukov would go on to fight his way to Berlin and eventual victory over the Third Reich.[64]

But far to the west the general opinion in both military and ruling circles in London, Paris and Berlin was that Russia, weakened by the purges, was not in a strong position militarily. On paper, the Soviet Union had one of strongest armed forces in the world by 1939, but this was largely dismissed in Western Europe because its military leadership and fighting ability was seen as weak.

Some of this was based on reality. Some of it was wishful thinking – as we shall see.

The United States: Facing Its Destiny

There is a myth that in the inter-war years the United States withdrew into isolation from world matters. In fact, it refused to join the League of Nations because it was not prepared to subordinate its power to an international body. The US ruling class continued to carve out its economic and sometimes physical domination of the Americas and parts of the Pacific basin. New York financiers were no less zealous in administering the US loans which had re-floated the European economy prior to the Wall Street Crash.

However, Washington did turn its back on the idea championed by its wartime president, Woodrow Wilson, that it should take the lead in re-ordering the post-war world, policing disputes and brokering diplomatic deals. Wilson had wanted a relatively equal international order which he believed would lead to greater prosperity for US industry and finance, but he was unable to secure congressional support for the US joining the League of Nations.[65] His Republican rival, Henry Cabot Lodge, led the fight against joining the League of Nations on the basis that the US's freedom of action should not be limited by international commitments. He supported building a stronger navy and was an ardent imperialist. In a debate over membership of the League he stated:

> We are a great moral asset of Christian civilisation. How did we get there? By our own efforts. Nobody led us, nobody guided us, nobody controlled us ... I would keep America as she has been – not isolated, not prevent her from joining other nations for ... great purposes – but I wish her to be master of her own fate.[66]

The United States had already acted on this sentiment. In 1898 its navy intervened in the Philippines' independence struggle against the Spanish colonial empire, destroying Spanish naval forces and preventing reinforcements arriving. Spain ceded control of the archipelago to Washington. In 1907, in response to strained relations with Japan, President Theodore Roosevelt argued that the Philippines, 'form our heel of Achilles ... I would rather see this nation fight all her life than to see her give them up to Japan or to any other nation under duress'.[67]

In May of the following year Congress authorised construction of the Pearl Harbor base in Hawaii. The House Naval Affairs Committee claimed the new base would constitute 'one of the strongest factors in the prevention of war with any powers in the Far East'.[68] Originally US planners believed they could use the Philippines to resist any Japanese advance southwards, but after the First World War, with Japan in possession of Germany's former Pacific colonies, planners accepted that the Japanese could occupy the Philippines. The best to be hoped for was that resistance could last as long as possible with the territories being won back at a later date.

There was nevertheless a difference between US imperialism and its older rivals. Its principal aim was not carving out a formal empire but achieving free access for US capital to every corner of the globe. It sought to benefit from cheap labour and resources abroad, while at the same time blocking imports from low-cost countries. Its imperialism was perhaps more subtle, but it still rested on exploitation for the benefit of US capital. This 'open door' policy was first promoted in relation to China, which was seen as a great prize in Washington and Wall Street. Washington championed China's territorial integrity over the territorial 'concessions' demanded by the European powers, confident that if permitted open access to the Chinese market US industrial power would ensure its dominance.[69]

Both Wilson and Lodge took it for granted that US capitalism could become a dominant global power without territorial aggrandisement. The Marxist geographer David Harvey argues that this lack of a formal empire allowed the US to 'conceal its imperial ambition in abstract universalism ... to deny the significance of territory and geography altogether in the articulation of imperial power'.[70] Despite the fact that the US intervened militarily in Latin America, the Caribbean and the Pacific, its rejection of outright colonialism meant it could aim anti-colonial rhetoric at its European rivals and win some sympathy in the colonised states. At the same time, heavy US investment in Europe meant it was enmeshed in European affairs.

By 1932 the US had overtaken Japan in trade with China. The United States was dismayed by the Japanese invasion of China. After Japanese planes attacked a US gunboat on the Yangtze River, Roosevelt pressed the British for joint action short of war with Tokyo. Chamberlain eschewed any involvement in the Asian conflict while maintaining his policy of appeasing Hitler. That fuelled Roosevelt's suspicions of the British premier.

As the 1930s proceeded, some in the US ruling class urged friendship with the fascist dictators while others argued that German and Japanese ambitions threatened those of America. The ruling class was split further after Franklin Roosevelt became president in 1933 and began implementing a degree of state intervention to reinvigorate the economy. A vague left populism associated with this alarmed much of American capital. Hostility to Roosevelt grew in corporate circles when a light economic upturn gave rise to a series of mass strikes and factory occupations.

Roosevelt was no left-winger and to secure re-election in 1936 he backtracked on his state interventionist policies. But suspicion of him in business circles lingered. As late as 1940 when the new British ambassador Lord Halifax arrived in Washington, Republican congressmen warned him that Roosevelt was 'as dangerous a dictator as Hitler or Mussolini'.[71] The president came to regard both dictators as the key enemies of US ambitions and began to overcome his distrust of British leaders. Roosevelt's assistant secretary of state and chair of the president's Executive Committee on Commercial Policy, Cordell Hull, argued, 'Unless we can export and sell abroad our surplus production, we must face a violent dislocation of our whole economy.'[72] He specifically saw Germany, Italy and Japan as the threat.

In 1937 Treasury secretary Henry Morgenthau warned that the Axis powers might take over Mexico. As Hitler began his expansion into Austria and Czechoslovakia, US business began to rally behind Roosevelt through concern they would be excluded from Eastern Europe and the Balkans. By 1938 Germany was regarded in Washington as the main threat to the US. That year saw Roosevelt sign the Naval Expansion Bill, ensuring the largest peacetime military expenditure in US history. In a developing naval arms race the US outspent all its rivals.[73] Yet Roosevelt was still suspicious of powerful forces in London:

> Roosevelt believed Chamberlain was an agent of the 'City' and that pro-German financial interests – Chamberlain, Simon, Hoare, the Astors, Lothian, Geoffrey Dawson and Lord Halifax – were preparing to save the Empire by a deal with Hitler to permit German expansion into Central and South Eastern Europe.[74]

In 1939 a league table of military powers placed the US in nineteenth place, behind Portugal. Yet the US's mighty industries meant this situation was to completely change. In 1937 the US produced 4.8 million vehicles; Germany 331,000; Italy 71,000, and Japan 26,000. The basis existed for the mass production of tanks and the creation of mechanised infantry armies. By 1944 the US was producing 600,000 army trucks, Germany 88,000. Between 1939 and its entry into the war, Washington increased its armed forces eight-fold, from 190,000 to 1.5 million.[75]

The US was also prepared to ensure exports of war materials benefited those it favoured. A series of Neutrality Acts passed in the 1930s prohibited US intervention on behalf of any belligerent, whether aggressor or defender. Arms sales were allowed if they were on a 'cash and carry' basis, which benefited Britain and France who could expect to control the Atlantic supply route and who might have sufficient dollars or gold to purchase US arms.

When war began in Europe the White House shared the view that America had much to lose from German hegemony in Europe and Japanese control of China and South East Asia, and that it could also gain from giving support to

Britain and France. Economic aid to both would come at a price. At this stage direct US military intervention was not on the horizon. By aiding Britain's resistance and building up US military forces, Roosevelt hoped to check Hitler and deter Japan.

Yet there were those in US ruling circles who did not perceive Hitler as a threat. As late as June 1941 Roosevelt's vice-president, Truman, was quoted by the press saying, 'If we see that Germany is winning we ought to help Russia and if Russia is winning we ought to help Germany and that way let them kill as many as possible.'[76] Such views were at variance with the growing realisation in the White House that Hitler threatened US interests. On 31 January 1939 Roosevelt called the Senate Military Affairs Committee to a meeting in the White House. He confided that he wanted the American people 'to gradually realise' the 'potential danger' that European dictators represented. Roosevelt outlined his thoughts about the strategy that he believed Hitler to be following and told the Senators, 'Beginning about three years ago, there was rather definite information as to what the ultimate objective of Hitler was, a policy of world domination between Germany, Italy and Japan.' Presenting the likelihood of a war between Hitler's Germany and Britain and France he argued that it could not be assumed that the two allies would defeat Germany and Italy, saying, 'The best opinion is that it is a fifty-fifty bet.'

Continuing, he argued that if Germany emerged the victor the next step in Hitler's domination of Europe would be for 'all the small nations' to 'drop into the basket of their own accord because it is silly for them to resist'. According to the president, Nazi Germany would then demilitarise those nations. Although they would be left with their flag and the guise of sovereignty, Roosevelt explained that the result would be total economic and military domination of the defeated countries.

Following this Roosevelt predicted Hitler's next step: 'Africa automatically falls.' Roosevelt then argued that having achieved domination of Europe and Africa, 'the next perfectly obvious step' would be for Hitler to look west across the Atlantic and move against Central and South America. The president solemnly characterised the problem facing the United States: 'It is the gradual encirclement of the United States by the removal of first lines of defence.'

Roosevelt described his preferred policy as one of 'self protection' rather than neutrality. Stating that he intended to prevent any munitions from going to Germany, Italy, or Japan, the president asserted in relation to Britain and France, 'I will do everything I can to maintain the independence of these other nations by sending them all they can pay for.'[77]

Earlier the president had predicted an economic boycott and blockade of Germany enforced by the Royal Navy and 'that with England, France, and Russia all pounding away at Germany from the air, Germany would find it difficult to protect itself even with its present preponderance in the air'. This, Roosevelt argued, 'would cost less money, would mean comparatively few casualties, and would be more likely to succeed than a traditional war by land and sea'. He might have added that it would avoid direct US involvement in any war.[78]

In June the assistant secretary of state for Latin American affairs, Adolph Berle, was even more candid:

> We have no necessary interest in defending the British Empire ... But we do have a very real and solid interest in having the British and not the Germans dominant in the Atlantic ... we shall be meeting imperialist schemes in South and Central America not on a paper basis, as we do now, but backed up by an extremely strong naval and military force. This can only mean that the next phase of the United States will be militarist and no mistake about it; or, still worse, that we shall be forced into empire to preserve ourselves, much as the British were.[79]

Until May and June 1940 Roosevelt and key sections of the Republican Party were ready to pin their hopes on the British and French keeping the Third Reich in check. Then on 16 May as the German Panzer forces crashed through the French lines and began their drive to the English Channel, Roosevelt asked Congress for 1 billion dollars to spend on defence. They approved this in just two weeks, throwing in an extra half billion dollars. Over the coming months they would agree to another $6.5 billion military spending and to increase the size of the navy by 70 per cent.[80]

Both the army and the navy shared concerns about the possible threat from an Axis-dominated Europe in which the British and French navies might be employed against the United States. American forces planned, accordingly, to occupy British and French bases in the western Atlantic. If the Axis was able to utilise the British and French fleets it would give them naval equality with the US fleet and within six months the Axis would be in a position to operate in the Western Hemisphere. Only 'one force', said Henry Stimson on the day following France's surrender, 'remained between the Nazis and the Western Hemisphere – the British Fleet'. Faced with this 'appalling prospect' the United States would stand alone if that fleet were lost.[81]

Key decisions had been taken regarding military expansion. The first was to begin construction of a fleet capable of operating in the Atlantic and the Pacific; second, to construct an army of 2 million (and the basis for a future expansion to 4 million); third, to create an air force of 7,800 frontline aircraft backed up by the capacity to produce 18,000 aircraft annually by 1942.[82] In June 1941 Roosevelt requested a paper on 'a strategic concept of how to defeat our potential enemies'. The response was written by Lieutenant General Albert C. Wedemeyer of the War Plans Division. The task before the US was very clear:

> We must prepare to fight Germany by actually coming to grips with and defeating her ground forces and definitely breaking her will to combat ... Air and sea forces will make important contributions, but effective and adequate ground forces must be available to close with and destroy the enemy inside his citadel.[83]

Wedemeyer set the date of 1 July 1943 as the deadline for the creation of an even bigger military, 8.8 million strong. The strategic decision was made that in the event of war with both Germany and Japan, Hitler must be defeated first, and only then would the Japanese be finished off. The US army was to be directed to Europe. The US navy would deal with a Pacific war until victory in Europe allowed ground forces to be moved eastwards. The US army was thus designed for an eventual invasion of occupied Europe – armoured forces to defeat Hitler's Panzers, aircraft to support their advance, and infantry in numbers to consolidate and hold what the tanks won. The US needed time to achieve this build up; the longer Britain resisted, the more time Washington would have.

In mid June Roosevelt added to his cabinet two prominent Republicans who agreed on the need to confront Hitler. Henry Stimson became secretary of war and Frank Knox secretary of the navy. Stimson confided in his diary that the administration agreed Britain was 'our last line of defence outside our own powers'.[84]

By the autumn of 1940 there was regular contact between the US and British military, and intelligence was being shared. The US had to act to secure the Atlantic as German submarines hunted the supply ships delivering arms to Britain. In April 1941 the US occupied bases in Greenland, moving into bases in Iceland three months later.

The Japanese attack on Pearl Harbor on 7 December 1941 would bring the US directly into the war.

CHAPTER THREE

The Axis Powers

Germany: Nazism Equals War

Hitler was the last resort of a desperate German ruling class, scared – and scarred – by more than a decade of revolutionary upheaval and economic crisis. As Leon Trotsky argued: 'The established bourgeoisie does not like the fascist means of solving its problems ... The big bourgeoisie dislikes this method, much as a man with a swollen jaw dislikes having his teeth pulled.'[1] Yet, while Hitler was far from the first choice of German big business, he was not completely rejected by them either.

Hitler came from a firmly middle-class family in the Austro-Hungarian Empire, his father holding a middle-ranking job in the imperial bureaucracy. He volunteered to fight for Germany at the outbreak of war in 1914 and was a decorated frontline fighter who became increasingly nationalistic and anti-Semitic as the war went on. He blamed the revolutionary movement that broke across Germany in 1918 for Germany's defeat in the war. That same year saw the German high command use the troops it had withdrawn from Russia to launch a series of offensives on the Western Front. For a moment the English Channel ports and Paris beckoned, but the Allies eventually held and stopped the offensive, and then began to press back, enjoying superiority in men (the Americans were present in big numbers) and material.

The morale of the German high command collapsed and they began to openly say they could do no more, despite the fact they were still deep inside France and Belgium. On 3 November the naval command ordered the home fleet at Kiel to sea in order to engage the Royal Navy, who were blockading the coast. For them it was 'one last battle' with which to preserve their honour, for the sailors it was a death sentence. They mutinied, took over the fleet and port, and sent emissaries out across Germany.

In the autumn of 1918, hunger and discontent over the collapse in living standards led to a growing tide of strikes and protests on Germany's home front. The arrival of the sailors led to the creation of workers', soldiers' and sailors' councils, which looked very much like Russian soviets. The Kaiser fled into exile in Holland and the high command demanded a new civilian government make peace. Even before an armistice was signed soldiers were marching towards the border and home. As crowds gathered in Berlin the Social Democrats declared a republic, fearful that the revolutionaries gathered round Rosa Luxemburg would declare a socialist republic.

The Social Democrats would join with the established parties and the high command in order to stop a Bolshevik-style revolution, murdering Luxemburg.

But from the end of the war in November 1918 until the autumn of 1923 Germany would live through a series of revolutionary convulsions, with the far left probably having a majority of the working class on side by the latter date but allowing the opportunity to slip through its fingers. This left Germany divided, with a ruling class who had lived through the fear of revolution, which was never far from the surface, a middle class who had already experienced a degree of radicalisation, to the right, and a working class divided between the majority Social Democrats and minority Communists, with the former defending the existing republic and the latter demanding revolution.

Hitler was appalled by all this, and after recovering from his war wounds joined the fledgling Nazi Party in Munich in 1920, enjoying access to important circles. Military friends flew him to Berlin where he met the head of the Freikorps. These were paramilitary units formed to avoid restrictions imposed on German armed forces by the Versailles peace treaties and as a counter to the mutinous and left-leaning army units. The Freikorps terrorised both the far left and the Slavs on the eastern borders. Hitler also met General Erich von Ludendorff, Germany's de facto joint Chief of Staff with Marshal Paul von Hindenburg from 1916 until the end of the war.

In Munich Hitler frequented the beer halls, which were cheap eating places for the middle class and white-collar workers, and would quickly win control of the Nazi Party. He also moved in wealthy circles, mixing with business people and aristocrats who bemoaned the demise of the old order. The people Hitler met with were largely on the fringes of the dominant bourgeois circles, but they provided finance for the Nazi Party and access to higher circles for its leader. Common to this milieu were a desire to rebuild and expand Germany's empire in Central and Eastern Europe, hatred of Weimar Germany and its generous welfare provisions, and violent anti-Semitism.

These ideas influenced students and the former wartime junior officers and NCOs who made up the Freikorps. They imagined a community of the Volk (a stronger term than simply the people, implying racial purity) free from class divisions such as those that, they believed, had wrecked Germany's war effort in 1918. In 1920 they attempted a military coup, the failed 'Kapp Putsch'. Many of them sported the swastika. In November 1923 Hitler tried to emulate Mussolini's 'March on Rome' with an attempt to take control in Munich, but the 'Beer Hall Putsch' failed and Hitler spent a rather comfortable spell in jail (where he wrote *Mein Kampf*). Over the next decade he would build the Nazi Party into a disciplined machine, loyal to him, and achieving hegemony on a splintered far right. The party was overwhelmingly middle class, but retained the support of sections of business, the aristocracy and the military elite.

Economic Stabilisation, Then Collapse

By 1923 Germany had experienced hyper-inflation, French occupation of the Ruhr industrial region, and a revolutionary crisis. It took an inflow of foreign credit totalling billions of marks to rebuild German industry between 1924 and 1930. During those years, under first the US brokered Dawes Plan and then the Young Plan, Germany paid 86 billion marks in reparations to the wartime victors. At the same time Germany's foreign borrowing totalled 138 billion marks, mainly from the US. The US lent money to Germany to pay its reparations to Britain and France which then used the money to repay their debts to America. The stabilisation of Western capitalism in the 1920s depended on this merry-go-round.

The consequent revival of the German economy left it highly dependent on US loans and on exporting to America. It also led to a new wave of rationalisation with production of consumer goods taking second place. The creation of Stahlverein, brought together major companies Thyssen, Stinnes and Otto Wolff. Productivity increased by more than 50 per cent, costs were substantially reduced, productive capacity was raised and labour costs per unit of production cut. But these advantages relied on there being a market for German steel and iron. Germany's export markets were too limited for the size of its expanding industries, and even prior to the Wall Street Crash exports were often 'dumped' on overseas markets.[2]

Initially it seemed Germany might be spared the worst of the developing world recession, but then in April 1931 the Austrian credit bank of Rothschild collapsed; it had been central to the financial systems of Central and Eastern Europe. Foreign creditors, chiefly the Americans, panicked and immediately withdrew all their short-term investments. In a few weeks the Reichsbank lost 3 billion marks in gold and foreign currency. The collapse spread with the bankruptcy of the Wool Trust of Bremen, which pulled down with it the Danat Bank, one of the big five, and the main instrument for financing heavy industry and the Steel Trust. The government was compelled to intervene to safeguard the other big banks, particularly the Dresdner Bank. Foreign creditors were not reassured and in July a German government moratorium on the whole of Germany's short-term foreign debts became necessary. The whole system of international investment and credit was starting to unravel.[3]

German industry had relied on exports to Britain and Europe but was now being frozen out of these markets. The United Steel Trust banked on producing at 80 per cent of its capacity. The minimum production level was regarded as 67 per cent. By the autumn of 1931 orders equalled just 40 per cent of productive capacity, and by 1932 this had fallen to 20 per cent. Heavy industry in Germany had traditionally favoured protectionism – now it looked at expanding physical control of markets and raw materials.[4]

The heads of heavy industry turned their backs on the policy of the dominant German politician of the 1920s, Gustav Stresemann, who was twice briefly chancellor in the 1920s and held the post of foreign secretary through numerous governments from 1923 to his death in 1929. Stresemann had striven to achieve conciliation with France, hoping Paris might allow Germany a free hand in Eastern Europe. Since the late nineteenth century, German foreign policy had been based on gaining economic and political hegemony in 'Middle Europe'. For most this meant those countries along the River Danube (inter-war Austria, Hungary, Yugoslavia and Romania). Now, with any hopes of an alliance with

France gone, the need to create '*Lebensraum*' (Living Space) in this region became the rising demand among industrialists, financiers and the generals.

In March 1931, in a precursor of future expansionism, the German government attempted to bring about a German-Austrian customs union which would have challenged France's system of alliances with the Eastern European states created by the post-war settlement, the Little Entente. The customs union was ruled out by the International Court of the Hague in September 1931 as being incompatible with the post-war settlement. This was regarded as a severe set-back by German industrialists. As Paul N. Hehn points out:

> Heavy industry had already turned against a French-dominated customs union ... The expansionist Lebensraum ideology enunciated by Hitler in *Mein Kampf* must have been regarded as manna from heaven by the profit-strapped German business class. That Hitler meant Lebensraum in the USSR, i.e., the Ukraine, and not in South Eastern Europe, few noticed.[5]

German industry had begun investing heavily in South Eastern Europe from the late 1920s. Companies like IG Farben, Siemens, AEG, Vereinigte Stahlwerke and Vereinigte Glanzstoff-Fabriken became active in Yugoslavia, Czechoslovakia and Romania. IG Farben, the chemicals cartel created in 1925, had been closely associated with Stresemann, who backed state subsidies for the company's production of synthetic petrol which, while expensive, reduced spending of foreign currency on oil imports. A board member and future chairman, Carl Bosch, enjoyed a close friendship with the chancellor Heinrich Brüning. Brüning raised pump prices for petrol to some of the highest in the world to attempt to cover the costs of producing synthetic fuel. Widespread opposition to this price-hike encouraged the company to turn to supporting the rising star of Adolf Hitler, despite Nazi propaganda attacking the firm for being linked to 'Jewish financial capital'.[6]

Even before the economic crisis, industrialists in the key industrial regions of the Rhineland and Westphalia had been demanding the dismantling of the welfare state created by the Weimar governments. The Weimar Republic had been based on an alliance between the parties of the centre, voted for by the middle classes, and the Social Democrats, rooted in the working class. That alliance was now collapsing. Middle-class voters, facing real or imagined economic ruin, began shifting rightwards, finding solace in Hitler. Big business demanded the exclusion of the Social Democrats and the unions.[7] In 1930 the 'grand coalition' government led by the Social Democrat, Hermann Müller, was brought down by these pressures.[8]

The Social Democrats were the one party committed to maintaining the Republic but from now on they were excluded from office. They also began to suffer a loss of support on their left to the Communists who hated a republic born in the blood of Rosa Luxemburg and her comrades back in 1919. A succession of administrations followed promising 'strong government', but all failed to halt the growing shift to both the extreme right and left, reflecting a polarisation of German society. The first was led by a Centre Party politician, Heinrich

Brüning, with a reputation for business and financial skill and whose war record made him acceptable to President von Hindenburg. While imposing massive cuts in welfare spending, Brüning began the process of German rearmament with the construction of two battle cruisers.

After the proposed customs union with Austria was blocked, Brüning threatened to stop reparation payments and hinted at halting repayment on all foreign debts. The subsequent run on the mark reduced German gold reserves by 40 per cent. Brüning could not carry a majority in the Reichstag. He and Hindenburg decided to call new elections, but these only benefited the Nazis and, to a lesser extent, the Communists. Brüning could not form a coalition government and instead relied on presidential decrees, declaring that he ruled by 'authoritative democracy'.[9]

After the severe economic crisis in the summer of 1931 all the major banks were under effective state control. Bankruptcies affected the insurance and engineering industries and the government had to buy a tranche of shares to bail out the Vereinigte Stahlwerke. Private holdings of foreign currency were effectively nationalised, with the government forcing people to exchange it to Reichsmarks. Restrictions were also placed on imports, all in a desperate bid to stem a growing trade deficit. Brüning slashed welfare spending and cut wages, causing widespread anger among the working class. The Social Democrats had been prepared to give tacit support to Brüning, but working-class anger over such cuts ruled this out any further. As middle-class voters moved rightwards, the centre right and liberal parties followed in their wake, calling for a more right-wing government.

Brüning had ruled out job creation – a policy which the Nazis began to promise. Their policies of rearmament, destroying Weimar's welfare system and expanding Germany's borders eastwards were now attracting elite support. In January 1932 Hitler was invited to address the Düsseldorf Industry Club. This was his first chance to convince some 600 representatives of big business that he and his party were serious contenders for power. His speech concentrated on what he and they shared in common. Hitler was beginning the process of winning these industrialists and bankers over.

Meanwhile Hindenburg determined to remove Brüning, appointing the relatively obscure Franz von Papen in his place in June 1932. The new chancellor had little support in the Reichstag and tried to exert his own style of personal and authoritarian rule. He staged a coup which removed the elected Social Democratic government of Prussia, the key German state, and lifted a ban on the Nazi Sturmabteilung (SA), the stormtroopers, hoping to win Nazi backing for his government. Hitler was not playing that game.

The von Papen government could not maintain a working parliamentary majority and he was forced to resign after the November 1932 elections. Kurt von Schleicher succeeded him as chancellor. A military man who had been the liaison between the army and the civilian government, Schleicher promised Hindenburg he would restore order. He hoped to form a bloc with disparate forces to attain a majority in the Reichstag – the Social Democrats, the trade unions, the Christian labour unions, and the supposedly more radical wing of the Nazi Party led by Gregor Strasser (although the latter was already losing his internal fight with Hitler and would soon be expelled from the party).

Hitler to Power

The November 1932 elections saw a fall in the Nazis' share of the vote accompanied by an increase in support for the Communists. The ruling class were scared by this and were beginning to view the Nazis as a useful weapon against the left. Initially, however, the ruling class was only prepared to countenance Nazi participation in a coalition government.

The Nazis and big business shared common aims. Firstly, to use repression to smash working-class organisation and to reverse welfare measures in order to increase exploitation. Beyond that both looked to expand production, to plunder, geographical expansion and war. Nazi political dominance sat comfortably with the continued economic dominance of big capital. A section of industrialists and bankers, whose mouthpiece was Hjalmar Schacht, moved towards accepting Hitler as chancellor. That month the steel magnate and Nazi Party member Fritz Thyssen, together with Schacht, organised a letter signed by business leaders urging Hindenburg to appoint Hitler as chancellor.

Schleicher's erstwhile comrades in the high command wanted a rapid shift to full-scale rearmament. The military commander in East Prussia, Werner von Blomberg had already met with Hitler and supported the Nazis being in government. On 16 December 1932 von Papen delivered an address on 'The New State' to 300 members of the elite 'Deutscher Herrenklub', open only to upper-class conservatives. Von Papen told the gathering that Germany required authoritarian rule embodied in an authoritarian ruler, that Schleicher did not command sufficient support to rebuild the economy, and that a new coalition was required to restore authority. The former chancellor was hoping to become leader of this coalition, and a meeting between von Papen and Hitler to discuss the latter joining such a government took place on 4 January 1933.

In the meantime von Papen played on Hindenburg's hatred of the Social Democrats to undermine the president's support for Schleicher and to urge the old man to appoint a coalition government involving the right-wing parties and politicians. The president was a Prussian landowner and the agricultural lobby was also pressing for a coalition government of right-wing nationalists and the Nazis. Hitler's confidence was such that in this swirl of negotiations he held out for the chancellorship. Hindenburg dismissed Schleicher and on 30 January 1933 appointed Hitler as chancellor, heading a coalition government in which the Nazis initially took just two cabinet positions. The Nazi accession to power rested on a pact between the Nazis, leading sections of big business and the German high command. This bloc would remain in place until the end.

While some hoped the coalition might house-train Hitler, the reality was that the Nazis' presence in government contaminated the whole of Germany's body politic, as Fabrice d'Almeida explains:

The nobility and upper bourgeoisie started out from conservative positions. Before the 1930s, few members of these groups defended Nazism. They were first led to support an alliance between Nazism and conservatism, and then allowed themselves to be infected by an ideological radicalisation.[10]

The motivation was both the need to restore profitability and hatred of the left. The shift to backing Hitler came late, and was pragmatic at the outset.

A month after he been made chancellor, Hitler summoned leaders of big business to a private meeting at Göring's villa. Attending were Krupp von Bohlen, head of Krupps and the Association of German Industrialists, Georg von Schintzler, second in command of IG Farben, and Dr Albert Voegler, chief executive of the Vereinigte Stahlwerke. Hitler announced that he wanted hefty donations to fight Reichstag elections to be held in March; in return he promised to end parliamentary democracy and to eliminate the left. Thyssen persuaded the Association of German Industrialists to donate 3 million Reichsmarks to the Nazi Party.

Hitler was won to the idea of producing synthetic fuel and limiting Germany's dependence on costly imports. In return IG Farben began funding the Nazi Party. In September 1933 IG Farben would request and receive from the new Nazi regime a state investment in synthetic fuel production of 400,000 marks, rising to 1.8 million marks.[11] In June 1933 Göring, von Blomberg, now minister of defence, and Erhard Milch, secretary of state at the air ministry, attended a meeting with Schacht where the latter outlined an arms programme of between 5 and 10 per cent of German GDP over the next eight years. The military had already been released from budgetary controls. It was allowed to pay for orders with IOUs. The arms, steel and engineering manufacturers were happy with this because they expected to benefit handsomely from an arms drive. Four months later Hitler announced that Germany was withdrawing from the League of Nations and world disarmament talks. Göring and von Blomberg expected Britain and France to take military action in response. Nothing happened.

At the close of 1933 two four-year plans were implemented, which set the target of creating by 1937 a standing army of 21 divisions, totalling 300,000 men (which could be expanded to 63 divisions in event of war), and for the Luftwaffe to have 2,000 frontline aircraft by 1935. In the second year of Hitler's rule, military spending accounted for over 50 per cent of total government spending. Two years later it stood at 73 per cent. The levels of military expenditure were unprecedented for any government in peacetime. In August 1934 President Hindenburg died and Hitler became head of state in his place. That day every member of the armed forces swore allegiance to Adolf Hitler as 'Führer of the German Reich and people and Commander in Chief of the armed forces'. The military high command agreed to this as part of a deal with Hitler – a month earlier, in the 'Night of the Long Knives', he had personally led the SS in a drive to eradicate the leadership of the SA who were demanding that their stormtroopers replace the existing army.

Characteristically Hitler also used the opportunity to remove and intimidate other opponents. Schleicher and his wife were murdered at their home; the former Nazi leader Gregor Strasser, who had quit the movement, was also killed. The SS stormed the vice-chancellery, arresting von Papen, gunning down his secretary and murdering other of his associates. Von Papen had demanded that Hitler show his supporters there would be no 'second revolution' aimed at the existing elite. Hitler was determined that the likes of von Papen would not tell him what to do. In the course of the 'Night of the Long Knives' the vice chancellor, under house arrest, resigned his position and a month later was appointed ambassador to Austria.

Self-sufficiency, Rearmament and Expansion

Germany was still burdened under foreign debt worth billions of US dollars. One billion Reichsmarks were paid each year in interest and repayments. Exports were hampered by the high exchange rate of the mark. The Third Reich had to operate very strict exchange controls in order to try to maintain a precarious balance of payments. In June 1933 a unilateral moratorium was announced on Germany's long-term debts, provoking the British government to threaten a trade war.

Various means were employed to get round this. Even before Hitler German governments had encouraged a barter system whereby German industrial goods were exchanged for agricultural products and raw materials from Latin America, Eastern and South East Europe. However, by the summer of 1934 the Reichsbank's foreign exchange holdings were virtually exhausted. The British, led by the governor of the Bank of England, Montagu Norman, a close friend of the Reichsbank president and Hitler's minister of economics, Hjalmar Schacht, negotiated the Anglo-German Payments Agreement of November 1934, which stabilised economic relations between Europe's two major economies. Germany received credits from the Bank of England and Britain became Germany's biggest creditor. The German government would continue to pay full interest in sterling on loans, satisfying City of London investors.

The City of London continued to provide the German economy with a vital line of credit all the way up to the outbreak of the war. This policy of economic appeasement of Hitler matched Baldwin and Chamberlain's policy of political appeasement. Nonetheless the Third Reich was pursuing a policy of 'autarky' (economic self-efficiency). In reality this did not mean cutting Germany off from the world economy. As Adam Tooze points out, 'A close look at the trade statistics reveal that "autarky" in fact amounted to a selective policy of disengagement directed above all against the United States, the British Empire and, to a lesser degree, France.'[12] In 1928 US exports to Germany had been worth 2 billion Reichsmarks. By 1936 they were down to 232 million Reichsmarks. Raw materials previously imported from the US and Britain were now obtained from South East Europe and Latin America.

Shortages of labour, raw materials and foreign currencies were also by 1936 threatening to cripple the German economy and the dictatorship's rearmament programme. The election of Popular Front governments in both France and

Spain in 1936 had bolstered Hitler's anti-communism while his anti-Semitism became more pronounced. In August that year Hitler prepared a memorandum on the German political and economic situation and the likelihood of war – which he concluded was inevitable. The enemy was Russia. The document concluded with words: 'i: The German armed forces must be operational within four years; ii: The German economy must be fit for war within four years.'[13] Hitler couched this as a war of civilisations. The launch of a four-year plan at the 1936 party rally, accelerating autarky and the arms drive, gave the signal for war. The armed forces, the party, the SS and industry became increasingly interwoven and mutually dependent.

Göring was in charge of the plan and he brought together military and party figures with executives from IG Farben to administer it. An IG Farben director, Carl Krauch, became Plenipotentiary for Chemical Production, which was later extended to include the mineral, oil, rubber, light metals and explosives sectors. Also brought in were Paul Pleiger and Hans Kehrl from the staff of Wilhelm Keppler, a committed Nazi even prior to January 1933, who was chair of two IG Farben subsidiaries, Braunkohle-Benzin AG and Kontinental Oil. Kontinental used Standard Oil's technology for production of gasoline from coal – the US government was unhappy about Standard Oil supplying this.

Göring's priority was military preparation, and no budgetary limits or requirements to balance civilian and military needs would be allowed to get in the way. The Wehrmacht now set a goal of 102 divisions with 3.6 million men by 1940. Seven armoured divisions had to be in place by 1939 – no small order given that in 1936 only light tanks armed with machine guns were in production. General Friedrich Fromm warned, 'Shortly after completion of the rearmament phase the Wehrmacht must be employed, otherwise there must be a reduction in demands or in the level of war readiness.'[14]

Göring presided over the creation of the giant state-owned Reichswerke-Hermann-Göring steel corporation, overriding opposition from the steel barons, who were compensated with lavish rearmament contracts. The Nazis were demonstrating that, however sympathetic they were to big business, they had their own interests and were prepared to pursue them relentlessly. Nonetheless, German industry was, to use Ian Kershaw's words, 'structurally implicated in the policy decisions which culminated in destruction and inhumanity on a scale unprecedented in Europe'.[15]

Hitler was following a continuity in traditional German foreign policy with his demands for *Lebensraum*, but there was also a break. In general Hitler was in step with the capitalist ruling class, but he had also created his own power base, the SS and to a lesser extent the Nazi Party. This allowed him to take crucial steps towards his own genocidal aims. Within the Third Reich the general thrust of 'working towards Hitler' meant the elites had to rapidly adopt his new policy initiatives and make them their own, as with rearmament, and even second guess what his next step would be. German expansion was an inevitability by the 1930s but under the Third Reich its direction and dynamic was no longer independent of Hitler's personal position.[16]

Industry benefited handsomely from rearmament but the Third Reich demanded in return that it should bend to the interests of the Nazi war machine. The individual interests of particular corporations had to be subordinate to the overall interest of the Nazi regime. Individuals who deviated from that paid a price, no matter how rich and powerful they were. In October 1933 Dr Hugo Junkers, a key aircraft designer and head of the family firm, was arrested and forced to sign the firm over to the state. His crime was to have squabbled with the Luftwaffe and air ministry over what types of planes should be developed.

Later, the steel boss Thyssen, a long-term supporter of Hitler, fell out with the regime and was forced into exile. By then he had been eclipsed by Gustav Krupp von Bohlen und Halbach. The steel and armament manufacturer had backed the Nazis in the spring of 1933 and a year later he became president of the association of German industrialists. By 1937 his eldest son headed the heavy industries owners' association, joining the Nazi Party the following year.

Nineteen-thirty-seven was the one year in which rearmament stagnated, largely because of a shortage of steel. One solution was to cut steel used for non-military purposes by 25 per cent, with serious consequences for the rail system and housing. By the summer of 1938 over 35 per cent of Germany's steel was allocated to the army. Politicians, industrialists and military chiefs all looked to securing Alsace-Lorraine and South East Europe as a means of accessing iron ore and increasing steel production.

The Nazis' aim of gaining *Lebensraum* was far more radical. Early in 1936, Richard Darre, head of the food administration, told his officials:

> The natural area for settlement by the German people is the territory to the east of the Reich's boundaries up to the Urals, bordered in the south by the Caucasus, Caspian Sea, Black Sea and the watershed which divides the Mediterranean basin from the Baltic and North Sea. We will settle this space, according to the law that a superior people always has the right to conquer and to own the land of an inferior people.[17]

Detlev J.K. Peukert argues that the contradictions so obvious at times under the Weimar Republic did not altogether disappear in the Third Reich, but were incorporated into the new state system. Above all he argues that because capitalist property remained intact, Nazi nationalisation was incomplete, and that led not to efficiency but to constant conflict between those charged with running the economy:

> there was now permanent confused petty warfare among rival power groups. Each of these groups (party administration, SS and police, business, armed forces) had its vassals and a relatively secure power base, but each tended to interfere with the area of responsibility of the others ... The 'nationalisation' of society by Nazism was followed by the 'privatisation' of the state.[18]

The different power centres within the Third Reich were in permanent competition with each other, 'working towards the Führer'. When he was told

Germany was an authoritarian state the French collaborationist prime minister Pierre Laval quipped that that might be so, 'but what a lot of authorities'.[19]

The German military high command was thoroughly politicised. Immediately after fighting ended in 1918, Germany's military leaders had set themselves the task of winning back all that had been lost at Versailles. In 1924 Lieutenant Colonel Joachim von Stülpnagel lectured the officers of the Reichswehr Ministry on the need for 'total war' against the French and Poles. This involved the mobilisation of all the people inspired by 'national hatred raised to the furthest extreme' involving 'sabotage, murder, and chemical and biological attack'. For Stülpnagel this also required ending parliamentary rule and imposing a 'strong central Reich authority' which could oversee the 'national and military indoctrination of our youth' so they would uncritically accept 'the categorical imperative of fighting and dying for the Fatherland'.[20]

Back in February 1933 the army's commander in chief, General von Blomberg, supported Hitler's assumption of full dictatorial powers and argued that the army 'had to serve the national movement with devotion'. He went on to instruct his soldiers that they had to learn the 'basic principles of the National Socialist State' because 'the ideas of both our corps spirit and National Socialism spring from the common experience of the Great War'.[21] This did not stop Hitler removing Blomberg from his position in 1938 and appointing himself as commander in chief. He now had control over the armed forces, foreign policy and much of the economy – not detailed, day to day control, but the leadership of all sections of the Third Reich nevertheless 'worked towards' Hitler.[22]

British intelligence and politicians made great play of their contacts with anti-war elements in Germany prior to war breaking out. Yet even the major components of the opposition circles which emerged post-Munich within the German military and upper classes accepted that Germany must be a great power, that Versailles must be revised and Berlin allowed control of Central Europe. They simply wanted to avoid a general European war. Klaus-Jürgen Müller points out that 'the term "opposition" is simply not appropriate in the sense of a resistance opposed to the system; it was rather opposition as an attempt to put through an alternative policy within the system'.[23]

Jews, Bolsheviks and Other 'Asocials'

Anti-Semitism was not central to the Nazis electoral campaigns prior to 1933. What it was crucial for was binding together the disparate elements of the movement by presenting an all powerful enemy which had to be and could be removed.

The German ruling class shared a desire to carve out an empire in Eastern Europe and Russia (and were happy when Western Europe fell their way), but Hitler's ambitions went way beyond that. For the Nazis war was not simply a means for economic or geographical gain. The mythology of the Third Reich portrayed an organic society, defined by race, in which all class and social divisions had been submerged. Opponents of this goal and those who did not fit the racial criteria were to be eliminated. This was to be a warrior community forged in war. For Hitler, Jews were not just 'racial aliens' but represented the greatest threat. Anti-Semitism was the key element in his racial programme, but 'racial purification' targeted the Roma, the mentally and congenitally ill, and homosexuals. Increasingly this racial policy would dominate Nazi policy, domestic and foreign.

The targeting of Jews as responsible for Germany's woes had surfaced as Germany began to face the possibility of failure during the First World War. Various mass organisations had existed prior to the war supporting imperial and expansionist ambitions. One was the Pan-German League, founded in 1891. Among its supporters was Emil Kirdof, who would be one of the few industrialists to back Hitler prior to the explosion in support for the Nazis. In 1917, after the Reichstag voted to open peace negotiations, the president of the Pan-German League, Heinrich Class, proposed 'to exploit the situation for fanfares against Jewry and the Jews as lightning rods for all injustice'.[24]

He and other leaders of the League helped found the German Fatherland Party (Deutsche Vaterlandspartei), which grew to 800,000 members by 1918. At its head stood Admiral Tirpitz, who had led Germany's 'naval race' with Britain, attempting to build a battle fleet to wrest control of the North Sea. Another leading member was Wolfgang Kapp, who would go on to lead the unsuccessful coup in 1920. So, even prior to Hitler's emergence, there was a great pool of nationalist and anti-Semitic right-wingers, including, of course, the Freikorps.

The German Psychiatric Institute, founded in 1918, urged mass sterilisation to solve Germany's problems. They compiled 'criminal-biological' data on individuals. In 1926, the Reich Ministry of the Interior allowed them the right to consult official records.

Hitler and the leadership of the Nazi Party were fired by the supposed comradeship of the trenches and by revulsion at the 'Jewish-Bolshevik conspiracy' which had stabbed the nation in the back when revolution at home ended the war in 1918. These and other 'traitors' had to be cleansed from the new Germany. In 1938 the SS (who controlled the police and security forces) gained control of anti-Jewish policy which rapidly accelerated in its virulence. The Kristallnacht pogrom of 9 and 10 November was the sort of 'wild excess' Schacht had opposed while he was economics minister (his concern was with possible economic repercussions abroad rather than Jewish loss of life).

The homosexual subculture which had developed in Weimar Germany was physically smashed by the Nazis on taking power, with bars and clubs shut down. In 1935 laws banning gay sex were toughened up still further so that the mere indication of sexual interest was a criminal offence. Two years later homosexuals and other 'asocials' were sent to concentration camps, where they were terrorised by guards and criminal prisoners. Worse was to follow.

As the British Marxist historian Tim Mason points out, Hitler had determined that in order to fight a second war, 'enforced ideological unity, and terror' at home were needed.[25] But Mason also demonstrates that fear of another 1918 led the regime to pull back from cutting wages or consumption too much or from moving to a full-scale war economy (to match Britain's) until after Stalingrad. It was not a case of 'bombs not butter' but of trying to provide bombs and butter when it was no longer possible.

One way of squaring that circle was by using slave and forced labour from the conquered territories, with very low productivity rates, rather than employing women or transferring workers into the armaments sector. If this suggests a rational, planned economy then the reality was that the component parts of the party-state and big business were left alone by Hitler to fight out it out over restricted labour and raw material supplies. It should be added that although Hitler destroyed the labour movement he did not need to lead an assault on working-class wages because that had already largely occurred under the von Papen government.

Labour shortages were a serious problem in the crucial coal-mining industry, and productivity levels were falling in the last two years of peace. In those years shortages were reported too in munitions plants and in construction (affecting the building of the Siegfried Line), and the Luftwaffe was worried by the lack of aircraft engineers. Arms suppliers were turning down orders, supply deadlines were being broken and production costs rising. As Mason argues:

> economic class conflict re-emerged in Germany on a broad front after 1936. This took forms which were not clearly political ... Further, this struggle for the basic economic interests of the working class does not appear to have been organised in any way. It manifested itself through spontaneous strikes, through the exercise of collective pressure on employers and on Nazi organisations, through the most various acts of defiance against workplace rules and government decrees, through slowdowns in production, absenteeism, the taking of sick leave, demonstrations of discontent, etc.[26]

All of this must be set against the wider impact of the Nazi dictatorship on German society, as the American economic historian, Paul N. Hehn explains:

> On the face of it, the population as a whole ... did not benefit from the Nazi economic recovery: its share of total production never reached the 1929–33 level of income, falling from 62–64 per cent of that period to 57 per cent in 1938 ... German working class gains can be attributed to the rise in the number of hours worked from 41.5 in 1932 to 46.5 and 47.8 in the last two years before the war. Property and entrepreneurial income in contrast rose from 30.4 per cent to 33.8 per cent and retained earnings of corporations from 0.4 per cent to 5.4 per cent in 1939.[27]

The Third Reich reduced investment in the public sector (public housing, social benefits, etc.), cutting spending on public housing from 1,330 million marks in 1928 to 250 million marks in 1939, creating an acute housing shortage. State spending was switched to rearmament. 'The chief beneficiary of this shift in public expenditure and investment was private business, particularly the large corporate and industrial sector.'[28]

Hitler's priority by 1939 was to avoid any prospect of social upheaval at home which might hamper a war of conquest abroad. The Third Reich combined terror against all forms of political opposition, in particular from working-class organisations, with attempts to incorporate the working class into the state project.

The Necessity of War

Labour shortages, lack of raw materials and the resulting production bottlenecks fed the necessity of going for a war in September 1939. Four months earlier Major-General George Thomas, former chief of the military-economic staff in the Reich War Ministry, had delivered a lecture on 24 May in the Nazi Foreign Office, claiming that the Third Reich could boast:

> the mightiest armament industry now existing in the world. It has attained the performances which in part equal the German wartime performances and in part even surpasses them. Germany's crude steel production is today the largest in the world after the Americans. The aluminium production exceeds that of America and of the other countries of the world very considerably. The output of our rifle, machine gun, and artillery factories is at present larger than that of any other state.[29]

Demand for copper, zinc, antimony and chrome had almost doubled. Thomas claimed that Germany depended on imports for 95 per cent of its bauxite, 80 per cent of its rubber, 70 per cent of its tin, two thirds of its oil and zinc, 50 per cent of its lead, 45 per cent of its fats, and between 10 and 20 per cent of its foodstuff.[30]

The need to secure raw materials began to take precedence over virtually everything else and became central to Hitler's foreign policy. Renewed recession internationally in 1938 undermined German exports, as did the shortcomings in industries like coal mining. Reduced exports meant there was a shortage of international currency to buy in vital materials. Hitler could lean upon Germany's neighbours to accept rigged rates of exchange or barter to overcome this but it was not enough. Hitler was modern enough to know that his dreams of conquest relied upon industry and necessities like oil, the thirst for which could not be quenched by his Romanian ally.

Maintaining an economy geared to the demands of war required an expansionist policy and a short-term deal with Russia, with Poland and the occupied territories supplying forced labour and Russia the badly needed raw materials.[31] In May 1939 Hitler stated:

> The ideological problems have been solved by the mass of 80 million people. The economic problems must also be solved. To create the economic conditions necessary for this is a task no German can disregard ... We must not allow the principle to prevail that one can accommodate oneself to the

circumstances and thus shirk the solution of problems. The circumstances must rather be adapted to suit the demands. This is not possible without breaking into other countries, or attacking other people's property.[32]

The Faustian pact between Hitler and big business guaranteed the Nazis political power alongside the continuance of the capitalist economic system. In the autumn of 1939 there was a consensus between German capitalism and the regime over the need to expand territorially to solve the immediate problems of labour and material shortages, the long-term aim of hegemony in Central and Eastern Europe, and the need to combat communism. The rather ineffective opposition that emerged from sections of German capital was not opposed to any of this, but to the possibility of Hitler taking Germany into a Europe-wide war.

In the beginning it seemed that Hitler would honour his pledge to President Hindenburg that the military were to be allowed their independence. Instead, the existence of the SS, a parallel party organisation, contaminated the military. As the Reich went to war the military effort assumed a terrible, murderous autonomy. German capitalists did not order or even approve mass murder but they too were pulled along behind the logic of Hitler's war.

Labour shortages were a constant problem. There was immigration from the countryside to industrial areas (making a mockery of Nazi rhetoric about returning the people to the land), and the German populations of Austria and Czechoslovakia were badly needed. Hitler's Italian ally, Mussolini, also sent workers – who were treated as racial inferiors rather than allies. Living standards for German workers returned to the levels of the mid 1920s, but accounted for a shrinking percentage of an expanding Gross National Product. In other words the destruction of working-class organisation led to increased economic exploitation.

Terror was a daily reality for workers. The Gestapo (Geheime Staatspolizei) was created as a national secret police force in 1934, under SS control. In 1936 the head of the SS, Himmler, took control of a newly centralised police force, the Ordnungspolizei ('order police'), and placed Reinhardt Heydrich, who was head of the SS's security service, the SD, in control of the Gestapo. In any community people knew friends and family who had been arrested and thrown into a concentration camp. The shadow of the Gestapo and their informers fell over working-class life. In the winter of 1939, after workplace unrest had become apparent, a Gestapo presence became a permanent feature in many key plants. Employers handed over names of absentees and 'troublemakers', who were then routinely dispatched to Gestapo prisons and concentration camps.

The lack of resistance to the Third Reich's expansion had created confusion among opponents of the regime. The underground Social Democrat network reported on conditions inside Nazi Germany. In March 1938 a Social Democrat described the popular mood in Breslau (today's Wroclaw) thus:

> The general opinion in the groups [on the street] was: 'Lets face it, Hitler is a great man, he knows what he wants and the world is scared of him.' Conversations the next day followed the same trains of thought. Hitler's

prestige has risen enormously again and he is now practically idolised. The objection that the western powers might still intervene and issue Germany with an ultimatum was laughed out of court. The western powers simply daren't do anything against Germany, and even if they do, Germany is strong enough to get its own way.[33]

However, there is considerable agreement among eyewitnesses that the outbreak of war in September 1939 did not lead to the sort of popular reaction which greeted the outbreak of the First World War. As Hitler's victories mounted, the regular reports from inside Germany sent to the Social Democratic Party leadership in exile noted 'unease, as hopes for peace were shattered, and a basic sense of uncertainty as to the ultimate outcome of the war'.[34]

The use of terror and the introduction of slave labour meant the workplace often took on the character of the concentration camp, and this would develop as the war prolonged. The slave labourers were regarded as disposable, forming another step towards genocide.[35]

Of the European powers only Germany wanted war, 'less because the German economy was fully prepared for war (certainly general and prolonged war) than because Germany was going through a severe economic crisis, of which one possible solution was a war of conquest'.[36] The Third Reich was arming in order to expand, but needed to expand in order to sustain that arms drive.

Tim Mason is surely right to conclude that: 'a Third Reich "at peace" is an unimaginable contradiction in terms'.[37] For Hitler the new German community would be built in struggle and maintained in struggle. He often expressed his fears that degeneration would set in if the Volk found itself at peace. For the German leaders there were only two possible outcomes – total victory or total defeat.

Italy: Big Appetite, Bad Teeth

The German chancellor Bismarck quipped, following Italian unification in 1861, that Italy was only ranked as a great power because the real great European powers, in their rivalry, vied with each other to make it their ally. The catastrophic performance of Fascist Italy in the Second World War might seem to justify Bismarck's remarks, but it is included here among the principal actors for two reasons. Firstly, fascism first came to power in Italy, in October 1922, and Hitler never hid his admiration for Mussolini. Secondly, the Italian Duce, like his German counterpart, held that war was necessary to forge not just a new empire but a new, vigorous race. It should be added that, despite the scathing comments often made privately about Italy's status in the corridors of power in London, Paris and Berlin, they all vied to secure Mussolini's allegiance in the 1930s.

Italy had been on the winning side in the First World War. It entered the war after a year, ditching its alliance with Germany and Austria to join Britain and France, after bargaining between the rival camps for the highest bribe. In the secret Treaty of London (only revealed by the Bolsheviks after the 1917

October Revolution), London and Paris promised Italy ownership of much of the Balkans, a tranche of territory in Turkey, more colonial possessions in North and East Africa, plus those parts of the Austrian Empire which contained Italian populations. The eventual peace treaties fell short of this. The US and France backed the creation of a state bringing together different Slav groupings – what would become Yugoslavia. The nationalist backlash among ex-officers, students and other sections of the Italian middle class was an important factor in the rise of fascism in 1920–22.

Italy was also the country in Western Europe which most closely approximated conditions in revolutionary Russia. In 1917 Italy's peasant conscript armies had almost fallen apart when they refused to resist an Austro-German advance following a breakthrough at Caporetto which was only stopped just short of Venice. Italy's rulers, rocked by this crisis, used intensified austerity and repression of labour unrest combined with vague promises of land reform in order to encourage peasant soldiers to fight.

All this ensured that the end of the war gave rise to a revolutionary crisis in the 'Two Red Years' (*Biennio Rosso*) of 1919 and 1920, culminating in a nationwide occupation of the factories in September 1920, which only ended when the government and trade union leaders traded economic concessions to secure a return to what they hoped would be normality. Almost instantly fascist bands emerged to wage war first on the rural agricultural trade unions before taking terror from the countryside to the towns.[38]

Italy as a unified state had existed for only six decades when Mussolini took power in October 1922. Its ruling class was far from homogeneous, and in the crisis of the post-war years it effectively ceased to govern. A motley band of fascists led by Mussolini was able to step into the void. Where the police and army had been unable to cope, squads of armed Blackshirts brought terror down on the agricultural trade unions and then on the urban working class. Italy's workers put up greater resistance than their German counterparts would later, but their socialist and trade union leaders made the same mistakes: they looked to the state to protect them and failed to co-ordinate the spontaneous resistance into a national effort.

Mussolini took power with the blessing of the king, big business and the army command. They might not like giving power to such a déclassé adventurer, but they were prepared to co-operate with him if they could retain economic control while he wielded total political power. Mussolini spoke of creating a new Roman Empire, but for much of the 1920s he implemented conventional free market economic measures and played the diplomatic game – staying friendly with the two dominant Mediterranean powers, Britain and France. He did, however, wage a brutal war to secure Italian colonial control of Libya using concentration camps and poison gas.[39]

In the 1930s Mussolini widened his ambitions to build Italy into a great power and to offset the effects of the Great Depression, which cut off its export markets and saw its rivals claw control of vital raw materials. He began using the state to defend Italy's uncompetitive industries and moved to seal off the economy by preaching self-sufficiency. Eventually between a fifth and a quarter of Italian industry was under state ownership, more than in any other Western state, yet this failed to restore the economy or staunch rising poverty and unemployment.[40]

Meanwhile arms spending as a proportion of national income increased from 3.4 per cent in 1927 to 5.4 per cent in 1931 and then mushroomed to 18.4 per cent in 1936. Between 1926 and 1940 Italy spent proportionally more than Britain on arms. The invasion of Ethiopia and the intervention in Spain carried Mussolini's spending beyond France's in real terms.[41]

In 1935 Mussolini decided to launch Italy as a great power by invading one of only two independent states in Africa, Ethiopia. In the build up to the invasion he told the Italian industrialist, Alberto Pirelli, that 'afterwards we shall conquer Egypt and Sudan', because he sought 'an empire that stretched from the Mediterranean to the Indian Ocean'.[42] Two months into the invasion the British and French foreign ministers, Samuel Hoare and Pierre Laval, agreed a deal with the former fascist *squadristi* commander Dino Grandi whereby Ethiopia would be partitioned, with Italy gaining the richest areas. When news of this deal leaked, the Baldwin government backtracked, and Hoare was forced to resign, while the French government was thrown into crisis and Laval met the same fate.

The League of Nations voted to denounce the invasion and demand economic sanctions against Italy, but Britain and France restricted themselves to denouncing the attack and imposing only ineffectual sanctions, with Britain refusing to block Italian troop movements and supplies through the Suez Canal. Mussolini told the Baldwin government that he would accept condemnation by the League of Nations and the imposition of limited economic sanctions in return for Britain not intervening. London agreed.[43]

Mussolini ordered the use of chemical weapons on a mass scale and terror against civilian targets. The Italian dictator sent a 'salutary warning' to the people of Ethiopia, stating that 'every civilian or member of a religious order, man or woman, suspected of having aided attacks [against Italian forces] is to be immediately shot without trial'.[44] Italian troops captured Addis Ababa, and Mussolini proclaimed the new Roman Empire, but up to 227,000 troops were needed to deal with continued resistance in the new colony.[45]

By May 1936 Baldwin's heir apparent, the chancellor Neville Chamberlain, was urging the cabinet to lift sanctions and to make a rapprochement with Mussolini a matter of high priority. A month later, when the League of Nations suggested tightening sanctions, Chamberlain said in a speech that the idea Ethiopia could regain its independence was 'the very midsummer of madness'.[46] Chamberlain had not informed the foreign secretary Anthony Eden of his speech, knowing that Eden regarded Italy as the key threat to Britain's dominance of the Mediterranean. Ten days after the speech Baldwin announced that Britain was dropping sanctions against Italy.

In post-war Italy it has become common to blame discrimination against the Jews and Italy's participation in what would become the Holocaust on Mussolini's alliance with the Third Reich, yet there is little evidence of German pressure on Mussolini to introduce anti-Semitic measures. The dictatorship's racial laws which deprived Jews of their citizenship (won at the time of Italian unification) and barred them from higher education and a whole raft of jobs were a product of Italian fascism. The regime had always been murderously racist but until 1938 this was aimed at Slavs on the country's north-eastern border, Arabs in its Libyan colony, and then the Ethiopians.[47]

The conquest of Ethiopia was justified on racist grounds and was followed by the creation of an apartheid regime. That meant a new objective of creating a racially pure state. If until now anti-Semitism had not been central to fascism it came easily to the Blackshirts. The majority of Italian Jews who died in the death camps were rounded up and deported by Italian security forces on the basis of Italian laws. Italy championed the Ustashi regime in Croatia, which had one of the worst wartime records in killing not just Jews but Greek Orthodox Christians and Muslims who found themselves under its rule, while Italian occupation forces also encouraged ethnic cleansing in Kosovo and elsewhere in the Balkans.[48]

Mussolini's eyes were bigger than his stomach. Given half a chance he wished to emulate Hitler in expanding his empire. But lack of finance and poor military ability meant his ambitions were restricted to the Mediterranean. The Germans calculated that the Italian economy performed at 25 per cent of its capacity. The percentage of Italian GDP devoted to the war effort peaked at just 23 per cent in 1941 compared with Germany's 64 per cent. In 1939 Italy possessed 469,000 motor vehicles as against 1.99 million in Germany, 2.25 million in France and 2.42 million in Britain. When war came the Italian army lacked not only trucks and armoured vehicles but even drivers and mechanics.[49] Italy had just three armoured divisions – which would be the sum total throughout Mussolini's war – and these were equipped with tanks which were death traps when confronted with enemy armour or anti-tank weapons. Its artillery dated back to the First World War, as did the tactics employed by the military commanders. The country possessed no aircraft carriers, its naval forces lacked radar, and there was no co-ordination between them and the air force. Its air force was not able to match its German or British counterparts, possessing no modern fighters.

Japan: War as the Only Escape

Modern Japan is the creation of the 1867 Meiji Restoration. Formally this was the restoration of imperial rule. However, political power moved from the old feudal elite to an oligarchy which wanted to industrialise Japan and create a modern empire in response to the threat of US intervention intended to open up Japan to its exports.[50]

The spur for this change occurred in 1853 when Commodore Matthew C. Perry took the US East India Squadron, made up of modern ironclad ships, into Tokyo Bay and trained his guns on the city, demanding that Japan open up to free trade with America. Under threat, when Perry returned the following year the Japanese signed a treaty accepting American demands. Military intimidation had worked, and Japan would not forget the lesson!

The bureaucracy that had run Japan, sidelining the emperor, was fatally wounded by the concessions granted to the United States. The social force that organised the insurrection that 'restored' imperial rule consisted of impoverished samurai warriors, armed with Western weapons, and funded by merchants and bankers.[51]

Japan now had to arm or face conquest, and that required industrialisation. The new imperial regime faced a race with the Western powers to acquire territory and influence in China, the Western Pacific and South East Asia. It had to create a modern army and navy to compete. The state funded and directed the creation of strategic defence industries and a modern communications infrastructure, as Jamie C. Allinson and Alexander Anievas argue:

> under military threat from the West, the primary task of reconstituting state and society along capitalist lines fell to the Meiji bureaucratic state class ... The Meiji state came effectively to function as capital ... The particularly rapid pace of Japan's transition to capitalism was indeed a conscious decision taken by the Meiji leaders.[52]

Japan was helped in this because the main European colonial powers had enough on their hands: Britain was preoccupied in China and India; France suffered a defeat in its attempt to control Mexico in 1867 and was also involved in a string of wars associated with Italian and German unification, culminating in its defeat in the 1870–71 Franco-Prussian war. The real threat facing Japan came from tsarist Russia and the United States.[53] By the 1880s Japan had a modern navy and army.

The contrast between Japan's position and that of Manchu China was dramatic. For centuries Japan had existed at the edge of a world in which China was the centre – the Middle Kingdom. Both countries had controlled Western trade and encroachments up until the nineteenth century, but China found itself faced with the might of British imperialism, which demanded access to its markets in order to sell the one thing it had to offer, opium. China refused and Britain took to arms. The crushing victories achieved by Britain over imperial China in the Opium Wars of 1838–42 served as a warning to Japan. Britain had overcome the efforts of the Manchu rulers to halt sales of opium, and had secured control of Hong Kong and other ports as 'concessions'. Other European powers demanded similar 'concessions'.[54] China's economy was wrecked, with a huge balance of trade deficit caused by the need to fund a mass drugs habit. The Manchu state dissolved, although formally China remained under imperial rule. With no central state China was ripe for the pickings of the imperialist powers.

A popular nationalist movement had arisen, the Guomindang (known too as the Kuomintang – the Chinese Nationalist Party), whose leading figure was Sun Yat-Sen. The nationalist party formed by Sun Yat-Sen adopted his 'three principles' – nationalism, republicanism and socialism. Its base was among the intellectuals, initially in the diaspora and then in southern and central eastern China. The Guomindang organised an uprising against Manchu rule but was not strong enough to control events in which its republican forces were joined by military uprisings and the withdrawal of support from the throne by the nobility. A republic was declared but in reality power in many localities fell into the hands of military officers tied to the nobility, the warlords.[55]

The Guomindang was gradually taken over by the wealthy capitalist class emerging on the eastern sea board and by the landowners. Both Japan and the United States had been sympathetic to the new regime. The former, though, began to sense weakness and that fuelled territorial ambitions; in response the US moved to buttress the Guomindang regime. Meanwhile the imperial Japanese government operated in partnership with the four great merchant families, Mitsui, Mitsubishi, Sumitomo and Yasuda – the *zaibatsu* – which grew immensely wealthy and powerful in finance, commerce and industry during the process of modernising Japan. The *zaibatsu* families would be rewarded by a grateful imperial government with political power and commercial privileges. Many of the government-initiated heavy manufacturing industries were later sold to *zaibatsu* families at generous prices, and the government maintained only indirect control over defence-related industries.

Japan was the first nation to undergo breakneck industrialisation, which saw it emerge within a few decades as a modern capitalist society. In Britain this process had occurred over centuries.[56] The principal founder of the modern Japanese army was Count Yamagata Aritomo, a field marshal in the imperial army, twice prime minister and one of seven advisers to the emperor who selected and appointed prime ministers. He warned the emperor in 1891 that Russian expansion into Manchuria and northern China required Japan to 'prepare adequate military power within the next eight or nine years'.[57] Russian control of Korea would pose a strategic danger to Japan itself.[58]

In 1894 China and Japan went to war over Korea. Within six weeks the Japanese controlled the peninsula and were advancing into Manchuria, even threatening Beijing. China was forced to make peace, granting Japan effective control of Korea, Taiwan (Formosa), the Liaotung peninsula which included Port Arthur in Manchuria, and the Pescadore Islands. The arrival of a Russian fleet forced them to give up Port Arthur and southern Manchuria. This indignity would lead Japan to look for an ally among the great powers. Its gaze fell on Britain.

In 1902 the Anglo-Japanese Alliance was signed. Russia was alarmed by this and three years later moved troops into southern Manchuria and to the border with Korea. Japan responded with a surprise attack on Russia's far eastern fleet, effectively destroying it. Japan took direct control of Korea. The Russian base at Port Arthur was eventually captured after a long siege during which the Russian armies were driven back across the imperial borders. The Russian western fleet that eventually arrived was destroyed in a decisive victory for Japan's navy. The other powers were astounded at Japan's success. In the subsequent peace treaty the Japanese gained much territory from Russia but could not win control of Manchuria, which was returned to the Chinese.

The Anglo-Japanese Alliance was re-affirmed four years later. Britain recognised Japanese control of Korea and both countries agreed to come to each other's aid if either's imperial possessions in the region, including India, were attacked. In 1911 the treaty was again revised so that Japan took responsibility for dealing with Germany in the region and protecting British imperial interests there. As naval historian Timothy D. Saxon argues, Tokyo's strategy up until 1918 was to stay close to Britain as the best way to expand:

> Japanese naval assistance in the Mediterranean Sea in 1917 boosted the strength of allied naval escorts during the darkest days of the war. Beyond the Mediterranean, an argument can be made that without Japanese assistance Great Britain would have lost control of the Pacific and Indian Oceans. That would have isolated the British Empire's two dominions in the Far East, Australia and New Zealand, from the campaigns in Europe and the Middle East. Other British colonies, from Aden and India to Singapore and Hong Kong, would have been exposed. Despite this help, Japan, at best a mistrusted and suspect ally of Great Britain in 1914, emerged from the conflict distrusted by its allies, the United States and Britain.[59]

Anglo-Japanese co-operation in the First World War continued with military intervention against Bolshevik Russia, but in the new post-war world Washington viewed the rise of Japan as a threat to its interests in China and the Pacific. The British faced the choice of retaining US goodwill or maintaining their Japanese alliance. They chose the former, dropping the Anglo-Japanese Alliance and then agreeing to the Washington Five Power Naval Treaty which ensured that Anglo-American fleets would outnumber the Japanese in the Pacific.

Japan was hit badly by the Great Depression. Its recovery came by way of a policy of autarky, intended to seal its empire from overseas competitors, which required state intervention driven by further militarisation and the expansion of the overseas empire to guarantee raw materials and markets.

The Japanese economy was reliant on high levels of both imports and exports. Its silk industry – which had tripled its output in the past decade and a half, satisfying the demand for stockings in the US – lost 90 per cent of its sales in America almost overnight. The price of rice collapsed too.[60] Japan's vulnerability to trade wars and protectionism was demonstrated by the fact that in 1930 it imported 100 per cent of its aluminium, 85 per cent of its iron and steel, and 79 per cent of its oil.[61] American import controls in the same year increased the price of Japanese exports to the US by 23 per cent. Japan's total exports to the United States fell by more than a quarter.[62] As Kenneth Douglas Brown argues:

> There is little doubt that the deterioration of international trade relations provided further justification for Japan's growing conviction that the only way to safeguard essential raw materials and markets was to secure its own economic self-sufficient empire ... By the end of 1931 Japan's gold reserves stood at less than half their 1929 level ... Japan quit the gold standard and allowed the yen to fall by 60% against the US dollar. Between 1930–31 and 1937–38 government spending grew by almost half.[63]

Taking up this point, Akita and Woods argue that 'Japan's closed door policy in the 1930s had clear Keynesian pump-priming goals – farm village relief, a military build up and a "big push" in heavy industries, thus to pull Japan and its colonies out of recession.'[64] By 1930, recession and two banking crises had led to the *zaibatsu* increasing their domination of the economy. The *zaibatsu* did not specialise in one sector of the economy but grew through agglomeration, with a family-run holding company typically controlling financial, manufacturing, mining, shipping and trading units. These core companies in turn controlled hundreds of sub-contractors. Ties with the state grew stronger still in the 1930s as the *zaibatsu* switched from light industries like textiles into chemicals and heavy industries.

The effect of the Great Depression, as elsewhere, was to accelerate the centralisation of capital:

> By 1937 the *zaibatsu* controlled between them over a quarter of the country's mining operations and more than a third of its shipbuilding. They also had a substantial grip on the major sources of capital, holding 61% of the insurance business and about a fifth of banking capital. Mitsui alone held 7.7 per cent of all Japan's industrial capital, Mitsubishi 5.5% and each controlled a hundred different enterprises.[65]

Japan's overseas territories had great advantages for the *zaibatsu* who co-operated with the military there. Korea was a 'capitalist paradise' with little tax and little or no regulation of working conditions or business practices.[66] The military and the *zaibatsu* encouraged the development of industry in Japan's overseas empire: 'steel, chemicals, and hydroelectricity facilities in Korea and Manchuria and even car manufacture for a time in Manchuria'.[67]

By 1937 Korea and the newly acquired territories of Manchuria and Taiwan took 38 per cent of Japan's exports, and by 1940 *zaibatsu* accounted for 75 per cent of capital investment in Korea.[68] At the end of the 1930s the Japanese economy was nearly double the size it had been before the 1929 Crash. It was the most successful capitalist economy of the decade. But success only increased the appetite of its rulers.

Japan regarded China as a key market. So did the United States. International recession sharpened this rivalry. Washington's preferred option was to buttress Beijing's government of Chiang Kai-shek, leader of the nationalist Guomindang movement. The Guomindang had begun as a broad-based nationalist movement seeking national unification to wrest China out of the hands of competing warlords following the demise of imperial rule, and an end to foreign occupation of key coastal territories. Chiang was its senior military figure, receiving training in Moscow. In 1927 he led a Guomindang army from Guangzhou (Canton) on the Northern Expedition aimed at capturing Shanghai and then Beijing. After the capture of Shanghai, Chiang massacred the Communists who had allied with the Guomindang. The Communist Party, after losing control of Canton, eventually retreated into the countryside.

As the Northern Expedition had advanced, Chiang offered the warlords a choice – join him or fight him. If they chose the former they were appointed governor of their province and their army was simply placed under Chiang's overall control. It was a policy which ensured warlord power remained, and would sow future problems.[69] Chiang used hit troops to suppress the peasant uprisings in 1927–28, as his biographer Jay Taylor points out: 'the KMT [Guomindang] adopted the more conservative policy of returning land to the original owner and putting off redistribution until the utterly devastated local economy had recovered'.[70] Chiang's regime was deeply corrupt, and in league with the warlords who ran vast areas of the country. Aware of this weakness, the Japanese military and sections of the ruling class pressed for the occupation of Manchuria, which could provide badly needed raw materials and be used to open up markets in China.

As the army expanded into China, the *zaibatsu* went with it, taking over Chinese mines, utilities and textile mills, and using Chinese and Korean slave labour in their own mines at home. By the time Japan entered into war with America, Mitsui had become the biggest private business in the world, employing about 1 million non-Japanese Asians.

Nine states, including the US, Japan and the main European powers, had signed an agreement to uphold China's territorial integrity, and the League of Nations forbade military attacks on member states. Yet Britain and the US did nothing about Japan's aggression; when the League of Nations imposed sanctions they and other powers ignored them. Britain's concern was to maintain its colonial possessions in the region and the ports 'leased' to it by China, which allowed it and other powers an 'open door' to trade in China.[71]

The successful conquest of Manchuria encouraged Tokyo to believe it could make similar piecemeal gains to secure dominance over northern China and East Asia. That required facing down both the US and the USSR. Japanese industry, associated with the army, invested heavily in Manchuria. Japan severely limited imports and encouraged low-cost exports: Japanese cotton goods undercut both the British and Indian cotton industries. But there were many divisions within Japan's ruling class. Party politics had effectively ceased to matter after the last prime minister representing a party, Inukai Tsuyoshi, was assassinated in May 1932 by right-wing extremists. Political parties survived but were out of power, with 'national unity cabinets' ruling. An attempted *coup d'état* by one section of the army on 26 February 1936 resulted in the military being given greater power within the state in the interests of 'national unity'. Then, in May of that year, a rule that only serving officers could become military ministers was reinstated – the military now had an effective veto over the cabinet, and the power to topple governments.[72]

To further complicate the picture, there was a split running through the army between one group fixated on war with Soviet Russia and another that wanted to use Manchuria and Korea as the base for imperial expansion into China. The different factions within the armed forces employed violence against each other and the political leaders who crossed their paths. Meanwhile, within nationalist China, Chiang Kai-shek concentrated on trying to eliminate the

Communists, who were based in rural areas of south-east China. The party had been centred on the coastal cities until Chiang had destroyed their base there in 1927. It was forced to establish itself in areas where the Guomindang had little power, fighting guerrilla warfare. Over time it would be transformed into a peasant-based party.[73]

In 1933 and 1934 Chiang sent his best troops to encircle the Communist-controlled rural Jiangxi Soviet, in what was named the Fifth Encirclement Campaign. The Communists were split between those who accepted the advice from Moscow in advocating a war of position with fixed defences, and those like Mao Zedong and Lin Biao who advocated guerrilla warfare.

After Guomindang troops took several key positions, in 1934 Lin recommended evacuating the Jiangxi Soviet, but he was opposed by the majority of Red Army commanders. Eventually the Communists had no option but to break out, beginning the 8,000 mile Long March to eventual sanctuary in remote Yan'an in Shaanxi province in north-western China, which the survivors reached in December 1936.[74]

Meanwhile Chiang Kai-shek faced student demonstrations over his failure to oppose Japanese provocations on the border with Manchuria. Rising nationalist sentiment and internal rivalries in the Guomindang meant he had to put up resistance to the Japanese if he was to retain his position.[75] A clash in July 1937 at the Marco Polo Bridge outside Beijing led the Japanese to attack northern China, expecting to occupy it within weeks. The Japanese Imperial Army took the city after four days of fighting, with orders issued to kill all captives. Accordingly they began to murder 300,000 out of 600,000 civilians and soldiers in the city. After a Chinese sentry shot two Japanese soldiers in Shanghai, the fighting spread there, with the Japanese employing bombers against civilian areas. After this the war spread across eastern China.[76]

In December 1937 Japanese forces took the Guomindang capital, Nanjing (Nanking), and carried out a massacre of civilians, known as the Rape of Nanjing. It represented the single worst atrocity of the era in either the European or Pacific theatres of war. Estimates suggest that 100,000 to 300,000 people were massacred, and tens of thousands of women, men and children raped.[77]

Despite the war with Japan the Communists were the main enemy for Chiang, he hoped the Americans would eventually deal with the Japanese. He openly stated: 'First pacify the interior then resist the external [threat].'[78] Chiang opted to retreat further and further into the country in the face of this invasion. In the process whole areas of the country slipped back into warlord control. But despite their leaders, Chinese resistance to the Japanese occupiers grew.

The Communists worked hard to ally and incorporate the guerrilla bands which had sprung up and the units of the Guomindang which were left behind enemy lines. Writing of a crucial area in North China, Shantung, Chalmers Johnson points out that the rise of Communists in Shantung followed:

> Two major influences in Shuntung promoted a spontaneous nationalist reaction to the Japanese invasion. One was scandal and treachery by the legal

Shantung provincial government ... the other was a long tradition of rural military organisation, and of peasant rebellion.[79]

The Guomindang administration and its forces did not resist Japanese occupation but largely chose to flee to join Chiang.

The Japanese in Hopei and Shantung occupied the towns and cities and defended the lines of communication between them but were not present in the villages. From 1938 onwards the Communists infiltrated the rural areas. They were aided by an influx of nationalist students who had fled Beijing and Tsingtao and would rally to the Communists.[80] Tokyo responded to the growing resistance by throwing in more troops, becoming consumed in an unending war. Japanese casualties totalled 140,000 dead and half a million wounded in 1937–38. Japanese occupation forces numbered 1 million.[81]

The Communists role in resisting the Japanese and the strategic decision of the Mao Zedong leadership, which had taken control of the party in the mid 1930s, to base it among the peasantry led to a dramatic growth, as the historian of the Communist Resistance, Tetsuya Kataoka, points out:

> When war broke out, the CCP had 30,000 men in the Eighth Route Army. In early 1938, the New Fourth Army was organised in central China with an initial force of about 12,000 men. Starting from a combined force of about 40,000 men, the Communist forces grew to 160,000 by early 1939.[82]

The composition of the party changed too:

> In the Fall of 1938, Yang Shang-k'un, the secretary of the Northern Bureau, took a trip through north China ... On the basis of a rough survey he found that 60 to 80 per cent of Party members in North China was of peasant background; 5 to 10 per cent of worker origin; and a quarter were intellectuals in some places ... Among the cadre as many as 70 per cent were from intellectual backgrounds.[83]

The party which was emerging was one with a leadership of middle-class intellectuals presiding over a peasant army. Military discipline was the most effective way of maintaining control.

From 1936 onwards Japan was allied to Germany, following its signing of the Anti-Comintern Pact (the public purpose of which was to oppose Communist propaganda and subversion, but which Tokyo saw as a military agreement). Four years later Japan, Germany and Italy signed the Tripartite Pact pledging that if one of them declared war, each of the others would too. Berlin and Rome would honour that pledge in regard to the United States. The Japanese army had meanwhile attacked Russian-controlled territory. After a severe defeat in Manchuria at the hands of the Red Army in July 1939 an armistice was signed between the two powers.

To the south the Sino-Japanese war continued. Its outcome was to have a profound impact on the world in which we live today.

CHAPTER FOUR

The Countdown to War

Across the world millions of people watched the spread of conflict in the 1930s with a growing fear that the clock was ticking for the outbreak of a new global war. Germany under Hitler was intent on expanding the borders of the Third Reich into Central and Eastern Europe, Fascist Italy under Mussolini was determined to act on his promise of a new Roman Empire, and Japan was already involved in a war of occupation in China.

Among the working class and sections of the middle class anti-fascism was a growing force. After the German debacle, when the most powerful working class in the world had allowed the Nazis to take power without resistance, there was physical resistance to fascism in Austria, France and Spain. This contrasted with the policy of appeasement promoted by British, French and, to a lesser extent, US leaders. Tory MP Henry 'Chips' Channon put the case for appeasement in 1936, couched in firmly anti-communist terms: 'We should let gallant little Germany glut her fill of the reds in the East and keep decadent France quiet while she does so.'[1]

The Rhineland

The first test of appeasement came in the Rhineland. On 7 March 1936 Hitler ordered his troops to re-occupy the Rhineland – under the terms of the Versailles Treaty it was a demilitarised zone abutting France's eastern borders. The 1925 Locarno Treaty saw Britain and France pledge to take joint military action if Germany altered the boundaries set at Versailles. The British prime minister Stanley Baldwin rejected any idea of France and Britain standing up to Hitler because that would lead to war, and if Hitler lost, 'it would probably result in Germany going Bolshevik'. He added that it might also lead to France going Communist.[2] Lord Lothian quipped that Hitler 'was only going into his own backyard'.[3]

When the government in Paris contacted Whitehall about whether they should mobilise the army, the British government effectively vetoed it and instead offered Hitler a reduced demilitarised zone just 20 miles wide on both sides of the Rhine. Downing Street would not even consider economic or diplomatic sanctions. The French commander in chief, General Gamelin, told his government that Hitler had nearly a million men under arms with 300,000 already in the Rhineland, and any response would require full-scale mobilisation, which the politicians baulked at. The historian Alastair Horne points out that at this time, 'the new Wehrmacht was still a relatively feeble, small and light armed force'.[4] Hitler had ordered a withdrawal if his troops met any resistance. As Hitler later admitted:

> The 48 hours after the march into the Rhineland were the most nerve-racking in my life. If the French had then marched into the Rhineland we would have had to withdraw with our tails between our legs, for the military resources at our disposal would have been wholly inadequate for even a moderate resistance.[5]

By the time the British foreign secretary Anthony Eden and his cabinet 'minder' sat down with Hitler's envoy, Joachim von Ribbentrop, to finalise matters, the re-occupation was a matter of fact. Ribbentrop offered solemn promises from Hitler that he would abide by international treaties and the British dropped the whole matter. The lack of any reaction by Britain and France encouraged Hitler to continue re-arming and to begin talking about his claims on Austria and Czechoslovakia.

Popular Fronts in Spain and France

The lead up to the outbreak of the Second World War must be understood against the background of two events in 1936 – the outbreak of civil war in Spain and the election of a Popular Front government in France followed by mass strikes. In July 1936 the Spanish military rebelled against a left-wing, Popular Front government, allying Socialists, Communists and liberal Republicans together with Basque and Catalan nationalists, elected six months before. The mass response of republican workers ensured the coup was defeated in Madrid, Barcelona, Valencia and other towns and cities. In Barcelona and across Catalonia workers and peasants took control of workplaces, the land, communications and much more. Alarmed by such revolutionary events in Spain, Lord Halifax, then Lord Privy Seal in the British government, argued that Britain should regard Germany 'as an ally of ours and all order-loving folk' because it could act as a brake on such insurgency.[6]

The military rebels held the central province of Castile as well as the north-east, but they desperately needed the assistance of the Spanish army in Morocco, a colony. The head of the rebellion there, General Franco, had led the brutal suppression of a revolutionary uprising in Asturias two years before. He would quickly outmanoeuvre his rival generals to become head of the uprising and of the nationalist state they declared. From the first both Hitler and Mussolini acted to aid Franco, immediately sending planes to ferry his troops from Morocco to Spain. Two German battleships screened the naval convoys across the Straits of Gibraltar to prevent the republican-controlled navy intervening. The Royal Navy positioned a battleship in front of the nationalist port of Algeciras to prevent republican ships shelling it.[7] Once Franco's troops landed in Spain they advanced steadily, massacring opponents, and threatening Madrid.

North of the Pyrenees a similar Popular Front government, led by Léon Blum, had been elected just weeks earlier, and it initially provided badly needed arms to the Spanish Republic. But it quickly found its ally Britain opposed to this, with foreign secretary Anthony Eden telling them that the British would, on balance, prefer a victory for Franco (he would later change that assessment). In France the generals opposed aiding the republicans, and the powerful engineering and armaments cartel, the Comité des forges, warned of a right-wing backlash. The Catholic writer François Mauriac warned Blum in *Le Figaro*, 'Take care! We will never forgive you for such a crime.' Mauriac would later shock his fellow Catholics by taking an anti-Franco position because of the brutality of the nationalists.[8]

The British and French governments then brokered a deal with Germany, Italy and Russia whereby they all agreed on an arms embargo to Spain to be policed by their navies. Hitler and Mussolini agreed and then simply ignored what they had promised. In contrast the Blum government stopped weapons crossing the border, and even attempted to prevent anti-fascist volunteers travelling to Spain to join the fight against Franco.

In the wake of the September 1938 Munich accords, where France and Britain effectively surrendered their ally Czechoslovakia to Hitler, the Socialist Party split. The former premier, Blum, was committed to defending Czechoslovakia and French rearmament. His main rival Paul Faure stated that fighting to defend Czechoslovakia was not worth the life of one Macon winegrower. But another Socialist, the teacher's leader Ludovic Zoretti, went further, writing that France should not 'kill millions of people, and destroy a civilisation to make life a bit easier for 100,000 Sudeten Jews'. Another Socialist deputy, Armand Chouffet, went further still stating: 'I've had enough of the Jewish dictatorship over the Party ... I won't march for a Jewish war.'[9]

The British pressurised Blum to stop arms deliveries. The French government proposed that France, Britain, Germany and Italy follow a policy of non-intervention. Eventually a commission was created representing these four states plus Portugal, to monitor and block military aid to either side. The Germans, Italians and Portuguese ignored it and the British did nothing to stop them.[10]

Across the Atlantic President Roosevelt supported non-intervention and an arms embargo, passing legislation to ban arms sales to either side in Spain. This did not stop American business sending aid to Franco's side. The president of the Texas Oil Company (today's Texaco) was an open admirer of Franco, and on hearing of the uprising diverted five tankers to fascist-controlled Tenerife, where there was a refinery. Texaco and Standard Oil supplied nearly three and a half million tons of oil to Franco on credit, while the Republic imported one and a half million tons, mostly from Russia.[11] Later Ford, Studebaker and General Motors supplied 12,000 trucks to Franco's forces, three times more than the Axis powers did, while the chemical giant Dupont sent them 40,000 bombs via Germany to avoid contravening the US Neutrality Act.[12]

The battle for Spain united Germany and Italy. The lesson Hitler and Mussolini drew from the experience was that Britain and France would do little in the face of fascist aggression. The Germans in particular learned valuable lessons from

Spain and used the conflict to train their forces, testing tanks, aircraft and aerial bombing in what the German tank commander General von Thomas would call 'a European Aldershot'.[13] Mussolini benefited little despite sending 80,000 men to fight with Franco in Spain. In March 1937 at Guadalajara Italian forces suffered a decisive defeat at the hands of republican forces, which included a large contingent of Italian anti-fascists. Italian fascism had suffered its first defeat and it echoed back into Italy. The Italian intervention also demonstrated that the country did not have the industrial capacity or the weaponry to wage modern war.[14]

Soviet military experts, along with their French counterparts, took from Spain the lesson that large tank formations could not achieve success against artillery and defensive positions. The Germans, on the other hand, became more convinced that armour backed up by close air support could achieve a rapid breakthrough.

But above all Hitler tested 'British mettle' in Spain and his attitude to Britain turned from 'esteem to scorn'.[15] Hugh Thomas argues that the Anglo-French failure to impose the arms embargo plus the Munich settlement of September 1938 led Hitler to believe that London and Paris would never risk war. 'The Germans were also encouraged to think that they could act with impunity by the cooling of Russian interest in Spain in the autumn of 1938, and indeed various gestures, especially after Munich, by the Russian government towards Germany herself.'[16]

The Spanish war was a clear ideological clash between fascists and anti-fascists which threatened to spread beyond the Pyrenees. The republican struggle in Spain and the mass strikes in support of France's Popular Front government raised the spectre of revolution in Western Europe. British policy towards Spain was guided by appeasement and anti-communism. Harold Nicolson, an MP in the Tory dominated coalition, opposed appeasement and had a greater grasp of *realpolitik* when he argued that, 'The second German war began in July 1936 when the Germans started with their intervention in Spain ... the propertied classes in this country with their insane pro-Franco business have placed us in a very dangerous position.'[17]

France Divided

Meanwhile the Popular Front government in Paris fell apart. Once the strike wave of June 1936 had receded the employers went onto the offensive and the far right began to enjoy support from the military. The Socialist leaders and future Popular Front prime minister, Léon Blum, believed a number of senior military figures were sympathetic to the far right. As early as March 1935 Blum warned that 'Important military leaders – including Marshal Pétain and General Weygand – were more than doubtful ... a great number of officers were suspect.'[18]

One of Pétain's staff, Major Georges Loustaunau-Lacau, co-ordinated the clandestine *Corvignolles*, cells of serving officers pledged to act to suppress

Communism. Another secret network, the *Cagoule* or CSAR (*Comite Secret d'Action Revolutionaire*), was uncovered in 1937, which aimed to overthrow the French Republic and install a far right regime. During the German occupation the *Cagoule* worked with the SS, assassinating a former minister and torching six Paris synagogues. The French officer corps were highly politicised. Later Marc Bloch recalled that so reactionary were the newspapers around his own officers' mess in 1939 that the highly conservative *Le Temps* might have been taken to represent the political views of the extreme left.[19]

The Popular Front fell from office in June 1937 as the radicals ditched Blum and their Socialist allies. The ruling class demanded a crackdown. In November 1938 the right-wing government of Edouard Daladier picked a fight with the main left-wing union federation, the CGT, by scrapping the 40-hour week, the main gain of the 1936 strikes. The CGT responded by calling a general strike which lacked support and was broken by police action. France in the late 1930s was a dangerously divided country, polarised along class lines.

Halifax Meets Hitler

Meanwhile in Britain, in May 1937 Stanley Baldwin had stood down as prime minister to be succeeded by Neville Chamberlain. This strengthened still further the policy of appeasing Hitler. Chamberlain took a direct hand in foreign policy, in alliance with the Lord Privy Seal, Lord Halifax, often bypassing the foreign secretary, Anthony Eden. The decision to appoint the pro-fascist Sir Neville Henderson as ambassador to Germany in 1937 meant Downing Street would be fed pro-Nazi views. In June 1937 Henderson told the Anglo-German Fellowship:

> In England ... far too many people have an entirely erroneous conception of what the National-Socialist regime really stands for. Otherwise they would lay less stress on Nazi dictatorship and much more emphasis on the great social experiment which is being tried out in this country. Not only would they criticise less, but they might learn some useful lessons.[20]

Henderson added, 'I would view with dismay another defeat of Germany which would merely serve the purposes of inferior races.'[21]

Halifax believed he could 'square Hitler'. Henderson encouraged Halifax to visit the Führer. An invitation for him to attend an international hunting convention in Germany came in October 1937, and an invite to meet Hitler at his Alpine retreat soon followed. Eden wanted any visit to be limited to warning Hitler to stay clear of Czechoslovakia and Austria. Chamberlain and Halifax, egged on by Henderson, wanted to reach an 'understanding' with the German head of state. On 13 November the London *Evening Standard* wrote:

> The British government have information from Berlin that Herr Hitler is ready, if he receives the slightest encouragement, to offer Great Britain a 10

year 'Truce' in the colonial issue ... In return for this agreement Hitler would expect the British government to leave him a free hand in Central Europe.[22]

On the eve of his departure Halifax wrote to ex-prime minister Baldwin, saying of Hitler and the Nazis, 'I cannot myself doubt that these fellows are genuine haters of Communism, etc! And I daresay if we were in their position we might feel the same.'[23] Halifax's main briefing was a memorandum written by Henderson which laid out the cold logic of appeasement. Henderson argued that Hitler's desire to incorporate Austria into the Third Reich, regain Germany's colonies taken from them in 1918, and the drive to obtain living space, *Lebensraum*, in Eastern Europe did not 'in themselves ... need injure purely British national interests', adding that they would 'restrain both Russian intrigues and ambitions'. This amounted to giving Hitler a free hand in Eastern Europe.[24]

Halifax's meeting with Hitler began with the British envoy praising him for 'performing great services in Germany', such as repulsing Bolshevism, adding that critics of Nazism back home 'were not fully informed about what was taking place in Germany'. It was Halifax not Hitler who raised alterations to the division of Europe agreed at Versailles in his opening statement:

> All other questions fall into the category of possible alterations in the European order which might be destined to come about with the passage of time. Amongst those questions were Danzig [the 'free city', formerly part of Germany], Austria and Czechoslovakia. England was interested to see that any alterations should come through the course of peaceful evolution and that methods should be avoided which might cause far-reaching disturbances.[25]

Hitler's interpreter, Paul Schmidt, recounted Halifax's message thus:

> The government of Britain, he noted, though not always the people, recognised 'the great services the Führer had rendered in the rebuilding of Germany'. Unlike the Anglican Church and the Labour Party and uninformed public opinion, the government appreciated that Hitler, 'by destroying Communism in his country ... had barred its road to Western Europe, and that Germany therefore could rightly be regarded as a bulwark against Bolshevism'.[26]

Chamberlain declared the visit

> a great success because it achieved its object; that of creating an atmosphere in which it was possible to discuss with Germany the practical questions involved in a European settlement ... What I wanted Halifax to do was convince Hitler of our sincerity and to ascertain what objectives he had in mind and I think both of these objects had been achieved.[27]

Halifax became foreign secretary in February 1938 following Eden's resignation after Chamberlain pursued an alliance with Italy and invited the Italian ambassador Grandi to talks in Downing Street. In his diary, Oliver

Harvey, Eden's private secretary, noted: 'the PM hates American co-operation and wants to make peace with the dictators'.[28] In July the new foreign secretary met an emissary of Hitler, who reported to Hitler that Halifax 'before his death would like to see as the culmination of his work the Führer entering London at the side of the English King, amid the acclamation of the English people'.[29] When the *Manchester Guardian* revealed this years later in 1957, the 75-year-old Halifax was unavailable for comment.

Anschluss

The next step in Hitler's programme of expansion was the incorporation of Austria into the Third Reich. Austria was a relatively homogeneous German state carved from the shattered Austro-Hungarian Empire after its defeat in 1918. This small state saw a strong and militant socialist movement pitched against a clerical pro-fascist elite. In February 1934 thousands of armed workers had come out in Vienna and other cities to fight the right-wing regime of Engelbert Dolfuss, but after four days they had been crushed. The triumphant pro-fascist state imposed a one-party dictatorship which looked to Mussolini's Italy to guarantee its independence from Germany. However, the growing convergence between Fascist Italy and Nazi Germany over the following years meant Mussolini was prepared to sacrifice his ally.

In March 1938 Hitler demanded that Austria join the Reich. When its leader Kurt Schuschnigg attempted to call a referendum on the issue, German forces moved across the border, meeting no resistance. The British government first heard of the Anschluss during a banquet Chamberlain and Halifax were attending in honour of Ribbentrop. The latter would write from his post-war prison cell while on trial at Nuremberg that Halifax had assured him previously, 'the British people would never consent to go to war because two German countries wanted to merge'.[30]

In France the former foreign minister, Yvon Delbas, told deputies, in response to Léon Blum's plea for a government of national unity, that 'the Communists, frightened by their defeat in Spain, and the Jews, hunted down everywhere, are searching for salvation in a world war'.[31] Days after Hitler entered Vienna, Halifax's deputy, Rab Butler, formed a publicity committee to ensure the media carried letters and articles favourable to the government's foreign policy and attacking Winston Churchill and other critics. Henderson wrote from the Berlin embassy to Halifax suggesting, 'That on some favourable occasion in the House of Commons or House of Lords we should say quite openly that we have no intention of trying to hamper Germany's legitimate freedom of action in Central or Eastern Europe.'[32] Shortly after, Henderson explained, 'I admit that personally I am only too glad to wish that she should look Eastwards instead of Westwards.'[33]

Even before German troops entered Vienna a pogrom engulfed the city's Jewish population. Nazi sympathisers led mobs in attacks on Jewish homes, businesses and shops, carrying out arrests and inflicting beatings. Five hundred

Viennese Jews committed suicide in despair.[34] The Nazi state was shocked at such unofficial 'Aryanisation', with individuals rather than the state plundering the Jews. The Nazi leadership wanted a more systematic approach to removing the Jews than such 'wild' pogroms.

Reinhard Heydrich, in charge of the SS in the city, threatened Austrian Nazis with the Gestapo for their lack of discipline. In contrast the SS implemented their 'Vienna model', devised by its Jewish 'expert' Adolf Eichmann, which 'encouraged' Jewish emigration in return for them signing over property, businesses and wealth to the SS. By autumn Viennese Jews were being removed to temporary accommodation pending 'voluntary' emigration.[35]

Czechoslovakia is Sold Away

The next and obvious target of Nazi aggression was Czechoslovakia – a country which both Britain and France had helped create in the wake of the First World War and which France was treaty-bound to defend. Czechoslovakia was alone in Eastern Europe in being a democratic state with a strong and vibrant left and labour movement. Its government was willing to enter into alliance with Russia to defend its independence. This created a suspicion in London and Paris that Berlin carefully exploited.

The Czech army could dispose 30 to 40 divisions and had built strong fortifications along its mountainous frontier with Germany. In addition Skoda was the biggest single armaments plant in the world.[36] This represented both a great threat and a great prize for Hitler. Within the Sudeten area, abutting the frontier with the Reich, was a predominantly German population that had been allocated to the new Czech state on its formation at the end of the war. Hitler now incited agitation for self-determination among the German population of the Sudetenland, threatening a 'humanitarian intervention' on behalf of the German minority in the strategically important Czech border lands.[37]

Clashes erupted between Sudeten Nazis and the Czech state forces. Britain began pressurising the Prague government to make concessions to the Sudeten Germans. The same month ambassador Henderson telegrammed London saying that the danger of war lay not with Hitler 'but in the forces working for war, namely German and Czech extremists, Communists, and other influences and the universal hatred of Nazism'.[38] If the British government seemed to believe it could feed Hitler territory in Eastern Europe in order to satisfy his hunger, events there were a more serious matter for its French ally.

The two pillars of French strategy in the event of war with Germany were that the impregnable fortifications along the Maginot Line would block any direct invasion of France, while alliances with various Eastern European states would ensure that German forces would be tied down in the East. After the First World War France had championed the creation of a ring of states on Germany's eastern borders which it believed it could use to curtail any future German military revival. The only one of these states with the ability to withstand Hitler's Germany was Czechoslovakia, which possessed sufficient industrial and military strength to resist until such time as its allies could mobilise to come to its aid. Czechoslovakia was also the only liberal democracy in the region.

There was a deep enmity between Poland and Czechoslovakia. As part of the post-war settlement the latter had been awarded the Teschen region, claimed by Poland, which remained a running sore. But the Prague and Warsaw governments were divided over more than Teschen. In 1920 when Poland invaded Soviet Russia, the Czechs had refused to allow French arms supplies to cross their territory in its support. The Poles were vehemently anti-Russian and until the summer of 1939 regarded Russia as a greater enemy than Germany. Polish foreign policy was to attempt to play its two neighbours off against each other. That did not stop it signing a pact with Hitler after he took power.

When, in 1935, the Nazi regime began demanding the transfer of the German-speaking region of Czechoslovakia, the Sudetenland, to the Third Reich, the Polish government echoed its claims that Czechoslovakia was an artificial state. The Polish foreign minister, Józef Beck, had just returned from a visit to Berlin convinced that Czechoslovakia was a Russian satrap. The president of Czechoslovakia from 1936 until his resignation in 1938, following the Munich agreement, was Edvard Benes, who the Polish government and many in London and Paris regarded as pro-Russian.

The fear caused by the great strike wave of June 1936 in France, and the revolutionary upheaval across the border in Barcelona later that summer, was still real in French ruling circles. Early in 1937 the chair of the French Chamber of Deputies foreign policy commission warned that war between Germany and Czechoslovakia might turn the latter into a second Spain. On the same theme an allied diplomat warned: 'Who knows if around Brno, a new Catalonia will not spring up.'[39] He was warning that a Czech industrial city might fall prey to the revolutionary impulse which had seen workers take effective control of Barcelona in the summer of 1936. The Czech working class was strong and well organised. A war in 1938 in defence of Czechoslovakia would become embroiled with that in Spain – creating, in other words, a European civil war between left and right. Britain and France wanted none of that. War over Czechoslovakia would have brought France and Britain into alliance with Russia, which pledged military help to Prague. This was something neither power desired, and both became desperate to escape their commitments to Czechoslovakia. Sensing this, Hitler stepped up his threats to intervene militarily on behalf of the Sudeten Germans.

In September 1938 *The Times* ran an editorial calling on the Prague government to cede the Sudetenland to Hitler. In those days the paper was regarded as a mouthpiece for the British government. Its editor, Geoffrey Dawson, was a close friend of Halifax. Clearly it was being used to test the waters for what would become Whitehall policy. Chamberlain accepted Hitler's claim that his intention was simply a reuniting of ethnic Germans in the region with their homeland, telling journalists invited to meet him at Lady Astor's home, 'Hitler wants all the Germans he can lay his hands on, but positively no foreigners.'[40]

On 7 September the British government resolved to inform Hitler that Britain demanded a negotiated settlement and if this was not forthcoming she would not 'stand aside'. Henderson was charged with delivering this warning during the

Nazis' annual Nuremberg rally. But he refused to present it, insisting that the British press 'write up Hitler as the apostle of peace'. Henderson got his way![41]

On 12 September Hitler demanded the right of self-determination for the Sudeten Germans. *The Times* once again backed this proposal. Britain and France now suggested a plebiscite to decide the future of the Sudetenland. Further clashes occurred between the Sudeten Nazis and the Czechs, who declared martial law in the region.

Chamberlain was so determined to forestall a threatened invasion that he wrote to Hitler: 'I propose to come over at once to see you with a view to try and find a peaceful solution. I propose to come by air and am ready to start tomorrow.'[42] Chamberlain told only three of his cabinet colleagues (Halifax, Hoare and Simon) of his intention to accept the invitation and did not inform his French ally at all. On 15 September 1938 Chamberlain flew to meet Hitler at Berchtesgaden. The *Daily Herald*, the official mouthpiece of the Labour leadership, saw him off with the words, 'Good Luck, Chamberlain'.[43] Chamberlain assured the Führer that, 'From the moment of my appointment as British prime minister I have been constantly occupied with the question of Anglo-German rapprochement.' Hitler told Chamberlain that he was about to order the invasion of Czechoslovakia in order to incorporate the Sudetenland into the Third Reich. Chamberlain responded saying, 'My personal opinion was that on principle I didn't care two hoots whether the Sudetens were in the Reich, or out of it, according to their own wishes, but I saw immense practical difficulties.'[44]

Chamberlain agreed to return to London to consult over this matter while Hitler agreed to put the invasion on hold until his return. Hitler concluded from the meeting that the London and Paris governments would not offer resistance until it was too late and that the British Tories would never enter into alliance with Moscow. Following his visit to Hitler, Chamberlain would write to his sisters, 'I have had a conversation with a man ... and one with whom I can do business ... I am the most popular man in Germany.'[45] Back in London Chamberlain won his cabinet and the French government over to an insistence that Czechoslovakia surrender territory to the Nazi regime or face an invasion on its own. Chamberlain announced a 'new understanding between England and Germany', saying of Hitler, 'it was impossible not to be impressed with the power of the man ... his objectives were strictly limited ... when he had included the Sudeten Germans in the Reich he would be satisfied'.[46]

The British prime minister returned to Germany on 21 September to organise the transfer of these territories. Hitler informed Chamberlain he was not prepared to wait on a plebiscite; he demanded that the Czechs evacuate their border defences and hand over the Skoda munitions works intact immediately. He finished by saying that German troops were ready to occupy a much greater area of the Czechoslovak state. Chamberlain protested that Hitler was raising fresh demands without agreeing to a general settlement, but in the early hours of the morning the two leaders had a private meeting which ended in an agreement that they would act together to prevent war in Europe.

Chamberlain agreed to return to London to discuss this new turn of events. He left telling his German hosts, according to their record of the meeting, that 'a relationship of confidence had grown up between himself and the Führer as a result of the conversations of the last few days'.[47] Hitler's translator, Paul Schmidt, recorded the Führer's closing words: 'Between us there should be no conflict ... we will not stand in the way of your pursuit of your non-European interests and you may without harm let us have a free hand on the European continent in Central and South-East Europe.'[48]

Hitler knew this was exactly what Chamberlain wanted to hear. The Englishman left believing he had reached a European settlement with the German leaders. He returned to London to tell the cabinet he was prepared to accept transfer of the areas the Germans now demanded, assuring them that Hitler 'would not deceive a man whom he respected and with whom he had been in negotiation, and he was sure that Herr Hitler now felt some respect for him'. He added that, 'He thought that he had now established an influence over Herr Hitler and that the latter trusted him and was willing to work with him.'[49]

But this time Chamberlain could not carry his colleagues. Halifax refused to accept such brazen blackmail from Hitler. The Royal Navy was mobilised, gas masks were issued to civilians, and war seemed probable. All the time Chamberlain was using back channels to reassure Hitler this was all for public consumption and that Britain would not fight to save Czechoslovakia. Three days after Chamberlain's second meeting with Hitler the Czech government refused the German demands. On 27 September Chamberlain broadcast to the British people saying, 'How horrible, fantastic, incredible it is that we should be digging trenches and trying on gas masks here because of a quarrel in a far away country between people of whom we know nothing.'[50] He ended by saying he was ready to travel to Germany to meet Hitler at any time. On 28 September Chamberlain opened a debate in the House of Commons on the issue. After he sat down, in a piece of theatre, he rose again to say he had just been handed a note inviting him to a conference the following day in Munich, with Hitler, Mussolini and Daladier, the French premier.

The Munich summit was of course a stage-managed affair. Mussolini, at Hitler's behest, had initiated the meeting and as a supposedly neutral referee carefully prepared his proposals with the Germans before presenting them to the Anglo-French side. As the leaders of the four powers pored over maps of Czechoslovakia, the one government not represented was Czechoslovakia's. At the close of the meeting the decision to surrender a fifth of Czechoslovakia to Nazi Germany was communicated to Prague.

Hitler and Chamberlain then had a private meeting at the latter's insistence, at which the British prime minister secured a piece of paper promising that Britain and Germany would never fight each other again. This was the paper he waved at Heston airfield as he announced he had secured 'peace in our time'. King George VI invited him onto the balcony of Buckingham Palace to be acclaimed – an unprecedented act. *The Times* editorial thundered, 'No conqueror returning from a victory on the battlefield has come home adorned with nobler laurels than MR CHAMBERLAIN from Munich yesterday, and

KING and people alike have shown by the manner of their reception their sense of his achievement.'[51]

For Britain and France, war with Nazi Germany in defence of Czechoslovakia would risk escalating the ongoing Spanish Civil War into a European civil war. Stalin had been prepared to fight to defend Czechoslovakia in alliance with Britain and France, but when that proposal was rejected it was apparent that the Chamberlain government was trying to encourage Germany to go to war with Russia. The head of the British Foreign Office reported of Chamberlain in May 1939, 'In his present mood, PM says he will resign rather than sign alliance with Soviets.'[52] The policy pursued by London and Paris, which urged the Czechs not to fight but to surrender the Sudetenland to Hitler, was endorsed by the US government.

Poland had delivered its own ultimatum to Czechoslovakia during the Munich crisis and its troops had moved in to occupy the Teschen district. After Munich the Russian vice commissioner for foreign affairs, Vladimir Potemkin, said to the French ambassador, 'My poor friend, what have you done? For us I see no other outcome but a fourth partition of Poland.'[53] The previous three partitions, in the eighteenth century, had been agreed between tsarist Russia, Prussia and Austria. Stalin wanted the Third Reich to focus its aggression elsewhere while the USSR provided the raw materials vital for war. Realising Britain and France viewed any alliance with Russia frostily he began to put feelers out to Berlin concerning the possibility of a pact between the two states.[54] Hitler had succeeded in dividing the states to his east and west which might have been united against him.

But Hitler was unhappy with the outcome of Munich; he wanted a war to annexe Czechoslovakia. The agreement with Chamberlain mattered little because he knew the prime minister could easily be replaced by Churchill or Eden. Hitler's ambitions went beyond winning hegemony over Central and Eastern Europe and he understood that Britain, France and the US had an interest in steering him into a war with Russia. Despite his promises at Munich Hitler moved at the beginning of 1939 to liquidate the rump Czech state, with German tanks moving in to occupy the country. Hitler himself visited Prague and spent one night there. There was no opposition, the Czechs were in no position to resist, but the response of the population was obviously sullen.

British intelligence noted as early as March 1938 that German troops were set to march on Prague. The US chargé d'affaires in Berlin reported to Washington:

> The British counsellor, who returned from London today, states that the British Foreign Office is inclined to regard any move by the Germans in Czechoslovakia with calmness and will advise the British government against assuming a threatening attitude when it in fact contemplates doing nothing. He stated in short that 'the British government were reconciled to a possible extreme German action in Czechoslovakia'.[55]

Chamberlain himself told the Commons the invasion was a 'shock to confidence', but added, 'Do not let us be deflected from our course.' He uttered not a word of sympathy for the Czechs.[56] When a Labour MP called on the government to warn Hitler not to attack 'the lives and liberties' of the Czech people, Chamberlain told him, 'I think it is wrong to assume that the German government have any such intention.'[57]

There was beginning to emerge, however timidly, an alliance between the Labour Party and a growing section of the Tory Party (grouped around Churchill, Eden and others who were breaking from appeasement) which realised that any further retreat would mark the end of Britain as a great power. Their difference with Chamberlain was that while he believed Britain's status as a great power could only be maintained by coming to a rapprochement with Hitler and Mussolini, they believed it required opposing their expansion. Churchill was no less an anti-communist than Chamberlain, but being in the minority position within the Tory Party and the ruling class he needed any ally he could find.

The left in Britain, in the form of the Communist Party and its allies on the Labour left, were on the streets opposing Munich and demanding aid for the Spanish Republic, but their loyalty to the Soviet Union meant they would soon, by the summer of 1939, drop anti-fascism in deference to Russia's foreign policy.

Chamberlain was kept abreast of the opposition to him thanks to the actions of Sir Joseph Ball, a former MI5 operative, now head of the Conservative Research Department. Through friends in MI5 Ball arranged for wire taps on the phones of anti-appeasement Tory MPs including Harold Macmillan, the future Tory prime minister, and the leader of the Liberal Party, Sir Archibald Sinclair, a confidante of Winston Churchill.[58]

Across the Channel the French premier Daladier used strong language against the Third Reich over the invasion of Czechoslovakia, but this was combined with growing anti-communism in government circles, a cooling towards Russia, with whom France had earlier signed a military treaty, and a refusal to act unless Britain did so too. Two months after Munich a young German Jewish refugee shot the secretary at Germany's Paris embassy in protest at the treatment of his family. Goebbels responded with orders (approved by Hitler) instructing party members to attack synagogues, Jewish businesses and homes throughout Germany. Reports of the officially sanctioned murder and arson on 'Kristallnacht' ('night of broken glass', referring to broken shop windows) on 9 and 10 November shocked people worldwide. Gestapo head Heydrich estimated that 7,500 shops were destroyed. Some 267 synagogues were set on fire and hundreds more attacked. The pogrom ended with 20,000 Jews being held in concentration camps. The Jewish population was required to pay 25 million marks towards damaged property and was fined one billion marks. Jews were expelled from hospitals, old people's homes and schools, and banned from public places.[59] Göring told the Council of Ministers the next day, 'I certainly would not like to be a Jew in Germany', and ended the meeting with this forecast: 'If in the near future the German Reich should come into conflict with foreign powers, it goes without saying we in Germany should first come to a showdown with the Jews.'[60]

The British air minister, Kingsley Wood, reported Chamberlain's reaction thus: 'Oh, what tedious people these Germans can be! Just when we were beginning to make a little progress'.[61]

The Final Hours Before War

Chamberlain continued trying to reach a European settlement with Hitler despite the fiasco over Czechoslovakia, but as an insurance policy efforts were begun to rebuild British and French defences and to make an alliance with Poland. If Hitler did decide to march westwards, seeking to incorporate the Low Countries or attacking France, such an alliance would threaten him with a two front war – something the British government believed Hitler would not risk.

The Polish state created in the wake of the First World War contained a significant German minority, concentrated in the industrial and mining region of Silesia. The Allies had also allowed the new state access to the Baltic Sea by carving out what was called the Polish corridor, a tranche of territory which divided the German region of East Prussia. Both states disputed control of Danzig (today's Gdansk) which had been placed under League of Nations control in an attempt to resolve the dispute. Britain pledged to act to defend Polish independence but did not promise to maintain its existing boundaries. Chamberlain was prepared to offer Hitler Polish territory if the Führer was prepared to enter another Munich-style agreement. As the British premier explained to his sister, 'what we are concerned with is not the boundaries of states, but attacks on their independence. And it is we who will judge whether this independence is threatened or not.'[62]

These pledges meant little unless Britain was prepared to enter into a pact with Russia, as Britain had no means to intervene against German aggression in Poland, given German control of the Baltic and the difficulty of sending aid from the Mediterranean given that Hitler was allied to Italy, Hungary and Bulgaria. Chamberlain was vehement there would be no alliance with Moscow. The permanent under-secretary for foreign affairs, Sir Alexander Cadogan, noted in his diary on 20 May 1939 that Chamberlain's 'instinctive contempt for the Americans' was matched by what 'amounted to a hatred of the Russians'.[63]

The French ambassador in Moscow noted the consequences of Britain's foreign policy in first scorning Stalin at the time of Munich and now allying with Poland against Germany but rejecting an alliance with Russia: 'After having pushed Stalin towards Hitler at Munich, it [was] now Hitler that they pushed towards Stalin.'[64] Hitler had reneged on his promise not to gobble up the rump Czechoslovak state in March 1939. Traditionally British imperial policy rested upon not allowing any European state to become too powerful to dominate the continental mainland. It was now clear Hitler intended to annexe much of Eastern Europe and the Balkans. Chamberlain may have been prepared to surrender Eastern Europe but the overall battle for world markets meant this threatened British economic interests. Greece was of strategic importance in terms of the Mediterranean-Suez Canal route to India, while the United Kingdom had significant economic interests in the Balkans, which British business did not wish to surrender and was now in fear that South East Europe would become, effectively, a German colony from which they were excluded. If Germany entered into an alliance with Greece that would threaten Britain and France's control of the vital Mediterranean sea lanes.[65]

In April 1939 Chamberlain, needing to ensure Britain was ready to intervene, if only to buttress his negotiating position with Hitler, agreed to the introduction of conscription. In retaliation Hitler renounced the 1935 Anglo-German Naval Agreement. Still Chamberlain hoped he might deter Hitler and tried to broker a Munich-style conference aimed at feeding Hitler a tranche of Polish territory. In July 1939 he told the owner of the *Daily Telegraph* that he had not 'yet given up hopes of peace' and that, 'if Hitler were asking for Danzig in a normal way it might be possible to arrange things'.[66] On 24 July Chamberlain's special adviser, Sir Horace Wilson, met with Dr Helmut Wohltat, one of Göring's team responsible for the four-year economic plan. With Chamberlain's approval Wilson jotted down on Downing Street headed paper the outline of an Anglo-German non-aggression pact, including trade relations and disarmament. The German ambassador in London met with Wilson and reported to Berlin that 'a programme of negotiations' would still be possible even after a German invasion of Poland. Wilson pressed for an Anglo-German agreement which 'would practically render Britain's guarantee policy [of Polish sovereignty] nugatory'.[67]

Chamberlain was prepared to countenance a rearmament programme if it would make Hitler 'realise that it never will be worthwhile' to go to war, telling his sister, 'What you want are defensive forces sufficiently strong to make it impossible for the other side to win except at such a cost as to make it not worth while.'[68] The British Chiefs of Staff had already come to the conclusion that no effective aid could be given to Poland in the event of a German attack.[69] Hitler, on the other hand, now saw that an agreement with Stalin would allow him to occupy Poland and then, if necessary, fight Britain and France on a single front.

Stalin had pressed for a military alliance with Britain and France in the event of a German attack in Eastern Europe. The Poles would not accept this because of their deep distrust of Russia. Eventually an Anglo-French military mission was dispatched headed by an obscure admiral, Sir Reginald Aylmer Ranfurly Plunkett-Ernle-Erle-Drax. It sailed to Russia on an old steamer, taking six days to get there. The admiral's instructions were to drag negotiations out – presumably by demanding he be referred to by his full name at all times.

On 23 August the Russian and German foreign ministers, Molotov and Ribbentrop, met in the Kremlin to sign a ten-year non-aggression pact. In return for a German credit of 200 million marks, Russia would supply raw materials – petrol, grain, cotton, phosphates and timber. A secret protocol to the pact divided Eastern Europe into German and Soviet spheres of influence. Finland, Estonia and Latvia were apportioned to Russia. Poland was to be partitioned in the event of its 'political rearrangement'. Lithuania, adjacent to East Prussia, would be in the German sphere of influence. In the south, Germany acknowledged Russia's interest, and German lack of interest, in Bessarabia, a part of Romania.[70] Hitler was amazed that the Russians did not ask for the release of the jailed German Communist leader Ernst Thälmann.

A day after the Molotov-Ribbentrop Pact, London signed an agreement with Poland affirming it would act if Poland was attacked. The prime minister told the US ambassador Joseph Kennedy that, 'I have done everything that I can think of and it seems as if all my work has come to naught.' The ambassador had argued with him to pressure the Poles to agree to German demands and noted that the prime minister was deeply depressed and that, '[he] says the futility of it all is the thing that is frightful, after all they cannot save the Poles, they can merely carry on a war of revenge that will mean the destruction of the whole of Europe'.[71] Kennedy reported to Washington that Chamberlain was 'more worried about getting the Poles to be reasonable than the Germans'.[72]

Meanwhile a Swedish businessman working in London, Birger Dalherus, was acting as a contact between British foreign secretary Lord Halifax and the Nazi second in command, Hermann Göring. In August 1939, with the private blessing of Hitler and Halifax, a meeting between Göring and his advisers and a group of seven British businessmen took place on a German island in the Baltic. During three days of talks the businessmen repeated the official British line that the guarantee to Poland still stood, but that Germany could obtain 'financial and industrial prosperity and the *Lebensraum* she had been seeking' if only she did not actually invade Poland. This could be achieved, it was suggested, through a new four-power conference, attended by Chamberlain, Hitler, Mussolini and the French prime minister Daladier, with the status of the port of Danzig (run under the auspices of the League of Nations rather than by either Poland or Germany) and the disputed Polish Corridor at the top of the agenda.[73]

On 29 August a friend of Lord Halifax noted in her diary, 'Edward thinks if we can keep Hitler talking for two more days the corner will be turned.'[74] Chamberlain continued to hope to broker a Munich-style conference via the Italians. The Italian foreign minister, Count Ciano, promised to convene a four-power conference on the Munich model. Halifax kept up negotiations with Göring through Dalherus, stressing that Britain wanted a peaceful resolution of Hitler's demands for the port of Danzig. Dalherus even phoned Göring from Halifax's office in the Foreign Office. But Hitler told senior Wehrmacht officers: 'Danzig is not the subject of the dispute at all. It is a question of expanding our *Lebensraum* in the East and securing our food supplies, of the settlement of the Baltic problems.'[75]

Pressure from London and Paris stopped the Poles from carrying out a full mobilisation of their army until 30 August, with the result that a quarter of their troops never reached their units following the German attack which finally occurred on 1 September. Britain did not declare war for a further two days despite treaty obligations, with Chamberlain and Halifax hoping for an Italian initiative. Britain demanded German troops withdraw from Poland; Berlin refused to answer.

On Saturday 2 September the House of Commons met at 7.30 p.m. Britain and France had now decided on a midnight ultimatum, but Chamberlain failed to announce this. MPs rose in rebellion.[76] Meanwhile Chamberlain's speech was passed to Göring via the Swedish go-between, Dalherus. There was no answer regarding a four-power conference. Ministers demanded a late-night cabinet which set an ultimatum for 11 a.m. the next day. The government whips advised that the mood among Tory MPs was sour. At 11.12 a.m. on 3

September Chamberlain broadcast that there was no response to the ultimatum and that Britain was now in a state of war with Germany.

A sense of doom was felt in the highest circles. The permanent secretary at the Foreign Office recorded in his diary for September 1939, 'Buck House to see King, called in about 6.10 and stayed till 6.50. He was depressed – and a little *défaitiste*.' As Andrew Roberts comments, 'Putting the word into French makes it no less extraordinary that within a week of the outbreak of war, the senior official at the Foreign Office could find the King-Emperor to be defeatist about Britain's war prospects.'[77] Chips Channon, Tory MP, society figure, and parliamentary private secretary to Rab Butler made his regrets clear about the declaration of war: 'I feel that our world, or all that remains of it, is committing suicide, whilst Stalin laughs and the Kremlin triumphs.'[78]

After the announcement of war Lord Halifax asked his permanent secretary what Britain's war aims were:

> I told him I saw awful difficulties. We can no longer say 'evacuate' Poland without going to war with Russia [Halifax sensed Hitler and Stalin had agreed to partition Poland], which we don't want to do! I suppose the cry is 'abolish Hitlerism'. What if Hitler hands over to Göring! Meanwhile what of the course of operations? What if Germany now sits tight? What do we do? Build up our armaments feverishly? What for? ... Must try to think this out.[79]

The British cabinet meeting discussed air attacks on Germany in support of the Poles. On 30 September the air minister, Sir Kingsley Wood, rejected setting fire to the Black Forest explaining, 'Are you aware it is private property? Why you'll be asking me to bomb Essen next.'[80] Essen was home to the giant Krupps arms plant. Similar arguments meant strikes on Ruhr armaments plants were also rejected. Instead the RAF dropped propaganda leaflets. One explanation for such a pathetic response was the hopes of Chamberlain and others that a compromise deal could be brokered with Berlin.

The French government and military were also at a loss how to proceed. The French had planned on maintaining a defensive posture until the British and the US came to their aid. Key to this policy was the construction, at great expense, of the Maginot Line covering the French border with Germany up to its junction with the Belgian frontier. The French high command argued that if Germany attacked it would be through the Belgian plain and French forces would advance to fight a war of manoeuvre. There were a number of fatal flaws in this plan. Firstly, it depended on Belgian co-operation but in October 1936 King Leopold III had revoked his country's alliance with France and declared it neutral. Secondly, the Germans knew of the French plan to advance north into Belgium to counter any thrust and planned accordingly. Lastly, the commitment of major forces to man the Maginot Line and the earmarking of the vast bulk of the remaining forces for an advance northwards into the Low Countries, meant little was left in reserve.

Despite evidence France would face a mobile enemy, the French high command drew from Spain the lesson – as its chief, General Gamelin stated –

that German tanks were 'inadequately protected, fit only for the scrap heap'. In response to a junior officer, Charles de Gaulle, who wanted independent armoured formations he argued: 'You cannot hope to achieve real breakthroughs with tanks. The tank is not independent enough. It has to go ahead, but then must return for fuel and supplies.' Gamelin added 'our doctrine is correct'.[81] French tanks were to be dispersed among the infantry to provide support in ways similar to the previous war. French forces would be strung out along the border with no concentrated reserve to respond to any break through.

France entered the Second World deeply divided. Indigenous fascism was too divided and weak to take power and the working class sullen and unenthusiastic about defending their employers' interests. The French establishment, frustrated with the failure of domestic fascism to pose an effective governmental option, increasingly began to speculate openly that Hitler might be a salvation from without. The stage was set for the great military collapse of the 1939–45 war.

France's ambassador to Moscow, Robert Coulondre, expressed a widespread view that war had to be avoided but if it came then a victory for Hitler was preferable to a possible Communist takeover of France: 'Vanquished, she was nazified; victorious, she had, especially following the destruction of German power, to sustain the growing weight of the Slavic world, armed with the communist flame throwers.'[82]

Appeasement Continues

The forces striving for appeasement were still at work. The Duke of Westminster convened a meeting to push for peace on 11 September at his London home, attended by the Duke of Buccleuch and Lords Rushcliffe, Arnold and Mottistone (John Seely, a former secretary of state for war).[83] The British government sanctioned the publication of 'The British Case', written by the top Tory Lord Lloyd in late 1939 and published at the start of the new year with an introduction by Lord Halifax. The book pleaded that there was 'no frontier in Eastern Europe which need be a cause for conflict between Britain and Germany' if only Hitler would co-operate with the British government. Lloyd made it clear that the British government was not fighting fascism or asking the German people to rid themselves of Nazism. Lloyd praises Franco for leading 'the nationalist uprising in Spain in 1936', ignoring the fact that his 'uprising' was against an elected government. Turning to Mussolini he declared, 'Above all, the Italian genius has developed, in the characteristic fascist institutions, a highly authoritarian regime which, however, threatens neither religious nor economic freedom, nor the security of other European nations.'[84]

The crux of the matter for Lloyd was that what prevented 'an honourable peace' between Britain and Germany was not the occupation of Poland but Hitler's pact with Stalin. He wrote: 'This was Herr Hitler's final apostasy. It was the betrayal of Europe. It meant the sacrifice on the altar of Communist ambition not only of Eastern Poland but of other independent states.' Hitler was criticised for sacrificing Europe's 'traditional institutions and habits on the bloodstained altars of world revolution'.[85]

In December 1939 four months into the war, Sir Alexander Cadogan, permanent under-secretary of state at the Foreign Office, had warned Lord Halifax of the need to be cautious about war aims: 'The difficulty that I see is that to proclaim "democracy" and "liberty" enables the enemy to say that we stand for the "Front Populaire" and the "Red" government in Spain. And millions of people in Europe (I would not exclude myself) think that these things are awful.'[86] So this was not posed as a war against fascism but instead as a war to save 'European civilisation'. Britain still hoped Mussolini, Franco and Portugal's 'authoritarian' ruler Salazar would come down on the side of 'European freedom'.[87]

Meanwhile Chamberlain continued to seek a rapprochement with Germany, though he now believed Hitler was unstable and should be replaced. British diplomats and spies sought ways to make contacts with 'good' Nazis and with the German high command. For seven months, from the outbreak of war in September 1939 until April 1940, Britain and France sat on their hands on the Western Front facing Germany in what became known as the 'Phoney War', reflecting the fact that London and Paris did not want to carry out any offensive actions against the Third Reich.

The French commander Gamelin had informed his British counterpart, Lord Gort, in July 1939, 'We have every interest in the war beginning in the east and becoming a general conflict only little by little. We will thus have the time necessary to put on a war footing all Franco-British forces.'[88] Britain and France, incredibly, pushed ahead with plans to attack not Germany but Russia. In November 1939 Stalin ordered the invasion of Finland after it refused demands to surrender territory bordering the USSR. The British and French planned intervention in support of the Finns. By March both countries were preparing to send 50,000 'volunteers' – in reality regular troops. In February 1940 General Gamelin approved plans for the bombing of the Soviet oil centre at Baku, supposedly to stop oil deliveries to Germany. By March plans were in place for a Franco-British attack using bases in Turkey, Syria, Iraq and Iran. Four French air corps and six British squadrons were earmarked for this operation. Only Finland's capitulation prevented both sides going to war with Russia. Days later German forces invaded and occupied Norway and Denmark.[89]

In the 1990s a new generation of Tory revisionist historians came out in defence of appeasement. John Charmley, for example, defended Chamberlain's policy on the basis that the Soviet Union was an 'equally sinister threat' as Nazi Germany, concluding:

> It might well have been in Britain's best interest to sit back and let the Nazis and Soviets fight themselves to exhaustion. Churchill neglected to ask himself, until too late, what the results of the total destruction of German power would be upon the balance of power for which he had wished to fight in the 1930s.[90]

Maurice Cowling developed this line:

> It is wrong to assume that a dominant Germany would have been more intolerable to Britain than the Soviet Union was to become, or that British statesmen had a duty to risk British lives to prevent Hitler behaving intolerably to Germans and others. We do not know that Hitler wanted war against Britain; we know only that he wanted war against the Soviet Union, and found himself at war with Britain and France when British indignation turned Chamberlain's political interference at Munich into a military commitment against him.
>
> Though the balance is a fine one, Russian (and American) domination of Europe after a long war, the destruction of Germany and the emasculation of the British Empire, were probably worse for Britain than German domination of Europe might have been if that had been effected without war or the emasculation of the Empire.[91]

The horrific reality of the German occupation of Europe is ignored. So to is the substantial evidence that Hitler would not have been content with controlling Europe but wanted global domination, and that required confronting Britain. The truth is that the consistent policy of appeasement pursued by Chamberlain had convinced Hitler that Britain would not go to war, and even if it did, it would fight half-heartedly.

One argument deployed in favour of appeasement and Munich was that it bought time for Britain to rearm. Yet the evidence does not support this. Between Munich and the declaration of war in September 1939, Britain's military expenditure was a fifth that of Germany's and its fighter production was half. British aircraft production only overtook Germany's in the spring of 1940 when numbers passed one thousand a month.[92]

All of this misses out the simple fact that the leaders of Britain and France (and indeed Russia) were not prepared to fight an anti-fascist war and risk unleashing the popular unrest that would come with it. That had already become clear in Spain during the civil war, but unfortunately the Republic's leaders focused on winning support from those same governments rather than building on the popular revolutionary upsurge which had thrown back Franco's campaign.

The British ruling class were aware of the decline of Britain as a world power, and feared their rivals, but they were also haunted by the memory of the revolutionary wave which had broken across Europe at the close of the 1914–18 war. They had been shaken by the upsurge of working-class struggle in 1919–20 and by the 1926 General Strike. That fear meant they could not grasp the sea change that had happened within Russia and still saw it as fomenting revolution – when, in fact, Stalin shared their hatred of any such upheavals.

CHAPTER FIVE

The Early War

The Fall of Poland

In August 1939 Hitler gathered his senior military commanders at his Alpine home, the Berghof, to tell them of his alliance with Stalin, his decision to invade Poland, and his belief that Britain and France were in no position to aid their Polish ally. He then told them frankly:

> 'I have put my death's head formations in place with the command relentlessly and without compassion to send into death many women and children of Polish origin and language ... Poland will be depopulated and settled with Germans ... As for the east ... the fate of Russia will be exactly the same ... After Stalin's death – he is a very sick man – we will break the Soviet Union. Then there will begin the dawn of the German rule of the earth.' After Hitler pledged to eradicate Polish women and children Hermann Göring jumped up onto a table and offered 'bloodthirsty thanks and bloody promises and proceeded to dance around like a savage'.[1]

The barbarity of Nazism would be inflicted on the population of Poland at terrible cost and with terrible consequences. In the first days of the invasion on 3 and 4 September German troops burnt down the village of Zloczew, killing 200 people. On 5 September mass reprisals began in the city of Bydgoszcz, after the killing of ethnic Germans blamed for sniping attacks on Poles. One thousand Poles were killed in the city and a further 5,000 in the surrounding region.[2]

Hitler wanted a quick victory over Poland before there was the possibility of Britain and France launching an attack. He was confident that Britain and France would return to the negotiating table once Poland was swallowed up. The German plan was to destroy the small regular Polish army near the border prior to its reserve being mobilised. Further, by overrunning the assembly areas for those reserves it would throw the mobilisation into chaos. The Polish command believed Danzig would be the initial target of any German attack and placed about a third of their army in the corridor between West and East Prussia; that allowed the Germans to attack from both flanks, inflicting a crushing defeat.

Air strikes destroyed most of the Polish air force on the ground. The Luftwaffe then concentrated on supporting the army's ground attack and preventing movement of troops and material. German forces from East Prussia attacked east of Warsaw. An armoured thrust from the west was diverted from entering the capital (with the realisation that tanks were unsuited for street warfare) and ordered to wheel round and advance to the east of the city, linking with the forces advancing from East Prussia. The Polish army was surrounded, trapped against the German border. Fighting continued but the outcome of the war was decided.

The role of the Luftwaffe was to provide support for ground forces, operating in close contact with them rather than acting as an independent strategic force as did the French and British air forces. The head of the Italian secret service, General Giacomo Carboni, produced a report for Mussolini's military co-ordinator, General Cavallero, which challenged beliefs, developed in the wake of the 1914–18 war, that stronger firepower gave the advantage to defence. He pointed out that in modern warfare large turning movements were possible at long range and could divide and defeat defending forces. This is what had happened in Poland. He also noted that control of the air had been central to the German victory and that commanders of major units had intervened directly on the battlefront using motor transport. Cavallero simply ignored the lessons Carboni had drawn.[3]

By 8 September the leading Panzers were on the outskirts of Warsaw, having covered 140 miles in only eight days. Two days later all Polish forces were ordered to fall back and regroup in eastern Poland for a last stand. Poland's hope rested on a major French and British offensive in the west to relieve the pressure. Thus far the French army on the Rhine limited itself to reoccupying some villages that had been evacuated. Yet facing them on a still incomplete 'West Wall' were just 35 German divisions, 25 of which were second grade or even lower. The French could field 70 divisions, which had superiority in terms of tanks and aircraft. The French commander, General Maurice Gamelin, assured Warsaw that the French army was fully engaged in combat, but on 13 September all military action on the Western Front was ended, with French troops ordered to fall back behind the Maginot Line.[4]

Warsaw was surrounded on 15 September and suffered punishing bombing raids without hope of relief. It surrendered on 27 September after 18 days of continuous bombing. German forces in the Brest Litovsk area came into contact with the Red Army advancing from the east. They were informed that the Russians were occupying eastern Poland as agreed by a secret clause in the Hitler-Stalin pact.

The brief campaign of conquest in Poland was a terrible warning of what would lie ahead as the Third Reich expanded eastwards. Five-hundred-and-thirty-one Polish towns and villages were burned and the Wehrmacht carried out 714 mass executions. Altogether, it is estimated that 16,376 Polish fell victim to those atrocities. Approximately 60 per cent of these crimes were committed by the Wehrmacht. Regular German troops carried out the massacre of Jewish civilians. Heydrich of the SS explained to the army, 'We want to spare the little people, but nobility, clergy, and Jews must be killed.'[5]

Hitler ordered Poland to be erased from the map of Europe. The Germans occupied western and northern Poland up to the River Bug. The industrial and coal-producing region of Silesia and north-western Poland were incorporated directly into the German state (these having been taken from Germany under the terms of the post-war Versailles Treaty). The remainder, named the General

Government, was run as a German colony. Poles were physically expelled from those regions incorporated into the Third Reich. Hundreds of thousands were driven from their homes by the SS, forced into cattle trucks and dumped in the General Government area. In the villages of Sola and Jeleśnia peasant women were shot as they tried to run away from their farms.[6]

Seven hundred thousand homes were confiscated from Polish and Jewish families and given to German families. In the district of Łódź alone the Nazis seized 70 banks, 3,500 textile factories and shops, 500 wholesale companies and 8,500 retail businesses, all of which were handed over to German firms, Nazi Party members, and Germans who resettled there. Poznań, a city of 270,000 people, was ethnically cleansed of its Polish population.[7]

Hitler appointed as Chief Gauleiter of Poland the former SA stormtrooper Hans Frank, who condemned its population to virtual serfdom declaring, 'Poland shall be treated as a colony, the Poles shall be the slaves of the Greater German World Empire.'[8] What that meant was a blitz on Polish culture and society – Polish universities were closed, all schools bar a few primaries were also closed, and the German criminal code was imposed, allowing death sentences for trivial offences against Germans. The population was put on a starvation diet. Poles had to sit at the rear of public transport and to give up their seats rather than allow a German to stand. Adults had to salute Germans in uniform and were beaten if they failed to do so; to take off their hats in the presence of German officials and stand aside to let them pass; they had to let Germans be served first in shops. Central Warsaw, designated by Hitler to become a minor German town, was given over to Germans and Poles were pushed further out. Polish agriculture was to be used to feed Germans. Frank made clear his attitude to those under his rule:

> I am not interested in the Jews. Whether or not they get any fodder to eat is the last thing I'm concerned about ... The second category is made up of the Poles in so far as I can make use of them. I shall feed these Poles with what is left over and what we can spare. Otherwise, I will tell the Poles to look after themselves ... I am only interested in the Poles as far as I see in them a reservoir of labour, but not to the extent that I feel it is a governmental responsibility to give them a guarantee that they will get a specific amount to eat. We are not talking of rations for Poles but only of the possibilities of feeding them.[9]

The League of Nations revealed that by 1940 the urban Polish population of the General Government area was receiving just 20 per cent of the recommended daily allowance of protein and less than 5 per cent of the necessary fats.[10] In November there was a mass round up of intellectuals, with 100 members of staff at Cracow University being sent to concentration camps, where 17 older professors died. When Germany attacked France, in order to forestall any unrest 30,000 members of Poland's elite were arrested, with 3,000 summarily executed. Justifying the mass round-ups and executions Hans Frank stated, 'I must quite openly admit that this will cost the lives of a few thousand Poles ... but all of us

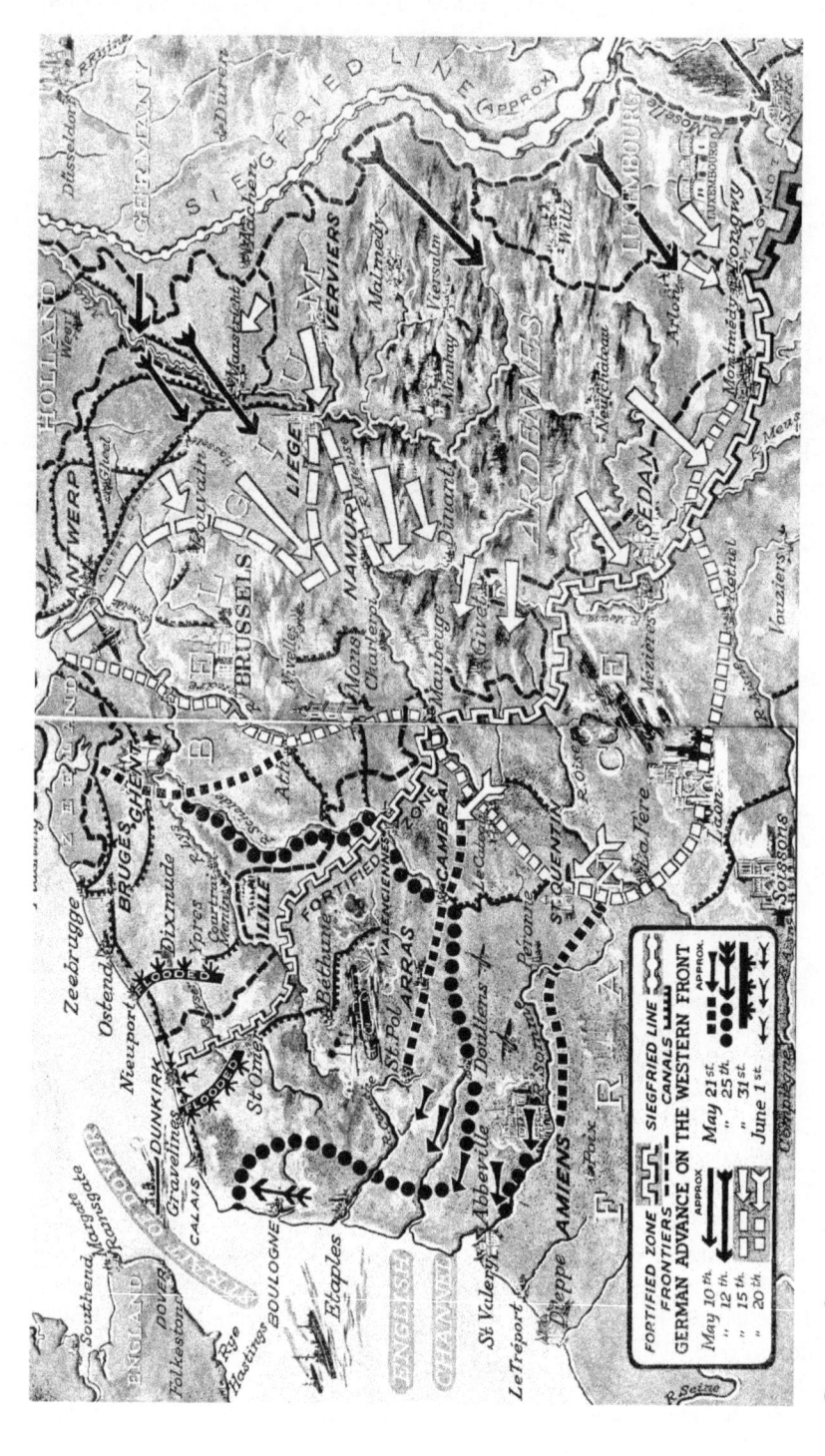

German advance through Belgium and France, 10 May to 1 June 1940

as National Socialists have a duty to ensure that no further resistance emerges from the Polish people.'[11]

For Poland's Jewish citizens an even worst fate lay in store. On 21 September 1939 Heydrich explained to SS commanders regarding the Jews that the object was a 'final solution, which will take some time'.[12] By the autumn of 1940, 80,000 Poles had been moved out of the area of Warsaw designated as the Jewish ghetto, with an initial 150,000 Jews being housed in the walled-off area. By March 1941 the population was 460,000, with one third of the city's population housed in 15 per cent of its housing stock. Mortality rates, which stood at 23.5 per thousand in 1940, soared to 90 per thousand in 1941 and a dreadful 142 by 1942.[13] Under Frank's direction over 6,000,000 Poles died, including 3,000,000 Jews.

The Occupation of France

The Hitler-Stalin pact removed a key part of the Anglo-French plan for dealing with Hitler: the re-imposition of the economic blockade they had enforced in the 1914–18 war. The alliance with Russia meant vital raw materials and foodstuffs flowed into the Reich. However, the pact allowed the British ruling class to package the war as one against Nazism and Bolshevism, with the emphasis tilting towards the latter. The *Daily Telegraph* declared, 'The object of this war is not to destroy Germany ... but to save her for Western civilisation against her own leadership because what has to be destroyed is the Bolshevik barbarism of the Eastern steppes.'[14]

The Allies hoped to fight a protracted war which would allow them to overtake German war production (they believed, erroneously, the German war economy was out-producing them). The British hoped the French army could hold the Germans in check and that the RAF could destroy much of the German economy through aerial bombing (during the war the British pioneered the development of heavy bombers). This, plus a naval blockade, they believed would lead to a German collapse after 18 months. The 'Phoney War' in which the Anglo-French armies faced their German opponents in a seeming stand-off from September 1939 until the spring of 1940 was a deliberate part of this policy. In reality such a collapse was not on the cards; the German economy was not fully mobilised until the second half of the war.

The French military mission to Poland, which since its ally had gained independence provided training and advice, had returned with graphic reports of the German strategy of using armour supported by aircraft to create a breach in the defensive line through which ground forces could then pour. Above all they reported that the Luftwaffe had destroyed the Polish chain of command and prevented the movement of defence forces. The air-force general in charge of the mission even predicted that a German attack westwards would fall on the centre of the French defensive line and not across the Belgian plain. He was sidelined and French intelligence reports were ignored.[15] In London Chamberlain drew the conclusion that Hitler's victory in Poland was due to the air force and Britain should prioritise building its fleet of heavy bombers above all else.[16]

The anti-communism of the Daladier government extended into the 'Phoney War' period. The French Communist Party's newspaper was banned following the Hitler-Stalin pact of August 1939 – despite the fact it had not caught up with the Moscow line and was urging the 'Union of the French Nation against Hitlerian aggression' rather than denouncing Anglo-French imperialism. Anti-Semitic, anti-British titles like *Je suis partout* and *Le Petit Parisien* continued to appear legally, while the Communists had to print and distribute *L'Humanité* underground.[17]

The party's general secretary, Maurice Thorez, had already enlisted to fight an 'anti-fascist war'. But now the Communist Party adopted an anti-war line under instruction from Moscow, arguing on 1 October 1939 that the French government should consider Hitler's peace terms favourably. Thorez had to skip the country to Moscow to avoid fighting an imperialist war, being stripped of his French citizenship by Daladier.[18] In September the Communist Party was suppressed and a month later 35 Communist deputies were expelled from parliament and arrested. By March 1940, 300 Communist-led local authorities had been suspended and 3,400 party members were in jail. Julian Jackson points out that 'anti-communism intensified dramatically during the Phoney War, forming a link between the final months of the Republic and Vichy'.[19]

Meanwhile the Daladier government cracked down not on the fascists and anti-Semites but on refugees, many of whom were Jewish, and Communists. Even before the war it had begun interning 'undesirables'. This category would expand to include Republican fighters fleeing Franco's victorious forces. All foreigners were included in a new register, which would prove very useful for the German occupiers after France fell. In March 1940 Paul Reynaud replaced Daladier as premier. He was personally resolved to prosecute the war and was admired by Churchill with whom he had been in contact pre-war. But he had no real base of support in the Chamber of Deputies. His government contained some who openly believed the war to be a mistake, and he was even forced to bring in right-wingers, one of whom was a member of the fascist Croix de Feu. Alastair Horne comments that it was 'roughly the same as if Churchill had taken Oswald Mosley into his cabinet'.[20]

Winston Churchill: Walking with Destiny

By now Winston Churchill had been brought into the Chamberlain government as First Lord of the Admiralty. On 8 April 1940 the British War Cabinet voted for Churchill's proposal to mine Norway's sea lanes to block exports of Swedish iron ore to Germany (Sweden was neutral but it co-ordinated its economy with that of Germany). This was a breach of Norwegian neutrality – something the Germans were quick to pin on Britain. The next day the Germans launched their own occupation of Denmark and Norway. The former was rapidly overrun, but the Norwegians resisted the attack, despite losing their capital, Oslo. The

British and French had overwhelming naval superiority in the North Atlantic and should have been able to intervene to stop German landings and destroy their supplies. In fact the whole operation foundered on a failure to ensure co-operation between naval, land and air forces. A series of botched landings ended with an inglorious evacuation of the Anglo-French forces leaving the Germans with an important strategic hold on a long North Atlantic coastline. Swedish iron ore supplies were never interrupted.[21]

The British Fleet Air Arm did carry out the very first successful air attack on a battleship; its aircraft flying from the Orkneys sank the German cruiser, the Königsberg. However, the British, as we shall see, failed to draw the lesson that heavy battleships were highly vulnerable to air attack if they did not have defending aircraft.[22] On 7 to 8 May the House of Commons debated the Norway campaign. Despite Churchill being responsible for the whole operation it quickly became a vote of confidence in the prime minister. Following one of the chamber's most dramatic debates the government won by 281 votes to 200, but 41 government supporters voted against it and 60 Tories abstained. On the following day Chamberlain was visited by a Tory grandee, Lord Salisbury, who advised him to quit. Chamberlain had asked the Labour Party to join his government but was now told that Clement Attlee and Arthur Greenwood, leader and deputy leader of the Labour Party respectively, refused to do so while Chamberlain remained as premier. The prime minister decided to resign. He went to see George VI who accepted his resignation reluctantly, lamenting: 'How grossly unfair I thought he had been treated and that I was terribly sorry that all this controversy had happened. We then had an informal talk over his successor. I, of course, suggested Halifax.'[23] The outgoing prime minister then met with Halifax and Churchill telling them they were the only two possible candidates to replace him. Halifax was his preference but he refused, citing the fact that he sat in the Lords not the Commons and admitting the idea of becoming a wartime leader gave him 'a bad stomach ache'.[24]

Churchill had had a peppered career, switching from the Tories to the Liberals before the First World War, and then back again after it. The Tories did not regard him as 'one of us', to coin a term of Margaret Thatcher's much later. From 1929 until 1939 Churchill held no position, either in the Tory shadow cabinet or in the National Governments of MacDonald, Baldwin and Chamberlain. Aside from warning repeatedly about the threat Hitler posed to British interests he had demanded there should be no concessions to Indian nationalism or the cause of opposing the abdication of King Edward VIII. To most Tory MPs he was regarded as untrustworthy and a has-been.

On 10 May Winston Churchill was appointed prime minister, to the disgust of much of his own Tory Party. Chips Channon wrote that it was 'perhaps the darkest day in English history' and in the evening joined Lord Dunglass (Sir Alec Douglas-Home, the later Tory prime minister), Jock Colville and Rab Butler in toasting the 'king over the water', Neville Chamberlain. Butler described the new prime minister's speeches as 'beyond words vulgar' and announced that, 'the good clean tradition of English politics ... had been sold to the greatest political adventurer in modern political history ... a half-breed American'.

A few days later Halifax, the man who had turned down the chance of the premiership, predicted 'the gangsters will shortly be in complete control'.[25] The Queen wrote to Chamberlain saying how 'deeply I regretted your ceasing to be prime minister. I can never tell you in words how much we owe you ... You did all in your power to stave off such agony, and you were right.'[26]

On his first day in office Churchill acted against two aristocrats who were associated with the pro-fascist, pro-peace fringe. He warned the Duke of Westminster, one of Britain's wealthiest men, about his activities, prompting him to depart for Ireland; he removed the Duke of Buccleuch as steward to the royal household.[27] The Labour Party joined Churchill's government with Attlee as Lord Privy Seal and Arthur Greenwood as minister without portfolio. Despite his own reputation for being tough on the trade unions, Churchill was prepared to gamble on the nationalism of the trade union bureaucracy by installing the Transport and General Workers Union chief, Ernest Bevin, as minister of labour. Other Labour appointees were Herbert Morrison as minister of supply, Hugh Dalton as minister of economic warfare and William Jowitt as solicitor general. Yet the government was essentially still a Tory one, and Chamberlain's rather than Churchill's. Halifax, Rab Butler and Chips Channon remained at the Foreign Office.

The Labour minister for economic warfare, Hugh Dalton, noted regarding Churchill's reception in parliament: 'It is noticeable how he is much more loudly cheered by the Labour Party than by the general body of Tory supporters. The relative silence of these latter is regarded by some as "sinister".'[28] This was obvious to Berlin, as a later account reveals. Goebbels noted in his diary after a discussion with Hitler early in 1942:

> Churchill has never been a friend of the Tories. He was always an outsider, and before the war was regarded as half crazy. Nobody took him seriously. The Führer recalled that all Englishmen whom he received before the outbreak of the war were in agreement that Churchill was a fool. Even Chamberlain said so to the Führer.[29]

Meanwhile the German military was about to achieve a stunning victory. In May 1940 the Wehrmacht concentrated its land and air forces for a breakthrough in the Ardennes, exploiting the fact that the French units were strung out across a long front with poor communications between them after their commanders decided the wooded and hilly terrain ruled out penetration by tanks. A secondary attack into the Low Countries was aimed at confirming the Anglo-French belief that the main thrust would be through Belgium and into Flanders, which accordingly led the Allies to advance north. The Germans relied on them responding in exactly this way, leaving a space for the decisive breakthrough in the Ardennes-Sedan region. The Germans forced their way past meagre reserve troops defending the River Meuse on 13 May and swept on into northern France heading for the Channel. Two days later the French premier, Reynaud, told Churchill the battle was lost. The French government made plans to evacuate Paris.[30]

The Luftwaffe operated using tactics developed in Spain and Poland: providing the armoured thrusts with close air support and attacking Allied airfields. Half of the French aircraft lost were destroyed on the ground. Others, including some of the most modern designs, were found by the Wehrmacht still in their crates. On the seventh day of the German attack amid panic over the breakthrough at Sedan and Namur, the French government ordered 40 squads of Gardes Mobiles to be withdrawn from the army to be sent to Paris to maintain order. The French and British forces never seriously launched a pincer attack on the ever-extending German lines of advance as the Panzer columns neared the Channel – even though German tanks were far ahead of their infantry support and were in danger of running out of fuel. The British army in France and Belgium (just nine divisions, less than the Dutch army and 40 per cent of Belgian forces) began to retreat on 16 May. In the first 11 days of the campaign British casualties totalled just 500. They left the bulk of the fighting to the French and Belgians.[31]

On 18 May Reynaud announced the appointment of General Weygand and Marshal Pétain to his government, hoping the men who had helped bring victory in 1918 could rally French resistance. Reynaud sacked Gamelin as supreme commander, replacing him with Maxime Weygand, 'a Catholic right-winger, with little enthusiasm for the war'. He took two days to arrive from Syria where he had commanded the occupying French army of the Levant.[32] Marshal Pétain was brought in as deputy premier. Both would undermine Reynaud and those wishing to resist:

> Weygand's defeatism may not have been known to him [Reynaud] until it was too late. But, from his position on the sidelines as France's ambassador to Franco's Spain, Pétain had made his views clear to anyone who cared to listen. Since the outset he had thought France's involvement in the war a mistake, even if she should be victorious.[33]

Pétain described Franco as 'the cleanest sword in the Western World'.[34] He returned from Madrid convinced that France must sue for peace. From the beginning of his taking command Weygand stressed his aim was to fight to preserve France's honour rather than to secure victory.

As early as 19 May the British general headquarters in France began planning an evacuation from Dunkirk. Two days earlier the rear general headquarters had been evacuated from Arras, the British supply hub, to the port of Boulogne without telling the French liaison officers who were stationed with them. When the French tracked their allies down to Boulogne 48 hours later they discovered the British rear GHQ was leaving for Britain. British forces did make one attack, around Arras on 21 May, after the cabinet instructed them to attack southwards. This caused considerable panic in the German command who understood a pincer move could cut off the Panzer vanguard. But the attack lacked artillery and air support and was not followed up. The next day the British continued to pull back towards Dunkirk.[35] On 24 May Churchill telegraphed the British commander in France, Lord Gort, 'Of course if one side fights and the other does not, the war is apt to become somewhat unequal.'[36] Clive Ponting notes that Churchill left this sentence out of his wartime memoirs.

On 25 May the British command in France ordered the evacuation of its forces. When he was told of this decision, the secretary of state for war, Anthony Eden, responded, 'It is obvious that you should not discuss the possibility of the move with the French and Belgians.'[37] The next day they ignored French orders to attack southwards. When asked about evacuating Belgian troops the Chief of Staff of the British Expeditionary Force replied 'we don't care a bugger what happens to the Belgians'.[38] The evacuation from the one remaining Channel port in Allied hands, Dunkirk, depended on a decision by the Germans to halt their advance and on the ability of the French to hold the perimeter of the evacuation area and a pocket around the city of Lille. The defence of the city continued until 1 June while French troops held the bridgehead at Dunkirk until 4 June, two days after the evacuation ended. The evacuation of British troops began on 27 May. It did not begin well. The Luftwaffe had dominance over the beaches because the RAF kept its fighters back in readiness for an expected attack on Britain. The Anglo-French alliance was now breaking down. The British believed the French would hold a perimeter round the port while they took ship. The French believed they were involved in a joint operation to defend a redoubt in their country.

The British commander, Lord Gort, had requested Canadian troops be sent to defend the perimeter while the British embarked. Protests by the government in Ottawa stopped this. The senior Royal Navy commander in Dunkirk commented on 29 May, 'The French staff at Dunkirk feel strongly that they are defending Dunkirk for us to evacuate, which is largely true.'[39] French troops were physically prevented from evacuating until 29 May, by which time a third of British troops had crossed the Channel. The British commander, Lord Gort, left without informing the French, and his replacement in charge, General Harold Alexander, told the French commanders he was withdrawing his troops from the frontline leaving the French to fight on. When the French general stated that Churchill wanted the perimeter to be held until the maximum number of French troops had been evacuated and the British commander should comply with that by holding the defence line, it 'caused Alexander to roar with laughter'.[40]

The German order to halt outside Dunkirk is generally held up as evidence that Hitler wanted to reach a compromise with Britain which would preserve its Empire while giving Germany control of Eurasia. This ignores the fact that Hitler had made clear his determination to liquidate Britain and its Empire before eventually confronting the US. Another interpretation is that Hitler believed that whatever Churchill said the British ruling class would sue for peace.

Churchill's determination to fight on after Hitler had conquered France, Belgium and Holland was not matched by the reality of the situation. In its evacuation from Dunkirk the British army lost nearly all of its equipment. As the military chiefs told the cabinet in May 1940, 'Should the enemy succeed in establishing a force, with its vehicles firmly ashore, the army in the United Kingdom, which is very short of equipment, has not got the offensive power to drive it out.'[41]

On the same day as Churchill had visited Buckingham Palace to be sworn in as prime minister the Germans attacked along their western frontier. Chamberlain met with the American ambassador, Joseph Kennedy, who expressed the view that Britain could not keep fighting without the French. Chamberlain noted in his diary, 'I told him I did not see how we could either.'[42] Churchill understood that surrender would destroy Britain as an imperial power. He strove mightily to preserve the Empire – but he had been dealt a bad hand with which to play.

Fight on or Surrender?

In the summer of 1940 the British prime minister was in a minority within the ruling class and his own Conservative Party. On 13 May, Harold Nicholson noted in his diary that, 'When Chamberlain enters the House he gets a terrific reception, and when Churchill comes in the applause is less.'[43] The following month Lord Dunglass told the wife of a Tory whip that 'since W[inston] came in, the H of C had stank in the nostrils of the decent people. The kind of people surrounding W are the scum.'[44] Tory MPs 'lost their heads' at Chamberlain's first appearance in the Commons following his resignation, cheering him to the rafters.[45]

The beginning of the collapse in France led to a sense of panic in Whitehall. On 19 May the British ambassador to France, Oliver Harvey, entered in his diary, 'Defeatism in London among the upper classes'.[46] On that day the Germans broke out of the Ardennes and began their race to the Channel. The appeaser Sir Samuel Hoare had been sacked from the cabinet by Churchill and had been unhappy at the suggestion he should go to Spain as British ambassador; when news of the German breakthrough reached him he went to the Foreign Office saying Churchill wanted him to leave immediately for Spain. Cadogan, head of the Foreign Office, wrote in his diary, 'Dirty little dog has got the wind up and wants to get out of this country!' When Hoare expressed worries to his wife about the difficulties of moving to a new country she replied, 'It may be easier than to adapt oneself to serving in an old country in new conditions.'[47]

On 17 May President Roosevelt raised with the British ambassador, Lord Lothian, his request that the British fleet should sail to US ports rather than risk falling into German hands. Churchill, who was in secret correspondence with the White House, replied:

> If members of this present administration were finished and others come to parley amid the ruins, you must not be blind to the fact that the sole remaining bargaining counter with Germany would be the fleet, and if this country was left by the United States to its fate no one would have the right to blame those then responsible if they made the best terms they could for the surviving inhabitants.[48]

Roosevelt then raised the idea of the British fleet seeking shelter in Canada. A week later, on 24 May, he telephoned the Canadian prime minister to request the dispatch of a secret envoy to discuss security matters. MacKenzie King, the premier in Ottawa, felt the US was 'trying to save itself at the expense of Britain' and told Roosevelt he would have to talk to Churchill.

On the morning of Saturday 25 May Halifax re-opened an old channel through the Italian ambassador suggesting Mussolini might broker peace talks with Berlin. He met with the ambassador, Giuseppe Bastianini. Halifax's private secretary, Rab Butler, had already promised the ambassador Britain would 'eliminate all inconveniences lamented by [Italy]'.[49] The Italian representative asked Halifax, 'whether he might inform his government that His Majesty's Government considered it opportune now to examine the question at issue between our two countries within the larger framework of a European settlement'. Halifax replied that he was ready to discuss a 'general European settlement'. He was then asked whether he was prepared to hold discussions 'involving not only Great Britain and Italy, but other countries', replying that such talks, obviously referring to Germany, would be 'difficult to visualise ... while war was still proceeding'. Bastianini responded that 'once such a discussion began, war would be pointless', adding that Mussolini desired a settlement to 'protect European peace for the century'. Halifax stated the British government's purpose was 'the same'.[50] They ended with agreement about the importance of holding talks aimed at a European settlement. In 1948 Halifax's biographer, Lord Ismay, persuaded Churchill to cut out a passage in his wartime memoirs in which, referring to Halifax's talks with the Italian ambassador, he wrote that, 'the foreign secretary showed himself willing to go a long way'.[51]

On Sunday 26 May the Bank of England's gold and other reserves were shipped to Canada. Ottawa was warned to expect the imminent arrival of the Royal Family. There followed three days of intense discussions in secret sessions of the War Cabinet about pursuing negotiations with Hitler. Halifax and Chamberlain were the effective leaders of the Tory Party, whose MPs held the majority in the House of Commons – and the majority of those opposed Churchill. Halifax stated, 'We had to face the fact that it was not so much now a question of imposing a complete defeat on Germany, but of safeguarding the independence of our Empire and if possible that of France.'[52]

On the morning of Sunday 26 May Churchill warned that Belgium was about to capitulate, France was facing collapse and British forces must risk evacuation by sea. Halifax reported on his discussions with the Italian ambassador to the War Cabinet: 'Peace and security in Europe were ... our main object, and we should naturally be prepared to consider any proposals which might lead to this, provided our liberty and independence were assured.' This meant agreeing to Mussolini brokering a Munich-style conference with the German Führer in attendance. Churchill riposted, 'That we could never accept. We must ensure our complete liberty and independence.' He was opposed to any negotiations that might 'lead to a derogation of our rights and powers'.[53]

After some discussion the War Cabinet broke for lunch with Churchill meeting the French premier Reynaud and Halifax lunching with Chamberlain. Reynaud reported that the French could now only deploy 50 divisions to counter the 150 advancing German divisions (the French figure did not include their forces effectively trapped 'defending' the Maginot Line). The Germans had the power to pierce any French defensive line, Reynaud reported, and while he would not surrender he might have to resign to allow his replacement to do just that.[54]

Following the bad news from France Halifax returned to a possible approach to Italy, asking Churchill, 'if he was satisfied that matters vital to the independence of this country were unaffected', would he be 'prepared to discuss such terms?' Churchill replied that he 'would be thankful to get out of our present difficulties on such terms, provided we retained the essentials and the elements of our vital strength, even at the cost of some territory'.[55] In his diary Neville Chamberlain quoted Churchill as saying:

'If we could get out of this jam by giving up Malta and Gibraltar and some African colonies he would jump at it.'[56]

Churchill moved to break off discussions arguing the War Cabinet should wait and see how many troops were evacuated from Dunkirk. The session ended agreeing to continue later that evening, but there was a further informal War Cabinet at which no minutes were taken and the cabinet secretary, the top civil servant whose job that was, was excluded. This was highly unusual in Whitehall's history. That evening the War Cabinet agreed that Halifax should draft an approach to Mussolini. Churchill won agreement that the secretary of state for air, Archibald Sinclair, a friend of the prime minister, should be asked to attend the next day's session in his role as leader of the National Liberal Party.

On the following day came news that Belgium had surrendered. Halifax pressed Churchill on whether he would accept any peace terms if they guaranteed Britain's independence. The Labour leader, Attlee, argued that Britain should show the utmost resolution even if France gave up the fight. Churchill seized on this and came out against an approach to Rome to broker peace talks: 'Nations which went down fighting rose again, but those which surrendered tamely were finished.'[57] Chamberlain, who had by now despaired of Italian mediation, also came out against making an approach. Churchill stated that if France surrendered he would not join them in asking for Hitler's peace terms, but if he were told those terms he would consider them.

Halifax was not finished. The next day, Tuesday 28 May, the War Cabinet met once more. Halifax argued that the French were keen to broker peace negotiations through Mussolini and that Britain could get the best terms from Hitler while France was still fighting and before Britain's aircraft factories were bombed. Churchill replied:

> If we once got to the table, we should then find that the terms offered us touched our independence and integrity. When, at this point, we got up to leave the Conference table, we should find that all the forces of resolution which were now at our disposal would have vanished.[58]

The foreign secretary insisted he saw nothing wrong in joining with France in trying to get Mussolini to mediate with Hitler. Churchill now asked for an adjournment. Shortly afterwards he addressed a gathering of those government ministers who were not members of the inner War Cabinet. There he declared surrender was not an option. Labour minister Hugh Dalton recalled that Churchill ruled out entering into negotiations with Germany, stating: 'We should become a slave state, though a British government which would be Hitler's puppet would be set up – "under Mosley or some such person". And where should we be at the end of all that.' Dalton noted, 'It is quite clear that whereas the Old Umbrella [Chamberlain] – neither he nor other members of the War Cabinet were at this meeting – wanted to run very early, Winston's bias is all the other way.'[59]

Churchill was applauded. He had taken the argument from the inner sanctum of the War Cabinet, where he faced dogged opposition from Halifax, and won the backing of a wider layer. Returning to the Cabinet, Churchill won assent for his proposal that any request for negotiations with Berlin should be put off for two or three months. Even so, the Tory appeasers were not quite finished. The French surrender encouraged the peace faction to once again broker talks with Germany.

France Collapses

Meanwhile German forces launched an attack southwards. The French government evacuated Paris and fled to Bordeaux in June 1940. Reynaud and others committed to prosecuting the war talked of moving to France's North African colonies to continue the resistance. Pétain called upon Paul Badouin, a supporter of seeking a separate peace treaty with Germany, to explain he wished to save the French army rather than let it fight to the last man. Weygand and Pétain now openly backed the separate peace lobby. Reynaud's days were numbered. Pétain and co played on fears of social unrest brought on by a failure to stop the fighting:

> Weygand told the cabinet that defeat could be followed by a repeat of the 1871 Paris Commune, when the city's workers took power after France had been defeated by Prussia. On 13 June he told the cabinet that the Communist leader, Thorez, had installed himself in the presidential palace, the Élysée. The interior minister, George Mandel, went to the phone and returned to report this was all untrue. Thorez had in fact fled to Moscow.[60]

Twenty hours later, on 13 June, Reynaud broached with Churchill the idea of France capitulating. Pétain scorned British declarations that they would resist come what may. Eden noted that the Marshal was 'mockingly incredulous'. Weygand announced they would sue for peace in a week and that Britain's neck would be 'wrung like a chicken'.[61] Pétain told the cabinet an armistice was 'necessary' and that whatever happened he would remain in France. This was a threat to Reynaud, and others considering retiring to North Africa to continue resistance, that Pétain would take charge of metropolitan France.

On 16 June Pétain read out a letter to the French cabinet announcing he would resign rather than serve in a government which would not end hostilities immediately. Reynaud resigned. The president swore in Pétain as premier. The next day, 17 June, he broadcast to the French people saying hostilities must cease. The effective announcement of surrender before any terms had been reached with Hitler meant the Germans could advance further, encountering little or no resistance and exploiting the chaos in the French army. One and a half million of the 2 million French soldiers captured by the Germans during the war were taken in the week between that broadcast and the subsequent signing of the armistice.[62]

Pétain formed a government that was viciously anti-Semitic and blamed defeat on the left and 'moral decline'. His vice premier, Pierre Laval, declared in July 1940 that, 'Parliamentary democracy lost the war; it must give way to a new regime.'[63] In just six weeks French resistance had collapsed. The right and the military chiefs who had never wanted war with Hitler took control of the government and brokered a humiliating peace deal which they tried to portray as a dented shield protecting French civilians and prisoners of war from worse terms. On 9 July deputies met in the spa town of Vichy to vote full powers to Pétain. Fifty-seven per cent of the Socialist deputies and 58 per cent of the Radical deputies, regarded as liberal and left of centre, voted full powers to Pétain.[64]

The next day Pétain abolished the Republic and appointed himself head of state with full powers to appoint and dismiss ministers, parliament was adjourned until further notice, and Pétain was given an exclusive monopoly on legislative, judicial and executive powers. Julian Jackson argues, 'The Vichy regime was largely a reaction against the revolution that the Popular Front had represented in the eyes of much of the French bourgeoisie.'[65] Pétain implemented anti-Semitic and fascist measures without directives from Berlin. By the end of 1940, 55,000 to 60,000 people were held in French internment camps – Jews, Communists, Spanish Republicans. The French State headed by Pétain was committed to 'Work, Family, Nation' rather than 'Liberty, Fraternity, Equality'. It was repressive and authoritarian from the start. In October 1940 Pétain left a meeting with Hitler at Montoire to declare, 'A collaboration has been envisaged between our two countries. I have accepted it in principle.'[66] Vichy would not go to war with the Allies, but thought collaboration might gain them a favourable position in Hitler's New European Order.

Vichy controlled the centre and south of the country. The rest, including the coast, was under direct German control. Pétain's government was made up of traditional right-wingers, particularly military men, and relied heavily on the Catholic Church. The hard-line, pro-Germans were kept at arm's length until Vichy's bitter end. They included the two main fascist parties, Jacques Doriot's Parti populaire français, and the ex-Socialist Marcel Deat's Rassamblement national populaire. Along with the writers of *Je suis partout* they gravitated to Paris and the Germans, who happily played them off against each other and against Vichy.

The Vichy government was prepared to materially help the German war effort. They ordered French forces in North Africa to supply Rommel with 1,700 vehicles, small quantities of arms and 3,600 tons of fuel when he entered war with Britain in the region. The Vichy prime minister, Pierre Laval, committed the regime to the Third Reich when he declared in June 1942, 'I desire a German victory because without it a Bolshevism will be installed everywhere.'[67] Yet the simple reality was that the Nazis were little interested in France as an ally. Goebbels declared in July 1940:

> The new order for Europe is to be quite consciously placed under Germany's sole auspices ... in future France would only play a small role as a small Atlantic state ... everything which serves to encourage a political or economic revival of France will be destroyed ... The peace treaty will eliminate France not only as a great power but as a state with any political influence in Europe.[68]

Meanwhile, all the competing power structures of the Third Reich had set up camp in Paris in rivalry with each other. The various French fascists groupings aligned themselves to these factions, who used them for their own ends. In October 1941 the SS in co-operation with French fascists bombed several Paris synagogues. Two months earlier the *Cagoule*, now re-named the Mouvement social révolutionnaire, had assassinated the former Popular Front minister, Marx Dormoy, who had exposed their existence four years before. But in general, the occupying authorities frowned on French groups of whatever loyalty having arms, and prevented the various paramilitary groups Pétain sponsored from acquiring them.[69]

Vichy accepted article 19 of the Armistice which facilitated the handover to the Nazis of all German citizens who had sought refuge in France. Those returned to their death included Herschel Grynszpan (whose shooting of a German diplomat in 1938 was seized on as justification for the Kristallnacht pogrom) and the social democrat economist, Rudolf Hilferding. The Jewish Affairs counsellor at the German embassy in Paris reported in February 1942, 'The French government would be happy to get rid of the Jews in any way whatsoever, without too much fuss.'[70]

There were only 2,400 German police in France, mainly occupied in dealing with 'terrorist' Resistance groups. After the war one of the SS commanders in Paris noted that, 'If the French police had not helped us, we couldn't have done anything at all.'[71] By the close of 1941 Vichy held 11,000 Jews in its camps; in the occupied zone the Germans held another 7,000. The first mass round-up of Jews, or 'rafle', was carried out on 14 May. Following a second round-up, 4,000 Jews, mainly from Paris, were held in dreadful conditions on a semi-derelict housing estate in Drancy, in the northern suburbs. The round-up was carried out by French police under Vichy laws. In March 1942 gendarmes loaded the first batch onto trains which took them to the boundary of Alsace Lorraine, annexed to the Reich, where they were handed over to the Germans and sent east to the death camps.[72]

One part of the British Isles did come under German occupation. On 19 June 1940 the War Cabinet agreed that the Channel Islands, which belonged to the king but were not part of the United Kingdom, could not be defended and that they should be 'demilitarised'. The Germans only found this out after they had begun bombing the Islands from the nearby French mainland. The government in London provided no means to evacuate the population, leaving the matter to the Island authorities, which resulted in chaos. The Germans occupied the Islands on 30 June and 1 July and the local authorities remained in place, co-operating with the occupiers in administering the territories and quite voluntarily passing anti-Semitic laws under which Jews were deported to the death camps.[73]

Britain Alone

Britain was left to fight alone in the summer of 1940. Its army had scrambled out of continental Europe leaving its equipment behind. Churchill told his junior ministers that Dunkirk was 'the greatest British military defeat for many centuries'.[74] The government's Director of Statistics later told a newspaper editor:

> The Dunkirk episode was far worse than was ever realised in Fleet Street. The men on getting back to England were so demoralised they threw their rifles and equipment out of railway carriage windows. Some sent for their wives with their civilian clothes, changed into these, and walked home.[75]

At the outbreak of the war, children had been evacuated from cities and towns believed to be targets for German bombing. One Londoner evacuated to the south coast recalled the state of the troops returning from France:

> I saw literally hundreds and thousands of lorry-loads of soldiers coming through the village, coming back from Dunkirk. Soldiers with no uniforms, in shirts, in a hell of a state ... I felt certain the war was over, that we had lost. Us kids were horror-stricken ... You couldn't believe it was an army. The next thing there was going to be an invasion and we were going to be finished. I was sure of it.[76]

The German conquest of France, Belgium, Holland, Denmark and Norway opened the possibility of waging submarine warfare in the Atlantic on an even greater scale than in the First World War. Far from Britain blockading Germany, the U-boat campaign in the Atlantic threatened a blockade of Britain, cutting its vital food supplies and the American military material on which it increasingly relied. On 27 May Romania agreed to Germany monopolising its oil exports. The Swiss government agreed to block all exports to Britain and to allow Germany to take all its highly valued machine tools and its 20 millimetre anti-aircraft guns. Victory in the west had brought immediate benefits to the German war effort.[77]

On 17 June Lord Halifax's deputy at the Foreign Office, Rab Butler, acting without the prime minister's consent, began the process of serious negotiations with Berlin through the Swedish ambassador, Björn Prytz, whom he chanced to meet walking in St James's Park. Prytz sent a telegram to Stockholm which read: 'Britain's official attitude will for the present continue to be that the war must go on, but [Butler] assured me that no opportunity for reaching a compromise would be neglected if the possibility were offered on reasonable conditions and that no "diehards" would be allowed to stand in the way in this connection.'[78]

During the conversation, Butler was called in to see Halifax, who sent the Swede the message that 'Common sense and not bravado would dictate the British government's policy.' Halifax added that he realised such a message would be welcomed by the Swedish minister, but that should be not be interpreted as 'peace at any price'. 'It would appear from conversations I have had with other members of parliament, that if and when the prospect of negotiations arises, possibly after 28 June, Halifax may succeed Churchill.'[79] On the same day the British ambassador in Sweden met the Swedish foreign minister. The Italian ambassador was then summoned to the foreign ministry. He reported to Rome: 'The British representative requested an interview with the Swedish foreign minister and notified him that the British government is inclined to enter into peace negotiations with Germany and Italy ... this declaration by the British representative is of official character.'[80]

While Churchill was making his oft-quoted speeches throwing defiance at Hitler, a peace party of appeasers was trying to obtain a German package it could then force through the War Cabinet, where it hoped it could win the vote. The British ambassador in Switzerland held a discussion in mid July with the German dissident, Prince Max von Hohenlohe, who it was hoped might oust Hitler and open peace talks. The ambassador said that Churchill was a drunk and unreasonable, but that Halifax and Butler were far more realistic.[81]

On 19 July in Washington the British ambassador, Lord Lothian, was told by an intermediary that his German counterpart had the German peace terms, which London could see. When he reported this to London Churchill ordered that the matter should not be followed up, but Halifax did not pass the order on. So Lothian met the man again, telling him 'dissidents' in the War Cabinet wished to know what Germany would offer a 'proud and unconquered nation'. Harold Nicolson, a junior minister at the Ministry of Information, wrote in his diary on 22 July, 'The German peace terms ... are most satisfactory.'[82] The German papers dealing with this matter disappeared after Berlin was captured in May 1945.

Churchill was conducting a vicious factional fight pitting him against the bulk of his own party. Chamberlain and Halifax operated together to check Churchill, co-ordinating holidays so one was always in Whitehall. Churchill had to rely on the Labour Party – ceding them effective control of the British domestic front – a ragbag of maverick intellectuals and the press baron, Lord Beaverbrook. The rhetoric championing continued resistance to the Nazis moved in a distinctly populist left-wing direction. The media magnate Lord Beaverbrook had been appointed to Churchill's War Cabinet. He utilised one of his titles, the London *Evening Standard*, to mobilise against the appeasers. On 15 June 1940 the paper responded to Italy's attack on France by declaring, 'It is a war not of nations at all. It is a mammoth civil war. Goethe and Garibaldi, a great German and a great Italian, are on our side.' Three days later it reacted to Marshal Pétain's surrender of France by proclaiming, 'Every rebel is our ally. We do not only fight a war. We must conduct a Continental revolution.'[83]

On 5 July the left-wing publisher, Victor Gollancz, published *Guilty Men*, written by three of Beaverbrook's journalists, including future Labour leader Michael Foot. It was a popular and hard-hitting indictment of the Baldwin and Chamberlain government's policy of appeasement and their lack of preparation for war. It demanded the ousting of the 'Old Gang' of Chamberlain, Halifax and the rest and, as Foot later recalled, was supportive of Churchill:

> Three or four of us sat down one afternoon at The Evening Standard office ... and decided to write the book. It was critical of the existing government while praising the ones who were really doing the job of saving us – Churchill was number one amongst these, and Beaverbrook himself. He had not had a good pre-war record on appeasement, but in the war he had a good one, and he was in the cabinet, so we were naturally favourable to him. The 'guilty' men were those whom we thought should not be allowed still to stay in the government, because of their appeasement records before, and because of their incompetence then to deal with the situation, and of course because of the new people who were coming in, who should really be taking over the job.[84]

Though full of praise for Churchill, the pamphlet was boycotted by many booksellers. But it sold in bundles on the streets: 'And there were some people who tried to suppress it, including Smith's who were the distributors, i.e. WH Smith, the bookseller. They were trying to stop the distribution. But they couldn't succeed and when they tried, we sold the book on barrows, up in Fleet Street and elsewhere.'[85] *Guilty Men* proved to be one of the most successful pamphlets in British history despite it being sold 'like a pornographic classic', as Michael Foot observed.[86] Despite the ban by WH Smith's and Wyman's it had sold 200,000 copies by December 1940. As Angus Calder wrote:

> A Gallup poll at this time suggested that three quarters of the public now wanted Chamberlain removed from office. There were strong feelings against the lesser 'Guilty Men', Halifax, Wood and Margesson [the Tory chief whip]. Churchill could not remove them; partly because they were able ('If one were dependent on people who had been right in the last few years,' he remarked at the time, 'what a tiny handful one would have to depend on'), and still more because the Tory benches might turn on him.[87]

Within the normally closed political world of the British ruling class the pamphlet represented an unprecedented glasnost in which a minority section of the Tory Party round Churchill relied on their media friends and the Labour Party to oust their opponents. Angus Calder writes, 'The "old gang", the old system, the "Old World" (as men came to call it) had failed ... Hatred focused on Chamberlain, Hoare, Simon, and beyond them the Conservative Party, and beyond them the businessmen whom they represented in parliament.'[88]

Through foul means and fair Churchill won out within the government and the Tory Party in the summer of 1940. He would make Halifax deliver the speech which rejected Hitler's call on Britain to make peace, and then in December removed him from government by dispatching him to Washington as Britain's ambassador there. Shortly after Butler was removed from the Foreign Office and sent off to the ministry of education, effective demotion (Butler would serve as a senior minister in subsequent post-war Tory governments).[89]

Powerless to strike at the Third Reich, except through costly and ineffective air raids, Churchill needed to assert British military defiance. On 3 July he had ordered a naval attack on the Vichy French fleet anchored at Oran in Algeria. The French had insisted that their fleet would not be used by the Germans (when the Germans later occupied their Mediterranean bases they scuttled the ships) and had conveyed this to the British. The attack on Oran was a signal to Hitler, Roosevelt and the defeatists in his own government that British resistance would continue. Roosevelt was consulted about the attack on the French fleet at Oran and approved – the US also feared it might fall under German control.

Back in Britain there was a growing flight abroad. Three MPs were among those who fled to North America. On 24 June, Chips Channon took his son Paul (a future minister under Margaret Thatcher) to Euston to be put on the train to Liverpool and then by sea to New York. Channon wrote in his diary, 'There was a queue of Rolls Royces and liveried servants and mountains of trunks. It seemed that everyone we knew was there.'[90] Lord Mountbatten sent his wife and two children and Duff Cooper sent his son (John Julius Norwich) to safety in the United States. The press baron Viscount Rothermere took his son, Vere Harmsworth, out of Eton and sent him to Connecticut.[91]

Despite Churchill being a blue-blooded High Tory, the rhetoric of *Guilty Men* and the propaganda of the BBC, ever loyal to whoever was in government, and the newsreels helped spur a growing radicalisation. The author J.B. Priestley gave a series of radio broadcasts in the summer of 1940 that won a mass audience and worried Churchill with their radical tone. In July Priestley attacked the idea of property as being 'old fashioned' and suggested it should be replaced by 'community'. Pointing to a house with a large garden near his own home, which lay empty after the owner had fled the blitz for America, he said:

> Now, according to the property view, this is all right, and we, who haven't gone to America, must fight to protect this absentee owner's property. But on the community view, this is all wrong. There are hundreds of working men not far from here who urgently need more ground for allotments so that they can produce a bit more food. Also, we may soon need more houses for billeting. Therefore, I say, that house and garden ought to be used whether the owner, who's gone to America, likes it or not.[92]

Tom Wintringham, an ex-Communist and commander of the British contingent of the International Brigades, coined the term 'a People's War' that summer, a term previously associated with popular mobilisation of the people, such as that which defended revolutionary France in the 1790s.[93] The socialist novelist George Orwell took things further: 'The defeat in Flanders will turn out to have been one of the great turning points in English history. In that spectacular disaster the working class, the middle class and even a section of the business community could see the utter rottenness of private capitalism.'[94]

The social research organisation *Mass Observation*, which closely surveyed British public opinion, reported in November 1940, 'In the last few months it has been hard to find, even among women [!], many who do not unconsciously regard this war as in some way revolutionary or radical.'[95] In the summer of 1940 Orwell even speculated that the popular mood of defiance to Hitler might lead to socialist revolution, with the Home Guard acting as a people's militia. This had been formed in May 1940 to resist any invasion, and was made up of men who were not available for conscription because of their age and occupation. In reality any spontaneity in that hastily recruited force was quickly squashed and it was run on the class lines so apparent in the British army. The BBC TV comedy 'Dad's Army' captures it perfectly, with the bank manager as the captain in charge and his clerk as sergeant. There was a radical spirit of resistance in that summer of 1940, but in the absence of any radical force to give conscious expression to it, that spirit would fuel the growing desire for a Labour government pledged to construct a welfare state.[96]

The Battle of Britain

In July the Luftwaffe began an air assault on Britain, which would intensify through August and September. The British would call this The Battle of Britain. In reality the Germans had no coherent plan; they pursued neither a strategy of achieving air superiority over south-east England in preparation for an invasion nor one of bombing the British into surrender. The latter was never a serious option – they lacked the heavy bombers to achieve it. An invasion was achievable if the British had lost control of the skies – there was no army with the equipment to defeat a serious German force and the Royal Navy would have been vulnerable to air and submarine attack in the Channel.[97]

The man in charge of resisting a German invasion, General Ironside, was not confident:

> Although he had a nominal 26 divisions available, there was only enough equipment for two of them and even they were so short of transport that they were virtually immobile. Ironside had little choice therefore but to adopt a system of static defences along the beaches to stop the Germans getting ashore. There were defence lines further back but they existed largely on maps rather than on the ground.[98]

Ironside would later be sacked because of his connections to fascists and right-wing supporters of peace with Hitler.[99]

Despite his spirited verbal defiance, Churchill shared the foreboding. 'At the end of June Churchill told the commander of the north Kent coast defences that if the Germans did get ashore he was not confident of holding any defence line.'[100] In fact the German army rejected any invasion plan. General Jodl argued on 30 June, 'A landing in England, therefore, should not have as its objective the military defeat of England ... but rather to give it the coup de grace.' In other words any invasion could only follow victory in the air.[101]

The RAF's frontline strength on the eve of the Battle of Britain – 1,200 planes of which 800 were Hurricanes or Spitfires (of which 660 were operational), the two most effective British fighters – was on a par with what the Luftwaffe could deploy. There was never a coherent plan behind the German air assault on Britain and no credible plan for a landing in southern England. The chief of the Luftwaffe's operational staff admitted in the autumn of 1940 that an air force four times the size of that deployed by the Luftwaffe in the summer of 1940 would have been required to bring Britain to its knees.[102] This is not to dismiss the reality that if sizable numbers of German troops had landed in southern England there would have been little chance of stopping them.

Britain was producing more fighters than the Germans and was able to sustain its losses and defeat the enemy fighters operating at the limits of their range. The Germans had success in attacking forward RAF fighter bases (at Manston in Kent ground crew took to the shelters and refused to leave, allowing locals to loot tools and supplies). But they then switched to bombing attacks on London (the RAF had carried out ineffective attacks in Germany, including on Berlin). As the British would soon discover, daylight bombing was not possible against intact ground and air defences; the daylight bombing campaign was defeated by September. The Germans switched to night bombing – the Blitz.[103]

Göring had promised Hitler that his Luftwaffe would bring Britain to its knees, but by November 1940 he had left France for his East Prussian estates and was dictating his orders to air-force commanders over the phone via his nurse! Again, little strategic planning seems to have gone into directing the Luftwaffe's missions. London was subject to nightly attacks from 7 September until 13 November. After that, attacks mainly switched to provincial cities, though the most spectacular attack was on London on 29–30 December, destroying three quarters of the City of London. As the US air attaché in London noted, 'The whole bombing campaign against England has been so erratic and so varied in its objectives that I cannot believe it is being directed by a trained soldier or airman.'[104]

In the eight months from 7 September 1940 to 10 May 1941, when the last large-scale raid on London took place, the German bombing killed 40,000, with 800,000 homes destroyed. The November 1940 attack on Coventry left 550 dead. Allied raids on Germany over the course of the war left in total 500,000 civilians dead, 800,000 injured and 7.5 million homes destroyed. The weight of bombs dropped by the Luftwaffe on Britain was 3 per cent of what would fall on Germany.[105] Despite the lurid and widespread pre-war predictions of the destruction aerial bombing would inflict on great cities like London, little had been done to prepare the city for such attacks. In February 1939 opinion polls showed 70 per cent of the population wanted deep underground shelters, and three months later 53 per cent disapproved of the Chamberlain government's refusal to build them. Lack of funding plus shortages of labour, steel and cement were partly the reason for that, but class came into it too: 'Some pundits came forward to warn against encouraging a "shelter mentality" – that is, they feared that if warm, dry underground shelters were provided the working classes would abandon their slum dwellings, set up house in the shelters and refuse to come out to man the war factories.'[106] Instead, much cheaper trench shelters and brick surface shelters were provided. Five thousand of the surface shelters built in London lacked cement and offered little or no protection. People grasped this quickly:

> A Ministry of Home Security report in the spring of 1941 observed that 'out of 30 cases of destroyed [surface] shelters of which we have detailed information 22 were wholly unoccupied' – a pencilled marginal note in the typed office copy of this report asked, 'What happened to the other 8?' but the records supply no specific answer to this inopportune question.[107]

Safety was available for those who could afford it. The Dorchester, one of London's top hotels, was held to be one of the safest buildings in the capital, having been built from reinforced concrete. A Tory MP, Victor Cazalet, was a director of the company that owned it and in mid September 1940 he converted the Turkish baths into a bomb-proof shelter for his friends, who included Lord and Lady Halifax, Duff and Lady Diana Cooper, and Sir George Clerk, the former ambassador to France.[108] Guests would still gather in evening dress for dinner even though an anti-aircraft battery across the road in Hyde Park kept up steady fire. The society photographer, Cecil Beaton, remarked that the hotel was 'reminiscent of a transatlantic crossing in a luxury liner, with all the horrors of enforced jocularity and expensive squalor'.[109]

In September 1940 the Communist councillor for Stepney, Phil Piratin, led 70 East Enders in an occupation of the Savoy Hotel's deep shelter. In November the home secretary, Labour's Herbert Morrison, announced that the London Underground stations would be opened and deep shelters constructed. Morrison got his revenge on the Communists in January 1941 by issuing an order banning their newspaper, the *Daily Worker*, and the muck-raking *The Week*, edited by a Communist Party supporter. The House of Commons was only informed the next day.[110] Within less than six months the ban would be revoked, since by then the Communists were pro-war and opposed to strikes, as Churchill became Stalin's comrade in arms following the Nazi invasion of Russia. Hitler's decision to turn east ended the bombing assault on Britain, at least until his new super-weapons arrived in late 1944, and ended any immediate danger of invasion. Britain had survived, and would subsequently become the base from which Allied forces re-entered Western Europe in June 1944. That survival was Churchill's victory.

Churchill's War

In June 1940 Winston Churchill told his son Randolph, 'I think I can see a way through ... I shall drag in the United States.'[111] In truth Churchill had no strategy to prosecute war with Hitler's Germany or, in the summer of 1940, the military means to do it. His one hope was to pull the US into the war even though he knew the price to be paid would be the dismantling of the British Empire by peaceful means. Churchill had no option other than to try to survive and wait for something to turn up:

> Britain had no forces left on the mainland of Europe and the army, even when rebuilt after Dunkirk, would never be strong enough to invade the continent in the face of a vastly superior German army – about four times the size of British forces. Churchill accepted that Britain would never be the equal of Germany militarily. He told Beaverbrook bluntly in June 1940, 'we have no continental army which can defeat the German military power.' At the end of the year he informed Roosevelt that Britain would never be able 'to match the immense armies of Germany in any theatre where their main powers can be brought to bear'.[112]

His other hope for success lay with the RAF's bombing campaign against Germany. In July 1940 he told Beaverbrook that the only way Hitler could be beaten was through 'an absolutely devastating, exterminating attack by very heavy bombers ... without which I do not see a way through'.[113] Luckily for Churchill the conquest of Britain was not a primary objective for Hitler. For him the prize was *Lebensraum* in the East, with its vital raw materials. If Hitler was to maintain the momentum achieved by the victory in the west he had to end his reliance on Stalin as a supplier of those materials, scupper any potential Russian threat along a border stretching from the Arctic Ocean almost to the Bosphorus, and clear the decks for a final reckoning with the United States. Hitler reasoned that a lightning campaign against Russia would remove Britain's 'continental mercenary' and free the Japanese to strike at the Americans. He concluded, 'When hope in Russia falls away, America too falls away, for an immense revaluation of Japan in East Asia follows.'[114] Later that year Hitler spelt out that 'the decision over European hegemony [will] come in war against Russia'.[115]

Churchill was also lucky in that until the spring of 1941 the British were not fighting any part of the German army, and that from then until the end of 1942 the British army never fought at one time more than four German divisions out of a total of more than 200. British forces had concentrated where their actions could bring maximum political gain against an enemy they could defeat – namely in Egypt, where an Italian attack was expected. From mid 1940 Egypt had become a war base second only in importance to the UK itself. Italian forces in Libya, Eritrea and Ethiopia threatened the key link in Britain's imperial chain of communications, the Suez Canal.[116]

In August 1940, with German forces sitting on the other side of the Channel and with Britain on invasion alert, it was decided to send 70,000 troops and three regiments of tanks to Egypt. The Admiralty had already based half the fleet in Gibraltar for use against the Italians in the Mediterranean, rather than in home waters ready to repel a German invasion.[117] As France collapsed into defeat Hitler had urged the Italians to strike from their Libyan base towards the Suez Canal. He pointed out that there were just 36,000 British and Commonwealth troops in Egypt and that the British military leadership was 'miserable'. The British had just one poorly equipped armoured division and lacked modern fighter aircraft. The Egyptian army was not reliable and the British were concerned about what it might do if they were seen to be facing defeat.[118]

Following Mussolini's declaration of war in June 1940 the Italians failed to invade and capture Malta, which had a garrison of just 12,000 men, despite having complete air control over the island – though they did bomb it to smithereens. The British thus retained a navy base vital to their control of the Mediterranean.[119] A rapid Italian attack on Egypt backed up by a naval attack on Malta and Alexandria could have carried the day prior to the arrival of the reinforcements being sent from Britain. Mussolini did not concentrate on the war in North Africa, opting instead to divert aircraft, armoured vehicles and trucks first to Albania for an attack on Greece and then to Yugoslavia.[120]

Meanwhile, after two naval engagements with the British in which the Italians came off worse, despite having naval superiority, the Italian fleet gave up offensive actions. In September 1940 the Italian army finally advanced but only as far as the Sidi el Barrani camp, 50 miles inside Egypt, with the British withdrawing unscathed. There the Italians stopped.[121] In December the British deployed heavy tanks to surround Sidi el Barrani. After its fall they advanced rapidly into Libya with one armoured column sweeping round through the desert to cut off the Italian retreat along the coast road. Mass surrender there was followed by the removal of Italian forces from Cyrenaica, the eastern half of Libya, with over 100,000 Italians taken captive. The Italians had 129,000 largely non-combatant troops and 209 near useless tankettes defending Tripoli. The British were in a position to end the North African campaign; instead Churchill would order forces to be switched to another front.[122]

In October 1940 Mussolini had ordered Italian forces in Albania to attack Greece, desperate as he was to emulate German successes. He believed the stories he had been fed that the Greeks would not resist and a pro-Italian government would be quickly brought to office in Athens. Just five Italian divisions joined the invasion force. The Greeks not only repulsed them but also advanced deep into Albania. Mussolini had to request that the Germans intervene to bail him out. Hitler had no desire to be dragged into a war in the Balkans – his priority was the planned invasion of Russia, but he agreed, anxious to prevent the Axis being humiliated. German forces attacked south into Yugoslavia and Greece. This marked the end of any separate Italian aspirations; they were now very much the subordinate partner in the alliance and any hopes of territorial gain were much reduced with Germany dominant in the region.[123]

Bulgaria was a German ally and joined the invasion. The Yugoslav king and government had promised free transit for the Wehrmacht, but in March 1941 nationalist Yugoslav officers, urged on by Britain, had launched a successful coup and the new government allied itself with Britain (and tried to do so with Russia to no avail). A rapid and successful German invasion followed.[124]

Back in Greece German forces took the second city of Salonika. The Greek commander in the region surrendered and the king fled to Egypt, leaving no instructions and great bitterness. The British forces dispatched from North Africa failed to halt the German invasion of Greece and then bungled an attempt to defend the island of Crete. This catastrophe is brilliantly described in Evelyn Waugh's novel, *Men at Arms*.[125]

Hitler now controlled the Balkans. Germany and Italy divided up Yugoslavia, with Germany taking the bulk of the key industrial and mining areas. Ante Pavelić, the head of the Ustashi, a Croatian fascist movement, took control of a rump Croatian state. In December 1941 the Ustashi let slip 'with a smile' that the total number of Jews within their territory had fallen from 35,000 to just 12,000. 'A few months later an Italian official put the number of survivors at 6,000 out of 40,000, with the rest, he informed Ciano euphemistically, "wasted" by the Croat authorities.'[126] By the end of the Ustashi regime in 1945, 'some 30,000 Jews, roughly 27,000 gypsies, and an estimated 487,000 to 530,000 Orthodox Serbs perished under the Croatian regime'.[127]

Since the end of the war there has been a sustained attempt to divorce Italian fascism from the crimes of its Nazi comrades. Despite its apparent weakness, Italian fascism proved its brutality as an occupying force in the Balkans. David Rodogno argues that, 'In the actual practice of repression, the Italian army's actions were no different in degree or kind from those of the Wehrmacht; the SS and the German police engaged in similar operations.'[128] Mass reprisals for the killing of Italian service personnel became common, as did mass detention. Italian forces took civilian hostages, burned villages, took reprisals against the families of Resistance fighters, deported civilians en masse, de-forested zones in which partisans operated, and seized or killed farm animals.

Churchill's decision to divert forces from Libya to Greece prevented the British from liquidating the Italian colony. Mussolini had to request German aid there too, and in February 1941 General Lieutenant Rommel landed south of Tripoli to take control of Axis operations. Rommel achieved immediate success and threatened to invade Egypt. That, in turn, encouraged Arab nationalists to seek to profit from Britain's discomfort.[129] Iraq was treaty bound to side with Britain in any new war, but its government had refused to join the conflict. In the spring of 1941 nationalist and pro-Axis officers launched a coup, with the pro-British king fleeing to a Royal Navy warship in the Persian Gulf. The Germans prepared to intervene on behalf of Iraq's new rulers, with the support of the Vichy French authorities in Syria. The potential loss of Iraq threatened Britain's air and land link with India and the oil supplies crucial to its Mediterranean campaigns.

A failed Iraqi attack on an RAF base allowed Churchill to order British forces from India and Palestine to invade to forestall any German intervention. By mid May British troops had occupied Basra and by the end of the month had taken Baghdad, despite fierce resistance.[130] Then on 25 August 1941 British and Soviet forces invaded Iran, overthrew the pro-German Shah Reza, and replaced him with his son, Mohammad Reza Pahlavi.[131]

A number of Luftwaffe squadrons that had been in North Africa were now switched to the invasion of Russia (to be covered in the next chapter). This helped the British recover lost ground, and they briefly drove the Axis forces from eastern Libya. But the strengthening of the Luftwaffe that winter reversed the situation. Rommel was set to inflict a further humiliation on Britain. He wrote of the British army's 'immobility and rigidity', of 'the ultra-conservative structure of their army' and of 'the machinery of command – a terribly cumbersome structure in Britain'.[132] In this respect Britain remained trapped in the legacy of the First World War, with a senior officer corps who were still upper class, had little military knowledge, and were remote from their men. Even Britain's most successful general, Montgomery, who relied on building up technical and numerical superiority before any offensive, failed to capitalise on his successes.[133]

Great claims were made for Britain's bombing campaign against Germany, but an official British history of the air offensive concluded that, 'Area attacks against German cities could not have been responsible for more than a very small part of the fall which had occurred in German production by the spring of 1945, and … in terms of bombing effort, they were also a very costly way of achieving the results they did achieve.'[134] Britain had established one advantage – courtesy of its defeated ally, Poland. The Poles had discovered that the Germans used an encoding machine to devise their codes for radio communications. In July 1939 they acquired one of these Enigma machines and handed it over to the British. The code-breaking establishment at Bletchley Park – forerunner of today's GCHQ – succeeded in breaking the code in April 1940 (although initially only the Luftwaffe's version). The intelligence advantage was vital, although the British had to conceal how much they knew so as not to alert the Germans. The intelligence was not always acted upon in the field. When the Germans invaded the island of Crete in May 1941 the British command was alerted to an imminent parachute attack. They chose to defend the coastline, thereby gifting eventual success to a perilous German landing.[135]

Britain's industry was ill equipped to deal with the demands of modern warfare, and it relied on America for steel. By late 1942 production of ammunition was falling; by mid 1943 so was production of military vehicles, and by the year's end production of artillery and small arms was also declining. By D-Day two-thirds of the British army's tanks and trucks were American. Yet Britain had a far more centrally controlled war economy than did the Third Reich. In 1940 Britain produced 6,000 armoured vehicles other than tanks to Germany's 500, and 113,000 military trucks to Germany's 88,000. It deployed a far more mechanised army. Unlike Nazi Germany, Churchill's government fully tapped the reserve labour force of women, introducing workforce conscription to replace the men conscripted into the armed forces. In 1939 there were 1 million women in the workforce; by June 1943 there were 3.25 million. Women were the single biggest source of extra labour in Second World War Britain.[136]

Meanwhile, a government led by a hard-line Tory was soon to initiate some of the most radical reforms in Britain's history, in recognition of the popular mood in the country. Ministers understood that the broken promises of a 'land fit for heroes' in the previous war had created mass cynicism. In order to sustain the war effort something more than vague promises of change had to be offered to the population. Despite the dire financial situation facing the country, on 1 December 1942 Lord Beveridge presented his official report outlining plans to implement a welfare state once victory was achieved. It promised 'freedom from want'. Beveridge stated it was a 'revolutionary moment in the world's history, a time for revolutions, not for patching'.[137] The report sold half a million copies in a matter of days. Churchill was unenthusiastic and the Tory Chamberlainite rearguard even more so. In the end the coalition government accepted the report in principle but put off any legislation until after the war. The people understood that if they wanted the report implemented they would have to vote Labour into government when the opportunity arose – as they duly did in 1945.[138]

The US Milks Britain Dry

The German victory in Western Europe encouraged Roosevelt to push forward with American rearmament. Even as the German attack began in May 1940 he announced that the US would build 50,000 aircraft a year. It was a figure plucked from thin air – 'less a planning target than a statement of American industrial supremacy'.[139] By the end of 1940 Roosevelt had decided that the Churchill government was prepared to resist and that if Britain fell to Germany it would threaten the US's position. Britain relied on US imports to provide 25 per cent of its steel and other necessities such as the machine tools used to build the Merlin engines for the Spitfire. Steel imports were already the biggest single cargo on the Atlantic run by the second half of 1940, and would rise to equal a quarter of the UK's own domestic production.[140]

Britain's investments in the US and its gold and financial reserves simply could not meet the cost of the material being shipped in from the US. Britain first used up the gold reserves of the various allied governments exiled in London, but by the summer of 1940 it had to go cap in hand to Roosevelt to ask for the means to prosecute the war. In August 1940 the US supplied 50 First World War destroyers in return for long-term US bases in Newfoundland, Bermuda and five West Indian colonies. In addition London gave its word that the home fleet would be evacuated to the US if a German invasion looked likely to succeed. The number of ships supplied to Britain was half that originally requested by London. The number of bases handed over was twice the initial British offer.[141]

On 14 August, after the deal was signed, a top UK scientist left for the US with samples and information about Britain's most important discoveries and projects, from microwave radar to designs for a jet engine and for Germany's magnet mine. The US was also given access on a daily basis to the British code-breaking centre at Bletchley Park. That December James S. Pope, managing editor of the *Louisville Courier Journal*, declared:

The phrase of the moment is 'Aid to England'. I, for one, am sick of it ... In heaven's high name, how have we aided England? When? Whose sacrifice produced the aid? ... We have sold England an indeterminate number of military airplanes. She has paid cash. She has come and got them. We have sold England, I understand, some old rifles and various shipments of ammunition. She paid cash. She came and got them ... Finally, in a moment of benign generosity, we traded England some rotting destroyers for some air and naval bases so valuable to our defence that even Mr Churchill had difficulty justifying the deal to his Parliament. We are going to sell her more and more planes, if our factories will just decide to produce them fast enough. We are going to sell England practically anything she wants – if we don't want it first ... And Napoleon called England a nation of shopkeepers! ... We are in the throes of a pleasant national orgy of 'aid to England'. Ain't it wonderful?[142]

By the autumn of 1940 dollar reserves were exhausted. The US Treasury secretary Morgenthau requested a complete list of British holdings in the Western Hemisphere, differentiated according to liquidity. Roosevelt's re-election in November 1940 was followed within a month by a letter from Churchill pointing out Britain's bankruptcy, and its dependence on US imports and shipping, with a plea not to liquidate all of Britain's assets in the US. Churchill ended the letter by saying Britain was in Roosevelt's hands. Matters were put more bluntly by Lord Lothian when he returned to Washington from London later that month, telling journalists, 'Well boys, Britain's broke: its your money we want.'[143]

Within weeks a US warship was dispatched to South Africa without London being informed in advance. They were told on 23 December that the Americans were taking £50 million of gold, Britain's last tangible assets.[144] Meanwhile the US was letting Indian industrialists know about their interest in entering the Indian market by removing its dependency on sterling. The British government had no choice but to swallow its anger and pride. In January 1941 Roosevelt presented a bill to Congress granting aid to Britain. There was no consultation. Washington would decide what it would loan Britain. Until Lend-Lease became law in March, British spending was unilaterally limited to $35 million a week. Under the terms of Lend-Lease Britain was barred from exporting to new markets or to existing markets such as Argentina. A year later Britain had to pledge to end 'discriminatory' trade and finance schemes after the war – in other words, the Sterling Bloc had to go.

In early 1941 Canada began selling off British assets in order to pay off UK debts to the US. On 10 March, Halifax (now British ambassador to America) was given an ultimatum: the British must sell one of their important companies in the next week as a mark of good faith. A major subsidiary of Courtaulds was sold at a knockdown price. By the spring of 1941 Roosevelt noted, 'We have been milking the British financial cow, which had plenty of milk at one time, but which has now about become dry.'[145] Items such as tobacco for civilians were removed from Lend-Lease, forcing Britain to pay for them by exporting goods across the Atlantic. Washington unceremoniously scrapped Lend-Lease within days of the war ending, forcing the new Labour government to beg for a US loan.

In March 1941, nine months before Pearl Harbor, a secret conference in Washington between the British and American Joint Chiefs of Staff decided on a 'Europe First' policy:

> The decision there made, incorporated in the ABC-1 Staff Agreement of 27 March 1941, was this: If and when America enters the war, she will exert 'the principal United States military effort' in the European theater. America will try by diplomacy to prevent war with Japan, but even if that proves impossible, operations in the Pacific will be conducted in such a manner as 'to facilitate' the effort against the European Axis.
>
> The reasons behind this decision, which the Americans initiated, were: Germany had a far greater military potential than Japan; Germany already controlled almost the entire Atlantic coast of Europe and threatened the Americas; England was already fighting Germany and could be assisted immediately, whilst Japan at that time was fighting only China, which foreign aid could not reach; Germany had a dangerously superior capability for the manufacture of munitions, and, if given time, might well invent a new and unbeatable weapon – as she did, with the guided missile.[146]

In addition to the 'Europe first' strategy, the meeting agreed to create an Anglo-American Combined Chiefs of Staff. Yet two months after the talks, the US War Department stated that, 'British forces are to be considered as an American Expeditionary Force.'[147]

The US was brought into the war by a Japanese attack, but its plans were for war with Germany. The war in the Pacific would remain a lesser priority until Hitler was beaten. Roosevelt prioritised the war in Europe because an American presence on the continent would ensure US post-war dominance. In September 1941 the British had concluded that with the maximum mobilisation they might deploy 90 modern divisions while the Germans were already fielding 150. The British Chiefs of Staff stated that Britain could not 'raise and land on the Continent an army comparable in size with that of Germany' and that the policy should be one of 'wearing down' the Germans. This meant there was a divergence between the policy adopted in Britain and that being developed in Washington. The British developed many different specialist units, which could strike at isolated outposts of the Third Reich. Rather than risk a landing in France the British looked to strike at points in the Mediterranean. The Americans, like Hitler, regarded the latter as a secondary front; their primary aim was a landing in Western Europe followed by a decisive confrontation with Hitler's forces. US planners concentrated on three forces: the armoured divisions that would spearhead this attack, the air force that would aid their penetration, and the infantry that would consolidate and hold what the tanks took. Churchill wanted to avoid an invasion of Western Europe because in such a venture Britain would be relegated to a junior partner.[148]

Meanwhile the German submarine campaign in the Atlantic had slashed British imports to a third of their pre-war figure by the beginning of 1942.[149] The Royal Navy was designed to fight set-piece naval battles where big ships engaged each other at long range, as in the 1916 Battle of Jutland. It was short of modern vessels – of its 61 cruisers a third had been launched in 1919 or earlier. Six of its ten aircraft carriers were old or converted and it was desperately short of long-range reconnaissance aircraft. It had neglected developing magnetic mines and discovered that the Germans could lay mines faster than the Royal Navy could sweep them. Up until 1943 it was even short of torpedoes. The Germans could read British naval signals up until mid 1943. Aircraft were crucial to dealing with German submarines but there was no co-ordination between the navy and RAF Coastal Command until 1941, and even when that was established Bomber Command would not release long-range aircraft for duties in the Atlantic.[150]

The Royal Navy refused at first to adopt the convoy system, with warships ushering civilian vessels across the Atlantic, which had proved so successful in the latter stages of the First World War. Instead it reverted to the older strategy of keeping its warships separate in 'hunter groups', which would supposedly seek and destroy enemy submarines. A lack of suitable escort vessels lay behind the British desire for vintage US First World War destroyers bought at such a high price.[151] Britain was lucky that Germany had begun the war with just 57 submarines of which only 23 were capable of ocean-going operations. Until 1941 U-boat losses outstripped replacements; but after that date new submarines were able to operate in the Atlantic with devastating results. This precluded a build up of US forces in Britain ready for an invasion of Europe. Prior to their entry into the war the US navy passed on information on German submarine positions to the British, and they occupied Greenland to provide a base from which to protect shipping. In May 1941 a US aircraft carrier, three battleships, and cruisers and destroyers were transferred from the Pacific to the North Atlantic. The US reintroduced the convoy system after severe losses in the weeks after they entered the war. It also used radar and long-distance aircraft to protect shipping.

Things were also going badly in the one theatre where British forces confronted the Axis. In May 1942 Rommel attacked the British line in the Libyan desert. The British dispersed their tanks, Rommel concentrated his. The British expected the attack in the north, it came in the south. As they fell back they left a garrison of 35,000 to hold the port of Tobruk, which was of symbolic importance. It fell in just one day. It ranked alongside the earlier surrender of Singapore as one of Britain's greatest humiliations in the war. In North Africa British forces were facing just four out of a total of 200 German divisions, the vast bulk of which were engaged in Russia. Sir Alexander Cadogan, the permanent head of the Foreign Office, wrote in his diary, 'Our army is the mockery of the world.' The Chief of the Imperial General Staff, Alan Brooke, confessed in his diary, 'I certainly never expected we should fall to pieces as fast as we are.'[152]

Studies of the desert fighting have shown that German soldiers were better able to deal with emergencies, with NCOs and even private soldiers taking decisions in the absence of officers. British units too often ceased fighting if they lost their officers.[153] By July 1942, Rommel's offensive in the Western Desert threatened Britain's control of Egypt. There was panic in Cairo on 1 July – the British Embassy and GHQ burnt piles of classified papers, showering the city with ash and charred documents. British forces formed a defensive line anchored on the town of El Alamein, 66 miles west of Alexandria. If that line was breached Rommel would be through to Alexandria, the Nile Delta and then Cairo. But the British forces managed to halt Rommel's advance. The German and Italian forces were at the end of a very restricted supply line, as three quarters of the Axis ships attempting to reach North Africa were sunk. Their tank units were much depleted. Luftwaffe squadrons had been drawn off once more to aid the renewed German offensive in Russia.[154]

The British commander in North Africa, Montgomery, won success through an unoriginal frontal attack backed by heavy artillery, which resulted in heavy losses – the British lost six times more men than the Germans and Italians, and over 600 tanks compared to Rommel's 180. Montgomery was able to deploy 300 new Sherman tanks sent from the US and he enjoyed near complete control of the air. El Alamein was Britain's one success against the Germans – although half of Rommel's troops were Italian. The British won through overwhelming numerical superiority (220,000 men against 96,000), a four to one superiority in tanks and artillery as well as a reserve of 1,200 tanks against the Germans' 22, and air superiority. But Montgomery did not follow up the German retreat with any urgency and the Axis forces retreated eastwards in good order.[155]

In November 1942 two invasion fleets carrying US forces approached North Africa aiming to seize Algeria and Morocco, French colonies run by Vichy. General Henri Giraud, whom the Americans believed could rally the French army in Algeria and Morocco, accompanied the US invasion force. Giraud had escaped German capture in 1940 and had reported back to Pétain, whom he supported despite opposing co-operation with Germany. Eventually he was smuggled out of France by British intelligence and brought to the US commander, Eisenhower, in Gibraltar. Roosevelt wished to build up Giraud as an alternative to de Gaulle, who was distrusted by Washington. De Gaulle was not told about the landings in North Africa until they were about to take place. Giraud refused to go to Algiers to join Resistance forces after he was denied command of the whole North African invasion. When asked why he did not go to Algiers he replied:

> You may have seen something of the large De Gaullist demonstration that was held here last Sunday. Some of the demonstrators sang the 'Marseillaise'. I entirely approve of that! Others sang the 'Chant du Depart' [a military ballad]. Quite satisfactory! Others again shouted 'Vive de Gaulle!' No Objection. But some of them cried 'Death to Giraud!' I don't approve of that at all.[156]

The Allies then discovered that Pétain's deputy premier, Admiral Jean François Darlan, commander of Vichy's armed forces, was in Algiers visiting his sick son. On 8 November Resistance forces in Algeria succeeded in capturing the Vichy command, including Darlan. As US troops came ashore, fighting continued between Vichy forces and the Resistance. After three days US General Mark Clark arrived with instructions from Eisenhower to secure a ceasefire, leaving Darlan in control of Algeria and Morocco. Darlan retained Vichy's anti-Semitic racist laws (which deprived Jews of French citizenship) and deported de Gaulle's supporters to camps in the Sahara.[157]

Darlan quickly became an embarrassment to his US controllers and was assassinated by a young Frenchman on 24 December. Speculation soon mounted that British intelligence was behind the killing. Giving power to a collaborator like Darlan smacked of appeasement and was deeply unpopular. General Giraud replaced Darlan as chief of French North Africa and Roosevelt and Churchill brokered an agreement between him and de Gaulle that both would lead the Free French forces. De Gaulle would eventually manoeuvre his more senior rival out of that position.[158]

Meanwhile US troops moved east into Tunisia, where the Germans and Italians had retreated intent on a last stand in North Africa. As the Axis forces fought to defend Tunisia, an SS special commando unit exterminated 2,500 Jews. The unit had been sent by Hitler following Rommel's capture of Tobruk in June 1942, with the Führer ordering them to 'destroy Jewry in the Arab world'.[159] After suffering some setbacks the Americans finally linked up with the British Eighth Army advancing westwards and forced an Italo-German surrender. The fact that the Axis had lost a quarter of a million soldiers and their equipment, plus their air and naval support, led the US to press for a landing in France.[160] Churchill successfully counter-posed an assault on Sicily and thence on to Italy. This reflected the centrality of the Mediterranean to the British Empire. By January 1943 there were 400,000 tonnes of ammunition stockpiled in Egypt with 750,000 personnel stationed there. Britain's resources were stretched to breaking point elsewhere, particularly in the Far East, but the concentration of men and materiel in Egypt demanded continued operations in the Mediterranean:

> In 1941 the British could have cleared the Italians from North Africa with just two divisions. By 1943 that required 21 British and US divisions and meant Allied forces were concentrated in a theatre Washington saw as secondary. The British had accumulated such vast piles of materiel in North Africa, at such great effort, that it would be hugely expensive and time consuming to transfer them elsewhere. That was an additional factor in their efforts to prioritise Mediterranean operations.[161]

Yet Churchill's successful argument for the invasion of Italy would be his last in determining the Allied strategy in Europe. As the advance in Italy became bogged down, Washington forced the June 1944 Normandy landings on the British. British planners were painfully aware that while their forces (which included large Canadian, Indian and Polish elements) would have parity with US forces at the time of the initial landings, that would quickly cease to be the case as the Americans would come to dominate. Britain constantly manoeuvred to oppose a landing in France, putting forward all sorts of alternative schemes – including an invasion of neutral Portugal. Even after the US insisted on 'Operation Overlord', the invasion of Normandy, going ahead, Churchill could ask in February 1944, 'Why are we trying to do this?'[162]

On D-Day itself – 6 June 1944, the day of the Normandy landings – the British provided half the troops (including Canadians and Poles). This was the maximum force it could mobilise. From then until the end of the war British troop levels declined while America's mushroomed until they had five times as many troops fighting the Germans. Churchill described the relation between US and Britain as 'a noble brotherhood of arms'. The truth was somewhat different. After America's entry into the war Churchill knew that Britain could not hope to dominate a land war in northern Europe.[163]

The world at war, March 1942

CHAPTER SIX

Russia: The Crucible of Victory

To the Gates of Moscow

A German attack on Russia was only a question of time. Victory there was key to Hitler's vision of the Third Reich and to the eventual global domination he craved. Domination of Europe would be followed by a showdown with the United States.

Nevertheless, in 1939, the regimes in Moscow and Berlin were prepared to explore a rapprochement – or at least use the possibility of it to scare the other powers. Even before the September 1938 Munich conference, from which Russia was excluded, Stalin had made it clear that the USSR 'had no obligation to Czechoslovakia in the event of French indifference to an attack on her', and that the USSR consequently had the right to renounce its pact with the Czechs.[1] The decision of Britain and France to acquiesce in the dismemberment of Czechoslovakia at Munich in September 1938 fuelled Stalin's distrust of the two Western powers and encouraged him to seek an accord with Hitler. During the 18th Congress of the Soviet Communist Party in March 1939, Stalin claimed that Britain and France were trying to incite a conflict between Germany and Russia and warned that Russia was not going to 'pull the chestnuts out of the fire' for anyone. On 1 April, Hitler echoed Stalin's words, saying he had no desire to 'pull chestnuts out of the fire' by fighting the West's battles against Russia. Hitler's foreign minister Ribbentrop ensured that the heads of all the European diplomatic missions were aware of Hitler's pronouncement.[2]

Meanwhile Stalin continued on the opposite track of pursuing an agreement with the Western democracies. In March 1939 he made one final offer to Britain and France proposing a pact guaranteeing the integrity of each European country – from the western boundaries of the USSR to the Atlantic – and committing the three powers to act if any were attacked by Germany. Two months later the British replied saying they could not agree such a pact but were prepared to hold talks with Moscow. Matters dragged on until foreign minister Molotov insisted that they had to centre on a military pact. On 12 August 1939 the Soviet defence minister, Voroshilov, and all the Russian military chiefs, assembled in Moscow's Spiridonovka Palace to meet the Anglo-French military delegation. The talks broke down almost immediately when the British revealed they could agree to nothing and could only report back to London.

Germany had already put out feelers to Moscow about an alliance three months earlier – Hitler was determined to avoid a two-front war when his planned attack on Poland went ahead. In late July the German trade minister proposed a political settlement of Eastern Europe – in other words, a partition of the region. As the deadline for Hitler's attack on Poland neared, the Germans rushed to convince the Kremlin of the benefits on offer: a non-aggression pact between the two states, a secret agreement on the territorial division of the region, and generous trade arrangements.

On 19 August Stalin agreed that the German foreign minister Ribbentrop should come to Moscow to finalise the pact. He arrived on 23 August to find the city decorated with swastika flags previously used on the sets of anti-Nazi films. Stalin himself was present alongside Molotov to greet the Germans. They agreed to a division of Poland, with the Russians joining the attack on that country, and, after some argument, Stalin was accorded the Baltic states (Lithuania, Estonia and Latvia). When the agreement was finalised Stalin invited Ribbentrop to celebrate; the Soviet dictator toasted Hitler, Ribbentrop toasted Stalin.

Attacks on fascism ceased to appear in the Russian press and the world's Communist Parties switched from supporting a people's war against fascism to opposing imperialist war. Eight hundred exiled German Communists were transferred from the Soviet Union to the Third Reich into the welcoming hands of the Gestapo. In December 1939 Stalin assured Hitler that the alliance between Russia and Germany was 'cemented in blood'.[3]

The Ribbentrop-Molotov pact permitted Stalin to expand the USSR's borders westwards, beginning with eastern Poland. In September 1939, the Russians forced the three Baltic states to agree to have Russian military bases on their soil. Taking advantage of the German conquest of France in June 1940, Molotov demanded each of the Baltic states replace their government with pro-Soviet ones and accept a massive increase in the Russian military presence in each country. Hardly waiting for a reply the Red Army moved in to occupy Latvia, Estonia and Lithuania. Stalin made a similar grab further south. The Romanian territory of Bessarabia had been placed within the Russian sphere of influence under the terms of the Hitler-Stalin pact. In June 1940 the Russian dictator issued an ultimatum to the Bucharest regime demanding they hand over Bessarabia and northern Bukovina. The Romanians, on advice from Berlin and Rome, agreed. In the short term Hitler accepted these coups d'état, but the Baltic states were regarded as a crucial part of the future German empire while Romania, an ally of Berlin, was a key provider of oil for Germany. In September 1940 Finland and Romania were admitted to the Tripartite Pact.[4]

For Hitler it was a question of expediency, allowing him to fight a single front war in the west before he turned his guns eastwards. But now the Russian ambition to control Romanian oil and much else in Eastern Europe endangered Germany's access to key raw materials. Further, the existence of an independent Russian state keen to exert influence in Eastern and South East Europe was a threat which had to be eliminated. Dependence on Russian supplies of oil, grain and other vital raw materials contradicted the aim of creating a self-sufficient Third Reich. By 1940 Russia supplied 74 per cent of its phosphate imports, 67 per cent of its asbestos, 65 per cent of its chrome ore, 55 per cent of its manganese, 40 per cent of its nickel and 34 per cent of its oil imports.[5]

The Führer's date for an attack on Russia was set as the spring of 1941. But there was also something else underlying the decision to extend the war eastwards. The Nazis rise to power centred on anti-communism and the need for Germany to expand. In terms of the movement's mass membership, Hitler had not delivered on his promise prior to taking office that he would oversee a complete revolution in Germany. In order to prevent demoralisation and desertion, anti-Semitism became central because the one thing Hitler could promise and in part deliver was the destruction of European Jewry, the majority of which was located in the East. As Ian Kershaw explains, 'If Nazism were to sustain and reinvigorate itself, were not to lose its ideological cutting edge, the war had to continue.'[6] The crusade against 'Jewish Bolshevism' was central to the Nazi project. As Hitler concentrated on planning an assault on Russia his racial policy would become inextricably intertwined with the campaign. A genocidal war was envisaged from the outset.

He and his generals were confident that the 'Jewish-Bolshevik elite' presided over a rotten system that would cave in under heavy blows. They allocated four months to achieve the destruction of the Red Army. The plan was to advance eastwards seizing a vast area up to a line running from Archangel in the Arctic to Astrakhan, where the Volga reached its delta with the Caspian Sea. The plan, as Richard Overy points out, was

> to populate it with fortified garrison cities, keeping the population under the permanent control of the master race, while a rump Asian state beyond the Urals, the Slavlands, would accommodate the rest of the Soviet people ... 'Russia,' Hitler is reported as saying, 'will be our India!'[7]

Britain and France shared Hitler's low estimation of the Red Army. That was confirmed by its woeful performance in the Soviet-Finnish Winter War, which had begun in November 1939. Stalin had demanded territory north of Leningrad in order to secure the city's defences, plus a naval base at the entrance to the Baltic. When that was refused he ordered an invasion, confidently expecting an easy conquest. One million men took on just 200,000 Finnish troops. Huge concentrations of infantry were sent forward without proper support, only to be surrounded by mobile Finnish units or butchered from well-prepared defence lines. In four months 127,000 Russians died having failed to secure a breakthrough. It took the influx of 26 new infantry divisions and tanks plus a massive artillery barrage to breach the Finnish defences and force the government in Helsinki to sue for peace in March 1940 (just as the British and French were readying to send troops to aid the Finns). Foreign minister Molotov admitted that a further 49,000 Red Army soldiers were killed and 158,000 wounded.[8] The debacle in Finland further convinced the Germans that victory in Russia would be quick.[9]

The experience of this disastrous war forced Stalin to relax his grip slightly on the officer corps. He reintroduced the old tsarist ranks of general and admiral in May 1940 and two months later introduced a severe disciplinary code modelled on that of the old Imperial Army. One thousand men were promoted to general or admiral and traditional uniforms were restored. But his cronies still exerted a reign of terror and there was no attempt to learn from the success of German armour in May and June 1940.[10] Furthermore Moscow was keen to develop its alliance with Germany in the wake of the Wehrmacht's spectacular victory over France. In November 1940 Molotov arrived in Berlin for talks with Ribbentrop and Hitler, hoping to extend the Ribbentrop-Molotov pact. Molotov cut to the quick, asking a series of questions: did the 1939 German-Soviet agreement establish Finland as being within the Russian orbit?, what role did Hitler envisage the USSR playing within the New Order in Europe, what was the position regarding Moscow's interests in Bulgaria, Romania and Turkey (particularly regarding access to the Mediterranean).[11]

Ribbentrop rather lamely responded by inviting the Soviet Union to join the Tripartite Pact uniting Germany, Japan and Italy, but Molotov would not respond until his questions were answered. Hitler intervened, pronouncing, 'After the conquest of England, the British Empire will be apportioned as a gigantic world wide estate ... In this bankrupt estate Russia will get access to the ice-free and really open seas.' The Russian did not take the bait and pressed the Führer about the presence of German troops in Finland, an ally of Hitler, and German guarantees of Romania's borders, which, he pointed out, 'displeases us'.[12] Later Molotov presented Ribbentrop with Moscow's demands, which included access to the Dardanelles, Swedish neutrality, access to the Baltic Sea, and assurances about the future of Romania, Hungary, Bulgaria, Yugoslavia and Greece. This discussion took place in an air-raid shelter after British bombers disrupted a diplomatic reception. The Russian leadership were angling for a share of control of Eastern Europe and the Baltic – something unacceptable to Hitler who regarded them as being under German hegemony. Later Hitler would tell Martin Bormann of his reaction when reports of this further exchange reached him, 'The Third Reich, defender and protector of Europe, could not have sacrificed these friendly countries on the altar of Communism ... War with Russia had become inevitable, whatever we did.'[13]

The damage caused by Stalin's military purges cannot be overestimated; at the time of Barbarossa only 7 per cent of army officers had any higher military education and 37 per cent had not completed intermediate training.[14] The purges continued right up until June 1941, though on a greatly reduced scale after 1938. Prior to the annexation of eastern Poland and the Baltic states, Russia's contingency plans for a war with Germany, dating back to the days when Hitler was seen as an enemy not an ally, centred on holding the prepared defences of the Stalin Line, behind the pre-1939 frontier. After the occupation of the new territories, Stalin ordered that the Red Army had to defend the new border with Germany. This was much longer, 2,800 miles, and the Russians hurriedly built new fortifications and airfields under the noses of the Germans. The Stalin line to the east was stripped of its artillery and equipment.

The new plan was that the Red Army could hold or absorb any German attack until the reserves could be mobilised for a decisive counter-attack. Accordingly Stalin vetoed plans to move vital industries eastwards, away from danger. Some 70 per cent of Russian industry lay in the Ukraine and the Moscow and Leningrad districts, dangerously exposed to invasion.[15]

In May 1940 Stalin recalled Georgi Zhukov to Moscow, following his success against the Japanese in the Far East. Zhukov was promoted to become a full general and in January 1941 Stalin appointed him Chief of the General Staff.[16] In March that year Stalin agreed to the creation of 20 armoured divisions and 106 new air regiments deploying new aircraft models. Half the armoured divisions still lacked tanks by the time of the German attack in July, and all lacked training and spare parts. Worse, they were all distributed along the border, easy prey for the Luftwaffe. There were also serious shortages of trucks, tractors and motorcycles, while artillery units lacked ammunition. Just weeks before the German attack, Zaporozhets, head of the Political Propaganda Administration, reported, 'The fortified districts located on our western frontiers are for the most part not operationally ready ... The fortified districts are not manned by the requisite number of specially trained troops.'[17]

The subsequent argument deployed by the Kremlin to justify the Hitler-Stalin pact was that Russia bought vital time to prepare its defences. As we shall see, there was no evidence of any serious planning being made to beat off a German attack; the Russian dictator refused to countenance that the Führer would break his word. Nevertheless the swift German conquest of France in May–June 1940 shattered Stalin's hopes that the war in the west would become a long struggle of attrition leaving none of the combatants free to attack Russia.

If anyone bought time with the agreement it was Hitler. Not only did it free him to launch a one-front war in the west, it also ensured there could be no repeat of the 1914–18 economic blockade of Germany – Eastern Europe and the Soviet Union could supply German needs:

> During the seventeen months of the pact Germany was supplied with: 865,000 tons of oil, 648,000 tons of wood, 14,000 tons of manganese ore, 14,000 tons of copper, almost 1.5 million tons of grain and much more besides. In addition Soviet traders bought up material on the world markets to be transhipped to Germany, including 154,000 tons of rubber, which came via Japan. Other military assistance was granted. The German navy was given a base to use near Murmansk for refuelling, Soviet icebreakers were offered to clear a way through Arctic waters for German merchant raiders, hunting down Allied sea traffic. Soviet weather ships sent back meteorological reports for the German air force during the Battle of Britain.[18]

While politicians in London, Paris and Washington had believed they could deal with Hitler in conventional diplomatic style, Stalin went further in thinking he could trust Hitler to honour his treaty commitments. Responsibility for the disaster that befell Russia in the summer and autumn of 1941 must be laid squarely at the feet of Stalin.

Right up until the first shots were fired by German invaders, vital Russian supplies crossed the border into occupied Poland. News of the invasion was suppressed for hours as Stalin desperately tried to broker a fresh deal with Hitler. Meanwhile Russian troops were killed while awaiting orders to resist the invaders, and aircraft were destroyed en masse as they sat on their runways.

Distrustful of virtually everyone else, Stalin seems to have trusted Hitler, believing he would be satisfied with their bargain, ignoring the clear warnings that the Führer wanted a genocidal war of conquest in Russia and the East. Until 21 June 1941, the day before the invasion, Stalin refused to accept that Hitler was about to launch an attack. Two months before the invasion German reconnaissance planes began systematically photographing the frontier areas and the Western USSR to map Soviet defences. Within weeks one plane had crashed in Russian territory complete with its cameras. Stalin ordered no one should fire on the spy planes.

Red Army commanders were aware by the beginning of April of a military build up on the other side of the frontier. Stalin was receiving warnings from Washington and London – both keen now to rebuild friendship with Russia – that invasion was imminent. He rejected them on the grounds that both wanted a Russo-German war. Russian intelligence supplied a torrent of accurate information indicating invasion was imminent. Stalin ignored it all. Until the last minute he believed his pact with Hitler would hold because Hitler, with the British undefeated, would not dare to fight a war on two fronts.[19]

Hitler envisaged the creation along the Urals of an Eastern Frontier for the Third Reich, behind which the Slavs and their Jewish string-pullers would be contained. This would be no Maginot Line but a human defence chain made up of warrior farmers, Germans settled on the Third Reich's eastern border. Hitler even talked of his hopes to colonise the Ukraine with 20 million settlers drawn not only from Germany but from Scandinavia, Western Europe and even America. He described how he saw the fate of any remaining Slavs:

> We shan't settle in the Russian towns and we'll let them go to pieces without intervening. And above all, no remorse on this subject! We're absolutely without obligations as far as these people are concerned. To struggle against the hovels, chase away the fleas, provide German teachers, bring out newspapers – very little of that for us! We'll confine ourselves, perhaps, to setting up a radio transmitter, under our control. For the rest, let them know just enough to understand our highway signs, so that they won't get themselves run over by our vehicles ... There's only one duty: to Germanise the country by the immigration of Germans and to look upon the natives as Redskins.[20]

The invading German troops would be fed at the expense of the local population. Göring talked of 'the biggest mass death in Europe since the Thirty Years War', while others quoted a figure of 10 million dead through starvation.[21]

Seven months before the invasion began, Colonel-General Halder delivered a report at a conference attended by the Führer to discuss the attack on Russia. 'The Red Army is leaderless', argued Halder. Germany was superior in leadership, equipment and fighting troops. The Red Army would be broken into fragments, which would be encircled and destroyed. Disaster would quickly befall the Soviet Union. Halder was to be proved wrong.[22]

The general view in London and Washington was that the USSR could not withstand a German attack. The Chief of the British Imperial General Staff,

General Sir John Dill, predicted that the Germans would go through Russia like 'a hot knife through butter'. The Labour left-winger, Stafford Cripps, now ambassador to Moscow, told the British War Cabinet, 'Russia cannot hold out against Germany for more than three or four weeks, by which time the enemy might be in Leningrad [today's St Petersburg], Moscow or Kiev.'[23]

Until just minutes before the attack, with the sound of Panzer engines audible across the frontier, Russian raw materials continued to feed Hitler's war efforts in line with the 1939 pact. The attack fell on Russian troops and border guards who had been refused permission to prepare their defences in case it provoked the Germans. John Erickson details the state of the Russian army in June 1941: 'No reserves of spare parts or concentration of repair facilities ... tractors, lorries and motorcycles were in grievously short supply', while artillery units 'faced a critical shortage of ammunition'.[24]

The 22 July 1941, the day on which Hitler launched Operation Barbarossa, was the high-water mark for German military power. In total the Germans and their allies deployed 3 million soldiers, 3,600 tanks, 7,200 artillery guns, 1,800 planes and 750,000 horses. Italian, Romanian and Hungarian divisions joined the invading Germans. The Bulgarians were content with seizing the territory they coveted from the Soviet Union and doing little else. Franco sent 45,500 'volunteers' of the Spanish Blue Division. These units were far less mobile and poorly armed and would become something of a liability for the Wehrmacht.[25]

While the Germans had no advantage in numbers of tanks or aircraft, they did have in the way they utilised them, concentrating their armoured forces and co-ordinating them with air cover. German armoured columns raced through the Russians' linear defences. Tanks and aircraft were either destroyed by the Luftwaffe where they stood or simply thrown away in ill conceived and unsupported counter-attacks. Russian infantry were ordered simply to march into the advancing Germans in a body with no artillery or armoured support. The Red Army had no means of co-operating with the air force. Much of its equipment was destroyed in those summer months and millions of Russian troops were simply over-run. On the first morning of the invasion 1,200 Red Air Force planes were destroyed as the Luftwaffe attacked their airfields. The Germans thus achieved air supremacy.[26]

The Russian mechanised corps lost 90 per cent of their strength in the first week.[27] On 23 June the Russians decided to form the Stavka (high command), a collective body over which Stalin supposedly presided, imposing tight centralism on the military. Stalin, however, withdrew into near-isolation until 3 July. When he reappeared at his first command meetings he was quiet and very nervous. In the first days of the war he sent radio messages to Berlin requesting peace and approached the Japanese to act as peace-brokers. When he emerged to give his first address to the population the official rhetoric had undergone a transformation. Gone was any mention of the Communist Party, instead he declared that Russia was fighting a 'patriotic war', and that his words were addressed to the Russians.

In order to survive Stalin was forced to limit the terror and play the nationalist card. In addition he placated his officer corps. The restoration of badges of rank and epaulettes based on the old imperial designs was, John Erickson comments, 'no mere ornament, for it marked, physically and visibly, a major transition in the Red Army'. Communist Party control over army units was also loosened in response to long-standing complaints from officers.[28]

But the decisive factor in bolstering the resistance of the Russians and other peoples classed as 'sub-human' by the Nazis was the extermination and mass slavery programme which came with German occupation. As the *Ostheer* (Eastern Army) advanced deep into Russia, the Nazi rulers gathered on 16 July to discuss how the newly occupied territories would be administered. Alfred Rosenberg suggested dividing Russia into small nations, 'so as to free the German Reich of the Eastern nightmare for centuries to come'. Hitler answered that, 'Small sovereign states no longer have a right to exist ... the road to self-government leads to independence. One cannot keep by democratic institutions what one has acquired by force.' He added, 'While German goals and methods must be concealed from the world at large, all the necessary measures – shootings, exiling etc. – we shall take and can take anyway. The order of the day is first: conquer; second: rule; third: exploit.'[29]

Hitler had already ordered that the Geneva Convention would not apply to prisoners in the East, that any commissars (which meant any Communist Party members, Jews or intellectuals) should be shot on the spot, and that Leningrad would be levelled when captured. He told his senior commanders prior to the invasion:

> The war against Russia will be such that it cannot be conducted in a chivalrous manner. This struggle is one of ideologies and racial differences and will have to be conducted with unprecedented, merciless and unrelenting harshness. All officers will have to rid themselves of obsolete ideologies. I know that the necessity for such means of waging war is beyond the comprehension of you generals but I ... insist absolutely that my orders will be executed without contradiction. The commissars are the bearers of ideology directly opposed to National Socialism. Therefore the commissars will be liquidated.[30]

As Alan Clark writes of the German army in Russia: 'Mass murder, deportations, deliberate starvation of prisoners in cages, the burning alive of school children, "target practice" on civilian hospitals – atrocities were so common that no man coming fresh to the scene could stay sane without acquiring a protective veneer of brutalisation.'[31]

Genocide flowed from the Nazis' racial theories. The Jews had to be exterminated; the Slavs were *Untermenschen*, sub-humans, who could be killed at will. This brutality affected the whole conduct of the war. Millions of Soviet prisoners suffered the ravages of the cold, starvation, disease and brutal mistreatment. Eventually it was decided to ship them back to the Reich to use as slave labour – the huge death toll being matched by low productivity. In the first four months of occupation Kiev's population fell from 850,000 to 400,000, and further still to 295,000 by mid 1943.[32]

The losses inflicted on the Red Army in the summer of 1941 were immense. In June the Germans took more prisoners at Minsk than the numbers evacuated from Dunkirk a year earlier. In August nearly half a million men were captured around Smolensk, Uman in the Ukraine and Gomel in Belorussia. A month later 665,000 were taken at Kiev and some 663,000 were captured as the Wehrmacht approached Moscow in October. Yet the Red Army proved capable of resistance in the most appalling conditions. Soviet resilience around Smolensk, key to the central thrust on Moscow, held up the German advance on that axis for a month, allowing the capital's defences to be prepared, while the main German effort in the south was deflected into clearing out Russian resistance in the Ukraine.[33]

With his armies at the gates of Moscow and Leningrad Hitler proclaimed victory. On 3 October he spoke in Berlin's Sportspalast, boasting that Russia was as good as finished and would not rise up again:

> The number of Soviet prisoners has grown to 2.5 million. The number of captured or destroyed cannon in our possession amounts to about 22,000. The number of destroyed or captured tanks in our possession totals over 18,000. The number of destroyed, damaged, and shot down aircraft is 14,500. And behind our troops the space is twice as large as that of the German Reich of 1933 when I assumed leadership, or four times as large as England.[34]

But the German advance on three fronts, towards Leningrad, Moscow and into the Ukraine, was too dispersed. The Panzers ran ahead of the infantry, who had to advance over huge distances on foot, so that when the tanks reached Leningrad they had to wait for troops to catch up, allowing the Red Army to fortify the city. The reality was that for Barbarossa to succeed the Red Army had to be destroyed quickly so it could not retreat eastwards in any kind of order. It was clear that the Red Army, though badly mauled, had survived the initial blows.

Fatal flaws became obvious as the Wehrmacht advanced deep into Russia. The eventual goals of Operation Barbarossa were imprecise. Originally any drive on Moscow had been of secondary importance; the strategy was to occupy the Baltic states, remove any threat to the Romanian oilfields, and secure the vital economic heartlands of the Ukraine, to which Hitler attached great importance. There were fears that an attack on Stalin's capital might simply push the Red Army eastwards without securing its destruction by encirclement operations. Meanwhile, Hitler ordered that Leningrad should not be attacked directly but rather besieged so that sickness and hunger would lead to its fall and destruction. Until the autumn of 1941 Hitler refused to prioritise between the three thrusts on Leningrad, Moscow and the Ukraine. It was the extent of Russian resistance and the onset of winter that dictated that a decision had to be made. By the close of 1941 German forces concentrated on capturing Moscow.[35]

Hitler was gambling that Russian losses in men and materiel could not be replaced. The Soviet state-run economy had moved to evacuate industrial enterprises eastwards en masse. As David M. Glantz and Jonathan House note:

In total, 1,532 factories, including 1,360 related to armaments, were transferred to the Volga River, Siberia and Central Asia between July and November 1941. Almost 1.5 million railcars were involved. Even allowing for the hyperbole so common to Soviet accounts, this massive relocation and reorganisation of heavy industry was an incredible accomplishment of endurance and organisation.[36]

The working day was increased in length from seven to eight hours but in practice was 11; holidays were abolished, and a seven-day week introduced. As the historian A.D. Harvey points out:

> The Soviet Union fought the mad-dog idealism of the Nazis with weight of material and machines, outproducing even the United States in tanks and artillery; the Russians produced 29 times more ordinance in 1941–45 than in 1914–17; three times the quantity produced by Britain and the US ... by 1942 war production was five times the 1940 level in the Urals and 27 times the 1940 level in Western Siberia.[37]

Yet as the Germans neared Moscow the Soviet dictator was prepared to countenance surrender. In October 1941 Stalin approved approaches to Germany via Sweden to ascertain what peace terms might be available. When there was no response to his overtures Stalin was forced to make further changes to the regime's tone in order to stiffen resistance. Russian nationalism was given official approval, controls on the Russian Orthodox Church were loosened and promises were made that life would improve once victory was secured. When Stalin spoke in Red Square on 7 November to mark the anniversary of the 1917 Revolution, he told the assembled troops, 'The war that you are fighting is a war of liberation, a just war. May you be inspired in this by the valiant image of our great ancestors – Alexander Nevsky, Dimitri Donskoi, Kuzma Minin, Dimitri Pozharski, Alexander Suvarov, Mikhail Kutusov.'[38] This was an appeal to Russia's Czarist and feudal history. As the realisation spread that German victory meant mass slavery and potential genocide, not just for the Jews but all of the Slavic population, Russian nationalism became central to Stalin's propaganda. Vodka was also made readily available to the troops.[39]

Stalin was also falling back on other tried and tested methods, ordering a purge of 'unreliable elements' – a policy of execution for deserters, panic-mongers and those who abandoned their positions (often this was simply as a result of getting lost or being cut off). Meanwhile Stalin agreed to release officers being held in the Gulag. Many went from slave labour to frontline commands. The future Marshal, Konstanin Rokossovsky, had survived two mock executions and emerged from the prison camps with nine missing teeth and three broken ribs to take command. He fought all the way to Berlin under the sentence of death which could be invoked by Stalin at any time.[40] Stalin had already ordered drastic reprisals against the families of commissars and officers who surrendered or deserted, denying them state support and benefits. As panic gripped, Moscow party officials were shot along with 'defeatists'. On 16 October the NKVD shot over 200 people in the city, the highest total since the last purge in 1938.[41]

Against this background Hitler urged the Wehrmacht to take Moscow. By now there were too few tanks available and his forces, expecting a quick victory, were not equipped for a harsh winter. The Red Army too was short of tanks and its troop levels had fallen to their lowest ever at 2.3 million. Artillery, infantry weapons and trucks were also in short supply. The Germans got near to the city's outskirts and threatened to break into the rear of its defences, leaving its defenders marooned. On 15 October the Russian government began evacuating eastwards to Kuibyshev. Molotov told the British and US ambassadors to leave. Panic spread as people besieged the train stations and the city's key factories were hit by absenteeism. Martial law was declared. Stalin himself delivered a broadcast making it clear he was staying in the city. Zhukov took over the defence of the capital.[42]

In September 1941 a Russian spy in the German embassy in Tokyo was able to pass on the information that a Japanese Imperial conference had decided to attack south into the Pacific against the US and the European imperial powers rather than attack the USSR. Units were switched west to defend Moscow.[43] The December 1941 surprise Japanese air attack on the US Pacific fleet anchored at Pearl Harbor confirmed this intelligence. It also meant Stalin was fighting alongside Britain and the United States, after Hitler declared war on America in accordance with his treaty commitment to Japan.

By now the numbers fighting outside Moscow on both sides were so reduced that the Russian reinforcements played a crucial role in tipping the balance towards the defending forces. For some 700 miles of the front the Germans had no reserves and their offensive was petering out into 'penny packet' attacks which were blocked by Russian resistance. Moscow was not taken and the Red Army counter-attacked. Russia's survival depended on the fact that it was fighting a war on a single, albeit massive, front against Germany. But there was also a difference between the two warring dictators. As the war progressed Hitler took more and more control over it. Stalin, in contrast, after he had regained his nerve in the summer of 1941, was far more open to the advice of his generals. Russia's war was fought under a relatively collective leadership.[44]

Defeat outside Moscow only led to an increase in the level of violence inflicted by the Nazis on the Russian people. On the day Hitler declared war on the US in solidarity with Japan, he also issued his 'Night and Fog Decree': all those placing German security in danger who were not executed immediately should vanish without trace, with their family being told nothing of their fate.[45] The failure to take first Leningrad and then Moscow left Germany fighting a war it could not win. Hitler had gambled on defeating the Soviet Union in six months; his gamble failed – just at the point a European war was to turn into a world war involving the US. The Germans were fighting a war on a long front with extended supply lines. Stalin was fighting a war of national defence on home territory. Despite his own incompetence and that of the state bureaucracy, the Red Army fought ferociously because it was aware of the savagery the Nazis were inflicting in the occupied territories.

Stalin and the USSR had survived but at terrible cost. Russian industrial output halved between June and November 1941 as German forces overran an area containing 45 per cent of the USSR's pre-war population. By December 1941 the Russians had lost 4 million men, 8,000 aircraft and 17,000 tanks. That was equivalent to the Red Army's strength at the beginning of Barbarossa.[46] The Russian regime had been able to raise new armies, often lacking training and equipment, but those units that survived became highly battle trained. Nevertheless, in 1942 the new factories in the east helped double pre-war aircraft production and quadruple tank production. This was achieved, as John Erickson notes, with a labour force reduced from 27 million to 19 million, 'fed by a "differentiated ration system" and housed ... primitively'.[47]

The Russians had developed the most effective tank of the war, the T-34, whose wide tracks were well suited to the mud and ice of the eastern front. Industry concentrated on mass producing limited designs of weapons – but that proved more effective than the German practice of producing too many weapons which were too complicated to use. German forces at the beginning of 1942 were suffering shortages of infantry and material, lost in the retreat from Moscow. One reaction was to step up propaganda emphasising the racial aspect of the eastern campaign – stressing the inhumanity of their enemies, the impossibility of surrender, and giving the green light to atrocities. Glantz and House point to the paradox that, 'The Soviet-German struggle led the Soviets to de-emphasise ideology in favour of nationalism, while it prompted the German army to embrace a Soviet-styled system of political officers and indoctrination.'[48]

There were two different dynamics at work. Hitler was fighting an imperialist war which was also a genocidal one. Stalin was fighting a war based on nationalism. Success in the battle for Moscow meant Stalin felt emboldened in talks with the British foreign secretary, Anthony Eden, to secure an assurance that he could keep the territories gained under the Molotov-Ribbentrop Pact (although the eventual Soviet-Polish frontier was not agreed), along with a promise of a second front, an invasion of Western Europe, in the coming year.[49]

Meanwhile Moscow was encouraging partisan warfare in the German-occupied zones, carefully controlled from Moscow. The basis for these units was often cut off Red Army units. The difficulties were severe – informers, lack of food and weapons, German reprisals, plus initially they were given little or no advice except for proclamations reissued from the post-1917 civil war. They gradually became more effective and made contact with the Red Army and the regime, which used them to retain some presence in the occupied zones. The German response was to increase reprisals – yet this simply helped stiffen civilian resistance to the Nazis.[50]

Stalin ordered a rapid offensive after Moscow, but he underestimated the ability of the Germans to resist and ignored the heed of his commanders, who wanted to concentrate armour in order to provide the sort of cutting edge they had witnessed German Panzers deploy. Instead the Red Army reverted to the full-frontal attacks that had proved so disastrous in the previous summer. The failure of Stalin's offensives encouraged further changes in the Russian command structure. Zhukov had become effective head of the Supreme High Command and Stalin's troubleshooter. In January 1942 he issued directives demanding offensives at limited points to allow concentration of armour and artillery. The Red Army commanders also began to win independence from party commissars and from Stalin's cronies. Increasingly they won a 'long, silent and bitter' struggle against party interference in military affairs.[51]

Hitler now faced the prospect of a protracted war in Russia with Britain still in the field and Japan and the US joining the conflict. He addressed fears that an alliance with Japan would undermine the position of the 'white races' in Asia:

> Interests of the white race must at present give place to the interests of the German people. We are fighting for our life. What use is fine theory if the basis of life (*Lebensboden*) is taken away? ... In a life and death struggle, all means available to a people are right. We would ally ourselves with anyone if we could weaken the Anglo-Saxon position.[52]

The Decisive Point in the Second World War

Hitler drew up a new plan for Russia, as Alan Clark describes: 'He intended to smash the Russians once and for all by breaking the power of their army in the south, capturing the seat of their economy, and taking the option of either wheeling up behind Moscow or down to the oil fields of Baku.'[53] Stalin was convinced the southern attack was a feint, and that the main thrust would be directed at Moscow once more; he duly demanded a concentration of Russian forces there, returning to old form in overruling his commanders who grasped that the main German thrust would be in the south.[54]

The summer 1942 southern offensive carried the Wehrmacht to the Volga and into the Caucasus. Hitler stressed the need to advance on Grozny and Baku to seize the oilfields but also demanded the capture of Stalingrad. This meant German forces would become divided as one prong advanced towards Grozny and the other drove on to Stalingrad where it became bogged down in a battle of attrition.[55]

Stalin feared a rebellion among the mainly Muslim peoples of the Caucasus. Beria, the NKVD commander, was rushed there with special security forces to quell any movement with mass murder and deportation, sweeping aside the nominal rights of these Soviet Republics.[56] In the event, the German advance became concentrated on the River Volga at Stalingrad where both sides were drawn into desperate street fighting. The Red Army was driven back until they held just a narrow strip of territory within the city, along the western bank of the Volga. Reinforcements and supplies were ferried across the river under German fire. German tanks were not suited to street fighting and were highly vulnerable in constrained spaces where movement was restricted. The Russian commander at Stalingrad, Chuikov, ordered his men to 'hug' the enemy – staying so close to their opponents that airstrikes became impossible.[57]

Stalingrad had never been one of the goals for the German summer offensive, but Hitler was now determined to capture the city. The Sixth Army soon found its offensive capability mightily reduced, as John Erickson describes:

> At the end of September General Halder noted the 'gradual exhaustion' seizing the German Sixth Army at Stalingrad: companies were reduced to a strength of 60 men, the armour, also suffering heavy losses, was caught up in a 'dead *Schwerpunkt*' [full stop] and burned to pieces in street fighting for which it was wholly unsuited.[58]

Halder was dismissed as Chief of Staff, one of his crimes being to urge withdrawal from the city. His successor argued for the same policy and was initially supported by the head of the Sixth Army, von Paulus, until he was promised great glory if he captured the city.

On 13 September during a break in a Stavka meeting discussing the defence of Stalingrad, Stalin overheard Zhukov and Colonel General Vasilevskii discussing 'another solution'. He demanded to know what they were talking about. They explained that they believed the Germans were overextended and that the Red Army should concentrate for an attack on the weakly defended German flanks encircling the city, besieging the besiegers. The German position at Stalingrad formed a salient which stretched eastwards to the River Volga. Many of the troops defending the flanks were Romanian and Italian, lacking anti-tank weapons, armour and motorised transport. The Russian defenders of the city would have to keep up their resistance meanwhile and not be told of this plan – they would be the anvil on which a Russian counter-attack would hammer down. This was the plan adopted in what would be the decisive battle of the Second World War.

While Chuikov held out in the remaining pockets of Stalingrad in Russian hands, the counter-attacks to the north and south were prepared.[59] By September 1942 larger mechanised corps had been formed in which tanks were supplemented by multiple rocket launchers, anti-aircraft and anti-tank units, armoured cars plus communications, engineering, medical, transport and maintenance units. Resources were still tight but eight such corps deploying around 230 tanks were in existence by the close of the year. These were now deployed against the German flanks west of Stalingrad. On the eve of the assault the Red Army calculated that its total field armies numbered 6,124,000, supplied with 78,000 guns and mortars (excluding the new multi-barrelled Katyusha rockets), 7,000 tanks and 3,200 aircraft. They estimated total German forces as numbering 5 million.[60]

Between 19 and 30 November the Russians attacked, crashing through German and Romanian lines, encircling the German Sixth Army and its satellite units within the Stalingrad perimeter. A quarter of a million German troops plus Romanians, Croats and other allied formations were encircled in the ruins of Stalingrad, the stage was set for Germany's first military defeat of the war and the elimination of one of its armies, something unthinkable a few short months before when Germany seemed unbeatable. As Clark states, 'the turning point in the Second World War had arrived'.[61]

The main German forces had been pushed far back westwards, though Russian tactical mistakes would eventually allow a German counter-attack at Kharkov to succeed. Hitler had ordered von Paulus to create a fortress at Stalingrad. He claimed the Luftwaffe could supply the 250,000 men cut off in the city. It was never conceivable. The Red Army tightened their squeeze on the city and drove back attempts to relieve the defenders. On 2 February, in defiance of Hitler's orders and with the Red Army nearing his headquarters, von Paulus surrendered.

After the defeat at Stalingrad German forces were fighting to hold back the Red Army in a brutal war, worse than that their fathers had fought in 1914–18. The losses would be astronomical, the barbarism absolute. Zhukov was made a marshal of the Soviet Union along with the commanders of the air force, artillery and armour. There were to be further enormous losses, but the Russians had begun an advance which would carry them to Berlin. It seems Hitler sensed the wheel of fortune had turned and that he faced defeat. Accordingly he began withdrawing into himself, distrustful of the generals he blamed for defeat and listening more to old friends and his courtiers. In 1943 he would make only two big public addresses plus a radio broadcast. He would spend little time in Berlin until the final days of the Third Reich.[62]

Germany now faced a war on two fronts and with two great powers, the United States and Russia, each of whose military and industrial power was greater than its own.[63] The Red Army was modernising rapidly with effective commanders at every level – far more free to take tactical decisions than their German counterparts. Infantry corps had armour, engineers, anti-aircraft units and mortars attached. 'From being little more than a collection of infantry and field guns with a few tanks and anti-tank guns, a typical rifle army grew into a complex structure that could integrate a variety of combat arms and services – in essence a combined-arms army.'[64]

By 1942 Russia outstripped the Third Reich in virtually every area of arms production, despite losing 25 per cent of its economic capacity: 'The margin for small arms and artillery was 3:1. For tanks it was a staggering 4:1, a differential compounded by the superior quality of the T-34 tank. Even in combat aircraft the margin was 2:1.'[65] Western writers often stress the importance of US Lend-Lease, an extension of the scheme aiding Britain, to the Russian war effort, but this did not have any significant effect until 1943.

Three hundred military schools had been set up to train officers along with 50 tank schools. Artillery was concentrated on particular fronts or allocated to individual armies with a variety of guns and rocket launchers, allowing for tactical flexibility. At the cutting edge were the new tank armies supported by mechanised infantry and mobile artillery, working in close co-ordination with the air force, plus signals, transportation and maintenance units.[66]

As well as such modern methods of war the Red Army also employed methods directly out of the tsarist military manuals. In the First World War the imperial army created penal battalions, punishment brigades for deserters and those who had breached the harsh discipline code. These reappeared in the Second World War, used in advance of attacking formations and denied camouflage outfits. As in 1914–17 they were kept in their positions by special units, under orders to open fire, preventing retreat or desertion.[67]

Underlying the Russian revival was their ability to relocate industrial production to the east, this having collapsed to a fraction of the pre-invasion level by the end of 1941. Between June and December, over 1,500 enterprises, along with millions of workers were moved east to the Urals, the Volga region, Eastern Siberia and Kazakhstan. By 1942 these regions supplied three quarters of all the Red Army's weaponry and virtually all the USSR's iron and steel. Conditions at work were grim: Russian workers received a quarter of the rations available to Germans and a fifth of those available to British workers. They worked longer hours too.

In the summer of 1943 the Germans massed for a final major offensive on the Eastern Front aimed at the city of Kursk. Unlike previous operations this was a much more limited effort in which the hope was that a tactical victory might lead to a turnaround in the wider strategic picture. The new German commander in the East, von Manstein, warned Hitler that while in April 1943 both sides could muster an equal number of tanks, any delay in launching an offensive would mean the Red Army being able to deploy 60 new armoured brigades.[68] The Russians held territory which 'bulged' into the German lines, raising the possibility of the Germans attacking its flanks from the north and south. The battle would involve the greatest tank forces ever committed to the field. Hitler told his star tank commander, Heinz Guderian, that the thought of the coming battle made 'his stomach turn over'.[69]

This time Stalin believed the intelligence predicting the attack, given to him by his own intelligence service as well as by the British. Accordingly the Russians amassed their forces in the region ensuring they held a three-to-one advantage in manpower and 50 per cent more tanks. According to Soviet archives their frontline forces numbered 1 million troops, 13,000 guns and mortars, plus over 3,000 armoured vehicles. Held in reserve was another front army numbering 445,000 soldiers, 6,500 guns, plus 1,500 tanks and self-propelled guns. Facing them were 435,000 German soldiers, 10,000 guns and mortars plus just over 3,000 tanks.[70]

Lend-Lease material was also coming from the US and Britain. Russia had little need of tanks or aircraft, but American trucks, food, petroleum products, chemicals, machine tools, boots and metals (steel, aluminium, copper and zinc) were vital to its war machine.[71]

The Germans deployed the new Tiger and Panther tanks in the hope they could outgun their enemy, but the Russians had improved their main workhorse, the T-34, introduced a new heavy tank, the Joseph Stalin, and a self-propelled gun designed to deal with the Tiger. Huge numbers of weapons and ammunition were stockpiled ready for the Wehrmacht's attack. A powerful strategic reserve was created, awaiting the moment when the Red Army could move from the defensive to the offensive.

There were few battles which could match the scale of that at Kursk. The Germans lost over 1,000 aircraft, enabling the Russians to take command of the air. German armour was attacking well-prepared defensive positions, and while they made some gains the cost was high, and the advance was ground down. To their shock, after an already gruelling fight, the Germans now faced the might of the new Russian tank armies. As the German attack petered out the battlefield was littered with burnt out and broken down tanks. While the Russians rushed to repair those they could, the Germans were unable to do the same. After their victory at Kursk the Russians claimed 70,000 Germans had been killed and over 3,000 tanks and assault guns destroyed.[72]

Russian advance, 14 May to 3 September 1944

The defeat of the German offensive was immediately followed by a huge Russian attack, using the reserves held back until this moment. They advanced along a 1,500-mile front, to a depth of 650 miles at its deepest. Belgorod, Orel, Kharkov and eventually Kiev were liberated. The Red Army would not stop now until it reached Berlin.

The Third Reich was no longer capable of replacing its losses on the Eastern Front. The 12th Infantry Division, which had crossed the Russian frontier in June 1941 with 14,500 men, had lost over 16,000 men by October 1943, 118 per cent of its initial number of combat troops and 156 per cent of its officers (the division had received replacements in an attempt to offset losses with an estimated 30,000 soldiers and 700 officers serving in the division during the Russian campaign).[73] The Grossdeutschland Division was virtually destroyed in the period from the commencement of the invasion to the end of the unsuccessful Russian winter offensive in February 1942. It was reformed with 18,000 men in May 1942. The historian Omar Bartov estimates that between then and late September 1943 the division lost nearly 18,000 men, some 600 of whom were officers.[74]

From Kursk onwards the Red Army was almost continually on the offensive, and accordingly suffered heavier losses than the German defenders. In the wake of the victories at Stalingrad and Kursk, Stalin agreed to meet his American and British allies in Tehran (which Russian and British forces had occupied, fearing the Iranian government was pro-German). There Roosevelt accepted Stalin's demand for an invasion of Western Europe, despite Churchill's opposition (as we have seen, he counter-posed further operations in Italy and the Mediterranean). Returning to Moscow, the Russian dictator told Zhukov he believed Roosevelt's pledge that there would be an invasion of France, but if he broke his word 'our own forces are sufficient to complete the rout of Nazi Germany'.[75]

Genocide

The invasion of Russia opened the way towards the Nazi extermination programme aimed at destroying European Jewry and other groups like the Roma. The programme took its final shape as Russian resistance turned into a Red Army advance that the Germans could not stem. The genocidal impulse of Nazism had been apparent in the conquest of Poland. From the opening hours of Barbarossa it was starkly obvious to all fighting on the Russian front.

Revisionist historians and Holocaust deniers argue either that Hitler knew nothing of the death camps or that there was no extermination policy. There was probably never a specific command from Hitler ordering the mass killings of the Holocaust. Yet it was not Hitler's style to issue such clear orders but rather to let the rival components of the Third Reich 'work towards' his wishes.

At the end of 1940 the Führer stated his wish that his Gauleiters (regional party leaders) in the East should have 'the necessary freedom of movement' in dealing with the Jewish issue. Above all no one in the party, the SS, the military or any other branch of the Third Reich could have been unaware from the outset that Hitler combined his need to win the war with his mission to destroy world Jewry. In his notorious speech to the Reichstag on 30 January 1939, Hitler 'prophesied' that war would lead to the 'annihilation of the Jewish race in Europe'.[76] Anti-Semitic violence, which led remorselessly towards the extermination policy, grew after the SS gained dominance in Jewish policy in 1938. The decision to invade Poland marked another huge step towards barbarism.[77] In the East from the beginning the Nazi occupation was murderous. As early as 1939 a leaflet issued to army companies by the Supreme Command defined the Third Reich's war aims as, '1: Wiping out all after-effects of the Jewish influence ... 2: The struggle against World Judaism [which] we fight the way one would fight a poisonous parasite ... the plague of all peoples.'[78]

The involvement of the Wehrmacht in the subsequent occupation of Poland helped radicalise it and ensured its involvement in developing genocidal policies, as Ian Kershaw argues:

> Eighteen months' involvement in the brutal subjugation of the Poles – even if the worst atrocities were perpetrated by the SS, the sense of disgust at these had been considerable, and a few generals had been bold enough to protest about them – had helped prepare the ground for the readiness to collaborate in the premeditated barbarism of an altogether different order built into 'Operation Barbarossa'.[79]

Many of the men Hitler would rely on to hold down the occupied territories in the East were veterans of the fighting there which followed the formal cessation of the First World War – Erich Koch, who would rule the Ukraine, Hans Frank, governor general of the General Government area in Poland, Arthur Greiser, boss of the Warthegau, and Rudolf Höss, who would become commandant of Auschwitz.[80] The Gauleiters of the occupied territories found Jews from Germany and the Polish territories incorporated directly into the Third Reich being deported eastwards into their areas. They began to initiate 'local actions' against them and to demand their further removal. In these territories, free from the legal restraints that still applied in the Reich and removed from public view, the SS and party chiefs had a free hand.

In October 1939 Himmler ordered the removal of all Jews and Poles from the north-west of Poland, which had been annexed to Germany. Several hundred thousand were sent east into German-occupied Poland. A policy emerged of concentrating Jews in ghettoes like that created in Lodz in December 1939.[81] In January 1940 the SS decided that those capable of working should be consigned to forced-labour camps and those unable to work should be left to starve in the ghettoes. The extermination programme centred on the death camps was still two years away, but Kershaw views this as one more shift towards genocide, arguing that, 'this decision, taken at a meeting of top SS leaders in January 1940' meant acceptance of 'inevitable deaths through exhaustion, hunger and disease'.[82]

Prior to the launch of Barbarossa, Hitler had assured Hans Frank, governor of the General Government area, that the Jews would be removed from his territory in the 'foreseeable future'. The notion was that five to six million Jews would be dispatched east of the Urals to die from sickness or forced labour.[83] Hitler made parallels with the destruction of the Native American population, 'Here in the East a similar process will repeat itself for a second time as in the conquest of America.'[84]

In the summer of 1941 Himmler phoned Rudolf Höss and told him, 'The Führer has ordered that the Jewish question be solved once and for all and that we, the SS, are to implement that order ... Every Jew that we can lay our hands on is to be destroyed now during the war, without exception.'[85] The ultimate aim of the Nazi occupation in Poland and the USSR was to remove or destroy the existing population and to resettle the area with Germans. Thirty-one million people, mainly Slavs, were targeted to be deported east of the Urals – 85 per cent of the native population of Poland was to be removed along with 64 per cent of the population of the Ukraine and 74 per cent that of Belorussia. In the Ukraine all grain was to be sent to the Reich and supplies to Ukraine's cities simply stopped. Göring boasted to the Italian foreign minister, Ciano, that Germany planned on starving 20 to 30 million Soviet citizens to death.[86]

From the first days of the invasion of Russia the Nazis had justified their aggression by claiming it was a pre-emptive action designed to forestall an invasion of Germany by a 'sub-human', 'Judeo-Bolshevik' horde. German troops were given free reign to carry out acts of barbarism. For instance, rape by a German soldier in occupied France was a moral offence; in Russia, if rape was punished, it was on the basis that sexual intercourse with a Slav or Jew was a 'race crime', a health hazard, or 'collaboration' with partisans.[87]

The Chief of the Army General Staff, Halder, noted these points in his diary from a speech Hitler made to 250 senior officers on 30 March 1941:

> Colonial tasks!
> Struggle between two world-views. Crushing verdict on Bolshevism: akin to social gangsterism. Communism an enormous future danger. We must move away from the notion of comradeship among soldiers. The Communist is not a comrade, never has been nor will be. It is a war of annihilation.[88]

Two days after the launch of the German invasion of Russia, Heydrich of the SS received an order from Göring, on instruction from Hitler, instructing the SS man 'to make all necessary preparations regarding organisations and financial matters to bring about a complete solution of the Jewish question in the German sphere of influence in Europe'.[89] Prior to the launch of the invasion of Russia, four *Einsatzgruppen* (task forces) were formed by the SS, each consisting of between 800 and 1,000 men, to execute Jews, Communist officials and commissars:

> The middle ranking commanders for the most part had an educated background. Highly qualified academics, civil servants, lawyers, a Protestant pastor, and even an opera singer, were among them. The top leadership was drawn almost exclusively from the Security Police and the SD ... they were in the main well educated men, of the generation just too young to have

fought in the First World War, they had sucked in *volkisch* ideals in German universities in the 1920s.⁹⁰

At first the killings were of male Jews. But after the first month of the invasion the death toll mushroomed. In August Jewish refugees, expelled from Hungary and Romania, were trapped in the small town of Kamenets-Podolsk in West Ukraine. In three days *Einsatzgruppe* D and Hungarian units executed 20,000. In September 1941 the *Einsatzgruppen* carried out mass executions at a ravine, Babi Yar, outside Kiev; 33,000 Jews were killed in two days. The ravine was used as a grave for those executed by the Nazis throughout the occupation. Following its recapture the Russians estimated that there were approximately 100,000 corpses at Babi Yar, and this was the figure cited during the Nuremberg Trials. According to testimonies of workers forced to burn the bodies, the numbers ranged from 70,000 to 120,000.⁹¹

A year later the *Einsatzgruppen* murdered some 16,000 Jews in one day at Pinsk using grenades, axes, dogs and even an SS cavalry unit. The clear instructions to SS *Einsatzgruppen* units to shoot Jews marked another major step towards Nazi genocide. Their leaders always claimed this was Hitler's instruction. Perhaps 2 million Russian Jews were executed by these units. *Einsatzgruppe* A alone reported the killing of 229,052 Jews by the beginning of January 1942.⁹²

The Wehrmacht collaborated with this programme of mass execution and was itself responsible for the extermination of two thirds of the Soviet prisoners of war who fell into German hands. By the end of December the Wehrmacht's records show they had taken 3.35 million prisoners yet only 1.1 million were still alive and just 400,000 of them were capable of work. On 5 October 1941 a Wehrmacht corporal serving in Belarus, Richard Heidenreich, noted in his diary, 'There were about 1,000 Jews in the village of Krupka and they all had to be shot today.' The entry explains how:

> The column was marched to the bog. They were ordered to sit. There was a ditch full of water. The first ten had to undress to the hip and then climb into the ditch. We, who were shooting, stood over them. Ten shots sounded. Ten Jews knocked off. This went on till they were all done. The children clung to their mothers, the women hung on to their men.⁹³

Hitler's allies needed little encouragement to unleash murder on the Jews. Days before the attack on Russia, the Romanian regime sanctioned a pogrom in its border town of Jassy, marking the doors of Christian homes to prevent them being attacked. In the subsequent attacks, following rumours Russian parachutists had landed, between 13 and 15 thousand Jews were killed. After the Romanians took Odessa a delayed action mine was detonated under the Romanian military HQ. The Romanian dictator, Marshal Antonescu, ordered the mass execution of Jews; his troops killed 20,000 – hung from lamp posts and telegraph poles, blown up in a warehouse, or taken outside the city to be shot in fields. Before the Romanians switched sides and joined the Russians in 1944, they were responsible for the deaths of up to 300,000 Romanian and Ukrainian Jews.[94]

The scale of the killings was beyond even the capacity of mass killers like the SS to deal with, and the disposal of such numbers of corpses caused all sorts of problems. Prior to the invasion of Russia the Nazis had looked to forcing the Jews and other 'undesirables' beyond the borders of the Third Reich. In 1939 and the first half of 1940 there had been discussions about deporting all Jews to Madagascar or Africa, but Britain's continued resistance in the early summer of 1940 scotched these plans. The failure to achieve a rapid victory in Russia meant deportation to east of the Urals was also ruled out. Industrial mass murder was now launched on European Jews. Already Hitler's special directive, 'Guidelines in Special Spheres re Directive No. 21 (Operation Barbarossa)', had stated:

> In the operations area of the army, the *Reichsführer-SS* [Henreich Himmler] has been given special tasks on the orders of the *Führer*, in order to prepare the political administration. These tasks arise from the forthcoming final struggle of two opposing political systems. Within the framework of these tasks, the *Reichsführer-SS* acts independently and on his own responsibility.[95]

Himmler was given responsibility for 'security' in the eastern occupied territories; his job was to solve the 'Jewish question'.[96] After the war General Alfred Jodl stated that once the Wehrmacht had failed to take Moscow in late 1941, 'Long before anyone else in the world, Hitler suspected or knew that the war was lost.'[97] If this was true, it meant Hitler was determined that at least one goal of the racial war he had unleashed could be realised: the destruction of the Jews.

In October 1941 Himmler banned Jewish emigration and German and Austrian Jews were expelled to Poland. That month the Reich Commissar in the Baltic states was given permission to exterminate Jews incapable of work and those who had been deported eastward from Germany. Plans for the construction of giant forced-labour camps were being drawn up by the SS's economic administration, the Reich Security Head Office (a merger of the SD, the Gestapo and the Criminal Police), and the resettlement agency, the RKFDV. That autumn the order was given to begin construction of the concentration camps, each to house 50,000 inmates, at Lublin-Majdanek and Birkenau, adjacent to the existing Auschwitz camp. By the end of the year the target for the number of inmates in each camp was raised to 125,000 and 150,000 respectively.

Meanwhile the extermination of Jews living within the pre-war boundaries of the Third Reich had been launched. On 25 and 29 November *Einsatzgruppen* shot 5,000 Jews who had been deported to Lithuania from Berlin, Breslau, Munich, Frankfurt and Vienna.[98] Within the Third Reich the Nazis had already employed mass murder in pursuit of their 'National Community': 'The goal was a utopian *Volksgemeinschaft* (national community), totally under police surveillance, in which any attempts at non-conformist behaviour, or even any hint of intention of such behaviour, would be visited with terror.'[99] The dictatorship had also begun the mass elimination of 'anti-social elements and parasites' within the Volk itself – the physically and mentally ill, the Roma people, tramps, alcoholics and homosexuals.

The 'Euthanasia Action' liquidated 70,000 patients in German psychiatric and other hospitals between 1939 and 1940. Between 5 and 8 thousand children were put to death, mainly by lethal injection. The prosecutors of this programme became key figures in the Holocaust. In March 1941 Victor Brack, the official in charge of the 'Euthanasia Action', proposed methods of sterilising 3,000 to 4,000 Jews a day. Among those compulsorily sterilised were the offspring of relationships between German women and African troops during the French occupation of the Rhineland. By 1945 between 200,000 and 350,000 German citizens had been sterilised by the Nazi regime.[100]

The Roma were targeted because they were regarded both as aliens and as being 'asocial' – refusing to accept work discipline or the norms of everyday life as laid down by the Third Reich. In October 1939 a decree was issued requiring them to be put in 'assembly camps'. The next spring deportations began into occupied Poland. In the autumn of 1941, 5,000 Austrian Roma were placed in the Lodz Jewish ghetto. In December of the following year Himmler's 'Auschwitz Decree' ordered the 'assignment of gypsy half-castes, Roma gypsies and Balkan gypsies' to Auschwitz-Birkenau. There they were not initially sent to the gas chambers but to a special 'gypsy camp'. Eventually, as the Red Army neared and disease spread, the SS broke up the camp and murdered its inmates in the autumn of 1944.[101]

At the end of November 1941 Himmler had sent out invitations for a conference at Wannsee which eventually took place on 20 January 1942. Its purpose was to organise the extermination programme for European Jewry and others. In between the conference being called and it actually occurring, Hans Frank, head of the General Government area in Poland, held his own conference in Cracow at which he stated, 'I want to say to you quite openly that we shall have to finish off the Jews, one way or another ... We have to annihilate the Jews wherever we find them and wherever it is possible.' Of the 3.5 million Jews in his territory, many expelled there from Germany, he said, 'We can't shoot these 3,500,000 Jews, we can't poison them, but we can take steps which, one way or another, will lead to an annihilation success, and I am referring to the measures under discussion in the Reich.'[102] On 12 December 1941 Hitler addressed the party's Reichsleiters (national leaders – second only to the Führer) and Gauleiters at a private audience in Berlin. Goebbels recorded the event in his diary:

> Concerning the Jewish question, the Führer is determined to make a clean sweep. He prophesied to the Jews that if they were once again to cause a world war, the results would be their own destruction. This was no figure of speech. The world war is here, the destruction of the Jews must be the inevitable consequence.[103]

Frank's deputy, Philip Bouhler, was one of the 15 men who assembled on 20 January 1942 at Himmler's Wannsee conference. The others were representatives of Alfred Rosenberg's East Ministry, Göring's Four Year Plan agency, the Justice Ministry, the Interior Ministry, the Foreign Office and the Chancellery. Heydrich chaired on behalf of the SS, and opened matters by stating that Hitler had given him 'the responsibility for working out the final solution of the Jewish problem regardless of geographical boundaries', adding that instead of emigration the Führer wanted mass deportation to the East.[104] The Wannsee conference also agreed to tell the Croat, Slovakian, Hungarian and Bulgarian governments that the Germans would deal with their Jewish populations.

No one present could have left the conference unaware that deportation meant a death sentence. According to the testimony of Adolf Eichmann when he was later put on trial in Israel, those present discussed mass murder, 'quite openly, quite differently from the language which I had to use later in the record. During the conversation they minced no words about it at all.'[105]

In the concentration camps there would be a constant tension between forcing prisoners to work as slave labourers for the war effort and the extermination programme, but this should not conceal the fact that everyone involved wished the eventual murder of all inmates. The gas chambers were already being designed. By the spring of 1942 six death camps had been set up in Poland: Treblinka, Sobibor, Belzec, Lublin, Kulmhof and Auschwitz. At the first four the extermination programme got under way using exhaust fumes to kill Jewish detainees, but Höss, the commandant at Auschwitz, thought this inefficient and initiated an alternative method – introducing Zyklon B poison gas into chambers disguised as shower blocks. He had finessed this method on Russian prisoners over the preceding months.[106]

By the summer of 1942 mass murder was well on track. Heydrich explained to one of his assistants, a Doctor Wisliceny, that he had been ordered to carry out the biological extermination of the Jewish race. Wisliceny replied, 'May God forbid that our enemies should ever do anything similar to the German people.' The reply came, 'Don't be sentimental. This is a Führer order.'[107] At the end of July Himmler wrote a letter to the chief of the SS head office stating: 'The occupied Eastern territories will be made free of Jews. The Führer has placed the implementation of this very difficult order on my shoulders. Nobody can remove the responsibility from me. Therefore, I forbid all discussion.'[108] Other groups were also victims of this genocide. In September 1942 the Reich minister of justice Otto Georg Thierack ordered that, 'Gypsies [in police custody] should be exterminated unconditionally.'[109]

The barbaric treatment of foreign slave labourers plus the mass killings of Russian PoWs helped contribute to the ease with which the regime could turn to industrial mass murder. Over 5.7 million Red Army personnel were captured by Nazi forces. At least 3.3 million died in captivity. Those executed totalled 600,000, with the rest dying of starvation, cold and sheer exhaustion. Just one third of Russian PoW's returned home as compared to two thirds of German military prisoners held by the USSR.[110]

The German High Command and officer corps had acquiesced in Hitler's coming to power and shared his determination to crush the left and remove the 'shameful borders' imposed by the Versailles peace treaties of 1919. They were keen to conquer Central and Eastern Europe, and above all they agreed to the armed forces' incorporation into the regime and their control by the Führer. Further, by the time of Barbarossa, the junior and middle-ranking officers came from the middle classes who had provided the cadre of the Nazi Party and had gone through the ranks of the Hitler Youth and the party's university section. The anti-Jewish measures were not central to German big business's concerns, but they were happy to benefit from Jewish expropriations, Jewish ghetto labour in Poland, and Polish slave labour in the Third Reich. But the Holocaust assumed priority for Hitler, the SS and large sections of his regime over all else, including what might have been beneficial to the war effort. As Mason points out:

> Among the first Polish Jews who were gassed in the extermination camps were thousands of skilled metal workers from Polish armament factories. This was in the autumn of 1942, at the turning point in the campaign against the Soviet Union, which was to increase still further the demands made by the Wehrmacht on the German war economy. The army emphasised the irrational nature of this action in view of the great shortage of skilled labour, but was unable to save the Jewish armament workers. The general who made the formal complaint was relieved of his post.[111]

The death camps were not such a secret. In August 1942 Himmler had personally told Mussolini that mass murder of the Jews was being carried out. Bosworth writes that, 'Mussolini had let him ramble on, without serious questioning or objection.'[112] The Fascist party secretary, Aldo Vidussoni, reported to Mussolini on a visit to the Russian front in September 1942, noting 'the elimination of the Jews'. In November 1942 Mussolini fobbed off complaints from the Italian industrialist Alberto Pirelli about German occupation policies in the East by stating, 'They were making them [the Jews] emigrate to another world.'[113] By the close of 1942 Mussolini had very accurate information on Hitler's death camps from the Vatican, the Croats, and from Italians involved in handing over Jews to the Germans. In January 1943 the German ambassador in Rome reported that all the Jews in Europe had to be exterminated by the year's close.[114] Shortly afterwards, Italian officers who had been present in Poland forwarded a description of the gas chambers.[115]

Elsewhere in Europe news of the mass murder of the Jews was spreading. In the autumn of 1943 a Spanish diplomat concerned about Spanish citizens deported from Salonika in Greece told a German Foreign Office official he could not stand by and watch 'Spanish citizens being liquidated in Polish camps'. A Greek train driver who took deportees as far north as Belgrade broke down on his return and told his son, the future novelist Giorgos Ioannou, that Jewish prisoners, denied water and packed in so tightly they faced suffocation, were dying before arriving in Belgrade and that the Germans stopped the train only to remove watches and valuables from detainees.[116]

In a number of speeches Hitler promised revenge on the Jews for supposedly starting the war. The references may have been obscure to those not in the know, but they were aimed at the growing numbers, both military and civilian, involved in the Holocaust. In the immediate wake of the final defeat at Stalingrad, Goebbels delivered a speech in Dusseldorf on 15 February 1943, promising 'total war' accompanied by the 'radical extermination and elimination of Jewry'.[117]

Eight months later, as knowledge of what was happening in the death camps rippled out, Himmler summoned SS officers to a meeting at Poznan in Poland. Stating that he wanted to talk frankly he said:

> Among ourselves it should be mentioned once, quite openly, but we shall never speak of it publicly ... I mean the evacuation of the Jews, the extermination of the race. It's one of those things it is easy to talk about – 'The Jewish race is being exterminated,' says one party member, 'that's quite clear, it's in our programme – elimination of the Jews, and we're doing it, exterminating them'.[118]

While he spoke in the third person Himmler was acknowledging that the SS were spearheading the extermination programme. Two days later Himmler and Albert Speer, the man Hitler had placed in command of Germany's war economy, addressed a meeting of Gauleiters and Reichsleiters in the same city. In the morning Speer delivered a speech threatening that the security forces would be brought in if the Gauleiters did not close non-military industries to release extra labour for the war effort. After lunch Himmler addressed a difficult issue – what to do with Jewish women and children: 'We, you see, were faced with the question, "What to do about the women and children?" ... The hard decisions had to be taken to have this people disappear from the face of the earth.'[119]

Hitler did not need to issue an order for the extermination of the Jews. The SS, the Nazi Party and his henchmen shared the determination to destroy European Jewry. This was a central objective uniting the disparate forces Hitler had bound together. As the tide of war turned against the Third Reich these murderous racists saw the mass murder of the Jews, and others, as the one historic victory they could deliver.

CHAPTER SEVEN

The End of the Third Reich

War of Materiel

In simple economic terms the outcome of the Second World War should not have been in doubt. In 1936–38 a third of the world's industrial production took place in the US. Add in the USSR's and Britain's shares and the figure was over half. Together the Axis powers' share was 17 per cent. In 1941 and 1942 the UK was out-producing Germany in military materiel.[1] By 1942 the US alone was exceeding the combined output of all the Axis states.[2] The Allies controlled 90 per cent of the world's oil output, with the US producing two-thirds of the world's oil in 1943; the Axis states controlled just 3 per cent.[3]

In all the belligerent countries state direction of the domestic economy gathered pace both before and during the war. In the US this effectively meant the war economy was run not by the military but by big business. Before Pearl Harbor, Roosevelt had created an Office of Production Management to oversee rearmament. On 5 January 1942 the man he had selected to head it, Ford and General Motors executive William Knudsen, gathered a room full of businessmen and read out a list of military requirements, asking for volunteers to meet the production demands.[4] In 1942 the US War Production Board was established. Over 1,000 corporative executives were seconded to run it, paid for by their firms. They decided on what materiel was produced, placing the orders with the companies they represented. Tax concessions and government funding paid for new plants and machinery.[5]

In 1941 Roosevelt also created the Office of Price Administration (OPA). Congress gave credence to this new government agency by passing the Emergency Price Control Act in January 1942, giving the OPA the power to control prices on everything except agricultural commodities and to ration items such as tyres, cars, shoes, nylon stockings, fuel oil, coffee, meat and processed food. At its height the OPA ensured 90 per cent of retail food prices were frozen. It could also prosecute corporations and retailers for violating these controls; in the last year of the war 71,000 retailers were fined a total of $5.1 million. Big business would challenge these controls, and lose, in the Supreme Court.[6]

A more amicable relationship was struck between the federal authorities and the oil industry. In 1941 Roosevelt had established the body which would eventually be known as the Petroleum Administration for War. It was headed by Harold L. Ickes, previously secretary of the interior, and met for the first time the day after the Pearl Harbor attack. Before the war Ickes had been regarded with suspicion by the oil industry. Now he appointed as his right-hand man Ralph K.

Davies, vice-president of Standard Oil of California. A further 1,500 executives and managers from the oil industry were selected to serve under Ickes.[7]

Meanwhile, despite his sympathies for Hitler, Henry Ford threw his weight behind the war effort. In September 1940 work had begun on a brand new aero-engine plant at River Rouge, and by the spring of the following year construction began on the Willow Run plant, which would mass produce heavy bombers.[8] In both the US and the UK the trade unions were invited to participate in ensuring an efficient war economy – in return for no-strike pledges enforced by emergency legislation. In Britain corporate executives were also recruited to direct war production, but when Winston Churchill formed his government in May 1940 he looked to another force. A number of leading Labour figures were appointed ministers, notably the party leader, Clement Attlee, and Ernest Bevin, who was general secretary of the powerful Transport and General Workers Union and had to be found a parliamentary seat. Churchill's idea was that Bevin would mobilise the trade union movement behind his government and the war effort. Within weeks the prime minister noted, 'Under his leadership the British working class are now giving up holidays and privileges to a far greater extent than in the last war.'[9]

Participation in wartime government shaped the Labour Party, wedding its leader both to a continuing alliance with the US and the need to defend Britain's imperial position in the world:

> The sharing of power also had important consequences for the Labour Party itself, particularly in the fields of defence and foreign affairs. The assumption of the wartime coalition – acceptance of the almost total dependence on the United States, the belief that Britain was still a great power and a strong ally of the Americans with a world-wide role to play – were to form the basis for the post-war bi-partisan foreign and defence policy.[10]

British strike figures fell from 1,354,000 days lost through industrial action in 1939 to 941,000 in 1940. Nevertheless, the class tensions of the 1920s and 1930s had not disappeared but were submerged. The strike figures rose to over a million in 1941 and in 1942 outstripped the total for 1939.[11]

All of the Axis powers lagged behind their opponents in the creation of state-directed war economies. Hitler hoped to wage expansionist wars without cutting domestic living standards, which continued to rise slowly until 1942. He was haunted by the revolution of 1918–19 which ended Germany's war and toppled the Kaiser. The Nazis suppressed all labour rights and organisation but were not prepared to depress living standards (though German workers had to work long hours in order to maintain them). Limits were put on the numbers of women working in industry, unlike in the Allied countries, because their place under Nazi ideology was in the home. Generous benefits were accorded to wives and families of servicemen. The various factions of the Nazi state were divided as to how to deal with the working class. One wing, represented by General Georg Thomas, head of the War Economy Office at the Ministry of War, wanted to prepare for war by systematic state control of the labour market, the conscription of civilian workers to work in war industries, decreed reductions in wages, and so on. Such measures were introduced in several steps in 1938–39, culminating in a War Economy Decree issued in September 1939.[12] Yet these measures, Tim Mason argues, failed thanks to working-class opposition:

> Despite the war and a 50 per cent increase in the income tax for the middle class, workers were not ready to resign themselves to even a limited reduction of wages, to the elimination of overtime pay or to the suspension of industrial safety regulations. The NSDAP [Nazi Party], worried because of the plebiscitary foundations of the regime, championed a moderate wage policy, and within a month everything had returned to normal ... The dissatisfaction and passive resistance continued, however, until mid November 1939, when the government saw itself forced to make further concessions in social policy. Bonus pay (except for the ninth and tenth hours of work) and holiday leave were restored, and this was quickly followed by the re-enactment of most of the industrial safety regulations.[13]

Working-class opposition, Mason argues, did not simply set limits to what the state demanded of them at work. Fear of it was a major factor in Hitler's decision to launch a war of rapid conquest in 1939–40. A series of campaigns of expansion and conquest could provide the resources to build up German military strength without pursuing the politically dangerous course of squeezing the working class too hard. The economies of conquered countries could be plundered to sustain the war effort.[14] Continuous war, as an end in itself, became the way out of an insoluble domestic situation. 'In terms of economic and domestic policy, the conduct of war has become the precondition of continuing to prepare for war.'[15] Mason seizes on a phrase of Hitler's – '*Flucht nach vorn*' (flight to the front) – to sum up this strategy: endless military expansion as a way of escaping the class contradictions which National Socialism had been unable to abolish.

In 1939 German tank output lagged behind that of both Britain and France, and its aircraft production was no greater than Britain's. The share of the German economy devoted to arms production was still less than Britain's in 1941. In 1940 German consumer expenditure was higher than its military spending. The German standard of living remained higher than Britain's until 1944. Military production was reduced after the fall of France, with Panzer production down to just 40 a month (compared to 2,000 at the high point of production in 1944).[16]

Unlike in the 1914–18 war, food supplies remained plentiful until the last months. As Detlev J.K. Peukert explains: 'Half of Europe was plundered so that the Germans could be kept supplied to a relatively high standard. Germany lived on credit, first its own, and then that of other countries.'[17] Occupied Europe was looted and exploited and forced labour was used on a mass scale (although its productivity levels were low). By May 1940 Germany was using 1.1 million forced labourers, mainly Poles. Adam Tooze describes their situation as 'penal apartheid':

Polish workers in Germany were confined to their workplace and allocated billet. They were to wear at all times an identifying tag bearing a large letter 'P'. To ensure that their status was always below that of their German co-workers, their wages were arbitrarily slashed to a maximum of 25 Reichsmarks per month. Polish workers were barred from all public conveyances and all social contact with Germans.[18]

Poles were banned from cinemas, dances, pubs, churches and theatres. Sexual intercourse with a German was punishable by death and 'shirking' at work punished by being dispatched to a concentration camp. By 1944 there were 12 million foreign workers in the Third Reich, making up a third of the workforce in the armaments industry and half in Krupps.[19] The presence of such large numbers of foreign workers required draconian measures to prevent Germans mixing with these 'inferior races'. In the first six months of 1944, 32,000 German citizens and 204,000 foreigners were arrested for breaching the stringent laws.

By the close of 1944 over 400,000 concentration camp inmates were working in German war industries. Concentration camps were built next to giant new industrial complexes; Oranienburg supplied the Heinkel plane plant, Buchenwald supplied Krupps, Sachsenhausen supplied Daimler Benz, and Dachau supplied BMW. The Mittelbau tunnel complex in the Harz Mountains was built with slave labour from the Buchenwald concentration camp. It would produce V2 rockets and jet engines for the Luftwaffe. The labourers who worked there slept in the tunnels, breathing fresh air at best once a week and denied sanitation and clean water. Thousands died. 'Shirkers' were hanged from the roof and left there to encourage survivors to work harder.[20]

Occupied Europe would eventually supply Germany with 27 per cent of its steel and 19 per cent of its labour force, allowing millions of German citizens to be conscripted into the armed forces. By 1943 half of France's workforce was engaged in producing for Germany's war effort, either within France or as foreign labourers within the Third Reich.[21] But the shift towards a war economy was too little, too late. Tank production peaked at an annual total of 27,345 in 1944. Yet the Russians had already topped 30,000, the British produced 36,000 and the Americans over 88,000 between late 1941 and late 1943.[22] In 1943 total Axis aircraft production was 43,000, total Allied production 151,000.[23]

In February 1942 Hitler had appointed Albert Speer as minister of armaments. Speer reduced the variety of weaponry being produced, finally prioritised war industry over consumer production, and put together a team of technocrats. By the end of 1942 he had formed 249 committees and sub-committees administering different sections of the war economy. Tooze points out that of the 100 top industrial firms of 1938 there was not one which did not hold the chair of one of these bodies. The Vestag conglomerate held 12 and Siemens eight. Tooze describes this as 'an alliance between Hitler's regime and the leading elements of German industrial capitalism, to secure their common survival'.[24] Weapon production tripled by 1944 before lack of raw materials began to halt production. The air ministry brought the three major aircraft developers, Junkers, Heinkel and Messerschmitt, under their direct control in

May 1941. The regime promised these were extraordinary measures and that it stood for a free market economy. In June at Berchtesgaden Hitler delivered a speech, written by Speer, to key figures from the armaments industry promising, 'When this war is decided by our victory, then the private initiative of German business will experience its greatest moment ... perhaps its greatest flourishing of all time.' Hitler reassured his listeners that 'the further development of humanity' was only possible 'through the promotion of private initiative, in which alone I see the precondition for all real progress'.[25]

Speer faced obstruction from the SS, Göring and other leading Nazis who diverted labour and materials to their own pet projects. In 1943–44 the propaganda minister Goebbels had 187,000 soldiers serve as extras in a film about the 1813 war against Napoleon. Released just four months before Hitler's suicide it was said fewer people saw it than acted in it![26]

German corporations were quick to move into the occupied territories to expand their markets, often buying up foreign competitors at knock-down prices. In a precursor of post-war European integration, coal production was co-ordinated between Germany, France and Belgium. The Third Reich did not exploit the full fruits of the occupied economies. The engineering industry of occupied Belgium produced two thirds of its pre-war output, falling to half for its iron and steel industry.[27] The occupying authorities were more interested in looting what they could and in milking money through rigged exchange rates. The occupied countries were also important for agricultural production, by 1943–44 supplying 22 per cent of German grain consumption, 28 per cent of fats, and 29 per cent of meat. But the savagery of the Nazi occupation in Poland and Czechoslovakia caused output to fall. The occupied countries paid for 40 per cent of the Nazi war costs in 1943–44.[28]

In the Balkans the primary German concern was to keep communications open and to allow Romanian oil to flow westwards. But mass resistance meant a vicious war of counterinsurgency accompanied by retributions against civilians. The Ustashi regime in Croatia and its counterpart in Slovenia needed no urging from Berlin to begin the mass murder of their Jewish populations. In Greece occupation would mean starvation; 360,000 people out of a population of 7.2 million died of hunger.

Speer was a notoriously unreliable and self-serving witness but he was surely right when he pointed out that:

> It remains one of the astounding experiences of the war that Hitler wished to spare his own people those burdens which Churchill and Roosevelt imposed on their peoples without second thoughts. The discrepancy between the total mobilisation of the labour force in democratic England and the sluggish treatment of this question in authoritarian Germany serves to characterise the regime's fear of a change in the people's loyalties ... Hitler and the majority of his political followers belonged to the generation which in November 1918 had experienced the revolution as soldiers, and they never got over it. Hitler often made it clear in private conversation that one could not be careful enough after the experience of 1918.[29]

What escapes Speer is that in Britain and the United States the working class, believing this to be a war against fascism, were prepared, mostly, to rally behind the war effort. In Russia it was seen as a war of national defence and, despite Stalin's dictatorship and the immense hardships, the regime could win a response from its workforce.

Tooze argues that in the medium term Germany was doomed to defeat by greater US industrial power, but this borders on economic reductionism. If Hitler had succeeded in toppling Stalin's regime, which was a possibility in 1941, or establishing a frontier in the far east with a rump Soviet state in either 1941 or 1942, it would have freed Germany to strike at Britain while its Japanese ally kept the Americans held down in the East. In 1942 the US was not yet ready to launch full-scale military operations and would, in the longer run, depend on Britain as their forward base in Europe. German success in the East could have allowed Hitler to break British resistance, if not by direct invasion then by forcing Churchill out and allowing a peace party to emerge.

All of this is of course speculation. Russian resistance would probably have continued even if only from east of the Urals. The point is that politics and war cannot simply be reduced to economics. Politics and events on the field of battle play a major part in the outcome of war. Churchill survived the spring and early summer of 1940 after the defeat in France, but it was not pre-ordained that he would triumph. If, for instance, Mussolini had concentrated his forces on taking Malta and then attacking Egypt before the British military build-up there, rather than dispersing his limited resources, he could have inflicted a serious defeat on Britain, forcing Churchill out. It is another 'if', but the point is that while Italy could not match Britain economically, by concentrating on one front it could have secured a key victory.

Nazi ideology meant that the Third Reich was not able to utilise Ukrainian and other nationalist sentiments against the Russians because these people were regarded as equally 'sub-human'. A combination of racism and the simple desire to pillage meant the Third Reich was unable to create a pan-European economy. The deep divisions between the component parts of the Nazi state – encouraged by Hitler – meant they were in competition, to the detriment of the war effort.[30]

In the end Hitler's Germany was primarily defeated by a country whose economic and military capacity should have been inferior to it, Stalin's Russia. One figure stands out: 'the Russians produced over 100,000 tanks and SUs (self-propelled artillery) from 1941 to 1945. The Germans produced only 42,000 tanks, assault guns and self-propelled tank destroyers from 1939 to 1945.'[31] Churchill's coalition government was relatively successful in mobilising the British population behind the war effort. Churchill left the direction of the home front to Labour politicians and Tories such as Butler, who was prepared to move away from free market policies and countenance greater state involvement in welfare and the economy. By 1941 all the major parties were agreed on the need for some form of welfare state and state measures to provide homes and jobs.[32]

Blockbuster films such as *Mrs Miniver*, *The Life and Times of Colonel Blimp* and Laurence Olivier's *Henry V*, pioneering radio comedies such as 'ITMA'

(Its that Man Again) and broadcasts by J.B. Priestley all helped rally support for the war effort.[33] Certain other policies directly benefited the population: Mass immunisation drastically cut mortality rates, particularly for children, and the state began providing free medical care and access to hospitals. People's health increased as rationing improved the daily diet for the majority of the population, while school meals were provided along with subsidised milk, vitamins, orange juice and cod liver oil.[34]

For the better-off rationing meant restrictions, though some were able to avoid these. The royal family's French chef, Rene Roussin, recalled what the two princesses, Elizabeth and Margaret enjoyed: 'A typical day's menu for them began with buttered eggs for breakfast; boiled chicken with sieved vegetables ... potato crisps, and hot baked custard for lunch; bread and butter, cake, jelly, and toast for tea; and just some kind of broth followed by compote of pear with whipped cream for supper.'[35] The king ordered six rashers of bacon and two eggs for breakfast each morning and grouse when in season each evening.

Jewish refugees had found it hard to enter Britain before the outbreak of the war. After Dunkirk, refugees from Germany and Austria were interned and shipped off to Canada and Australia. One Jewish refugee from Germany recalled, 'Churchill had the right kind of instincts "we've got to do something" and, like in Germany, you immediately turn on the Jews.'[36] In June 1940 together with his father (who had been held in Buchenwald) and his brother, he was taken by detectives from the family home in London to a detention camp in a Liverpool stadium. He and his brothers were shipped off to Australia – despite the fact the Australian government had refused to accept such refugees. They were eventually allowed into Australia after the government in Canberra insisted they had to be treated as prisoners of war. Meanwhile another ship carrying mainly German and Italian internees, the *Andorra Star*, had been torpedoed by a German submarine with just 586 detainees survivors out of 1,216 on board.

The leader of the British Union of Fascists, Sir Oswald Mosley, was released from (very free and easy) detention in November 1943, after his relations lobbied establishment figures. By the following year fascist groups had begun to operate again as Mosley prepared to relaunch the BUF in the form of the Union Movement. There was no official attempt to block any of this. One anti-fascist Jew wrote of 'going from a cinema showing newsreels of piles of Jewish men, women and children being bulldozed into lime pits in the concentration camps, and then passing an outdoor fascist meeting or seeing swastikas whitewashed on Jewish homes and synagogues'.[37]

Britain experienced a radicalisation during the Second World War, which was reflected in the growth of unofficial and illegal strikes, support for the Communist Party (which secured two MPs in 1945) and the radical Commonwealth Party, which enjoyed brief success in wartime by contesting by-elections where Labour, the Tories and the Liberals agreed to support the candidate of the party which previously held the seat.

Yet the biggest beneficiary would be the Labour Party, which established itself as the natural successor to the wartime coalition.

The End of Mussolini's War

Following Germany's defeat in the East, Anglo-American armies were set to enter continental Europe. The obvious target was Italy, because of the military build up in North Africa. Mussolini's regime was facing its final test. Food shortages were common and prices were rising rapidly. The official food ration gave Italian civilians a calorie intake similar to that in German-occupied Poland.[38] By January 1943 the ration card of a worker in the Biella wool industry was an inadequate 1,000 calories a day. There was an anti-regime mood among the Italian people even as Allied bombs fell on their cities, as the historian Tobias Abse points out:

> In Italy the bulk of the anger aroused by the bombing was not directed, as the Fascist authorities had hoped, against the British and the Americans ... it was aimed against the Fascist regime and its alliance with Nazi Germany, a phenomenon that is virtually incomprehensible unless we presume the persistence of the *tradizione sovversiva* [subervisive tradition] amongst significant groups within the working class.[39]

In 1921 and 1922 Italian workers, ill-served though they were by their leaders, had put up far greater resistance to Mussolini's takeover than their German brothers and sisters did a decade later. That meant that although they had been defeated Italian workers could retain a pride that they had fought and maintain the 'subversive tradition' which resurfaced as Mussolini's regime began to crumble. Italy was to experience something unique – a mass strike in a fascist state which led to the collapse of the regime. Abse points to the factors that led to the mass strike of March 1943:

> Food shortages, bombing and the military defeats in North Africa do not provide sufficient explanation for the emergence of working class militancy on this scale. The causes lay not just in the material conditions of 1943 but in the failure of Italian Fascism over two decades to win the lasting allegiance of a stubbornly recalcitrant working class.[40]

Such brazen defiance by the working class meant the dictatorship was paralysed by it and unable to suppress it.

On 19 July 1943 Allied forces landed in Sicily. Mussolini's dispersal of Italian forces all over Europe, with 1 million Italian troops elsewhere (over half a million in the Balkans and Greece, over 200,000 in Russia and 200,000 in France), meant the regime was woefully ill-prepared. But the Allied invasion of Sicily faced stiff German resistance. The Germans were able to beat a fighting retreat, helped by the Allies' failure to control the Straits of Messina, allowing the Wehrmacht an escape route to the Italian mainland. The Italian forces, however, began to disintegrate.[41] Mussolini failed to secure a de facto vote of confidence in the Fascist Grand Council and the king dismissed him on 25 July. As he left the palace he was arrested and bundled into an ambulance to be driven off into detention. The king appointed as premier the aged Marshal Badoglio, an architect of Mussolini's attack on Ethiopia, and began manoeuvring between the Allies and Germany to remove Italy from the war – and above all to preserve the monarchy. The new Italian administration carried out a series of uncoordinated negotiations with the Allies and pleaded for Allied troops to be sent to defend Rome. Even when they signed an armistice with the Allies, Badoglio and the king wanted it to be kept secret to avoid antagonising the Germans. Eventually Eisenhower ordered news of the armistice to be broadcast on Allied radio stations.[42]

German troops immediately flooded south over the Alps, securing Milan, Turin and Genoa and advancing on Rome. The king and Badoglio fled south to British-occupied territory, denuding the capital of troops needed for its defence in order to protect their escape route and failing to issue orders for Italian troops to resist the Germans. In Italy, Yugoslavia and Greece, Italian troops were in the main simply disarmed by the Germans and sent back to the Third Reich. But in some cases they fought back, as on the Greek island of Cephalonia where 5,000 men of the Acqui Division joined the local resistance in fighting the Germans. When they eventually surrendered they were massacred. In Rome troops and civilians defied the odds to battle German troops entering the city, but to no avail. The Italian resistance had, however, begun.[43]

Meanwhile British troops had crossed from Sicily into Calabria and landed at Taranto, beginning a painstaking advance up both sides of the peninsula. One of the ex-fascist commanders negotiating an armistice with the Allies had warned them, 'To possess Italy one must seize her boldly by the neck, not advance inch by inch up the leg.' This sound advice went unheeded.[44] The Allies landed at Salerno, south of Naples, ruling out a landing further north as being beyond the range of their air cover. The Germans were prepared and inflicted heavy damage from the hills around the beach-head. The Allies advanced north only once the great city of Naples had been liberated by a popular insurrection provoked by German repression.

After this Allied forces also landed, unopposed, at Anzio, south of Rome, but they did not follow this up with an advance on the city. This allowed German forces to contain the landing and almost drive the Allies back into the sea. The German line was eventually breached after a costly battle for the mountain town and abbey on Monte Cassino. Rome would eventually fall the day before the D-Day landings in Normandy in June 1944. By then hopes of quick success in Italy had long since faded.[45]

Italy was now divided into a German occupied zone, formally run by Mussolini after he was rescued from detention by German paratroops; an Anglo-American occupied zone; and, eventually, a small area in the south administered by the Italians. The Germans had annexed territories in the Alps and in the north-east and dispatched tens of thousands of Italian soldiers back to Germany as forced labour, with some being sent to fight with Mussolini's forces. In northern and central Italy assorted fascist units nominally loyal to Mussolini fought a brutal counterinsurgency against the growing resistance. In Venice it was the Italian fascists, not the Germans, who rounded up the ancient Jewish community. At

Risiera di San Sabba near Trieste the Germans built a death camp, the only one in Western Europe with a crematorium.[46] A veteran Communist, Rossana Rossanda, recalled:

> By the autumn of 1943 the deportations were no longer disguised as 'work in Germany'. Lorries packed with deportees were driven away in the middle of the night ... We saw the hanged in the public squares: their twisted necks, their elongated limbs ... the dead still bore the traces of what they had gone through, like the pile of bodies stacked, spread-eagled, their mouths and eyes wide open, in Milan's central square. The German and Italian forces kept them there all through a sweltering August day.[47]

The Americans became discontented with the whole strategy of advancing up the Italian peninsula, insisting seven of the best Allied divisions be moved from the Mediterranean back to England to prepare for the following year's invasion of France. The British-led campaign continued until the end of the war, at which point they were still far from entering the great northern plain or reaching the industrial triangle of Milan-Turin-Genoa. These would be liberated by Italian Resistance forces.

The Allied invasion of Italy had one other important ramification. Russia was barred from participating in the armistice negotiations and in the Allied administration which emerged. Stalin was to cite this every time Washington or London complained about his behaviour in Eastern Europe.

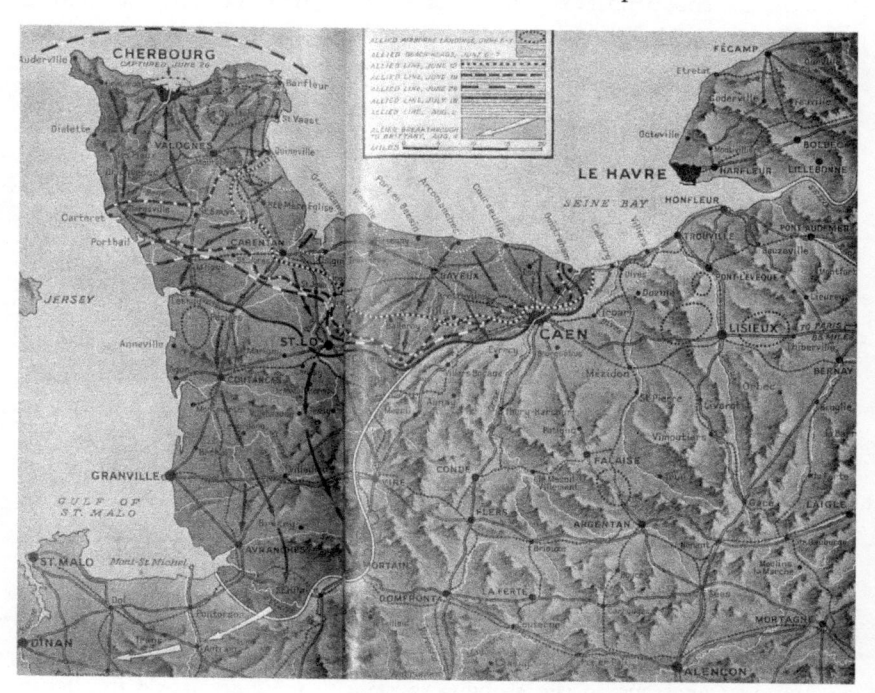

Normandy bridgehead, July 1944

The Invasion of North-Western Europe

By the spring of 1944 southern Britain was a vast concentration point for the Allied invasion of France. The US was determined to secure a military presence in Western Europe. From June 1941, as we have seen, the Americans were working on the basis that they would have to bring the Wehrmacht to battle in Western Europe. Despite their mutual distrust, Washington and Moscow shared one aim, to insist, over British objections, that a cross-channel invasion of Europe must be the absolute priority of the Western allies.

The British relied on the US, as Clive Ponting stresses: 'By the autumn of 1943 the United States supplied 77 per cent of Britain's escort vessels, 88 per cent of its landing craft, 68 per cent of its light bombers, virtually all of its transport aircraft and self-propelled artillery, 60 per cent of its tanks and 100 per cent of its heavy tank transporters and 10 ton trucks.' By 1944 Britain was dependent on the US for 28 per cent of its munitions, with Canada supplying another 9 per cent. The one thing Britain produced itself was its heavy bombers.[48]

In November 1942, the private secretary to Britain's foreign secretary, Anthony Eden, noted that, 'The Chiefs of Staff ... wish to do nothing till 1944 except carry out a few raids and give arms to Russia to carry on the fight. The Russian Army having played the allotted role of killing Germans, our Chiefs of Staff think by 1944 they could stage an onslaught on the exhausted animal.'[49] It was an attitude picked up by the US secretary of state for war, Henry Stimson, who, after a visit to London in July 1943 to assess opinion on a cross-channel invasion, reported back to Roosevelt:

> Though they have rendered lip service to the operation, their hearts are not in it ... the British theory (which cropped out [sic] again and again in unguarded sentences...) is that Germany can be beaten in a series of attritions in northern Italy, in the eastern Mediterranean, in Greece, in the Balkans, in Romania and other satellite countries, and that the only fighting which needs to be done will be done by Russia.[50]

He told Roosevelt that, 'the time has come for you to decide that your government must assume the responsibility of leadership in the great final movement of the European war'. The US Chiefs of Staff accordingly determined 'the allocation of additional forces in the Mediterranean is uneconomical and assists Germany to create a strategic stalemate in Europe'. They concluded Britain's favoured strategy would 'imperil the final victory'.[51]

In 1942 and 1943 Churchill still had sufficient weight to block American efforts to mount a cross-channel invasion, seeing off Operation Sledgehammer in 1942 and then Operation Round Up in 1943. But in May 1943 at a conference in Washington, Anglo-American planners put a date for exactly 12 months hence for a cross-channel invasion. Three months later, at a conference in Quebec, the US insisted that in addition to a landing in north-western France they would unleash a simultaneous invasion of southern France, transferring their forces from Italy to carry it out. The British were greatly dismayed. Churchill's stress on the centrality of the Mediterranean made sense in terms of narrow British interests, as historian Robert Holland points out:

> By 1943 Churchill appreciated that whoever might end up winning the war in Europe, it could not possibly be the United Kingdom. In the Continental heartland the British could never be more than subordinate to people more powerful than they were. Along the southern littoral it was different; there Britain could assert herself as a genuine principal ... where Britain might aspire to go on fighting a war on its own terms and in its own national interests.[52]

In other words, the British on their own could beat the Italians but not the Germans!

On 11 November 1943 the British Chief of Staff could still argue regarding Overlord (the code name for the cross-channel invasion) that, 'We do not, however, attach vital importance to any particular date or to any particular number of divisions in the assault and follow up.'[53] A memorandum prepared for the US Chiefs of Staff office argued with justification:

> It is apparent that the British, who have consistently resisted a cross-Channel operation, now feel OVERLORD is no longer necessary. In their view, continued Mediterranean operations, coupled with POINTBLANK [the bomber offensive against Germany] and the crushing Russian offensive, will be sufficient to cause the internal collapse of Germany and thus bring about her military defeat without undergoing what they consider an almost certain 'bloodbath'. The conclusion that the forces being built up in the United Kingdom will never be used for a military offensive against western Europe, but are intended as a gigantic deception plan and an occupying force [for when Germany collapsed] is inescapable.[54]

The Americans were very aware that the Russian advance in the east could mean that the Red Army would be well inside Germany if an invasion was delayed until 1945.

At the first three-power summit of the allies, held in Tehran later that month, Marshal Voroshilov turned on the British Chief of Imperial Staff, Sir Alan Brooke, demanding to know whether he regarded plans for an invasion of France to be the most important operation, as the United States did. Brooke had to answer 'yes'. Meanwhile Stalin was demanding of Churchill, 'Do the British really believe in "Overlord" or are they only saying so to reassure the Soviet Union?' Roosevelt remained silent until Churchill assented to the invasion of France.[55]

Six weeks before D-Day Churchill told the head of the Foreign Office, 'this battle has been forced upon us by the Russian and United States military authorities'.[56] Even 24 hours before the 6 June 1944 landings in Normandy, Brooke wrote, 'I am very uneasy about the whole operation ... At the best it will come very far short of the expectations of the bulk of the people, namely all those who know nothing about its difficulties.'[57] Brooke ventured that the invasion would be, 'the most ghastly disaster of the whole war'.[58]

Churchill and his military commanders were haunted by the fear of infantry casualties on the scale of the First World War. They were aware that in May 1944 British-led forces would reach the limit of their growth, 2.75 million men, and from then on could only fall in number. In contrast US forces stood at 5.75 million and were expanding still. On top of this, 'British production of ammunition had been falling since late 1942, of vehicles since mid 1943, of artillery and small arms since late 1943.'[59]

Other problems faced the overall Allied commander, General Dwight D. Eisenhower. Both the British and US air force commanders resisted prioritising air cover for the invasion over the bombing campaign against Germany and had to be forced into line. Tactically too the Allies lagged behind their enemy, who deployed infiltration tactics after D-Day and had perfected co-operation between armoured forces and the infantry.[60] British field commanders were lacking in tactical flair, and the rigid structure of the British army meant that NCOs did not seize the initiative if officers were killed or missing.

A German report from Italy in the summer of 1944 identified the problem:

The conduct of the battle by the Americans and English was, taken all round, once again very methodical. Local successes were seldom exploited ... British attacking formations were split up into large numbers of assault squads commanded by officers. NCOs were rarely in on the 'big picture', so that if the officers became a casualty, they were unable to act in accordance with the main plan. The result was that in a quickly changing situation, the junior commanders showed insufficient flexibility. For instance, when an objective was reached, the enemy would neglect to exploit it and dig in for defence. The conclusion is: as far as possible, *go for the enemy officers*. Then seize the initiative yourself.[61]

However, the German forces facing the Allied invasion were outnumbered and faced overwhelming firepower and airpower:

The Anglo-American invasion forces had overwhelming advantage as Overlord went into action: total superiority at sea, 12,800 aircraft against 500 and a 5:1 superiority in tanks. They were fighting less than a third of the available German combat units and most of these were in a poor state. The eight Panzer divisions committed to the battle in Normandy had just 17 replacement tanks between them and infantry and static units were even weaker.[62]

There were just 18 German divisions in Normandy. Another 19 were based in the Pas de Calais where the German high command believed a landing would take place, and 17 south of the Loire.[63]

On 6 June 1944 Allied forces made landings on five beach-heads on the stretch of the Normandy coast stretching from the Cotentin Peninsula (which sticks out into the English channel with the port of Cherbourg at its head) to the mouth of the River Seine. The landings took place in strict secrecy with the Germans unaware of what was happening until it was upon them. The invaders had superiority in numbers and control of the air. Hitler had ordered a concentration of German forces in the Pas de Calais region, just 22 miles across the Straits of Dover from England, believing that would be where the invasion would land. Even after news of the Normandy landings he kept insisting this was a diversion and the main thrust would come further north.

The US forces suffered heavy casualties at one of the beaches, codenamed Utah, but despite this secured the landing area. Elsewhere British, US and Canadian forces pushed inland. Yet despite being outnumbered and surprised, the German forces in Normandy were able to throw the invasion timetable into crisis and to cast a shadow over the reputation of Britain's Field Marshal Montgomery, who failed to break out of the eastern sector. In July 1944 a US staff officer noted the views of the American liaison officer posted to work alongside Montgomery's Chief of Staff:

> Monty, his British commander Dempsey, the British corps commanders and even those of the divisions are so conscious of Britain's ebbing manpower that they hesitate to commit an attack where a division may be lost. When it's lost, it's done and finished ... The Commanders feel the blood of the British Empire, and hence its future, are too precious for dash in battle.[64]

The British had determined artillery would play a key role and 18 per cent of their troops in the Normandy bridgehead were gunners. Even so this could not prevent shortages of infantry building up as casualties mounted and there were simply no further replacements from Britain or Canada.[65] By 11 June the Allies had established a bridgehead 50 miles wide and 12 miles deep into which they poured over 326,547 men, 54,000 vehicles and 104,000 tons of supplies. The plan hinged on Montgomery's force taking Caen in the first days of the invasion and then driving towards Paris. In fact Caen did not fall until 8 August. The invasion force found itself caught for two months in a narrow bridgehead, fighting an attrition battle.[66]

Ten days after the landings in Normandy the German commander in France, von Rundstedt, urged Hitler to withdraw German troops from south of the Loire in order to concentrate everything on preventing the Allies expanding their bridgehead. The request was refused. Major fighting formations were held back to deal with Resistance forces in areas of little strategic importance to the war. On 1 August the American general Patton broke German lines by advancing south into Brittany and then east towards the Seine. He then advanced north trapping the German forces in Normandy into a pocket round Falaise. Hitler had ordered them to stand and fight, but flight towards the Seine became the only option. Allied forces failed to plug all the escape routes but German resistance in France was effectively ended.

Patton employed the air force to protect his flanks against possible German counter-attack and he bypassed defended towns and cities. The plan was to avoid Paris and to advance to the German border, but a Resistance uprising in the city led to a change. Free French forces, fighting with the Allies under the nominal command of General Charles de Gaulle – a junior member of the French government who had fled to London in June 1940 in order to continue resistance to the Germans – were hurriedly dispatched to secure the French capital. In their wake came de Gaulle, who loftily dismissed the Resistance fighters who had effectively liberated Paris. De Gaulle was a Catholic who had a reputation as a man of the right.[67]

Meanwhile Patton reached Lorraine only to be halted by fuel shortages. Montgomery was now able to advance northwards liberating Brussels and Antwerp, though failure to secure the mouth of the River Scheldt hampered the use of its port and allowed German forces to retreat north into the Netherlands. The advance halted once more.[68] In September 1944 Montgomery pushed through a plan to use airborne troops to secure bridges over two arms of the River Rhine, at Nijmegen and further north at Arnhem. Allied forces would advance rapidly northwards to relieve the airborne forces. It was hoped this plan would achieve a rapid breakthrough to the Ruhr, bypassing the German Siegfried Line. The plan was flawed from the beginning. The advance north would take place on one road and required no delays. Dutch Resistance forces alerted the Allies to the fact that an SS Panzer corps was refitting at Arnhem. In the event the lightly armed airborne troops could not take and hold the bridge there and the advance from the south was unable to relieve them. The Arnhem campaign was a desperate throw of the dice by British commanders acting in an unusually rash way. It must reflect the fact they understood it was a last chance to secure a decisive British success. It's failure ensured their role as junior partners in the alliance.[69]

By winter the Allies were still short of making a decisive advance into the Third Reich. Hitler determined to strike a blow at them by attacking through the Ardennes, as in May 1940, with the aim of taking Antwerp. Twenty-nine divisions totalling 250,000 men, badly needed on the Third Reich's eastern frontier, were amassed at a weak point in the Allied lines and made massive headway towards the Meuse River during one of the worst winters Europe had seen in years, with bad weather preventing the Allies utilising their air superiority. Despite initial success the momentum could not be maintained, air operations resumed and Patton counter-attacked. By February the 'Battle of the Bulge' was over and German forces were preparing to defend the Reich.[70] At the height of the battle, Roosevelt and Churchill begged Stalin to commence a winter offensive in the east. Stalin responded by giving the go ahead for an offensive starting on 11 January which took Warsaw and East Prussia and carried the Red Army to within 100 miles of Berlin. Even if German forces had broken through and re-captured Antwerp it is difficult to see how this would have staved off German defeat. While inflicting a defeat on Anglo-American forces, it would not have removed them from the continent, and meanwhile the Russians were poised to strike at Berlin.

When the British and American forces resumed the offensive in February 1945 they were able to cross the Rhine. Eisenhower admitted that they did not encounter any serious opposition stating, 'The two US divisions that made the assault suffered only 31 casualties.'[71]

The Failure of the Bombing Campaigns

Between the wars the theorists of aerial warfare, the US's Brigadier General William 'Billy' Mitchell, Italy's Giulio Douhet and Britain's Lord Trenchard, 'the father of the RAF', believed strategic bombing would secure final victory in any inter-power conflict. Douhet believed it could break 'the will of the people' and fumed against attempts to use airpower for homeland defence or as tactical support for ground forces, branding such ideas as 'useless, superfluous and harmful'.

British prime minister Stanley Baldwin summed up widespread fears, stating in the House of Commons in 1932 that, 'the bomber would always get through'. He went on to add, 'The only defence is offence, which means that you have to kill more women and children more quickly than the enemy.'[72] Air Marshal Sir Arthur Harris, head of Britain's Bomber Command, was a zealot in support of the 'area bombing' of German towns and cities, constantly predicting the imminent collapse of Germany's morale and war effort.[73]

The RAF developed a dogma that effectively ruled out the possibility of air defence against attacking bomber fleets. It was so obsessed with developing its heavy bomber fleet that the Chamberlain government had to eventually insist on building fighter squads to defend Britain. The head of Fighter Command, Dowling, built a force sufficient to win aerial supremacy in late 1940, helped by radar, which could summon fighters into the air to meet their German opponents with full fuel tanks just as the Luftwaffe planes were forced to return home because theirs were running empty. But Dowling came under constant criticism because his critics in the RAF had wanted a different strategy, with many fighter squadrons in the air ready to meet the Germans in a big battle, and at the moment of victory he was sacked without ceremony.

The German Luftwaffe regarded ground support as being part of its task from its inception. For both the German and Russian air forces the priority was developing close co-operation with ground forces.[74] Britain and the US were alone in building and maintaining heavy, long-range bomber forces. While the 'Blitz' lives on in popular memory, the actual bombing of London and other British cities, while terrible enough, could not compare with what would be visited on Germany as the war drew to a close.

In the two years after Dunkirk an aerial bombing campaign was the only offensive action against Germany Churchill could deliver. Since the fall of France, the RAF had been bombing German cities. Yet an inquiry in the summer of 1941 found that only one aircraft in three got to within five miles of the target; over the Ruhr the figure was just one in ten, falling to one in 15 on foggy or moonless nights. Altogether just 20 per cent of RAF bombers dropped bombs within a 75 square mile area round their designated target.[75] The first RAF bombing attacks in the late spring and summer of 1940 were so off-target the

Germans had difficulty working out what the supposed targets were. Originally the British had believed precision bombing could wreck Germany's oil capacity and transport routes. They quickly discovered that daytime bombing was too costly and night-time bombing was imprecise. In the course of 1941 they moved to blanket bombing of German cities.

In July and August 1943 RAF mass bombing raids targeted the port city of Hamburg. High explosives and incendiaries created a firestorm of 1,000°C with winds blowing at 150 mph, killing 50,000 civilians and leading to a mass evacuation of the city.[76] The US air force took up and developed this campaign of blanket bombing of enemy cities. Up until 1944 the advantage lay

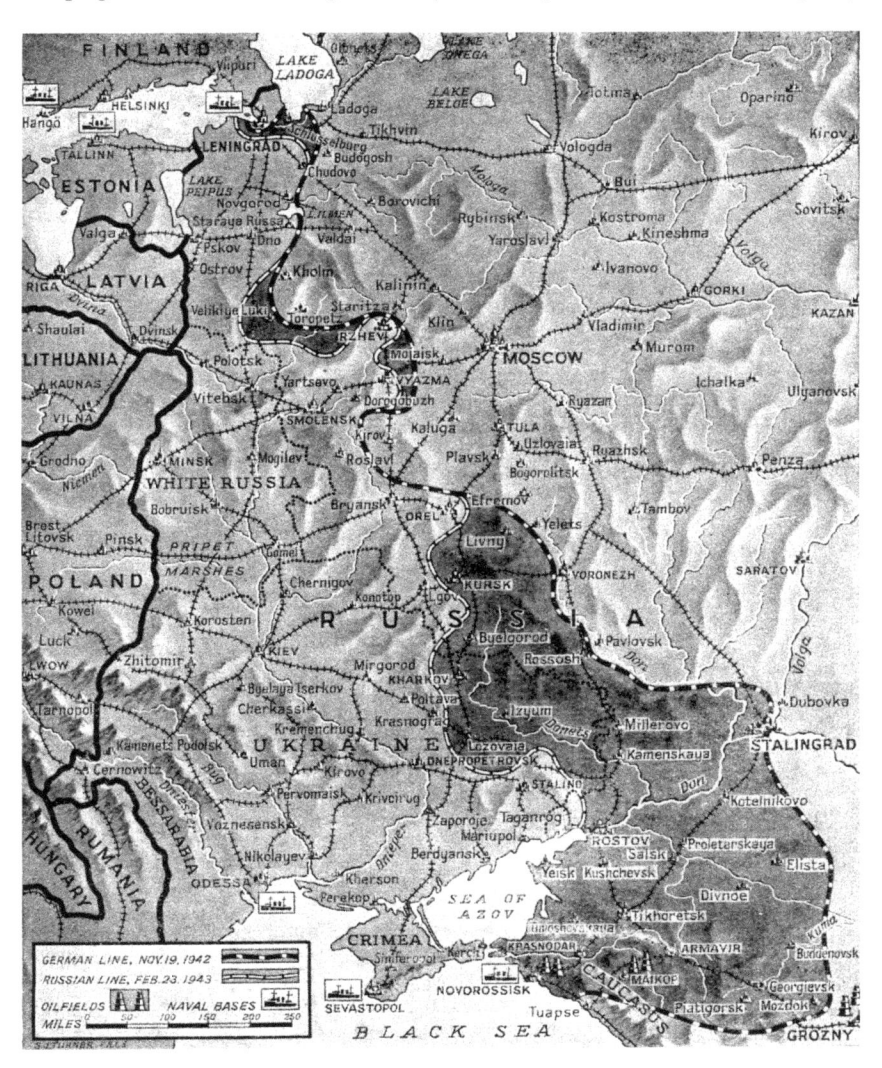

Eastern Front showing furthest extent of German push by November 1942 and position of retreat by February 1943

with the German air defences. The Americans' introduction of long-distance fighter planes, particularly the Mustang P-51, at the beginning of 1944 gave the Allies control of the skies above the Reich and allowed daytime bombing. This changed the nature of the campaign and, finally, meant it was effective in paralysing German industry. Between June and October 1944 the RAF and USAAF dropped half a million tons of bombs on Germany, more than they had delivered in total up to the beginning of the offensive. Over the next six months they dropped a further 545,000 tons.[77]

The autumn of 1944 saw the destruction of bridges and railways leading to the cutting off of the Ruhr from the rest of the country. The resulting coal shortages

Russian winter advance to 26 January 1945

closed down key factories. On 13 February 1945 an RAF attack on Dresden caused a firestorm. It was followed by a USAAF daylight raid. Some 40,000 people died. This single attack killed more than the total of 30,705 people who died in German attacks on Britain. Dresden was of little strategic importance, nor was it an industrial centre, and its destruction had no effect on the outcome of the war.

In total Allied raids on Germany left 500,000 civilians dead, 800,000 injured and 7.5 million homes destroyed. The weight of bombs dropped by the Luftwaffe on Britain was 3 per cent of what would fall on Germany.[78] The highest number of bombs dropped came in March 1945, by which time the outcome of the war

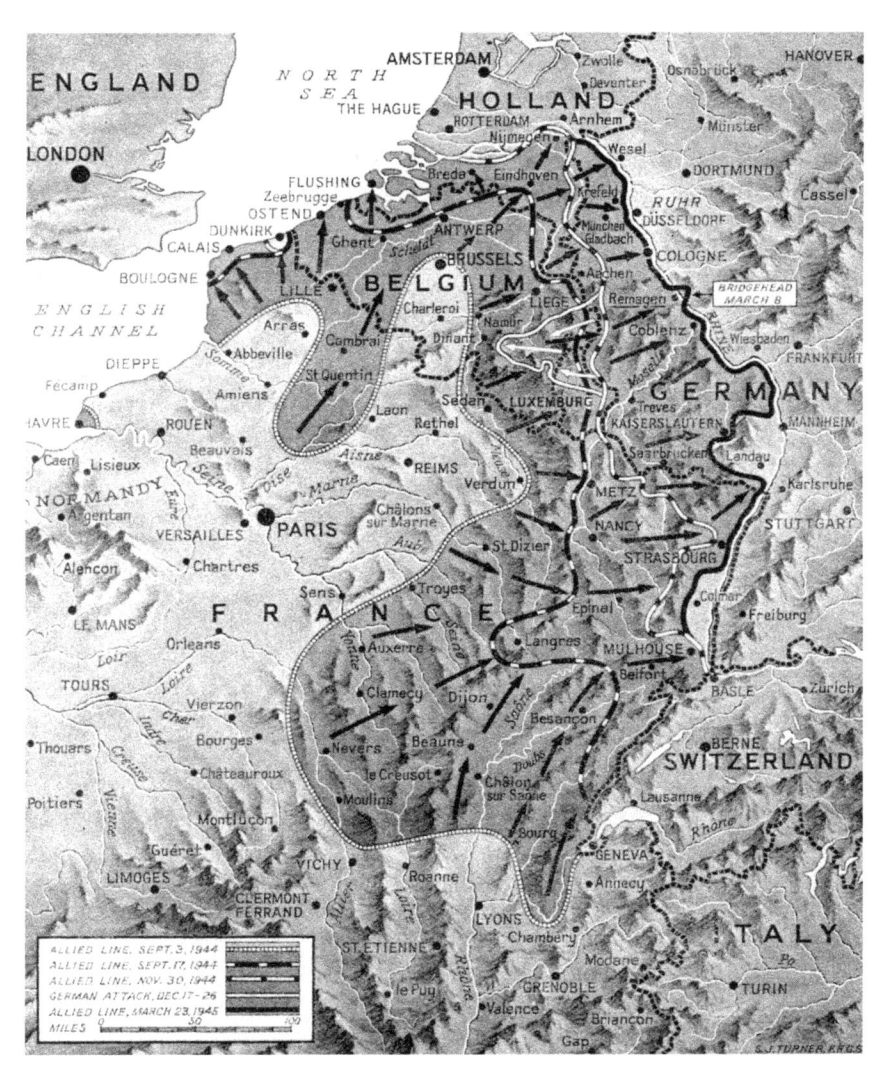

Allies on the Rhine to 23 March 1945

was certain and the German war industry was already effectively destroyed. The final attack was on Potsdam on 14 and 15 April 1945, killing 3,500 people.[79] In total the RAF lost more than 8,000 bombers in its campaign against Germany, with over 55,000 aircrew dying – more than the Luftwaffe's total wartime loss. The greatest single loss came on the 30–31 March 1944 attack on Nuremberg in which 94 aircraft were shot down. More than 800 RAF crew were killed, greater than the number killed in the Battle of Britain. In percentage terms these losses compare with those of the Flemish and Picardy trenches three decades earlier.[80]

The Destruction of the Third Reich

In the summer of 1944 Stalin and his top commanders – Zhukov, Vasilevsky, and the latter's deputy, Antonov – planned five staggered offensives from the front with Finland down to a drive on Romania. These would carry the war into the heart of Nazi-occupied Eastern Europe. The biggest effort was on the Belorussian front, Operation Bagration (named by Stalin after a tsarist military commander who faced the Napoleonic invasion in 1812). The Red Army could deploy a force greater than that with which the Germans had invaded Russia back in June 1941. The offensive began on the third anniversary of that invasion. The Russians had superiority in terms of tanks, self-propelled guns, artillery, mortars and rockets, aircraft and trucks with which to carry the infantry (many of these were supplied by the United States).

In just one week the 200-mile-long German frontline was broken. The Wehrmacht was driven back beyond the 1941 border, with the bulk of it retreating into East Prussia and the other segment being bottled up in the Baltic states.[81] Thirty German divisions were shattered, with 350,000 men lost. On 17 July, 57,000 German prisoners were marched through Moscow with generals at their head. Crowds watched in silence.[82] The Russians advanced 300 kilometres until their supply lines were too extended to permit further progress.

The Germans had no reserves in the Balkans, with all available forces consumed in combat with Yugoslav partisans. In September 1944 they lost control of the Romanian oilfields. The arrival of the Red Army on Romanian soil led to a coup in Bucharest. In August the new government switched sides, and its troops came under Red Army control. The treaty with Romania was signed by all three Allied powers but Russia had control of the country. Bessarabia and northern Bukovina were handed over to the USSR, while Transylvania was removed from Hungary and put back under Romanian control.

In Bulgaria the Communist-led Fatherland Front carried out a coup and suspended all military operations against the Red Army. Advancing Russian forces were welcomed as they crossed the frontier. In both countries the Communists were now part of a coalition government, but worked to ensure their supporters took key positions within the state security forces.[83] By the end of 1944 the Red Army was inside the Third Reich and with Berlin in its sights. Russian forces liberated the first death camp, Majdanek in Poland, in July. More than a million people had died there. It was the first of a series of terrible discoveries, with the horrors of Treblinka, Sobibor, Auschwitz-Birkenau, Belzec and Stutthof lying ahead of the Red Army.[84]

Meanwhile within the USSR the propaganda switched from a patriotic emphasis to a reassertion of the Communist Party's central role. The centrality of collectivisation was emphasised, scotching hopes that the state-run farms would be broken down into private holdings. More and more Soviet citizens were sucked into the labour force, which reached 23 million in 1944 (10 million in industry and construction). Women formed 50 per cent of the workforce. Coal, petrol, machine tools and cement were all in short supply. Despite that, 1944 saw 29,000 tanks and self-propelled guns produced (up 5,000 on the previous year), 40,000 aircraft, 123,000 guns and 184 million shells.[85]

The Germans had belatedly switched to a full-scale war economy, with production for war finally prioritised over the needs of the population. But although they could produce tanks, artillery and other equipment, they could not sustain the losses they suffered on the Eastern Front. An estimated 485,000 soldiers were killed or captured during that summer's offensive in the east. There was a severe manpower shortage. Tank production peaked in September 1944 but the new armour was used in abortive offensives in the Ardennes in the west and in Hungary in the east. The latter was at Hitler's insistence to protect the Reich's remaining oilfields, but it represented a diversion from the main Russian thrust which threatened the industrial region of Silesia and thence Berlin. Fuel shortages were now halting operations.[86]

The Red Army made huge gains throughout 1944, far greater than their expectations. The Wehrmacht was seriously damaged. Out of the total German units knocked out during the years 1941–44, more than half (65 per cent) were eliminated in the course of 1944.[87] In October 1944 the Soviet General Staff began planning the final assault on Berlin – 'the greatest campaign in military history'.[88] To the west the Allies had 87 units with over 6,000 tanks facing 74 German units deploying 1,600 tanks. Some 3 million Allied soldiers had landed in France and Belgium since D-Day. On the Eastern Front 6.5 million Red Army soldiers and 13,000 tanks faced 3 million Germans and 6,000 tanks. The eventual defeat of the German offensive in the Ardennes resulted in their switching the bulk of their forces to the defence of the Reich in the east. The Anglo-American armies had scheduled an attack across the Rhine for March 1945, but when the operation began there were just 26 German divisions left in western Germany, the bulk of these holding the ports in the north to allow an evacuation from the east. In contrast the Red Army faced 170 divisions. The British and Americans were able to cross the Rhine and begin a rapid advance eastwards as resistance disintegrated.[89]

Hitler had determined to take Germany down with him in flames. After the failure of the Ardennes offensive he told his aide, 'We'll not capitulate. Never. We can go down. But we'll take the world with us.'[90] The Nazi terror used in the occupied territories now came home. Anyone uttering defeatist talk or believed to be retreating in the face of the enemy was subject to instant execution. Corpses hung from lamp posts in German towns and cities under attack. As Berlin came under attack the SS carried out summary executions against members of the Volkssturm ('People's Storm', the German equivalent of the Home Guard), the Hitler Youth and regular forces who they believed were trying to desert their positions. School children were among those hanged.[91]

The Russian attack on Berlin centred on the highway from Warsaw to the German capital. The Russians concentrated 7,500 combat planes. The Red Army amassed 2.5 million troops for the attack on Berlin, others were engaged in operations elsewhere, including taking Czechoslovakia and Vienna. For the Berlin operation the Russians deployed over 4,200 guns and mortars, 6,200 tanks and self-propelled guns and more than 1,000 rocket launchers. Facing them at the outset of the battle were around 1 million defenders with 10,000 guns and mortars, 1,500 tanks and self-propelled guns and 3,300 combat aircraft.[92]

Stalin now permitted two of his marshals, Zhukov and Konev, to advance on Berlin, playing on their rivalry. Zhukov was placed in command of the central thrust on Berlin. He massed over 7 million shells designed to 'stun and shake' German troops. Searchlights were used to blind the defenders. A Soviet war correspondent recorded the beginning of the assault on the city on 22 April:

> On the walls of the houses we saw Goebbels's appeals, hurriedly scrawled in white paint: 'Every German will defend his capital. We shall stop the Red hordes at the walls of our Berlin.' Just try and stop them! Steel pillboxes, barricades, mines, traps, suicide squads with grenades clutched in their hands – all are swept aside before the tidal wave. Drizzling rain began to fall. Near Bisdorf I saw batteries preparing to open fire. 'What are the targets?' I asked the battery commander. 'Centre of Berlin, Spree bridges, and the northern and Stettin railway stations,' he answered. Then came the tremendous words of command: 'Open fire at the capital of Fascist Germany.' I noted the time. It was exactly 8:30 am on 22 April. Ninety-six shells fell in the centre of Berlin in the course of a few minutes.[93]

A day later the Red Army had cut off Berlin from any possibility of a German counter-attack from the west and its troops had begun to break through the defence line formed round the city's S-Bahn railway. As Zhukov's and Konev's troops battled their way into the German capital it was clear to the defenders that there would be no miracle to deliver Hitler from defeat. The 'wonder' weapons (the V1 and V2 missiles and jet fighters) had come too little and too late. The death of Roosevelt revived hopes that the 'un-natural alliance' between the 'Anglo-Saxons' and the Russians would fall apart, but they were soon dashed. Hitler believed his people had failed him and deserved the retribution that was to be visited on them.

As defeat neared the Nazi regime fell apart. The unfulfilled hopes of self-aggrandisement fuelled by constant factional struggles at every level of the party and the state meant that, one after another, virtually all the leaders of the regime, with the exceptions of Goebbels and Bormann, deserted the Führer in the final days before his suicide.

Further south, in Italy, justice awaited another fascist dictator. Allied forces had renewed their offensive into the Po Valley on 5 April. Beginning in

Ravenna and Bologna and spreading across northern Italy, the Resistance rose up to liberate their towns and cities in advance of the Allies' arrival. On 28 April Hitler's brother in arms Mussolini was shot by partisans and his body displayed in Milan. News of this penetrated Hitler's bunker. On 30 April 1945 Hitler shot himself. On 2 May German forces in the capital surrendered.[94]

In the battle for Berlin, Russian dead, wounded and missing topped 300,000. The Red Army paid a high price for the capture of the German capital. The fall of Berlin was a bloody battle. The poet and journalist Ilya Ehrenburg had urged in his manifesto to the Red Army: 'Kill! Kill! None of the Germans are innocent, neither the living nor those yet born! Follow the advice of Comrade Stalin and wipe out the Fascist Beast in his lair forever! Break the proud racial pride of the German women brutally! Take them in just revenge.'[95] Russian forces behaved with great brutality. One Russian commander pointed to the weight of fire the Red Army brought down on Berlin: 'The Allies dropped 65,000 tons of bombs – we fired 40,000 shells in two weeks.'[96] The honour of capturing Berlin went to the Red Army, but at great cost. John Erickson quotes the sardonic comment of one Red Army officer, 'yes we got to Berlin, but did we have to go via Stalingrad?'[97]

Russian casualties in the Second World War were 20 times greater than those of the US and Britain combined. The simple fact is that the war against Nazi Germany was won by Russia. Russian forces inflicted three-quarters of all German casualties. Total German losses were 13,488,000 killed or captured. Of these 10,758,000 were lost or captured on the Eastern Front. The USSR suffered at least 29 million casualties.[98]

The military historian, Richard Overy, concludes, 'Without Soviet resistance it is difficult to see how the democratic world would have defeated the new German empire, except by sitting tight and waiting until atomic weapons had been developed.'[99] This does not excuse Stalin's crimes or his responsibility for the disaster that so nearly befell the USSR in 1941, but it is a fact often denied by revisionist historians. Russia survived Stalingrad to virtually defeat Germany singlehanded, but it was a close-run thing. The Russian ruling class was able to use its state control of industry to simplify production so that until the war's end Russian factories concentrated on basic tank designs, making repairs and replacements easier.[100] Stalin's conduct of the war made victory harder. In 1917–18 the Bolsheviks had encouraged German soldiers on the Eastern Front to rally to the revolution. In 1941–45 all Germans, regardless of class, were classed as enemies and treated as if they were all Nazis.

Russia would emerge from the war as the key military power in Europe. By the Yalta conference American generals knew that in the event of a conflict with the USSR the Soviet armies would reach the shores of the Atlantic. This was also recognised by President Truman, who admitted in May 1945, 'It would be open to the Russians in a very short time to advance if they chose to the waters of the North Sea and the Atlantic.'[101] The Yalta summit brought out the fundamentally imperialist demands of Stalin. At a dinner hosted by Roosevelt the US official Charles Bohlen stressed America's support for the rights of small nations (this was in reference to keeping Poland out of the Russian bloc). Stalin responded, 'in prim but powerful style, making absolute assertion of the rights of the "Big Three" against all the bleating of the small powers that their rights were at risk ... the small must be ruled by the great, the delinquents brought to book'.[102]

At 2.41 a.m. on 7 May 1945 Generals Friedeberg and Jodl signed the surrender of Germany on behalf of Adolf Hitler's designated successor, Admiral Doenitz, at General Eisenhower's headquarters at Reims, northern France. The Americans drew up the surrender document with no reference to either of their allies; no senior British officer or minister was present – Field Marshal Montgomery had to stage his own separate surrender ceremony for the cameras. A relatively junior Russian officer was flown into Reims at the last minute. Stalin refused to accept this; the Red Army was still fighting taking Prague, and another surrender ceremony was staged in Berlin.[103]

Genocide: To the Bitter End

By the autumn of 1943 one and a half million Polish Jews had been slaughtered. The SS now pressed for the Final Solution to be extended to all parts of the Nazi empire – from Scandinavia to Italy. In August 1944 Eichmann reported to Hitler that 6 million Jews had been murdered – 4 million in the death camps and the rest in mobile operations.[104] By then two Jewish prisoners had escaped Auschwitz and had been smuggled to London. Jewish organisations pressed for bombing attacks on the rail routes bringing Jews to the camps and on the gas chambers, but the British and Americans claimed the camps were beyond the range of their bombers. That had not been the case in April 1944 when an Allied air attack was carried out on a synthetic fuel plant adjacent to the camp, or in September when American planes accidentally bombed the plant instead of a target further east.[105]

The Jews are often portrayed as passive victims of the Holocaust, but there was serious resistance. In April 1943 just 70,000 Jews remained in the Warsaw Ghetto, 'home' at one time to 380,000. They rose up as it became clear the SS were preparing to wipe them out. The level of resistance by poorly armed fighters shook the SS, who had expected an easy victory. The rebellion lasted three weeks. In the end, of the 58,065 who were rounded up, 7,000 were shot immediately, 22,000 were dispatched to Treblinka and Lublin, and the rest sent to labour camps.[106]

In September 1943 a first batch of 1,750 Red Army prisoners arrived at the Sobibor camp. All but 80 were gassed straight away but the survivors spread the reality of what lay ahead to the Jewish prisoners in the camp. A few weeks later the prisoners rose, killing ten SS guards with axes, knives and their bare hands, allowing 400 prisoners to escape. Some were hunted down, some killed by right-wing Polish bands, but others joined partisan groups and would rejoin the Red Army. Himmler ordered Sobibor to be shut down and all traces of the camp to be destroyed.[107]

Revolts occurred at Auschwitz too. One, carried out by Red Army prisoners, failed in the summer of 1942. Two years later, on 7 October 1944, several hundred prisoners working in Crematorium IV at Auschwitz-Birkenau rebelled after learning that they were going to be killed. During the uprising the prisoners killed three guards and blew up the crematorium and adjacent gas chamber. They used explosives smuggled into the camp by Jewish women who had been assigned to forced labour in a nearby armaments factory. The Germans crushed the revolt and killed almost all of the prisoners involved in the rebellion. The Jewish women who had smuggled the explosives into the camp were publicly hanged in early January 1945.[108]

Hermann Langbein was a member of the Combat Group which led the resistance at Auschwitz. The group was not able to stop the SS evacuating the camp as the Russians neared, forcing the prisoners onto a death march westwards. But, looking back, he was clear that in the most terrible conditions resistance was a necessity:

> When our Combat Group there, which had many failures, was able to influence the destiny of the camp, we knew that we were no longer mere objects in that 'univers concentrationnaire', in the hermetically sealed world created by the SS in which its misanthropic ideology about members of a master race and persons not worthy of living was to achieve an absolute triumph. We knew that we would not allow ourselves to be broken and would knowingly incur additional risks to pass muster before ourselves as active subjects.[109]

In the final two years of the war, as the Red Army advanced westwards, the regime envisioned a tide of retribution sweeping down on the German people. German soldiers knew what had been done in occupied Russia and they feared what the forces of occupation might unleash. In April 1945 a sixteen-year-old on a crowded S-Bahn train in Berlin heard a decorated soldier address terrified passengers thus: 'Silence! ... I've got something to tell you ... Even if you don't want to listen to me, stop whingeing. We have to win this war. If others win the war, and if they do to us only a fraction of what we have done in the occupied territories, there won't be a single German left in a few weeks.'[110]

Even as the end drew near the killings of Jews and others continued. In March, as the city of Danzig (Gdansk) was about to fall, Wehrmacht soldiers together with the SS massacred the prisoners held in the Stutthof concentration camp. Men of the local Volkssturm on the outskirts of Leipzig joined with the SS in herding forced labourers into a building, throwing in incendiary bombs, and gunning down those trying to escape.[111] Three days before the Red Army entered Auschwitz on 27 January 1945, the SS had tried to destroy the evidence of genocide, blowing up the gas chambers and crematoria. The remaining prisoners were forced to march westwards, leaving just 7,000 prisoners to be liberated. Despite the attempts to eradicate the evidence, Red Cross officials found 368,820 men's suits, 836,255 women's coats, 13,964 carpets, and seven tons of hair, plus pile upon pile of shoes, toothbrushes, spectacles and artificial limbs. Mass graves were soon uncovered too.[112] Of the 700,000 prisoners still held in the death camps, a third would die in a series of forced marches as their SS guards beat them westwards away from the Red Army.

War crimes accompany every war, but the Holocaust and the barbarism of Germany's war on the Eastern Front were in a different league. Yet apologists for the Third Reich, and those who wish to claim that Stalinism was more barbaric than Nazism, still trot out the arguments that the Allies committed equal or greater war crimes, or that the Waffen SS and others were defending European civilisation. In the late 1980s German revisionist historians such as Ernst Nolte began to produce apologies for the Third Reich. For Nolte the Holocaust was only one of a series of genocides that took place in the twentieth century. Auschwitz differed only in the use of gas and could be explained as a 'reaction born out of the anxiety of the annihilation occurrences of the Russian Revolution'. The death camps were simply a copy of Stalin's Gulag. Nolte further argued that the Holocaust was a pre-emptive reaction to the onset of 'Asiatic barbarism' represented by the Bolsheviks in their drive to exterminate their 'class enemies', which they threatened to repeat against a vanquished Germany.[113]

Andreas Hillgruber accepted that German troops had committed unspeakable crimes in the East but claimed that in 1944–45 they were defending the 'centuries old settlement area of East Prussia' from the onslaught of Bolshevism, and thus serving the 'national interest'. This argument was then extended to the Holocaust by arguing that the Stalinist regime was responsible for equal if not greater crimes of mass murder.[114]

Another attempt to excuse Hitler is to compare him, favourably, to Stalin. A.D. Harvey points to some differences between the two murderous dictators:

> First Stalin killed a lot of people. He destroyed an entire class – the peasant proprietors – and the upper reaches of several professions, most notably the military ... The scale of his mass murders is exceeded only by Hitler's massacre of the Jews, but while part of the loathsomeness of Hitler's Final Solution is that so many Germans took care not to know what was going on, Stalin's murdering, especially in the later stages aimed at the military, was accompanied by a stage-managed blaze of publicity.[115]

Stalin was a mass murderer. But there was another difference between him and Hitler. There was no equivalent of Auschwitz in the Soviet Union. Anti-Semitism existed there, as did racism against minority nationalities, but it did not develop into genocide. In Stalin's Russia, anti-Semitism was deployed and minority nations were scapegoated, but the terror of the 1930s could affect anyone, from Stalin's immediate circle downwards. Arrest and murder were almost casual affairs. Up until the outbreak of war it was the case that Stalin's regime was far more repressive, but under the impact of war the Third Reich seized the chance to implement genocide. Stalin's crimes did not involve the industrialisation of mass murder for its own sake.

After the division of Poland the Russian authorities deported around 400,000 people from the territory they occupied and carried out executions of Polish officers who fell into their hands.[116] Mark Mazower points to 'some overlapping' in the German and Russian treatment of the Polish elite, but also points to major differences:

> Soviet policy, while aiming to crush Polish nationalism, and to prevent any security threats it might pose, especially near the borders, did not aim to get rid of any particular national or ethnic group *in toto*. Its purpose was social revolution not national purification ... There was no equivalent on the Soviet side to the sporadic, unsystematised and almost invariably unpunished shootings of Jews which German soldiers and SS carried out.[117]

The Red Army and GPU were not implementing a revolution; they were acting as another imperialist force. But Mazower is right to point out that Jews were seeking to enter Russian-occupied areas to escape the Nazi terror. The Holocaust aimed at the mass extermination of the Jews, the Roma and other groups, deploying massive resources to seize every possible victim using industrial techniques of mass murder. The mass deaths in the Russian Gulags were a by-product of forced labour and terrible conditions; in the Nazi concentration camps mass extermination was the aim.

A similar revisionism has also been evident in Italy. Renzo de Felice, Mussolini's biographer, described the interregnum between the dictator's dismissal and the signing of an armistice with the Allies 45 days later as a 'national catastrophe'.[118] The resistance war that would follow was a 'civil war' whose outcome the mass of Italians were indifferent to, and in which there was no moral difference between the two sides. That rather overlooks that by late 1943 and certainly by 1944 no one who voluntarily fought alongside the Germans in the various Italian fascist forces could be unaware that Jews were being rounded up and probably murdered, and that anti-partisan operations included reprisals against Italian civilians.[119]

There is an importance in refuting these claims as they give considerable ammunition and encouragement to today's political heirs of Mussolini and Hitler. Since 1945 they have been desperate to escape the dark shadow of Auschwitz. It is of the utmost importance to stress the unique barbarism of the Holocaust and the simple fact that it remains the greatest crime in human history.

Where Was the German Working Class?

Throughout the final months, weeks and days of the Third Reich there was little evidence of what had once been the best organised working class in the world acting as a force against Nazi tyranny. But neither was there clear evidence that the German working class was ever won over en masse by the regime. Why did Germany not produce the sort of working class unrest such as the mass strike which swept northern Italy in March 1943?

The defeat inflicted on the German working class, and the destruction of its mass organisations, reduced it to an atomised grouping. The German working class experienced defeat in 1933 without resistance. In Italy workers could take pride in their efforts to confront Mussolini, even when defeated. In 1933 the German Communists had argued that Hitler's victory would be short-lived, offering the slogan, 'After Hitler Us'. Accordingly the party urged its members to maintain 'mass work', which left them terribly vulnerable to the savage repression unleashed by the Nazis. Further, the Hitler-Stalin pact had a major, demoralising impact. By the time the war began, the older workers who had experienced mass trade unionism and the existence of a labour movement were either cowed or waiting on deliverance from abroad. Younger workers had little experience to draw upon and relied on other forms of resistance – absenteeism, cultural protest, etc.

All three Allied powers wanted to take over a Germany free from any upheaval, such as that which had swept the country at the end of the First World War. Therefore they made no attempt to incite revolutionary feeling among the German people. Peukert goes so far as to argue that the British strategy, involving the aerial bombing of German cities, 'created a climate of resignation that led people not to rebel ... but merely to wait passively for the war to be over'.[120] The Russians on the one hand attacked all Germans as fascist criminals, and on the other attempted to build an anti-Hitler front organisation of captured generals whose message was a nationalist one. There was no effort to incite class warfare.

The Nazi regime was able to play on fears of Russian retribution for the evils inflicted by the Wehrmacht and the SS in the East together with the anger and fear caused by Allied bombing, but the state terror against the German population also continued right up to Doenitz's final surrender. When in the autumn of 1944 partisan-type groupings emerged in Cologne made up of the Edelweiss Pirates (teenage rebels against Nazi restrictions on their freedoms and cultural lives), escaped POWs and foreign workers, the Gestapo, Wehrmacht, the SS and the Hitler Youth were all mobilised to destroy them. The rebellions by such groups of young people seemed relatively isolated from the old, established Socialist and Communist traditions of the working class – testament to how effectively the Nazis had driven those who held such ideas into isolation or small, sealed circles.[121]

Among those sections of the officer corps and the old ruling class who had resented Hitler, the prospect of defeat led to the botched Stauffenberg bomb attack of July 1944. The conspirators included many implicated in serious war crimes on the Eastern Front. Stauffenberg, a member of the German officer corps, wanted the Reich restored to its 1916 borders (which would have included Alsace-Lorraine and much of Poland) plus the Sudetenland and Austria. The assassination attempt was followed by an attempted coup; the relative ease with which it was crushed by army units loyal to the Führer speaks of the degree to which the old elites had been compromised and co-opted by Hitler.[122]

CHAPTER EIGHT

Resistance in Europe

'I guess the whole world is on a leftward march', exclaimed US Senator Vanderberg in 1945.[1] By the closing months of the Second World War Resistance movements had spread across Europe, most of them aligned with the left. They were a major concern for the Germans and a major worry for all three of the Allied powers.

The experience of occupation breeds resistance, as has been repeatedly discovered since 1945. Resistance began early on in occupied Europe. In February 1941, for example, there were strikes in Amsterdam over the Nazi persecution of Jews, and in May in mining areas of Belgium and northern France. On the first anniversary of the German invasion, 100,000 miners walked out in the Belgian coal fields of Liège, Hainault and Limburg. In Holland in 1943 half a million struck after the Germans ordered that all former POWs should be sent to Germany as forced labour. The SS imposed martial law and over 100 strikers were executed. In 1943 resistance began spreading across Europe in response to the brutality of German occupation, and Hitler's defeat at Stalingrad.[2]

The collaboration of the European ruling classes with the Nazis, or at best their willingness to wait for liberation by the Allies, meant that resistance increasingly developed its own revolutionary dynamic. The electoralism of the Social Democratic Parties (the equivalents of the British Labour Party) made it difficult for them to organise effectively underground. As Eric Hobsbawm points out, 'Faced with a fascist takeover or German occupation, social democratic parties tended to go into hibernation.'[3]

In some cases, the Social Democrats were prepared to collaborate with the Germans. In Denmark the Social Democrats were in government at the time of the occupation and remained so until 1943. The main beneficiaries of this tendency were the Communist Parties, which in four crucial countries – Italy, France, Yugoslavia and Greece – dominated the Resistance. They had immense credibility because of their role in fighting fascism. In contrast the Socialist Democrats were not able to survive the inter-war repression in Italy and Greece, and in France they were tarnished by the involvement of so many of their leading figures with the Vichy regime.[4]

The dynamism, heroism and rootedness of the Communists meant they could quickly overcome the bitter taste left by their turn in 1939, following the Hitler-Stalin pact, when they switched from supporting an 'anti-fascist war' to advocating peace, before switching once more in June 1941 to full-scale support for Russia and its new ally, Britain. The Communist Parties were better suited to resistance work than other parties because of their experience of underground work, their organisation into a tight cell structure, and their internal discipline. They undoubtedly played a key role – and up to 60,000 French Communists may have lost their lives in the Resistance.[5]

The Communists' strategy post-June 1941 was a continuation of their 'Popular Front' line following Hitler's victory in 1933. Then the French Communists had led the way in creating an anti-fascist alliance with the Socialists and Republicans, in which they limited their demands to the defence of the French Republic and agreed to desist from criticism of their partners. Following the German attack on Russia the Communists became stridently nationalistic. The head of the Italian party, Palmiro Togliatti, broadcasting from Russia, appealed to 'Italians of all social conditions' including 'industrialists' and 'businessmen' whose trade had been damaged by the war. The Communist-led *Francs-Tireurs et Partisans* (FTP) raised the slogan *Chacun son Boche* (Let every man kill a Hun).[6]

In Italy, France and Greece the Communist Parties themselves were not at first fully under the control of their leaders, who were in Moscow. Thorez of France, Togliatti of Italy, and Zachariadis of Greece had to confront fast-growing parties which might not simply jump on Stalin's orders. They returned from Russia determined to bring their parties under tight control. Most party members believed that what their leaders said was designed to dupe the class enemy and that when the time was right they would make the revolution. In reality the parties were starting on the road towards integration into parliamentary, establishment politics and into the respective national lives of their own states. As the historian Gabriel Kolko puts it, 'Succinctly, the Russians were as committed to revolution as the West was to democracy.'[7]

Stalin saw that any revolutionary movement in Europe would clash with his own goals of securing a solid alliance with the United States and Britain, and control of Eastern Europe, goals that remained in place in the immediate aftermath of the war until the United States launched what would become known as the Cold War. Support for revolution abroad might also revive the revolutionary aspirations of the people of the USSR, which he feared. In May 1943 Stalin approved the dissolution of the Communist International, the body which had represented the goal of international workers' revolution. The spectre of 1917–19, when working-class unrest had erupted into revolution at the close of the First World War, hovered over all the war leaders during the Second World War. The Communist Parties now strove to portray the Resistance as essentially made up of nationalist movements and pledged to prioritise national unity among all anti-fascist forces. Yet many of those at the cutting edge of the fight did not fit into this picture.[8]

Exiled Spanish republicans in France and elsewhere continued to resist fascism. Some 10,000 died in German concentration camps, many having been taken from existing French camps and handed over to the Gestapo or Mussolini's OVRA. Hugh Thomas quotes a total of 25,000 republicans killed fighting Hitler and Mussolini during the Second World War. Spanish republicans were crucial to the French Resistance and provided much of the resistance inside the concentration camps. Volunteers who had fought Franco were often key figures in the Resistance movements which flared up in occupied Europe. 'Colonel

Fabien' (Pierre Georges), who would carry out the first Resistance killing of a German, served in Spain, as did 'Colonel Rol-Tanguy' (Henri Tanguy) who led the Resistance uprising which freed Paris in 1944. Luigi Longo, 'Gallo' in Spain, would lead the partisans in northern Italy, and Giovanni Pesce, a key Resistance fighter in both Turin and Milan, served in the International Brigades. Josef Tito had helped organise the flow of volunteers from Paris to the International Brigades in Spain. He would lead the victorious Yugoslav Resistance. The key military figure in the Albanian Resistance, Mehmet Shehu, also fought in Spain.[9]

Because of their strong Communist associations, the European Resistance movements and those among the Allies who wished to utilise them against the Germans were viewed with suspicion in London and Washington. In the autumn of 1942 British foreign minister Anthony Eden fumed about a 'very dangerous doctrine' being promoted by the SOE (Special Operations Executive, responsible for fomenting sabotage and resistance in occupied Europe). The danger was the SOE's willingness to 'collaborate with parties of the left'.[10] In his history of the OSS (Office of Strategic Services, forerunner of the CIA), Bradley F. Smith notes, 'Every manifestation of irregular warfare [was] watched with varying degrees of coolness or suspicion.'[11]

The best-known case was the Russian attitude to the Warsaw Uprising of August and September 1944. The Russian offensive in Belarus carried the Red Army to the River Vistula and to within 15 kilometres of Warsaw. German counter-attacks halted their advance and allowed the Germans to hold the city. Stalin had assembled a Polish government in Lublin, the first major city liberated by the Red Army. Its legitimacy was contested by the exiled government in London. In addition the Russians' proposal to move the country's borders westwards, rendering its eastern territories to the USSR, put them at odds with the British and Americans. The Polish Home Army, loyal to the London-based government, regarded the Russians as being as much their enemy as the Germans. There had already been clashes between them and the smaller Communist-led People's Army. The latter were loyal to Stalin and prepared not just to see post-war Poland as part of the pro-Soviet bloc, but to surrender the territory in the east that Stalin was demanding, which was anathema to the government in exile in London and the Home Army.

As the Red Army closed on the Polish border it offered the Home Army conditions for co-operation. They included:

> Operational subordination of the Polish Forces to the Soviet Command locally and also beyond the Bug River; recognition of the Polish Forces as a division under Polish authorities in Warsaw and London; the Division to be absolutely free to maintain contact with them; a regular Polish division to be formed out of the existing Polish partisan detachments; no partisan activity in the rear of Soviet Forces; full field equipment and armament for the Polish Division to be supplied by the Soviet authorities.[12]

The Home Army refused the terms unless they included recognition of Poland's pre-war boundaries. The Red Army was prepared to co-operate in combat with the Home Army as it advanced into Poland, but then demanded it either disband or be incorporated into the Polish units of the Red Army. Both the government in exile and the Home Army understood that they had to act in order to avoid this fate.

On 1 August the Home Army launched an insurrection in Warsaw, seizing large parts of the city centre but failing to take the four bridges over the Vistula, which could have provided a link to the Russians. The exiled Polish government in London approved the plan – they realised that if they did not mobilise the Resistance against the Germans Stalin would cast them as 'collaborators' and exclude them from any say in how Poland was run. However, they did not tell the Russians of their plans. The British were given notice but ruled out a bombing operation in support of the insurgents, or the dispatch of a Polish paratroop brigade fighting under British command.[13]

The Polish government believed the Germans would evacuate Warsaw. But the Wehrmacht had decided to hold the city and now armoured columns and SS units were sent in to re-occupy their positions. Polish fighters lacked sufficient small arms and ammunition. More crucially they had no heavy weapons to repulse armour. They were able to seize the city centre but the Germans destroyed the city with artillery and carried out retaliations on the population. Warsaw was now key to the right flank of the German defence line.[14] The Russian advance had halted at the Vistula but the Red Army was in touch with the Resistance in the city and could have provided the aid it badly needed. Instead, on 16 August Stalin sent a letter to the exiled government's prime minister, denouncing the rising as 'a reckless adventure' and breaking a Russian assurance given during talks in Moscow that arms would be provided to the insurgents. The British, after much urging, had sent flights to drop arms, often piloted by Polish airmen, but these were at the limit of the aircraft's range and were exposed to attack as they flew over German territory. Little reached the fighters in the city and the flights were eventually ended after losses became too great.

Churchill did urge Roosevelt on 25 August to press Stalin about permitting US bombers flying into Soviet airfields to be allowed to drop arms into Warsaw, but Roosevelt refused, stating he was 'taking into account Uncle J's present attitude towards the relief of the Underground forces in Warsaw'. He cited 'current American conversations on the subject of the subsequent use of other Russian bases'. These were bases in the Far East the Americans hoped to use against Japan.[15] When Stalin did allow the USAAF use of airfields in Eastern Poland to launch airdrops to Polish fighters in mid September, the area of Warsaw held by the Home Army was so small most of the material dropped fell into German hands.[16]

The Home Army was forced to surrender on 2 October. Warsaw was reduced to rubble after Hitler ordered its destruction. The Red Army liberated the city three months later. All three Allied powers viewed the growing Resistance forces with distrust. All three acted to limit their ambitions. This was true even in Germany as the war ended. Working-class organisations re-emerged, their ranks swollen by new activists. As Kolko notes of Germany in 1945:

Everywhere the Allied troops entered they found local Left committees ... running factories and municipalities which the owners and masters had deserted, via spontaneously created shop committees and councils. Some were old Socialists and Communists, many were new converts, but everywhere they moved to liberate concentration camp prisoners, organise food supplies and eradicate the Old Order. For the most part they scoffed at regular party doctrine and talked vaguely of new forms based on a united Left, unlike that which had helped open the door to Hitler.[17]

As the Allies entered German-occupied territories, all three powers acted in similar ways towards local resistance movements. Stalin was prepared to let 166,000 Poles die in the Warsaw Uprising. In Italy, at the close of 1944, Britain's Field Marshal Alexander broadcast openly on the radio saying Allied forces would advance no further that winter. It was a clear message to the Germans and their fascist allies that they could concentrate on anti-partisan operations, which they did. That winter was a hard one for the Resistance.[18] Basil Davidson, a former British Special Forces liaison officer with the Resistance in Liguria, said of the broadcast that it 'told the partisans to disband, and to the enemy to come up and finish them off while they were doing it'.[19]

Italy

Writing of Italy in 1945 Kolko asks, 'With red banners and power in hand 150,000 armed men disappeared overnight, and the almost morbid fears of the English and Americans proved entirely chimerical. Why?'[20] The answer lies in the politics which underlay this resistance movement.

Popular resistance to fascism began early in Italy. In March 1943 some 100,000 workers struck in Turin, mainly at Fiat, and the end of the year saw further strikes in the city and in Genoa.[21] The mass strike and then the Allied invasion of Sicily three months later led to the king dismissing Mussolini, who was arrested as he quit the royal palace. The king appointed Marshal Badoglio, the conqueror of Ethiopia, as the new premier, who immediately ordered there should be no demonstrations. That did not stop people taking to the streets to remove fascist symbols, free prisoners, and take over newspaper offices to allow an anti-fascist press to appear.

Such anti-fascist actions unnerved Churchill, who was staunch in his defence of the king and Badoglio, bemoaning to Roosevelt in August 1943:

Italy turned red overnight. In Turin and Milan there were Communist demonstrations which had to be put down by armed force. Twenty years of fascism had obliterated the middle class. There is nothing between the King with the Patriots who have rallied around him, who have complete control, and rampant Bolshevism.[22]

Almost immediately following the fall of Mussolini, Hitler ordered German forces to occupy most of the Italian peninsula, forming a frontline south of Naples facing Allied forces moving north from Sicily. While the Germans controlled most of the country, the Allies set up an occupation zone in the far south, where the king and Badoglio fled when German troops neared Rome.

The experience of occupation quickly led to the rise of the Italian Resistance. In Naples the population rose up in September 1943, against food shortages imposed by the Germans, and drove the Wehrmacht from their city.[23] By the end of 1943 there were some 10,000 partisans in various formations. Most were simply keeping out of the way of German attempts to conscript them as forced labour. Kolko writes that

> partisan formations were recruited largely from the working class and the poorer peasantry – the origins of over half of its members in the Piedmont ... on the whole it was clear that precisely those classes whom the fascists had muzzled after 1921 were in command of the biggest part of the armed resistance and that the basic tensions in Italian society that had existed before Mussolini were likely to re-emerge.[24]

Partisan attacks on German and fascist forces developed throughout late 1943 and 1944. Easter 1944 saw 10,000 German and fascist troops attack the mountains south of Forli in Romagna trapping and all but destroying the 1,000 Resistance fighters of the 8th Garibaldi Brigade. Two months later the German commander, Kesselring, told his commanders, 'The fight against the partisans must be carried on with the utmost severity. I will protect any commander who exceeds our usual restraint in the choice and severity of the methods he adopts against the partisans.' On 29 June 1944 German forces massacred 244 civilians in southern Tuscany; on 4 July they killed 176 in the same area.[25] By 8 July the Garibaldi Brigade had reformed in southern Tuscany. Some 3,500 German and fascist troops were sent to destroy them but this time the partisans withdrew, avoiding battle. The Nazis and fascists carried out reprisals against civilians burning 20 houses and massacring 64 people, 19 of them under the age of ten.[26]

A month later in the hills north of Lucca, in northern Tuscany, German forces evacuated civilians who had resisted an order to leave prior to an offensive against the partisans. The Germans applied methods refined in Russia, despite the partisans having withdrawn from the area. The village of Sant'Anna di Stazzema was swollen with evacuated civilians. The Germans burned houses, rounded up civilians and locked them in barns. Grenades were thrown in, machine guns fired and finally the barns were set alight. Five-hundred-and-sixty men, women and children were butchered.[27]

September saw 770 people killed in three days of reprisals in the Monte Sole area south of Bologna. Among the victims 45 were under two years old, 110 were under ten, 95 were under 16, 142 were over 60, 316 were females, and five were Catholic priests. The operation destroyed the Stella Rossa (Red Star) partisan group, which until then had controlled the area. It was the worst German atrocity in Western Europe.[28] Many other massacres occurred as the Germans sought to liquidate the Resistance, but the reprisals acted only to intensify it. Kesselring's intelligence office calculated that the partisans had killed 5,000 Axis soldiers between June and August 1944 and wounded or captured 50,000 more. Kesselring thought the figures too high: 'In any case the proportion of casualties on the German side alone greatly exceeded the total partisan losses.'[29]

By the end of that summer the Resistance in northern Italy was holding down 14 German divisions. Between 17 and 30 September 1944 partisans carried out 280 attacks on German forces killing 129 and wounding 3,663, as well as taking 8,241 prisoners.[30] The involvement of Italian fascist forces, whether operating under German or Mussolini's command, ensured that the resistance struggle took on aspects of a civil war. Nazi and fascist repression simply fuelled support for the Resistance and created the conditions for a radicalisation of anti-fascist forces. The Republican Action Party moved sharply left and Communist groups sprung up often drawing on the party's revolutionary tradition prior to its virtual destruction within Italy by the fascists. But this was at odds with the direction of the leadership of the Communist Party.[31]

On 3 and 4 March 1944, shortly before his return to Italy, Palmiro Togliatti, leader of the Italian Communist Party, met Stalin to discuss the Italian situation. Togliatti wrote a note summarising Stalin's main points: 'the Communists are even ready to participate in a government without the king's abdication, as condition that the actual government will take immediate action to prosecute a war to expel the Germans from the country'.[32] A day later Togliatti reported Stalin as saying:

> The existence of two camps [Badoglio and the king and the anti-fascist parties] weakens the Italian people. This is an advantage for the English who want a weak Italy in the Mediterranean Sea ... If the king goes against the Germans there is no need to call for immediate abdication ... The most important thing is the unity of the Italian people in the fight against the Germans for a strong independent Italy. Follow that line *without making any reference to the Russians*.[33]

Stalin and Togliatti were uniting with the same king who had helped bring fascism to power and who had fled Rome along with Badoglio rather than resist the Germans. The vast majority of those in the Resistance wanted an end to the monarchy.[34]

When Togliatti arrived in Naples on 1 April he pledged to end a situation with 'on the one hand a government with power but no authority, and on the other hand a popular movement with authority but no power'. The obvious solution from any revolutionary point of view was to ensure the latter took power. But Togliatti's solution was that all the anti-fascist parties and the Communists would support Badoglio's government if it presided over 'a truly effective war effort'.[35] Togliatti also claimed that the Christian Democrats, at that time far from a major force, represented the country's middle classes and had a mass base among the peasantry, so that the Communists, who represented the working class, had to forge unity with them above all else. The Allies and the

Vatican were determined to build up the Christian Democrats as a pro-western force, and now the Communists helped promote them too.[36]

Meanwhile, the British commander, Alexander, wrote of his concerns about the SOE 'arming nearly 100,000 so-called patriots', warning that it 'will produce [a] revolutionary situation unless we devise a system for immediately on the liberation of the territory taking them in to either our or the Italian army'.[37] A month after Alexander's broadcast announcing that the Allied advance in northern Italy had halted for the winter, representatives of the northern Resistance reached Rome to meet the Allied commission running Italy. Against their better instincts they signed a pact whereby in return for money, food and arms they recognised Allied authority and agreed to hand over control to Allied forces when they arrived. In other words, they agreed not to make a revolution.[38]

In March 1945 Kesselring began secret negotiations with Allen Dulles, head of the OSS, who was based in Switzerland. The Germans offered to surrender so as to forestall a Communist uprising or a Yugoslav advance into Italy. The Americans were prevented from making any agreement by furious protests from the Russians when they discovered what was going on. In late April the talks resumed with Russian observers present, and surrender terms were agreed. Alexander instructed the Germans to stay in position, to maintain 'law and order', and only to surrender to Allied troops – the Resistance was not to be allowed to liberate northern Italy.[39]

In the event the Resistance took matters into their own hands launching an uprising in Genoa on 23 April, and going on to liberate all the great cities of the north, before Allied forces arrived. The National Liberation Committees (CLNs) held effective power. These were based on the anti-fascist parties, giving equal representation to the Christian Democrats, the Communists and the Action Party, despite a huge majority of partisans identifying with the latter two parties. The Communists ensured that the CLNs disarmed the Resistance fighters and then dissolved themselves. As minister of justice Togliatti agreed to an effective amnesty for all but the very worst fascists, to the restoration of the independence of the judiciary (dominated by fascist appointees), and to a law which allowed ex-partisans to be tried for 'crimes against the state' – Mussolini's state.[40]

As reprisals took place against fascists (stories of which were later hugely inflated by the right-wing), Togliatti told Communists in Emilia, one of the 'hot spots', that:

> In the north, the Party must fight all forms of illegality. To guarantee the elections will take place in the next three or four months we must keep order through the actions of the Party. This is especially important in the Emilia province, where illegal acts were most serious ... You in Emilia have nowadays a special responsibility. You must give us the assurance that if there will be struggles they will unfold under our leadership.[41]

The number of Italians who died fighting the fascist and Nazi forces between September 1943 and May 1945 equalled those that died fighting for Mussolini between 1940 and 1943.[42] One member of British Special Forces who parachuted into Carnia in the far north-east reported thus:

> I think that period for Italy – history will prove me on this point – will possibly be a more glorious period than the Risorgimento. That's what I feel. The sacrifices made by the youngsters, instinctively they would throw away their lives. What we gave the Partisans was not very much, we gave them a few arms, and a few blankets, and a few canned goods, and that's all they got – plus their guts and ours.[43]

France

Events similar to those in Italy were unfolding in France. Food shortages had provoked riots during the winter of 1940–41 and continued into the next winter. There were already class divisions apparent in attitudes towards Vichy and the German occupation, as the historian of pre-war and wartime France, Julian Jackson, outlines:

> Early in 1941, the prefect of the Lot [department] noted that collaboration was supported by the bourgeoisie, the peasants showed no open hostility, and the workers were against it. In December of the same year, the prefect of the Limoges region reported: 'Very striking hostility to the [Vichy] government from most workers, small farmers, small shopkeepers and artisans; unreserved support from big business and big shopkeepers, magistrates and notables.'[44]

Jackson notes the 'indecent haste' of big business in securing contracts from the Germans and that business circles 'sympathised with its [Vichy's] social values'. By the end of 1941, 7,000 businesses were producing directly to meet German orders, and that figure had doubled by 1944.[45] The establishment was heavily compromised by its support for Vichy. Even the minority who opposed Pétain's capitulation were content to simply wait for an Allied invasion.

The German occupation became harsher with the move to a total war economy in 1942, which required more from France in terms of production, agricultural produce and manpower for the Reich. France provided 42 per cent of German transport planes by 1943. The extermination programme against the Jews began in 1942 and was extended to France. Collaboration now meant complete involvement in the Third Reich and its programme of mass murder. The Germans relied heavily on Vichy's security forces to 'maintain order' in France. Between May 1942 and May 1943 some 16,000 Communists and Gaullists were arrested by French police working in close co-operation with the Germans. During 1942, 36,802 Jews (6,053 of them children) were rounded up and sent to the death camps by French police (this figure includes 12,884 arrested by 9,000 police in the two-day *Rafle* [round up] in July).[46] Under Vichy 650,000 French civilian workers were compulsorily enlisted to Germany, 30,000

French were shot as hostages or as resisters, and another 60,000 were deported to German concentration camps.[47]

Real wage levels in the Paris region had fallen to nearly half their 1939 value by the end of 1943. That began to translate into industrial discontent. In the Nord-Pas-de-Calais region 39,000 miners struck in October 1943 and won increased wages, despite the usual arrests and deportations. The fact that the German authorities worked closely with the employers during the strike helped breed resistance to the occupation. Miners made up 47 per cent of those arrested in the area during the occupation, with other manual workers making up 29 per cent and the unemployed 12 per cent. Four fifths of manual workers and almost one half of all resisters were in Communist organised groups.[48]

Armed resistance began on 21 August 1941 when a young German naval officer on his way to work was shot dead at the Barbès-Rochechouart Metro station on the edge of Paris's Montmartre district. The killing, the first such assassination, was carried out by a 22-year-old Communist veteran of the Spanish Civil War, Pierre Georges, better known by his codename, Colonel Fabien. Two days before the attack two Communists had been executed after being arrested on a street demonstration. Five French hostages were executed after Fabien's attack. Not to be outdone Vichy tried and executed six Communists in August and September, even though they were not involved in military resistance.

The Communists would soon set up the *Francs-Tireurs et Partisans Francais* (FTP). Resistance actions quickly led to German reprisals. Hitler directly ordered the execution of 97 hostages after two officers were killed in Nantes and Bordeaux in October 1941. After the Bordeaux hostages were murdered, de Gaulle broadcast from London ordering an end to the assassinations by the Resistance. The Communists ignored him. At this time he had only rallied some of the smaller garrisons in the French colonial empire and he seemed insignificant. The introduction of labour conscription led to the rise of the *Maquis* – young workers and peasants who had fled to the remote country and employed guerrilla tactics against the occupiers. They become an important part of the Resistance.[49]

In January 1943 Vichy launched the *Milice française* (French Militia) under the command of Joseph Darnand, an activist in the pre-war fascist leagues. Recruits pledged 'to fight against democracy, against Gaullist insurrection and against Jewish leprosy'.[50] At first the Germans were reluctant to provide any French force with arms, even the *Milice*. The Militia quickly found itself suffering casualties at the hands of the Resistance. In October Darnand swore allegiance to Hitler and enrolled in the Waffen-SS. Arms then followed.[51]

In May 1943 the Communists joined with the Socialist and Radical Parties, the largest union federation, the CGT, and other groups to create a National Council of the Resistance. Its authority was not recognised by de Gaulle, in exile in London then Algiers. The Gaullists and the Communists both talked in nationalist terms; the significant difference was that the Gaullists generally followed a policy of waiting for the Allies to arrive, while the Communists prosecuted armed attacks on the Germans and their allies. By October 1943 the Communist FTP could rely on 12,000 activists across France. Beyond them were thousands more involved in distributing Resistance material. In the Cantal there were ten active sympathisers for each fighter. Arms were few, however, despite Allied promises.[52]

At the close of the First World War, the Russian revolutionaries had stressed the need to fight the main enemy – the ruling class at home, to reject chauvinism and to build fraternisation among the opposing forces facing each other in the trenches. The French Communists claimed to be followers of Lenin but their actions flew in the face of what he had argued, as they wrapped themselves in the tricolor and used nationalist rhetoric.

In contrast to the Communists, the tiny forces of the French Trotskyists were able to engage in limited but significant work of fraternisation with occupying German soldiers. As Ian Birchall points out, 'In terms of sheer quantity the PCF [French Communist Party] distributed far more propaganda aimed at German troops. But what they produced fell within the normal framework of military propaganda aimed at demoralising enemy forces.' For the Trotskyists, however, 'German workers in uniform were to be perceived, not as an object of a military tactic, but as part of the subject of revolutionary change ... A paper aimed at German soldiers, *Arbeiter und Soldat (Worker and Soldier)*, was produced by a young German Trotskyist, Paul Widelin, and distributed in Paris and especially in Brest.'[53]

In 1943 the Gestapo raided a meeting in Brest; 17 German soldiers and a French Trotskyist, Robert Cruati, were shot. In July 1944 Widelin was arrested by the Gestapo, tortured and left for dead. He was taken to hospital, but the Gestapo found him and this time succeeded in killing him. Undermining the morale of the German forces was no easy matter and made harder by the fact that none of the Allies, including Russia, had any interest in fomenting dissent among Germans, whether in uniform or not.[54]

The British and the Americans had different attitudes towards France. The former wanted to rebuild France as a power in the post-war world, but one owing its allegiance to Britain. Accordingly they had recognised the exiled General Charles de Gaulle as leader of the 'Free French'. Washington distrusted de Gaulle and was less keen on restoring French power. Until the eve of the invasion of France they looked to winning the support of senior figures associated with Pétain's puppet regime in Vichy. For his part, de Gaulle was determined to play off all the Allied powers in order to create a strong, independent France. That increasingly depended on bringing the internal Resistance to heel. De Gaulle's Free French movement relied largely on colonial troops from the minority of French overseas territories that had rallied to him, but was officered by military men appalled by both Vichy and the Communist-led Resistance. They had no faith in guerrilla warfare, pinning their hopes instead on French forces playing a powerful role in an Allied invasion of France.[55]

De Gaulle was soon to prove his worth to the Allies. In September 1943 there was a popular uprising on the island of Corsica involving Resistance forces and Italian troops who joined them after Mussolini's fall. Together they defeated the Germans, forcing them to quit the island. De Gaulle's Free French forces arrived from Algeria and abolished the liberation committees that were running the island. By the summer of 1944 the Americans and British needed someone to do the same in mainland France. Washington swallowed its qualms about de Gaulle. The US and the British would allow him to gain control of the country at the expense of the left.[56]

The Allies believed some 3 million people might aid their invasion effort in some way. This included 800,000 workers in Communist-led unions who could disrupt transport and other services. By the end of May 1944, a week before the D-Day landings, the Allies estimated there were some half a million potential Resistance fighters in France, but there was a chronic shortage of arms and ammunition. In Lyon 4,000 resisters had just 150 weapons. In Paris 16,000 had just 600.[57]

There were no clear directions to the Resistance forces from Allied command or from de Gaulle. In a number of areas the Gaullist Secret Army, often led by former regular officers, had developed plans to take over swathes of territory in expectation of a prompt Allied arrival. The Communist-led FTP scorned such tactics, arguing they left Resistance forces liable to German attack.

Free French units began concentrating in the Vercors, a high plateau south of Grenoble, on news of the landings to the north. By 9 June there were 3,000 fighters there. On 3 July, they proclaimed the restoration of the French Republic. The Resistance fighters expected arms from the Allies, but no deliveries of heavy weapons came; they expected an Allied landing on the Mediterranean coast, but this was postponed until 15 August; they expected Free French regular troops to be airlifted in, but that did not happen either.[58] At the end of July the Germans attacked using Alpine units backed up by Panzers and the Luftwaffe. The fighters did not have the means to resist such forces. Six-hundred-and-fifty paid with their lives.[59]

Meanwhile, the Germans reacted to Resistance attacks elsewhere with reprisals against civilians. At Oradour-sur-Glane, north of Limoges, the Waffen-SS Das Reich tank division, moving north to Normandy, killed 642 people, virtually the entire population.[60] The Allied invasion unleashed uprisings in Paris and various industrial towns and cities. A nationwide rail strike in August 1944 paralysed the country. Liberation committees took over the running of much of France. On 19 August 1944 the Resistance launched an uprising to free Paris before the Americans arrived. De Gaulle successfully persuaded the Allies to allow Free French armoured forces to move forward to be the first into the city. De Gaulle quickly followed in their wake. He imperiously took over the capital, treating the Resistance with disdain and demanding they demobilise and disarm.

The Communist Party accepted this. 'One state, one police force, one army', was the slogan offered by Maurice Thorez, general secretary of the French Communist Party, on his return to France in November 1944. General de Gaulle had allowed his return knowing he would enforce Moscow's line of coalition with nationalist parties. Under Thorez's leadership the party not only participated in de Gaulle's government but allowed him to veto its ministerial candidates.[61] De Gaulle himself was far from being a consistent democrat. Prior to the war, in 1934, he had advocated the formation of a shock army of six mechanised divisions. The priority of this proposed force was to prevent 'a situation of anarchy, perhaps of civil war'. He criticised the police's inability to maintain order, and claimed the army could not cope because 'its units are now all formed of voters or natives'.[62] De Gaulle became president of the new French Republic following liberation but stepped down in 1946, and with the onset of the Cold War his *Rassemblement du Peuple Français* employed 'shock troops' against the Communists in a series of bitter street clashes.[63]

In France the purge of Vichyite collaborators, the *épuration*, saw 10,000 people killed by local Resistance fighters. Thorez backed de Gaulle in demanding an end to the *épuration* and the dissolution of all extra-parliamentary institutions. During the official process of 'denazification' nearly 7,000 people were sentenced to death, but, as Kolko points out, 'only 770 were actually executed, and over 38,000 of the roughly four times that number who were tried for collaboration were sent to prison or forced labour for some term'.[64] Vichy's defenders, who would quickly re-emerge after the war, would claim the Resistance carried out up to 150,000 reprisal killings after the Liberation. They wanted to paint this as another Terror, similar to that of the Jacobins after the French Revolution. Probably some 10,000 reprisal killings were carried out – which pales before the 100,000 killings of French men, women and children carried out by the Germans and Vichy during the occupation.[65]

In Spain, Franco's forces carried out some 180,000 executions.[66] These were justified by the 'terror' which supposedly gripped the Republican zone. Yet their executions totalled 38,000, about half taking place in the first six weeks of the war following Franco's rebellion. All the parties in the Republic argued against such killings and strove to end them, with some success. In the rebel zone executions were officially encouraged and continued unabated throughout the war.[67]

A similar attempt was made to create a myth of mass reprisal killings by Communist partisans in Italy at the end of the war.

Belgium

In Belgium by mid 1944 collaborationist forces (the French-speaking Fascist Rex Party, the Flemish SS, and the right-wing VNV, Flemish National Union) were carrying out attacks on Resistance forces in what was becoming a civil war. In September 1944 British forces liberated Brussels and Antwerp. The Belgian Resistance numbered 80,000 – bigger proportionally than the French but much less disciplined by the Communists. The monarchy and the established parties including the Socialists had collaborated with the German occupiers. Nevertheless these were the very forces put in government by the Allies.

Despite instructions from Eisenhower and their own leaders to disarm, the Resistance fighters kept their weapons – they did not trust the new administration. They called a demonstration in central Brussels on 25 November. Belgian troops occupied the city's Grand Place, with British tanks and troops in support. When the demonstrators tried to enter the square troops opened fire, killing 35. A general strike was immediately called. Churchill warned the House of Commons that the revolution was underway.[68] However, the Communists and their allies soon gained control and called the strike off, entering the government 'in the interests of the common war effort'.[69]

Once again the working class were championing democratic change, which meant ousting the politicians who had worked for the occupiers, but found themselves opposed by the Allies and the Communist Party, acting in accord with Russian diplomatic needs.

Greece

Churchill had remarked to Anthony Eden in the summer of 1940 that only one major prize – Greece – could now be won by British arms alone.[70] Yet by late 1944 the Greek Communist-led people's liberation army, ELAS, claimed control of three quarters of the country.[71] Prior to the war Greece was ruled by the royalist, pro-German Metaxas dictatorship. The official political structures were polarised between republicans and royalists, themselves sub-divided into a myriad of factions. Metaxas's sympathies for Germany did not prevent Hitler sending in a German invasion force to bail out Mussolini's botched invasion in 1941.

After the invasion, King George II fled first to Crete and then on to Cairo, and Greek politicians, whether royalist or republican, began vying for favours from the German and Italian occupiers (often while maintaining covert contact with the exiled government in Cairo and the British). Nominally a right-wing Greek government ruled from Athens, but it was a puppet of the occupiers. Companies like Krupps and IG Farben followed close on the tails of the Wehrmacht, and a Krupps agent, seconded to the army, could soon report that, 'During the period 1–10 May 1941 in Athens, the entire output of Greek mines of pyrites, iron ore, chrome, nickel, magnesite, manganese, bauxite and gold was obtained for Germany on a long term basis.'[72]

German occupation produced familiar results – 'famine, inflation and expropriation', all of which led to 'a profound sense of alienation' and 'tore apart the existing structures of Greek society'.[73] In the winter of 1941–42 the daily diet in Athens and on the Greek islands fell to between 600 and 800 calories – less than half the recommended amount. But this situation also produced another familiar pattern – the growth of popular resistance, which bypassed the old established parties as it flowed leftwards.

The Greek Communist Party, which had operated underground pre-war, took the decision to launch a broad Resistance movement, EAM, the National Liberation Front. In April 1942 wildcat strikes forced the Germans to distribute food and then to release those strikers who had been arrested. In February 1943 students began street protests against the conscription of civilian labour for work in Germany. Strikes spread among civil servants, council and bank workers, with workers joining the students on the streets.

On 5 March EAM called a mass protest in central Athens with 7,000 heeding the call. Greek police opened fire. Five protesters died. The next day there was an effective general strike. The Greek collaborationist regime was forced to announce that no one would be conscripted to work in Germany. By the summer of 1943 EAM's armed wing, ELAS, the Greek People's Liberation Army, began carrying out attacks on occupying forces, winning control of parts of northern Greece and the Peloponnese. Historian Mark Mazower quotes a figure of 17,000 guerrilla fighters in the late spring of that year, the vast majority affiliated to ELAS.[74]

The success of the Yugoslav partisans and the presence of the Red Army in Bulgaria and Hungary threatened to cut off the German occupation forces in Greece. The Germans decided to withdraw northwards towards Croatia. Reacting to the news in September that the Red Army had entered Bulgaria, Eden telegraphed Churchill arguing, 'Even if they do not penetrate into Greek territory, their presence in the Balkans is bound to produce strong political reactions.' He added that unless British forces entered the region soon 'the influence of Great Britain will suffer seriously'.[75]

In one of the most extraordinary episodes of the war, in November 1943 a British SOE officer stationed in Greece travelled to Athens to meet the head of the German Field Police to discuss possible collaboration against Russian forces if they reached Greece. Officially the British agent was acting on his own initiative but his superior officer, with whom he was in radio contact, was sacked. The documentation regarding this affair remains closed.[76]

Britain was the power designated to deal with Greece. An exiled Greek army was based in Egypt but in March 1944 it mutinied in protest at the monarchy's refusal to promote active resistance and in support of the inclusion of EAM in the government. British forces dealt harshly with the mutineers, putting 20,000 in prisoner of war camps. Greece was of strategic importance to Britain. As one of its intelligence officers explained in May 1944, 'Our long term policy towards Greece is to retain her as a British sphere of influence, and … a Russian dominated Greece would not be in accordance with British strategy in the Eastern Mediterranean.'[77] But Churchill also had an eye on Resistance forces elsewhere in southern Europe. He argued that British intervention against the Greek Resistance was needed to deter 'radical uprisings' that 'may spread to Italy' and beyond.[78]

By the summer of 1944, EAM/ELAS controlled huge areas of the country, holding popular assemblies, granting votes to women for the first time, providing education and law courts. At the same time rival political groups, royalist and republican, moved towards open collaboration with the Germans. The British, despite their hostility to EAM/ELAS, were forced to provide arms in recognition of the role they were playing in fighting the Germans. EAM/ELAS were suspicious of the British, whose aid had generally flowed to royalist groups that were now collaborating with the Germans.

In July 1944 a Russian mission arrived at ELAS headquarters, but Churchill needn't have worried; as military historian John Erickson argues, 'The role of the Soviet mission to ELAS proved to be policing the unpalatable decisions already made in Moscow, deferring all and any plans for a Communist coup in Greece.'[79] The Greek Communist leadership met the following month and after a bitter debate agreed to join with the British-backed government in exile. In October 1944, as German forces began evacuating Greece, EAM took over the running of much of the country, but stood by an agreement with the British not to enter Athens, which the British would control. British forces landed in Patras on 3 October and then parachuted into Athens the day after the Germans left. As British troop numbers built up it was clear they were there not to fight the Germans, who had already left the country, but to prevent EAM taking power.[80]

Initially ELAS fighters were not interested in confronting the British but rather in pursuing those forces that had collaborated with the Germans; but a confrontation with the British could not be avoided. At this stage the Americans looked with some suspicion on Britain's involvement in Greece – not out of sympathy with the Resistance but out of discomfort at Britain pursuing its own interests. The US refused to release landing craft to take British troops from southern Italy to Piraeus. The US Chief of Naval Staff, Admiral King, said that the intervention in Greece 'does not appear to be a war in which the United States is participating'.[81]

EAM and ELAS had committed to avoid clashes with the British and offered to disarm as part of a general disarmament if the king stood down and was replaced by a regent. The dominant force in EAM/ELAS, the Communist Party, was clear that in line with Churchill and Stalin's negotiations, the country fell within the British sphere of influence. Churchill was determined to restore the king and to leave intact a vehemently anti-democratic elite. British troops were supplemented by the Security Battalions that had been recruited by the puppet regime installed by the Germans to fight the Resistance.

On 2 December the British-appointed government banned ELAS. EAM called a demonstration in central Athens for the following Sunday, which the government granted permission for. Hours before the Sunday demonstration, official permission was withdrawn. Crowds gathered in the city centre. At Constitution Square police opened fire killing 24 demonstrators and wounding 150. British troops stood ready to help.[82] Churchill telegraphed the British commander, General Scobie, with the instructions:

'Do not … hesitate to act as if you were in a conquered city where a local rebellion was in progress … We have to hold and dominate Athens. It would be a great thing for you to succeed in this without bloodshed if possible, but also with bloodshed if necessary.'[83] ELAS troops set off for Athens and 16,000 British troops were quickly cut off with little food. Spitfires and Beaufighters strafed working-class suburbs. The British suffered a major blow when ELAS fighters took their HQ and main air base at Kifisia, on 19 December 1944, with the capture of many British prisoners.[84] The British feared military defeat, with Field Marshal Alexander warning of 'a first class disaster'.[85]

Churchill arrived in Athens at Christmas 1944 and had to be driven in a tank, wearing a steel helmet, to a conference with a motley crew of Greek politicians and clerics. As the discussions began British snipers were at the windows as incoming fire hit the building. Churchill described the scene as 'intensely dramatic'.[86] His presence in Athens summed up Britain's position in the war:

Where the American and Soviet principals stared at large scale maps, moving vast armies this way and that, engaged in a struggle for mastery in the broad geo-political sense, the British leader was ducking and weaving in the fragmented world of Greek politics, dealing in scarce landing craft rather than whole divisions, but determined for all that to ensure Britain got her dues as she conceived them to be.[87]

Churchill installed a government excluding EAM. The new government began recruiting former collaborators, and Churchill told Anthony Eden: 'It seems to me that the collaborators in Greece in many cases did the best they could to shelter the Greek population from German oppression ... The Communists are the main foe ... There should be no question of increasing the severities against the collaborationists in order to win Communist approval.'[88]

The British rounded up and interned 15,000 leftists, putting 8,000 in camps in the Middle East. The Russians actively helped the British in their conflict with ELAS. Moscow insisted that the Greek Communist Party agree to a ceasefire. At the Yalta summit Stalin told Churchill he had no criticism of British policy in Greece, 'he simply wanted news of the situation'. As Erickson comments: '*The hint was broad and crude; if the British did not break the rules the situation in Greece would continue.*'[89] The subsequent agreement, brokered in February 1945, as the Allies met in Yalta, permitted the Communists to operate openly and pledged that there would be free elections. This was never acted upon. Instead former ELAS fighters suffered growing persecution and assassinations.

Formally EAM and the Communist Party were legal parties, but their activists faced jail sentences, newspaper vendors who sold their papers were beaten up, and general repression mounted. The key ELAS commander, Veloukhiotis, was expelled from the Communist Party for opposing the peace agreement. Two days later right-wing forces captured and decapitated him. It was widely believed he had been betrayed by his former comrades. ELAS fighters began slipping back into the mountains to avoid arrest and harassment, attempting to wage a new guerrilla civil war, which they lost.[90]

The British claimed that EAM/ELAS wished to take control of Greece and create a Soviet-style regime. Yet the Resistance had controlled the country in October 1944 and could have prevented British forces arriving. Similarly in December 1944 they had held Athens in their hand but agreed voluntarily to withdraw, leaving British forces in control.

Regarding Stalin's attitude to the Greek Communists, Erickson writes:

Stalin's 'Grand Strategy' did not admit of much generosity towards his communist associates if they stood in the way of the 'accommodation' he sought temporarily with his major partners in the alliance. Over Poland he chose to use the Communists as wedges to force 'accommodation' on his terms; in Greece they [the Communists] became prime instruments in implementing the bargain with the British at the cost of all their hopes for a 'takeover'; and over Yugoslavia Stalin showed himself highly suspicious of the uncompromising attitude of the partisan leadership.[91]

Churchill himself admitted that the alliance with Stalin was key to stemming revolutionary movements in Western Europe: 'At this time, every country that is liberated or converted by our victories is seething with communists. All are linked together and only our influence with Russia prevents their activity stimulating this movement, deadly as I conceive it to peace and also to the freedom of mankind.'[92]

At the Potsdam conference in July–August 1945 both the Americans and the Russians were prepared to point to the lack of democracy in Greece to discomfort the British, but that was as far as their concern went. The US ambassador sent a report to his country's delegation highlighting 'the deficiencies of present Greek regional administrative and judicial procedure ... for the civil liberties of leftists and slavophones [Macedonians]', and fingering the National Guard, many of whom 'had served as Gendarmes under both Metaxas and the Germans'.[93] He concluded that foreign troops were needed to maintain order. Molotov circulated a note criticising repression and calling for an agreement guaranteeing EAM legal status to be honoured. That was as far as the Russians went.[94]

Elections in 1946 were so badly rigged that the Communists refused to take part and clashes developed into a full-scale civil war. The Russians blew hot and cold over supporting the Greek Communists because they still hoped to maintain the wartime alliance, even though tensions were growing. In February 1947 the British could no longer afford the cost of sustaining the right-wing regime and passed the task on to the Americans, who by now were determined to stop what they perceived as a Communist takeover (though British troops remained until October 1949). By the start of 1947 the Communists were weaker and more isolated than they had been in 1944. Their leaders insisted on holding fixed lines in the northern mountains allowing the royalist forces to use bombing and US-supplied napalm against them. As Mazower argues, 'Ultimately the KKE [Communist Party of Greece] got the worst of both worlds: its half hearted commitment to legalism frustrated many activists inside the Party without removing the suspicion of its bourgeois opponents.'[95] He also points out, regarding claims that the Communists were out to seize power, that, 'On the contrary, what evidence there is suggests the KKE – in so far as its divided leadership was capable of any decisions at all in the absence of a clear lead from Moscow – had decided not to seize power at a time when it easily could have done so.'[96]

The apparent success of Churchill's intervention in Greece had an impact on British politics. For a further ten years Britain believed itself still to be the key player in the Mediterranean. In 1956, after the Egyptian president Nasser nationalised the Suez Canal, Churchill's coup in Greece was held up as an example to follow by those urging Anthony Eden to invade Egypt to retake the Suez Canal. They assumed, wrongly, that the US would eventually accept this course of action as they had Churchill's in Greece. The Suez fiasco ended Britain's imperial illusions. In Greece civil war and repression paved the way for the dictatorship of the Colonels which lasted from 1967 to 1974. Greek society still bears the scars.

Parcelling Up Europe

As the prospect of Allied armies advancing into Europe loomed, in August 1943 Stalin proposed that a commission of the three Allied powers would jointly run Italy following Mussolini's fall, as well as Romania, Hungary and Bulgaria. The US and Britain vetoed Stalin's proposal, being determined to exclude the Russians from Italy. But as Kolko writes:

> By blocking the possibility of a Soviet veto in Italy, the Anglo-Americans gave themselves a free political hand in that country but also revealed to Stalin the decisive political constraints the Americans and British were prepared to impose where their political and strategic interests were involved. Much more important, it confirmed the reality that military conquest rather than negotiations would define the political outcome of the war in Europe.[97]

Stalin now applied this principle vigorously. In Italy and Greece the British and Americans were given free hand – at whatever cost to the Communists. When in August 1944 Romania signed an armistice with the invading Russian army, Stalin announced he would apply the same arrangements there as the Anglo-Americans had applied in Italy. Both Western powers were excluded from any say over the running of Romania and by extension Bulgaria and Hungary, which lay on the Russians' line of advance.[98]

In Romania the Communist Party emerged from hiding to join a government which included the remnants of the old pro-fascist dictatorship under King Michael. The Communist Party, Erickson points out, was

> swelled with a horde of place-seekers, collaborationists and men on the run from their Iron Guard [the Romanian fascists] past ... it was one bloated with elements which only weeks earlier had manned or supported the Antonescu dictatorship – the same thugs, secret policemen and soldiers swelled with the riff-raff signed up by the Communist leadership.[99]

After the initial Russian occupation coalition governments were formed with Communists in a minority, but in control of the security forces. As long as politicians agreed to follow Moscow's diplomatic line they were acceptable. In 1947–48, as the Cold War developed, the Communists moved to exert complete control, bulldozing through 'mergers' with the Socialist Parties, excluding virtually all non-Communists, and then purging party members who had operated outside the Soviet Union during the war and were thus deemed too independent.[100]

The US and Britain blocked Russia having any say in the unelected occupation administration of Italy and other Western European countries but in Eastern Europe the US demanded elections. Stalin, naturally, had no interest in that. Above all he did not want strong governments in Eastern Europe – even if they shared the same ideology as him.

Yugoslavia

The most powerful European Resistance force to emerge in the Second World War was in Yugoslavia. The Yugoslav state had been created at the close of the First World War as one of the cornerstones of a pro-French alliance of Central and Eastern states designed to police a re-emergent Germany. On 25 March 1941 the Yugoslav government signed a pact with Germany and Italy allying itself with the Axis and permitting free passage of German troops en route to invade Greece. Two days later military officers staged a coup in Belgrade ousting that government and deposing the pro-German regent, Prince Paul, and replacing him with 17-year-old King Peter II.

The new regime pleaded neutrality, but British funds had been available to the plotters. On 6 April the Germans bombed the Serb capital and within a few days German, Italian, Bulgarian and Hungarian troops invaded. The government surrendered on 17 April. Yugoslavia was divided between its invaders, with Germany receiving the greatest territorial and economic control, to the chagrin of Mussolini, who viewed the Balkans as part of Italy's *spazio vitale*.[101]

Mussolini championed Ante Pavelic and his Ustashi, who, after the destruction of Yugoslavia, took control of a rump Croatian state and began the ethnic cleansing of Jews, Orthodox Christians and Muslims. By 1943 the German military estimated the Ustashi regime had murdered at least 400,000 people. The Germans too employed reprisals against opposition to their occupation of the bulk of Serbia. In October 1941, following a partisan attack on German soldiers near the Serbian city of Kragujevac, the Nazis shot and killed between 6,000 and 8,000 people in three days – 50 people for each wounded soldier, 100 for each dead soldier. Among those killed was a whole generation of boys taken directly from their secondary school.

Meanwhile two Resistance forces began to emerge. The first was based around former Yugoslav officers who were loyal to the exiled Prince Paul, essentially Serbian nationalists who were extremely anti-communist. The other was led by the veteran Communist Josip Broz Tito and began rallying wider forces loyal to the idea of a federation of Slav people within Yugoslavia. In October 1941 the German military commander in Serbia, Harald Turner, wrote of the German response to partisan attacks:

> The devil is loose here you probably know ... five weeks ago, I put the first 600 against the wall, since then in one mopping-up operation we did in another 1,000, in a further operation again some 1,000 and in between I had 2,000 Jews and 200 Gypsies shot in accordance with the quota 1:100 for bestially murdered German soldiers, and a further 2,200, likewise almost all Jews, will be shot in the next eight days.

Turner added that the Jews 'have to disappear'.[102]

During the winter of 1941–42 Hungarian occupying troops and security forces massacred several thousand Serbs and Jews in the area around Novi Sad.[103] The royalists Chetniks, as they became known, largely avoided military attacks against occupation forces, instead waiting for the British and Americans to arrive. Tito's partisans began widespread guerrilla warfare, from Ljubljana in Slovenia to the mountains of Montenegro, becoming known as the People's Liberation Movement. Tito's message of 'brotherhood, ethnic solidarity, and a common patriotic struggle to free the country from foreign domination' began to attract wider support. 'The Partisans were the lone force in Yugoslavia that refused to recruit on a religious basis and who always appeared to be on the side of the underdog – those fighting for their lives and livelihood against exploiters, exterminators, and invaders.'[104] The partisans were also fired by the desire to give solidarity to Russia, pan-Slavism playing a part in this as well as party loyalty to Moscow.

The partisans' base was overwhelmingly among the peasants who were attracted by the prospect of land reform, moderate though Tito's promises were, while the Chetniks represented the old landowning classes. As the partisans' support grew the Chetniks felt threatened and began to broker local deals with the Germans and Italians culminating in joint operations against Tito's forces. By the autumn of 1941 Tito's forces had begun operations in Serbia and established a headquarters with a printing press and arms factory at Uzice. When the Germans attacked Uzice, the Chetnik leader Mihailovic proposed a truce and then assisted their assault.[105]

The partisans survived the winter of 1941–42 against the odds. In June 1942 30,000 German and Croat troops were sent into the field against 3,500 partisans. Many partisans were killed, but Tito's force survived, a victory in itself. By the year's end there were 11,000 partisans in Bosnia and some 40,000 across the whole of former Yugoslavia. One reason for their survival was the failure of the two occupying Axis powers to co-ordinate counterinsurgency operations, reflecting the fact that Germany and Italy vied with each other for control of the Balkans, with the Germans enjoying overwhelming success. By November 1942 the partisans had sufficient support to convene a national assembly at Bihac which allowed them to create the Anti-Fascist Council of National Liberation of Yugoslavia, laying the foundations for the provisional government to be formed a year later.[106]

Following Mussolini's dismissal in July 1943 the Italian occupation collapsed. Many Italian troops attempted to flee home, most were rounded up by the Germans, while some joined Tito's forces, forming a Garibaldi Brigade. The partisans seized large stocks of Italian arms and took control of large areas of Croatia and the islands in the Adriatic.[107] The Russians had done nothing to encourage Tito's partisan armies in Yugoslavia, while praising royalist forces that talked resistance but co-operated with Germany and Italy against their Communist opponents. In 1942 the hard-pressed partisans had requested Russian aid and were refused, being advised instead to unite with the Chetniks and told that Moscow had sent a military mission to Mihailovic. Tito would receive more aid from Britain when Churchill, despite his monarchism, recognised that the Communists were the ones killing Germans. The British had glimpsed that the Yugoslavs were on a collision course with Stalin.[108]

Stalin was reported to have been enraged when in 1943 he received a telegram from the partisans asking, 'If you cannot send us assistance, then at least do not hamper us.'[109] Moscow suspected that the Yugoslavs were essentially nationalists who wanted to exercise hegemony in the Balkans, an area allocated to Russian control. The unity Tito had created among the component parts of the Yugoslav population was an attractive prospect for others in the Balkans. The crucial thing was that Tito had created his own popular base which meant he could deal with Stalin on equal terms. By the close of 1943 Tito could claim some 250,000 fighters. His Chetnik opponents were openly siding with the Germans.[110]

The scale of partisan support won recognition from the American news journal, *Time*, which featured their exploits in February 1943, reporting:

> Down through the rocky hills of Croatia and Bosnia last week swept a formidable Axis army. Its aim: destruction of the Partisan armies and liquidation of the free democratic state comprising roughly one-sixth of Yugoslavia – larger than Massachusetts, Connecticut and Rhode Island combined. The Stukas started off well by destroying the towns of Drvar and Tsetingrad.
>
> Not without reason had the German High Command decided to engage in a major operation against the Yugoslav Partisans at a time when every Axis soldier was needed in Russia. The Partisans had proved themselves a menace to Hitler's New Order. In a recent advance their armies, commanded by stalwart, black-haired Kosta Nagy, captured the town of Karlovac, 30 miles from the Croatian capital of Zagreb, and approached Banja Luka, Bosnia's second largest town, throwing the fear of the Lord into the hearts of the puppet government.[111]

The *Time* piece noted Eisenhower had issued a note of congratulations to Mihailovic, adding that when they approached the exiled royal government, 'Pressed by journalists, the émigré officials admitted they had no idea where Mihailovic was, that he had been inactive for months while Partisans were doing almost all the fighting.'[112] This was the key reason why the British switched to supporting Tito. In contrast, as late as August 1944, the US OSS had sent a military mission to Mihailovic, which attempted to open negotiations about a separate surrender with German commanders. The mission was hastily withdrawn after Churchill complained to Roosevelt. The British and Americans agreed to provide air support for an offensive in September by eight Partisan divisions (120,000 soldiers) across Yugoslavia aimed at cutting German communications in the Balkan theatre. Axis forces lost 4,187 killed, 2,000 wounded and 5,782 captured. By the autumn of 1944 the Yugoslav partisans had liberated much of the country and had defeated a final German offensive against them, estimating German losses at 43,000. The partisans were holding down 21 German divisions, equal to the German force confronting the Allied armies in Italy.[113]

Two million women joined the national liberation movement (encompassing fighters and non-fighters). According to the official figures issued post-war, out of 800,000 fighters, 100,000 were women; 70 per cent of the guerrillas were under the age of 20; all nationalities were represented; and the majority were from peasant backgrounds.[114] As the Red Army neared Serbia, Tito flew to Moscow to meet Stalin in September 1944. He told Churchill's representative to the partisans that he needed to repair relations with the Russian dictator. He also sought to determine the status of the Russian forces entering the country. The meeting saw the two leaders clash, but Tito secured Stalin's agreement that the Yugoslavs could run their country and that the Red Army would quit Yugoslavia once it was cleared of German forces. The Red Army helped take Belgrade, treated the civilian population with contempt and then went on its way, leaving renewed tensions between Belgrade and Moscow.

Tito was aware that Moscow was trying to subvert his supporters and to secure control over Yugoslav intelligence and military forces. Later the Yugoslav leader simply ignored a statement from the three Allied leaders issued from Yalta that he should include non-collaborationist right-wingers in his government. All of this would later erupt into a dramatic break with Stalin.[115]

Albania

The Yugoslav partisans played a crucial role in the development of the Albanian resistance, first against the Italians and then the Germans – although this would later be denied by the post-war Enver Hoxha regime, which sided with Moscow in the Tito-Stalin split. Albania had declared itself independent from the Ottoman Empire in 1912. Much of the country was occupied by the Italians during the First World War but they failed to secure annexation during the Versailles negotiations (although the victorious allies recognised Italy's 'prominent interest' in the country). The country was woefully underdeveloped and deeply divided. Ahmet Zog – who ruled inter-war Albania first as prime minister, then as president, and finally as King Zog – was forced by the onset of the Great Depression to beg for a loan from Mussolini. Under its terms Italy assumed effective control of Albania's foreign policy and awarded itself the right to intervene in its internal affairs. Not content with that, Mussolini annexed the country in 1939. There was little resistance and Zog fled into exile.[116]

The Italians had no real support in the country and the economy deteriorated. By 1942 Italian control was effectively restricted to the towns and cities. At this stage the Resistance bands were localised and based round particular influential families. The Albanian Communist Party was effectively founded in November 1941 after the intervention of Yugoslav emissaries united disparate factions. Fifteen people were present at the inaugural meeting which elected a central committee and chose Enver Hoxha as the party's general secretary. He has been described 'as a nationalist first, then a Stalinist communist, and finally as an intellectual'.[117] The Communists helped launch the National Liberation Movement (NLM), whose partisans began large-scale operations against the Italians, spurred on by the Red Army's victory at Stalingrad. By June 1943 it claimed 10,000 partisans in 30 bands and 20 divisions.[118]

The Italian collapse in the summer of 1943 led to the Germans occupying Albania to secure communications with Greece. Fifteen thousand Italian troops surrendered to the partisans with between 1,500 and 2,000 joining the Antonio Gramsci Battalion that fought with the Resistance.[119] The various royalist and regional Resistance groupings would be drawn into collaborating with the Nazis, who recruited Albanians for a special SS unit and for anti-partisan operations. By February 1943 the Germans could count on the co-operation of 10,000 Albanians formerly in Resistance bands. In Kosovo – the mainly Albanian province of Yugoslavia incorporated into 'Greater Albania' by Mussolini in 1941 – the Third Reich encouraged the ethnic cleansing of the Serb population (Kosovo would remain hostile to both Tito's and Hoxha's partisans).[120] Despite a number of effective anti-partisan operations by the Germans and their Albanian allies, the NLM gathered strength. The German historian, Bernd J. Fischer, explains why:

> The partisan goal of re-establishing an independent Albania under a social system based upon equality ... was something for which many were willing to sacrifice. Conversely, few were willing to make similar sacrifices for the reestablishment of the old social system under Zog, which had clearly failed.[121]

The other nationalist, anti-communist groups were tarred by their collaboration with the Germans, or at least their refusal to resist the occupiers. The German occupation also created widespread hunger, which boosted the NLM. British SOE liaison officers estimated that by May 1944 the partisans had nearly 20,000 fighters. By October 1944 the Germans were withdrawing from Albania. The partisans launched an attack on the capital Tirana, seizing the old city and restricting the Germans to the new one. A month later, using artillery, the partisans broke through into the new city and the Germans hurriedly withdrew north. Fischer concludes: 'In November 1944 then, the communist-dominated NLM remained the only anti-fascist group with political credibility. They had fought the Germans more or less consistently and often under difficult conditions, although they had by no means defeated the Germans.'[122]

Hoxha's priority was to establish an independent Albania. That would entail breaking with his Yugoslav allies, who had provided much needed aid and expertise, but who wanted to create a wider post-war Balkan federation.

Conclusion

The Resistance movements throughout Europe, largely led by Communists and peopled by the working classes or peasants, were fighting a real anti-fascist war. It had a revolutionary potential which surfaced only to be thrust back by the Communists in line with Stalin's wishes. All three Allies either used the Resistance to their own ends or actively crushed it. The key to ensuring that the revolutionary potential of the Resistance did not come to fruition lay with the leadership of the Communist Parties, who limited their goal to achieving, at best, parliamentary democracy. The one leader who did not succumb to Stalin's wishes was Tito, because he had his own nationalist project and the mass support he built allowed him to realise it.

CHAPTER NINE

Asia and the Pacific

The Early War in the East

The Japanese army wanted full co-operation with its Axis partners. The navy and the foreign ministry were prepared to act in concert against the Soviet Union but did not want to antagonise Britain and the US. The Hitler-Stalin pact cast a shadow over the army allowing the navy and the foreign ministry to attempt to improve relations with London and Washington. This quickly broke down over the issue of China, which the Americans saw as a crucial future market.

Already on 26 July 1939 the US had served notice on Japan that it would not renew the 28-year-old commercial treaty between the two countries. In December 1939 the Roosevelt administration prohibited US corporations giving Japan technical information and manufacturing rights for the production of high-grade aviation gasoline. In June 1940 Congress passed the National Defense Act, which gave the president power to prohibit exports to Japan, and on 2 July Roosevelt restricted the sale of arms and ammunition, and materials such as aluminium and parts for aircraft. US sanctions were potentially devastating. More than half of Japan's imports came from the US, with 40 per cent of its exports being sold there.[1]

German successes in the spring of 1940 reinforced Japan's alliance with Germany and Italy and brought the army back into dominance within the government. Berlin pushed for its ally to attack Hawaii and the Philippines, to which the army replied positively. Opinion in ruling circles now veered towards a drive south into South East Asia and its oilfields, but it could not get the army to halt or limit its operations in China. These splits were never resolved.

In the absence of a unified strategy for both the army and the navy, the two services worked out their own plans for operations against Russia and the US respectively and then submitted them for the Emperor's approval. The government could not decide which the most likely enemy was – or whether it should insist on planning for a war with more than one power. This meant it was unable to establish priorities regarding military spending; planning for a war against Russia required strengthening the army while a war against the US required a bigger navy. This did not stop Japanese military and ruling circles believing that swift military blows could win them a vast empire. The old colonial empires were clearly not in a strong position. Japan began testing the waters.

In April 1939 two Chinese nationalists, operating out of the British-held 'concession' port of Tianjin (Tientsin), assassinated a Japanese official. The local British administration refused to hand over the two men, so the Japanese blockaded the city and demanded a British withdrawal from it. The British could do nothing. Naval forces earmarked for any confrontation in the Far East were needed in the Mediterranean or nearer home to face Germany and Italy. The Japanese began strip-searching British citizens entering or leaving the city. British officials on the ground eventually handed over the two men for execution, thus ending the blockade.

Despite occasional rhetoric against European imperialism, Japan was engaged in its own imperial expansion and would treat 'fellow' Asians in ways just as brutal as the European colonial powers. A new government took office in July 1940. Even before the first full cabinet meeting the four principal ministers – the Premier, Prince Konoye, war minister Hideki Tojo, navy minister Zengo Yoshida, and foreign minister Yosuke Matsuoka – agreed that Japan's main objective was the establishment of a new order in East Asia, known as the 'Greater East Asia Co-Prosperity Sphere'. The first targets for inclusion were Hong Kong, Burma, French Indochina, Thailand, Malaya, the Dutch East Indies, the Philippines and New Guinea; later India, Australia and New Zealand were added to the list. This involved a closer alliance with the Axis, a non-aggression pact with the Soviet Union, and every effort to bring the China war to an end. Any nation that opposed this programme was the enemy of Japan.

Despite its title, the 'Co-Prosperity Sphere' involved a racist hierarchy in which Japan's 'superior' culture, a synthesis of east and west, presided over a series of other cultures akin to it but deemed inferior. Marriages between Japanese citizens and other races were restricted on the grounds that they would weaken Japan's unique fusion. Plans were laid to settle 12 million Japanese in Korea, Indochina, the Philippines, Australia and New Zealand, where they would occupy a dominant position.

Meanwhile the Japanese army in China suffered a rude awakening in July 1940 when the Communists' Eighth Route Army launched the 'Hundred Regiments Offensive'. The Japanese held the Communists in low esteem and had little intelligence about them, but 'more than 20,000 Japanese were killed in sporadic battles'. The initial Communist success was ended with the Japanese concentrating their forces, counter-attacking and defeating their opponents.[2] The collapse of French and Dutch colonial power in the region in the summer of 1940, and the concentration of British forces in Europe and North Africa, encouraged Japan further, but there was still no unanimity on where to strike: one faction argued for the need to concentrate on China, another for taking Siberia from the USSR, and a third, now the largest faction, for a drive southwards to control the Western Pacific.

In June 1940 the Japanese demanded that Britain withdraw its forces from China and block supplies from Hong Kong or Burma reaching Chiang's armies. Churchill argued for accepting this ultimatum, and after considerable discussion the British government acquiesced. The Japanese demanded of France, firstly, that Japanese troops be stationed in northern Indochina, adjacent to the China border, to intercept supplies to Chiang Kai-shek; secondly, to use airfields there to bomb the 'Burma Road', which carried supplies overland from Burma to

Chiang's forces. Vichy accepted these demands and a month later Japanese troops entered Indochina.[3]

In September 1940 Germany and Italy recognised Japan's construction of a new order in Asia, and in return Japan recognised the new order in Europe. Each signatory agreed to come to each other's aid 'with all political, economic, and military means' should any of them be attacked by a power with which it was not then at war. With Germany and Italy already at war with Britain and the Hitler-Stalin pact still in force this was clearly aimed at the US.

In his 'Fireside Chat' broadcast on 29 December 1940, President Roosevelt argued that the Tripartite Pact represented a threat to the United States and that in response the US must increase its aid to the free nations and make greater efforts to re-arm.[4] In the spring of 1941 the Japanese foreign minister, on a visit to Moscow, drew up a neutrality pact with Stalin. Both states agreed to respect each other's territorial integrity and to remain neutral in case of attack by a third power. The pact was only agreed to in Tokyo after bitter argument and opposition from the army. It benefited the Soviets who would soon withdraw forces from the Far East to defend Moscow from German attack, but the Japanese army would not consent to any weakening of its strength in Manchuria. The huge Japanese army in Manchuria was left sidelined until the final days of the Second World War when they were powerless in the face of a brief and successful campaign by the Red Army in August 1945.[5]

It was hoped too that a treaty with Moscow might lead to Chiang Kai-shek coming to terms. Next to the United States, Russia was his main support. Stalin did not believe the Chinese Communists could take power and did not want that to happen, in large part because they were a potential challenge to his own authority over the international Communist movement. But there was no rapprochement between Toyko and Chiang. Japan ended up fighting a war on two fronts: the navy would go on the offensive in the Pacific while the army maintained its effort in China. In fact, while the navy planned the 'southern advance' the army was planning a 'northern advance' – an attack on Russia.[6] The army made little effort to evaluate the US threat, concentrating their intelligence on Russia and insisting that the Americans were the navy's responsibility. In addition they dismissed the American ability to fight claiming that 'Americans are individualistic and they cannot stand a long drawn out war.'[7] On the basis of this the Japanese army believed the war with the US would be over by the spring of 1942, leaving them free to fight the Soviet Union, and at the beginning of that year planned to send four more divisions to Manchuria for that purpose.[8]

Japan's economy was a tenth the size of the US's with far fewer natural resources and no secure oil supplies. Its armed forces lacked tanks, their main infantry rifle dated back to 1905, and their artillery was of the same vintage. Japanese industry could not supply modern weapons in the quantities necessary to match the Americans. The Japanese ruling class, unlike the generals, did not believe they could defeat the US but they hoped they could inflict heavy enough blows to force Washington to accept Japanese hegemony in Eastern Asia and the Eastern Pacific.

There were some who grasped the limits of Japan's economic and military capacity to fight a prolonged war. In late 1940 a Japanese government report drawn up by army, naval and government research officers (in an unusual instance of co-operation) concluded that: 'Japan's national power could allow her to fight against the Allied powers for at most two years, and that the Soviet entry into the war would deliver a final blow to Japan.' When it was read by the war minister, Tojo, he responded: 'You did a good job, but your report is based on a kind of armchair theory, not a real war. As you can imagine, we had never expected to beat Russia before the Russo-Japanese war, but we won. War is not always carried out as planned. We will face unpredicted elements in war.'[9]

The economic war planning section of the War Ministry also reported to the Army General Staff in September 1941: 'The Japanese industrial capacity will peak in the near future, while Allied capacity will continue to increase. We cannot fight a long drawn out war with the Allies.' Marshal Hajime Sugiyama, the Chief of Staff of the Imperial Japanese Army said: 'The report is perfect and there is no room to argue. But the report is against our national policy [war with the Allies].' He ordered that the report be burnt.[10]

As John W. Dower argues, the various factions of the Japanese ruling class saw themselves threatened by 'truly alarming developments: political chaos, economically crippling anti-Japanese boycotts in China and internal communist revolts there', together with 'American and European protectionist policies, global trends towards autarchic "block economies" and coercive Western policies in the months prior to Pearl Harbor'.[11] Japan was at a crossroads.

The United States increasingly saw the rivalry with Japan as a clash between an autarchic model of capital accumulation and the US's 'open door' policy – the precursor of what today is called globalisation:

> It was the outbreak of war between China and Japan in 1937 ... which convinced American observers that Tokyo was aiming for autarky.
>
> For the next two years the American administration groped towards a response to this growing threat ... For nearly another year, it engaged in a programme of cautious pressure against Tokyo. Finally, in increased frustration it commenced eighteen months of economic 'cold war' ended only by the Imperial Navy's attack on Pearl Harbor.[12]

In July 1941 Roosevelt ordered all Japanese assets in the US to be frozen and, crucially, stopped all oil exports to Japan. The *New York Times* described it as 'the most drastic blow short of war'.[13] The US was joined in this boycott by Britain and the Dutch. Japan faced being cut off from 90 per cent of its oil supplies. In response, the Japanese government agreed on a 'southward advance' aimed at British and Dutch colonial possessions. But there was no co-ordinated army-navy policy. As one former navy minister explained regarding military operations, 'if the Chief of the Army General Staff says that we will do this, that is the end of it; and as far as the navy operations are concerned, if the Chief of the Navy General Staff says we will do this, that fixes it; and should there develop difference of opinion between the two chiefs, then nothing can be accomplished'.[14]

In August 1941 navy and army planners clashed over Japan's strategic priorities. The navy favoured a step-by-step advance from the Philippines to Borneo, then Java, Sumatra and Malaya. The army favoured the early seizure of Malaya, bypassing the Philippines, thus delaying war with the US. Unable to agree on either of these options, they went for simultaneous attacks along the two axes. This would create serious problems of co-ordination and timing and a dangerous dispersion of forces. At this time an attack on Pearl Harbor was not considered. In October 1941 negotiations with Washington effectively ended when the US demanded Japanese withdrawal from China. The ensuing crisis in Tokyo led to the fall of the government and its replacement by an administration dominated by the military under General Tojo.

The Japanese set a deadline for a conclusion to the negotiations with Washington: 25 November (the British and Americans found this out on 11 November). On 20 November the Japanese suggested a temporary agreement while talks were extended for another three months. Roosevelt rejected this (Churchill wished to accept but was not consulted).

On 26 November the US secretary of state, Cordell Hull, delivered the final Allied proposal demanding the withdrawal of all Japanese forces from Indochina and China:

[Major General Kenryo] Sato [Chief of the Bureau of Military Affairs] was informed of the note and commented on the 29th: 'Reading the proposal, it was far more belligerent than we had expected. Now we decided to wage war against the United States.' [Foreign affairs minister, Shigenori] Togo was shocked by the proposal because of the gap between his expectation of US appeasement and the harsh terms of the Hull Note, and gave up his diplomatic talks with the United States.[15]

The Japanese naval commander, Admiral Isoroku Yamamoto, had no illusions about the potential power of the US. The navy's assessment was that in 1941 it would have 70 per cent of the US's naval power and this would decline to 50 per cent in 1943 and 30 per cent in 1944. Asked about the chances of success against the Americans he replied: 'If I am told to fight ... I shall run wild for the first six months ... but I have absolutely no confidence for the second or third year.'[16] He was aware that in June 1941 naval intelligence 'estimated that Japan's oil stockpile was about 620 million barrels, which would be consumed within two years. More than 80 per cent of Japanese oil imports depended on the United States, but these imports were banned in August 1941. Put simply, Japan would run out of oil by the end of 1943.'[17]

Yamamoto had already submitted a plan for an attack on Pearl Harbor, arguing that the success of the southward drive depended on the destruction of the American fleet. He failed to convince his colleagues and threatened to resign from the navy. His threat overcame his colleagues' resistance. In mid October the Navy General Staff accepted his plan for a surprise carrier-based attack on

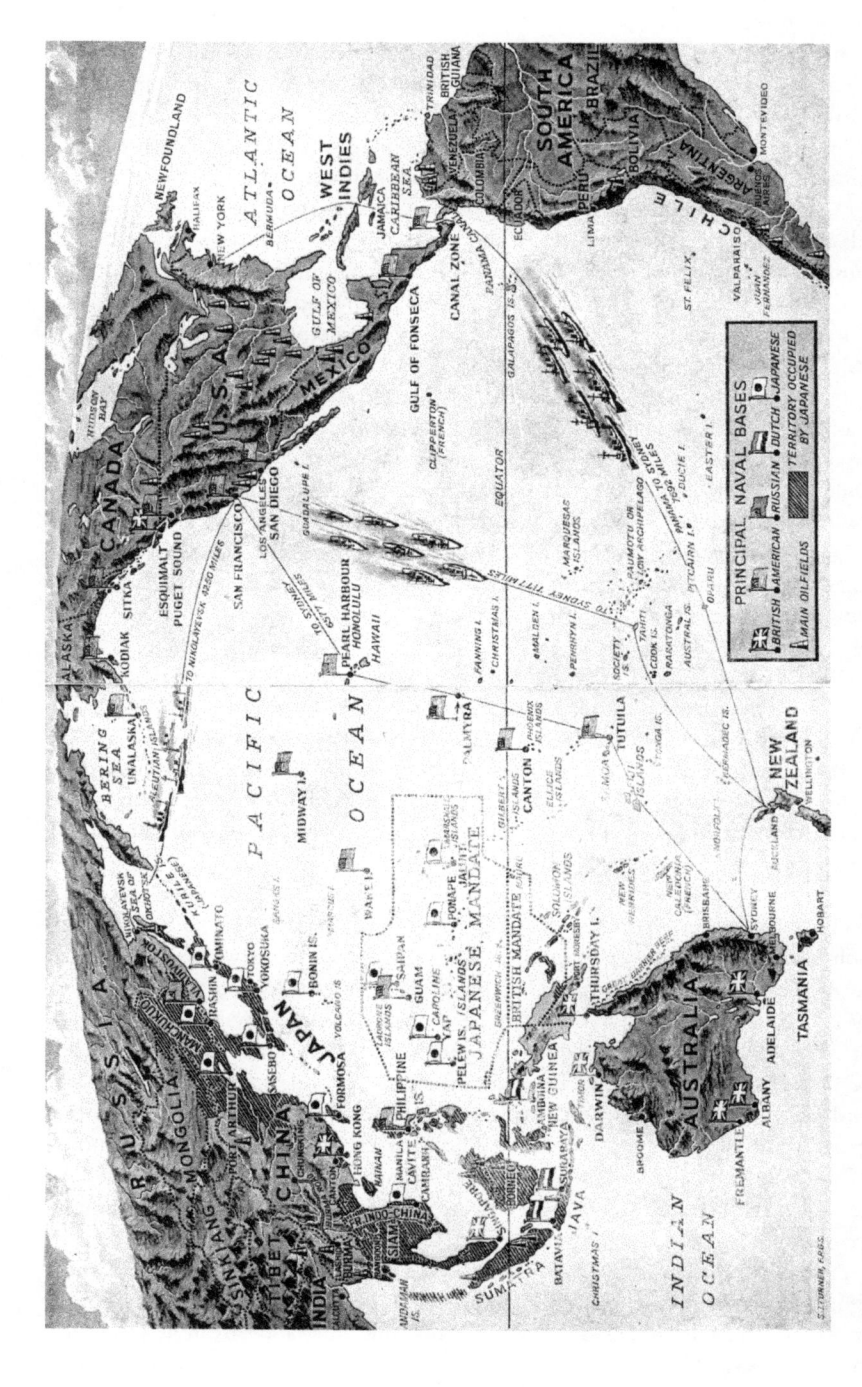

Pacific theatre of war at March 1942

Pearl Harbor and incorporated it into the larger plan for war. On 26 November the Japanese task force charged with attacking Pearl Harbor set sail. In the event the US aircraft carriers were at sea when the attack happened on 7 December and the oil storage units were not hit. The attack did not destroy US naval power in the region.

After Pearl Harbor, Washington portrayed Japan as the first 'Evil Empire'. In reality Japan was still an industrialising country when it went to war in 1941. It would find that the US, even when prioritising the war in Europe, could easily dwarf its military efforts.

War in the Pacific

The immediate cause of the spread of the war to the Pacific theatre was the Japanese attack on the US Pacific fleet's base at Pearl Harbor in Hawaii in December 1941, but as we have seen Japan was already long at war in China and had occupied France's colonies in Indochina.

The attack on Pearl Harbor was immediately followed by attacks on British-controlled Malaya, the US-controlled Philippines and, after their fall, Dutch-controlled Indonesia. The United States, Britain, and the forces loyal to the Dutch government in exile (Holland was under German occupation), together with the Indian army (India being a British colony was denied any say on whether it was at war or not), Australia and New Zealand were all now at war with Japan.

Japanese strategy was aimed at neutralising American striking power in the Pacific, the US Pacific fleet at Pearl Harbor and the US Far East Air Force in the Philippines, and then moving southward and westwards to occupy Malaya, Indonesia (then the Dutch East Indies), the Philippines, Wake Island, Guam, the Gilbert Islands, Thailand and Burma. Once in control of these areas, the Japanese intended to establish a defensive perimeter in the Western Pacific. The hope was that the US would wear itself out in frontal assaults against this perimeter and ultimately would accept a negotiated peace, leaving Japan in possession of most of its conquests. The initial part of this plan was highly successful. The opening campaigns of the Pacific war saw Japanese forces register successes as spectacular as those of Germany between 1939 and 1941, as will be detailed below.

In December 1940 the Germans handed over a captured document sent by sea from the British Chief of Staff in London to the British commander in chief in the Far East in which he said Hong Kong and Thailand were indefensible: 'There is no doubt that the document encouraged the Japanese war planners in their decision to advance into Southeast Asia.'[18] A month later Japanese army intelligence decoded a cable from the head of the British Far Eastern Command describing the British position in Malaya (Singapore island is at the bottom of the Malay peninsula) as 'highly vulnerable'.[19]

The British had a racist attitude to the Japanese. In 1935 the British naval attaché in Tokyo informed naval intelligence: 'The lack of command experience at sea of the more senior officers must be a serious handicap to fighting efficiency.

I cannot believe that the system is capable of producing really efficient ships companies for war purposes ... I think the IJN [Imperial Japanese Navy] is of the 2nd class.'[20] Not to be outdone the British military attaché argued: 'The Japanese are a slow thinking and naturally cautious people. This applies especially to the Army, in which the officer class is still very largely bound by tradition.'[21] Taking matters further the British commander in the Far East, Air Marshal Robert Brooke-Popham, commented after a visit to Hong Kong in December 1940, where he looked across the border into Chinese territory occupied by the Japanese: 'I had a good close-up, across the barbed wire, of various sub-human specimens dressed in dirty grey uniforms, which I was informed were Japanese soldiers.'[22]

The whole basis of British strategy in the event of war with Japan was that Singapore would become the crucial base for operations in the region. Within two days of the attack on Pearl Harbor on 7 December 1941, the Japanese had succeeded in destroying nearly all the RAF's frontline planes in attacks on air bases on the Malayan peninsula. After this Japanese troops began landing in Malaya. On 8 December the battleship *Prince of Wales*, one of the most modern in the Royal Navy, and the battle cruiser *Repulse* were sent north to block the landings. The two ships were all that the Royal Navy could provide to defend Singapore. The aircraft carrier that was supposed to provide air cover had broken down en route and the ships had no protection against air attack. Two days later both vessels were repeatedly attacked and then sunk by Japanese torpedo-bombers.

It was the Royal Navy's most devastating defeat of the war, a body blow to Churchill, and proof that capital ships without air cover were very vulnerable to air attack. The loss of the *Prince of Wales* and *Repulse* signalled something else, as acknowledged by the British Chief of the Imperial General Staff: 'It means that from Africa eastwards to America through the Indian Ocean and the Pacific, we have lost command of the sea.'[23] The loss of control of the Indian Ocean was a serious matter. The British moved quickly to occupy the island of Madagascar, having to defeat the French colonial forces which controlled it, to forestall the Japanese. It was the growing demand of Japan's naval war with the US in the Pacific which allowed the British to regain control of the sea lanes to India.

The British forces in Malaya, comprising 90,000 British, Indian and Australian troops, outnumbered the Japanese, who had 65,000 troops. But after their defeat at the Battle of Jitra, fought on 11 and 12 December, the British were in retreat. By 31 January 1942 British forces had evacuated Malaya, crossing over to the island of Singapore. Their commander, Lieutenant General Arthur Percival, spread his men along the 70-mile coastline. When the Japanese, concentrating their forces, penetrated the stretched defence line, they left many British troops isolated from the fighting. As the Japanese advanced through Malaya, Percival had said: 'It will be a lasting disgrace if we are defeated by an army of clever gangsters many times inferior in numbers to our men.'[24]

On 15 February 1942, to the surprise of the Japanese, who were by now desperately short of ammunition, Percival surrendered. Twenty-three thousand Japanese soldiers captured 100,000 of the island's garrison of British imperial and commonwealth forces. Percival ignored Churchill's insistence that they should fight to the last. Many of those captured had landed on the island after it had become clear defeat was looming and had never fired a shot. General Gordon Bennett, commander of the Australian 8th Division, decided that it was vital he report back to Canberra on how to defeat the Japanese, something he had failed to do in the Malay fighting. He defied orders to remain with his men, commandeered a boat out of Singapore and returned to Australia. He did not receive another command.

The Indian nationalist Subhas Chander Bose called Singapore 'the graveyard of the British Empire'.[25] Since the eighteenth century, British military power had swept all before it in Asia. Now, with one stroke, the myth of its invincibility was gone. Nationalists sensed they could throw off the shackles of colonial rule. In January 1942 the Japanese attacked the south of Burma. British forces were too few and had only outdated air support. The Japanese were able to take Rangoon, the chief port, by March, and, reinforced by the troops who had taken Singapore, they pushed the British back into India. Burmese nationalists fought alongside the Japanese and formed a government under their protection which was soon engaged in attacks on ethnic minorities.

The British were not alone in their humiliation. Within hours of the Pearl Harbor attack Japanese planes had struck the main US air base in the Philippines, destroying 100 aircraft caught on the ground. This raid was followed by a Japanese landing. In three weeks Japanese forces established complete aerial and naval supremacy, cut the line between the Philippines and Australia, and stood ready to advance on Manila.

The US commander, General Douglas MacArthur, decided he could not block the Japanese advance and withdrew his forces into the Corregidor fortress, on an island in Manila Bay and the Bataan Peninsula on the other side of the Bay from the capital, in the hope relief would come. When it became clear no help was coming MacArthur was evacuated to Australia and the US troops abandoned by him surrendered.

Dutch forces in Indonesia loyal to the government in exile numbered 98,000 men. But the Dutch fleet and the few British warships operating in these waters were wiped out in February 1942 and the Dutch surrendered the archipelago with its vital oilfields. Between the spring of 1941 and the spring of 1942 the Japanese navy was the most powerful in the world, with seven aircraft carriers deploying 474 aircraft. It needed to secure a quick victory in the Pacific before the US mobilised their industrial resources to build a fleet to match it. The gap between the wartime economies of Japan and the US was simply huge. As A.D. Harvey points out:

> The Japanese leaders ... had realised from the very beginning that the productive capacity of the Japanese munitions industry could not compete with that of the far more technically advanced industrial sector in the US, though they could not possibly have guessed how great their inferiority would be. Coal output per miner was 164 tonnes in Japan and 1,021 tonnes in the US in 1940, and in 1944 it had fallen to 119 tonnes in Japan while rising to

1,430 tonnes in the US. High explosive output per man was only 3.68 per cent of American levels, propellant powder output an incredible, humiliating 0.54 per cent – pro-rata one American working a 44-hour week produced eight times more propellant than 15 Japanese working a 67-hour week.[26]

The ability of the US to sink Japanese shipping quickly began to be felt:

> Only several hours after the attack on Pearl Harbor, the US navy decided to engage in unrestricted air and submarine warfare against Japan. The American submarine fleet achieved its first significant results during its mission to block Japan's maritime transport of reinforcements and supplies to Guadalcanal. From August to November of 1942, American submarines sank 62 Japanese ships (nearly 270,000 tons). Over the course of the entire war, the US navy's submarine attacks accounted for Japan's loss of 213 naval vessels and roughly 1150 merchant ships (totalling some 4,850,000 tons).[27]

The Japanese state was far from being the monolith it was portrayed as in US propaganda. The Japanese army had placed one of its leading lights, General Hideki Tojo, as premier from October 1941 to August 1944, but he could not manage a ruling class divided four ways between army, navy, civilian government, and huge business combines, the *zaibatsu*. Early military success only accentuated these divisions. The army simply took control of all raw materials in the territories they occupied, with the navy doing the same in the islands, and also taking control of the shipping. Both wings of the armed forces then cut deals with the *zaibatsu*.

Things got more complicated with the army and navy placing orders for two completely different aircraft designs for a two-engine bomber and a fighter plane. They also both insisted that the one company capable of producing radar build two different systems in a factory divided in two, where the engineers working for one service were barred from entering the area working for the rival service. The result was two entirely separate systems, neither of which worked properly.

Japanese plane design was excellent and Mitsubishi built one of the world's largest aeroplane plants. But in 1941 productivity in the aircraft sector was 44 per cent that of the US, falling to 26 per cent three years later. Japanese machine tools lagged behind American or German designs. There was not enough skilled labour. By 1944 the physical health of the workforce suffered from food shortages and the effects of bombing (absenteeism was at 20 per cent of the workforce in 1944 reaching 34 per cent a year later). Throughout it all, aeroplane plants had to produce two separate fighters and night fighters for the army and the navy.

From the beginning America's war against Japan took on a racial character. As one history notes: 'All Japanese people were lumped together as misshapen, ugly, stupid, dwarf people. They were like nothing so much as Mr Tolkien's orcs in *The Lord of the Rings*, creations of a people of sheer malevolence and hideousness.'[28] The US commander General Douglas MacArthur, who would be the occupation ruler of Japan after the surrender, viewed the war as a 'Christian mission', part of 'the white man's burden'.[29]

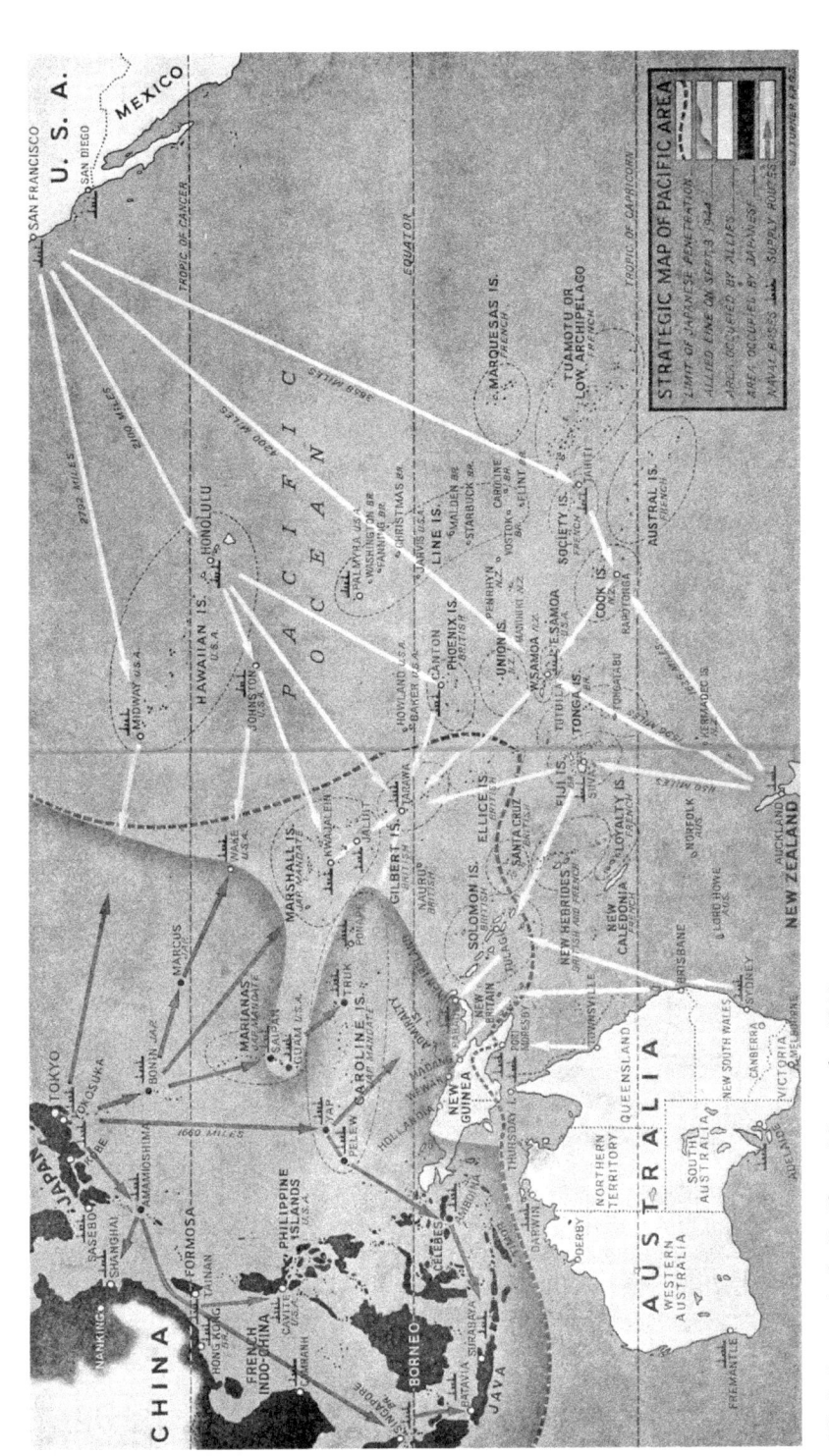

Allied advances in the Pacific to 3 September 1944

A US army poster urged workers to 'Stay on the job until every murdering Jap is wiped out.' Douglas Aircraft commissioned the 'Tokio Kid', which appeared on the back cover of its monthly magazine. A semi-human Japanese figure complete with fangs thanked 'slackers'. The Tokio Kid would branch out to appear on propaganda posters.

Hollywood, comic books and newspapers portrayed the Japanese as inhuman, apelike figures who threatened American civilisation, and women in particular. Disney sent Bugs Bunny to 'Nip the Nips', while Popeye routed the Japanese navy in 'You're a Sap Mr Jap', which spawned a hit record. Those of Japanese origins living in the US were on the receiving end of 'Jap hunts':

> At first the Japanese-American population were subjected to abuse, harassment and worse as individual American citizens 'took matters into their own hands.' Various curfews were imposed and Japanese-Americans were excluded from specified 'prohibitive zones', which grew in number and extent over the first few months after Pearl Harbor until these unfortunates were barred altogether from the western third of Washington and Oregon, the western half of California and the southern quarter of Arizona (which was judged to be relatively near to the Pacific coast). Then in June 1942 orders were given that led to further controls which effectively deprived all Americans of Japanese extraction of their liberty within any part of those four states.
>
> Eventually, 119,000 were taken away to be concentrated at ten internment camps established for that purpose at remote, inhospitable sites (where they lived in terrible hardship and a significant number died from their privations).[30]

No compensation was paid by the federal government until the 1980s. Americans of German or Italian extraction did not suffer internment.

The US on the Offensive

Japan was not in a position to strike directly at Britain or the US (despite invasion scares in the US after Pearl Harbor). They could only hope to sever the long-distance communications the powers would need to sustain their positions in the Pacific and South East Asia. They succeeded with Britain, though it was able to rely on the Indian army to repulse an attack through Burma. With the Americans they failed. Japanese invasion forces had limited supplies of food, slightly better supplies of ammunition, and little else. There were no field hospitals, stretcher bearers or first-aid teams, and few medical supplies.

As early as October 1942 Japanese troops fighting at Guadalcanal had much less ammunition than their American opponents and faced starvation as rice supplies failed to reach them. American losses were 1,979 killed and 6,000 wounded. The Japanese lost over 32,000 dead – more than half of them due to lack of medical care. Two years later, in the battles at Imphal and Kohima, in north-east India, half of the 115,000-strong Japanese army died from malnutrition or lack of medical care. On the Burma-Siam railway (immortalised in David Lean's film

The Bridge on the River Kwai), for each of the five POWs who died building the railway, three Japanese guards died.[31] In the Pacific theatre for every American GI there were four tons of supplies; for each Japanese soldier two pounds.[32] Ultimately the Japanese failed to press home their early advantage and failed to exploit the vast resources under their control.

In May 1942 the Americans fought their first major sea battle, engaging Japanese naval forces, who were defending an attack on New Guinea and the Solomon Islands as a prelude to an assault on Australia. In what became known as the Battle of the Coral Sea, neither side achieved a clear victory, but the Americans blunted the Japanese attack. A month later the Americans won a crucial victory at the Battle of Midway, the westernmost point of the Hawaiian Islands. The Japanese had planned on surprising and destroying the remnants of the US fleet, but the Americans had broken the enemy code and were ready. The two fleets did not sight each other, the issue was decided by airpower, as Dallas Woodbury Isom points out:

> The lethal damage that determined the outcome was done during a two minute period when three out of the four Japanese aircraft carriers were set ablaze by American divebombers.
>
> When the battle was finally over, all four carriers were at the bottom of the ocean. With four of the six fleet aircraft carriers in her navy now gone, along with about 250 carrier planes and more than 100 irreplaceable pilots, Japan's naval airpower was decimated. What little chance Japan had of winning the war in the Pacific went up in the smoke of her burning carriers.[33]

The outcome at Midway meant that the US could both prioritise the war in Europe and plan to go over to the offensive in the Pacific theatre.[34] Despite their defeat, Japanese forces launched a land offensive along the north-eastern coast of New Guinea, seizing Tulagi and Guadalcanal in the Solomon Islands, astride the US-Australian lines of communication. In hard fighting in the autumn of 1942, Australian, New Zealand and US forces halted the Japanese offensive on New Guinea and counter-attacked, eventually clearing out Japanese forces by the year's end. In the Solomon islands a US marine assault on Guadalcanal succeeded in taking an airfield being completed by Japanese.

The Japanese navy launched a night attack using surface ships with no air support, aiming to destroy troop transports. The attack destroyed one Australian and three American cruisers but not transports.[35] Japanese troops landed on the island but could not break through the defences to re-take the airfield. Starvation and disease affected them badly. Rations were reduced to one sixth of what was the norm on the frontline and 'most Japanese soldiers died of hunger and disease'.[36]

The Japanese naval commander, Admiral Yamamoto, once more hoped for a decisive battle in which he could destroy US naval power in the Pacific. Mustering all the ships he could, he moved to meet the US fleet which was gathering at Guadalcanal, confident of achieving victory. Nevertheless, at battle's end the Americans had won a conclusive victory ... they destroyed two Japanese battleships along with sundry other vessels and almost completely interdicted the Guadalcanal bound transports .... American pilots and antiaircraft gunners also took a fearsome toll of Japanese fliers, further eroding Japan's already tenuous air superiority.[37]

US naval planners now called for a major thrust across the central Pacific towards Taiwan, while General Douglas MacArthur, commander of ground forces in New Guinea, argued for a major offensive aimed at liberation of the Philippines. This was not simply about strategy. MacArthur believed the US had to undo the damage done by the loss of the Philippines in order to demonstrate its might, the navy wanted to attack Japan as quickly as possible in order to guarantee US hegemony of the Pacific. In the end the US Joint Chiefs of Staff, surveying the US's growing resources, settled this dispute by sanctioning both offensives.

Admiral Nimitz and General MacArthur began two campaigns of island hopping, advancing towards the Japanese home islands. By mid 1943 Nimitz in the Central Pacific could base naval task forces around new, larger and faster carriers of the *Essex* class (27,000 tons) and lighter carriers of the *Independence* class (11,000 tons), alongside which were a mix of destroyers, cruisers, battleships, submarines, minesweepers and support craft. In the Central Pacific these task forces could provide both air and naval support for long-distance operations, with the entire Pacific fleet ready to confront the main Japanese fleet if it threatened to give battle.

Nimitz aimed to advance via the Gilberts, Marshalls, Marianas, Carolines and Palau towards Japan itself. This was the axis most favoured by the US Chiefs of Staff. MacArthur aimed to advance from the north coast of New Guinea to the southern Philippines, relying more on land-based than carrier-based aircraft. The range of land-based aircraft set the limits to his advance. Nimitz's forces were charged with taking a succession of atolls and islands. That required sufficient naval power and carrier-based aircraft to establish air and naval superiority and the ability to take on the main body of the Japanese fleet if need be. The US benefited from being the dominant naval power, leaving Britain and Japan trailing in its wake. The key measure was the number of aircraft carriers.

The US navy had discovered that groups of aircraft carriers could advance deep into enemy-held territory, within range of Japanese air and naval forces, without land-based air cover. This made possible the long-distance operations required in the Central Pacific. The success of the island hopping assault on Japan depended on carriers that could neutralise enemy airfields and counter-attacks, and defend amphibious operations and convoys. Having achieved early success with carrier fleets, the Japanese now seemed to retreat towards reliance on capital ships, building only three new aircraft carriers. As serious was the weakness of its merchant marine. Pre-war Japan had relied on foreign trading vessels; now it did not have enough ships to supply the home islands and US submarines relentlessly destroyed those it had.

In September 1943 the Japanese drew a gloomy assessment of their ability to wage war. Ships and aircraft were needed to blunt and repel an American offensive. The army and navy estimated they required 55,000 aircraft in 1944, but total Japanese aircraft production in August 1943 was only 1,360 and in September 1,470. The shipping problem was no less serious than the shortage of aircraft. In a period of less than two years, 445 vessels had been sunk and another 414 damaged. Japan had to match US and British naval forces, maintain sufficient forces in Manchuria to deal with a possible attack by the Russians, and sustain large-scale operations in China. It was impossible. Accordingly the Japanese devised a defensive line extending from the Kuril Islands southward through the Bonins, Marianas and Carolines, New Guinea and the Sunda Islands to Burma. This line encompassed the 'Greater East Asia Co-Prosperity Sphere'. It contained the raw materials and food required by Japan to wage war. It also meant shorter lines of communication, allowing Japanese commanders to believe they could repulse any large-scale enemy offensive and ultimately launch a counter-offensive of their own. It was not to be. By late 1943 the Americans had already pierced the new defence line.

The US had initially hoped British forces would be able to launch an amphibious operation from India to retake Rangoon in Burma and to reopen a supply line northwards to Chiang Kai-shek's forces in China. But the British did not have the resources to do this. By the end of the year the Americans had concluded that their Pacific forces would reach the China coast before either British or Chinese forces could come in through the back door. At the Cairo Conference in November 1943, attended by Roosevelt, Churchill and Chiang Kai-shek, it was agreed that the main effort against Japan should be concentrated in the Pacific, with operations elsewhere given subordinate roles. In other words, the war against Japan would be conducted by the US. The declaration issued at the conference also stated that Manchuria and Taiwan would be returned to China, that Korea would be given independence, and other territories occupied in 1941 and 1942 would be returned to their former owners – that is Britain, France and the Netherlands would regain their colonial possessions. At the subsequent summit of Russian, US and British leaders in Tehran, Stalin pledged to attack Japan after victory over Germany.

Nimitz and MacArthur's dual advance gathered pace in 1944. Nimitz took Kwajalein in the Marshall Islands and that summer his forces conquered Saipan, Tinian and Guam in the Marianas. The Americans now had air bases from which they could carry out extensive air attacks on Japan. Meanwhile MacArthur advanced through the Bismarck Archipelago and thence westward along the New Guinea coast towards the Philippines.

In October 1944 the US Chiefs of Staff accepted Nimitz's proposal to shift the Central Pacific attack to Iwo Jima in January 1945 and then against Okinawa and northwards to Japan. Operations aimed at taking Taiwan and bases on the Chinese coast were dropped. MacArthur was directed towards the conquest of the Philippines, though this was now secondary to Nimitz's thrust. That October MacArthur's forces landed on the Philippine island of Leyte, through which Japanese oil supplies were transported. The Japanese gathered their remaining forces to try to prevent the landing. The Japanese air force had attacked the American fleet off the island of Taiwan and despite suffering a heavy defeat announced it had sunk 19 aircraft carriers and four battleships. The Japanese navy believed they could only have sunk four but in fact none had been sunk. On this false information they decided on what they believed would be the decisive naval battle of the war.[38]

The ensuing Battle of Leyte Gulf in October 1944 was the final major naval battle of the Pacific war. The Japanese fleet deployed just 90 planes on its four remaining carriers. The Japanese surface fleet was virtually destroyed. Simultaneously US submarines sank much of the Japanese merchant fleet. The loss of naval control of the Western Pacific meant that even though Japan controlled the oilfields to the south they could not get the oil, other raw materials or food supplies back to Japan.

Back in May 1944 the Japanese had overrun the US air bases that had recently been established in China, precipitating a near collapse of Chinese forces. US General Joseph Stilwell, the US representative in China, blamed Chiang Kai-shek for the fiasco. So did his superiors in Washington, who demanded that control of Chinese forces be ceded to Stilwell. Chiang, however, insisted that Stilwell was the problem and demanded his recall. Roosevelt complied and replaced him with General Albert C. Wedemeyer, but the Americans downgraded the importance of China and military operations there, increasingly looking to Soviet entry into the Far Eastern war in order to eradicate Japan's forces in China.

By the end of 1944 MacArthur's forces were firmly established in the central Philippines and preparing to land on Luzon, while B-29 Super Fortress bombers based in the Marianas were bombing the cities of Japan. The Japanese navy had been virtually defeated, and carrier forces of the US Pacific fleet had penetrated Japan's inner defence zone. Japan was facing defeat. American forces continued to make substantial progress during the first half of 1945, liberating the Philippines, destroying what remained of the Japanese merchant fleet, conquering the islands of Iwo Jima and Okinawa, and beginning the aerial devastation of Japan.

The British were effectively sidelined in the war with Japan. In 1943 Britain had been forced by the US to sign an agreement with China abolishing the extraterritorial agreements that had given Britain control of crucial areas of port cities such as Shanghai (where they had created an apartheid system excluding and discriminating against Chinese). In May 1944 Churchill told the dominion prime ministers that, 'we must regard ourselves as junior partners in the war against Japan'. In Burma, which the Japanese regarded as of secondary importance, the British-led forces had acquired great superiority over the Japanese, deploying six divisions against a single Japanese one, and they also had air superiority. Sixty per cent of these troops were from the Indian subcontinent, 12 per cent from Africa and just 12 per cent were British. The victory at Imphal-Kohima repulsed a Japanese invasion of north-east India in March 1944. The following year British-led forces advanced into Burma, eventually reoccupying Rangoon in May 1945. Churchill himself was clear about what really mattered for Britain. In September 1944 he told the assembled Chiefs of Staff that the recovery of Singapore was key because it was 'the supreme objective in the whole of the Indian and Far Eastern theatres ... the only prize that will restore British prestige in this region'.[39] In the event, British forces only entered Singapore after the Japanese surrender – Churchill's hopes of restoring imperial prestige were dashed.

Japan Defeated

General Tojo resigned from the Japanese premiership in July 1944 after failing to stop US bombing attacks on Japan. This represented a major defeat for the faction of the ruling class around the army. Their rivals, grouped around the navy, pressed for an end to the war. So fine was the balance between these factions that the new government could not move too openly or quickly towards negotiations with Washington for fear of a coup by their rivals. In September 1944 the Japanese ambassador in Sweden approached his British counterpart to suggest that peace might be possible with Japan giving up all it had conquered after the invasion of Manchuria. The British refused to follow up the approach, holding to a position agreed with Washington that unconditional surrender was the only option.

The US air force decided on a strategy of launching fire raids on Japanese cities. An incendiary attack was carried out on a mock-up Japanese town built at an air base in Florida. 'Results were deemed to be satisfactory.'[40]

In early 1945, General Curtis LeMay, commander of 21 Bomber Command in the Pacific, carried out a 130-plane daylight raid on Tokyo. Twenty-five thousand houses were destroyed. The USAAF bombing offensive now targeted highly populated residential areas aimed at causing great fires. Japanese air defences and civil protection was woefully inadequate, allowing the Americans to bomb with impunity.[41] On the 9 and 10 March 1945 a huge fire raid was carried out on Tokyo using an early form of napalm. Some 90,000 died in three hours, fewer than would later die in the atomic bomb attack on Hiroshima but more than in Nagasaki.[42]

From April to August 1945 the US air force began to work systematically through Japan city by city. Forty per cent of urban areas were destroyed, with 30 per cent of the population homeless at the war's end. In the biggest city, Tokyo, 60 per cent of homes were destroyed. Eight million refugees fled to the countryside. Four-fifths of Japan's shipping had been destroyed, along with one-third of machine tools and almost a quarter of rolling stock and motor vehicles. Absenteeism at work reached 50 per cent.[43] As the historian A.D. Harvey argues: 'By the time the atom bomb was dropped on Hiroshima Japan had already been completely defeated by conventional weapons; nearly all the major cities had been laid waste, most of the merchant fleet was at the bottom of the sea, and the surviving factories stood idle for want of raw materials.'[44]

For the final month of the war US naval forces operated from along the shores of the home islands themselves without losing a single ship. They bombarded steel works and destroyed the Hokkaido-Honshu ferry link which transported vital coal supplies. That alone demonstrated the inability of the Japanese navy and air force to defend the home islands. Sections of the Japanese ruling class feared revolution would follow defeat. In February 1945, Prince Konoye, a former prime minister and friend of Emperor Hirohito, had told him, 'What we have to fear is not so much defeat as a Communist revolution which might take place in the event of defeat ... we shall simply be playing into the hands of the Communists if we elect to continue a war wherein there is no prospect of victory.'[45]

The defeat of Germany in May 1945 strengthened the faction favouring peace. Meanwhile, in the same month, the US State Department's expert on Japan, former ambassador to Tokyo Joseph C. Grew, had persuaded Roosevelt that the emperor should be retained in position following American occupation of Japan. Grew had argued as early as 1943 that, 'to try and graft a democracy on Japan would result in chaos', and that the emperor should stay on the throne to secure 'a healthy structure in future'.[46]

US policy, shaped by Grew, was to utilise the emperor as a counterweight to the army, and to base occupation policy on close co-operation with the giant industrial corporations. Japan was seen as a counter to Russian expansion into Manchuria in the post-war world and as a more reliable future ally than China.

The need for Russian aid in the war against Japan still influenced American strategy. On 23 July 1945, US President Harry Truman met with Churchill and the Combined Chiefs of Staff and reiterated the policy to, 'encourage Russian entry into the war against Japan'.[47] The desperate Japanese resistance and the resulting American casualties in the fighting at Okinawa, as the Americans neared the Japanese island home chain, determined Truman's position at the Potsdam summit in July 1945. Truman wrote, 'There were many reasons for my going to Potsdam, but the most urgent to my mind, was to get from Stalin a personal reaffirmation of Russia's entry into the war against Japan, a matter which our military chiefs were most anxious to clinch.'[48]

By the summer of 1945, the Japanese navy, the leaders of Japan's corporations, and even the emperor and his circle, accepted that it was necessary to open peace talks, but they needed to do this without provoking a coup by the army. For eight months the Japanese government tried to broker peace talks through its Moscow embassy. The US was fully aware of this, having broken the Japanese secret codes. The Americans, it seems, did not believe the Japanese were serious about surrender talks. Also, whatever damage they could inflict on the Japanese home islands, there were still over 1 million Japanese troops in China, where the army still believed partial victory was possible. After bitter experience with Chiang Kai-shek, the Americans decided they could not afford, financially or militarily, to get sucked into a war on the Chinese mainland.

On 6 August 1945 an atomic bomb was dropped without warning on Hiroshima, destroying the entire city and killing 100,000 civilians. Three days later the US bombed Nagasaki, levelling it and killing 70,000 people. With the additional impact of slow radiation poisoning nearly half a million civilians died in the two attacks. The Americans now pressed for a quick Japanese surrender and Japanese leaders agreed, with the proviso that the emperor be retained. Admiral William Leahy admitted in 1946 that the Japanese had already been prepared to surrender before the bombs were dropped:

It is my opinion use of this barbarous weapon at Hiroshima and Nagasaki was of no material assistance in our war against Japan. The Japanese were already defeated and ready to surrender because of the effective sea blockade and the successful bombing with conventional weapons ... My own feeling is that in being the first to use it, we had adopted an ethical standard common to the barbarians of the Dark Ages.[49]

In 1963 General Dwight D. Eisenhower told *Time* magazine, 'The Japanese were ready to surrender and it wasn't necessary to hit them with that awful thing.'[50] Air force General Curtis LeMay, who had presided over the destruction of Japanese cities with conventional bombs, described the use of the atomic bomb as 'the worst thing that ever happened ... Even without the atomic bomb and the Russian entry into the war, Japan would have surrendered in two weeks.'[51] The official US Strategic Bombing Survey concluded after the war found that prior to the dropping of the bomb morale in Japan had already collapsed. Sixty-eight per cent believed the war was lost and just 28 per cent were willing to resist to the death.[52] The US government's real fear was that Russia would gain territory in Asia. Truman's aim in using the bomb was to send Russia a message. Gabriel Kolko writes that in May 1945:

the Allies had effectively defeated Japan and reduced its industrial capacity and manpower to nearly a last-stand posture ... The Americans now tried to weigh the atomic bomb both from the viewpoint of its use against Japan and its implications to future relations with the Soviet Union ... One must remember that at no time did the Americans see the bomb as a weapon for defeating the formidable Japanese army in China, and at no time did they consider it desirable that the Soviets invade the Japanese mainland. The bomb did not reduce the importance of Soviet entry into Manchuria and north China.[53]

The US secretary of state for war, Henry Stimson, recalled telling Truman in June 1945 that he 'was a little fearful that before we could get ready the air force might have Japan so thoroughly bombed out that the new weapon would not have a fair background to show its strength'. The president 'laughed and said he understood'.[54]

Meanwhile on 9 August, the Russians, acting on Stalin's pledge to the Americans, attacked the Japanese positions in Manchuria. The Russian advance finally achieved a rapid breakthrough. Russian forces entered Korea almost a month before US troops arrived, whereupon the Red Army withdrew to an agreed occupation boundary on the 38th Parallel. Russian troops also landed in the Kuriles, in the far north of the Japanese island chain. The Americans were now keen to secure a quick Japanese surrender – decisive action was required to pre-empt the Russian advance by ending the war. Truman needed to secure the US's dominant position in the post-war world.

One explanation for the dropping of the atomic bombs was that it was a warning to Russia. Stalin reacted by stepping up Russia's own atomic programme, which benefited from valuable spies in the United States. The Russian advance now meant Washington needed to bring the war to an end before Stalin's forces advanced further into Japan. On 15 August a recording of the emperor was broadcast on the radio conveying news of the surrender to the population of Japan, citing 'a new and most cruel bomb' and warning further resistance 'would not only result in the ultimate collapse and obliteration of the Japanese nation but would lead also to the total extinction of human civilisation'.[55]

On 2 September, after much preparation, on board the USS *Missouri* anchored in Tokyo Bay, General Douglas MacArthur accepted the surrender of the Japanese. The British, Chinese and Russians were effectively excluded from the ceremony. All were also excluded from any say in the American occupation of the country. In the Pacific there was little pretence that the Allies were on an equal footing, as Holland points out: 'For such heroes of America's Pacific struggle as Admiral Nimitz and (especially) General Douglas MacArthur, the Grand Alliance was, in the main, a ritual rather than a practical bond.'[56]

Japanese armed forces, who were faced with an imperial order, not just one from civilian politicians, surrendered unconditionally, but, unlike in Germany, the civil authorities retained their powers. The emperor would become the cornerstone of the US strategy to rebuild Japan. The Americans effectively buried his direct involvement in ordering not just the Japanese attack on Pearl Harbor but the savage colonial order it imposed in China, Korea and elsewhere.

Gerhard L. Weinberg puts the figure for the numbers of Chinese killed in the war with Japan at 15 million. Three million Japanese died in the Second World War. Japan was guilty of serious war crimes against people in its Greater East Asia Prosperity Zone, as John Dower argues: 'From the Rape of Nanking in the opening months of the war against China to the Rape of Manila in the final stages of the Pacific war, the emperor's soldiers and sailors left a trail of unspeakable cruelty and rapacity.'[57]

The Japanese biological warfare programme involved 'experiments' on prisoners first in Manchuria and then across the occupied territories. More than 5,000 people worked on this programme. Thousands were murdered in the name of science. The Japanese employed biological weapons against Chinese forces and civilians. After the war MacArthur granted an amnesty to the scientists and technicians involved in the programme. The information acquired from them was sent to the US and Britain – British forces even took over a fully operational laboratory in Singapore.

Despite these war crimes, the US saw Japan as a vital part of its new world order. Even in the immediate aftermath of Pearl Harbor, the State Department argued that post-war Japan should be brought into US orbit. Official Hugh Borton authored a memo, 'a framework for long-range planning for US-Japanese relations', which set the aim to 'reintegrate [Japan] into the world economy of economic interdependence'.[58] Japan remained under US occupation for six years and eight months, until April 1952. The US reshaped the existing institutions of the imperial state. As the historian of the US occupation, John Dower, notes:

> For all practical purposes, General MacArthur relied on the Japanese bureaucracy to carry out its directives, creating in effect a two-tiered mandarinate. When

the Americans departed, the native mandarins carried on, stronger than they had been even during the war. For ideological purposes, MacArthur also chose to rely on Emperor Hirohito, in whose name all of Asia had been savaged ... publicly praising him as the leader of the new democracy.[59]

Yet the US authorities faced an unexpected challenge: 'Support for socialist and communist agendas exceeded anything the Americans had anticipated, as did the explosive challenge of the nascent labour movement.'[60] US policy in Japan paralleled that in Italy, the Japanese Liberal Democratic Party playing a similar role to the Italian Christian Democrats. Both were forged in the Cold War, both enjoyed office for decades, both were reliable allies of the US, both were tied to big business, both were prepared to utilise organised crime, and both were made up of warring factions who fought over key positions. There was one difference: in Italy the Christian Democrats had to uphold the new post-war republic; in Japan the Liberal Democratic Party was a bastion of the old 'emperor system'. Japan became a frontline state in the Cold War, with ex-intelligence officers being recruited to the US-run Japanese Research Division to provide information on China and Korea. By the early 1950s Japanese airmen were flying covert reconnaissance missions over North Korea, northern China and the eastern Soviet Union.

CHAPTER TEN

The East is Red

China

The United States had a number of aims in the Second World War. They included the dismantling of the British and French trade blocs, achieving a permanent military presence in Europe, and control of Middle East oil. But there was another – hegemony over China. Washington championed an 'open door' to China, meaning it wanted free trade which would benefit the sale of American goods and the purchase of raw materials from China. To that end Washington opposed the ceding of Chinese territory to the European powers (such as Britain's control of Hong Kong) and more importantly Japanese attempts to control the country.

The Chinese government led by Chiang Kai-shek had hoped that elements in the Japanese ruling class who were open to rapprochement with China would come to power. Instead, as Japan was drawn into war in China in the 1930s it became more militarised.[1] In 1937 Chiang was forced to formally resist a full-scale Japanese invasion because he was under two pressures, neither of which would disappear until 1945, as the American historian of modern China, John W. Graver, points out:

> First, was the mounting force of nationalist pressure within China. The Japanese advance in North China in the early 1930s challenged the Nationalist government's legitimacy, deriving as it did from its claim to represent the 'redemption' of China from the depths of national humiliation...
>
> Second, by late 1936, the growing power of the militarist faction in Japan and the failure of Chinese diplomats to achieve a 'fundamental adjustment' in Sino-Japanese relations induced Chiang to abandon his earlier hope that more moderate forces might prevail in Tokyo ... Only after Japan suffered a military rebuff at the hands of China and its allies would it come to its senses.[2]

Any victories would raise Chiang's international prestige and sideline his internal opponents – the Communists, the warlords and his Guomindang (Chinese Nationalist Party) rivals.

The United States supported Chiang because they hoped Japan would become mired in a war it ultimately could not win. After Russia was invaded by Germany, Stalin, similarly hoping that if Japan was bogged down in China it would not join the attack on Russia, sent several thousand military advisers to Chiang as well as large amounts of arms, modern aircraft and several hundred pilots who flew missions against the Japanese.[3] Chiang was prepared to raise the possibility of his making a deal with Tokyo, or of Chinese resistance collapsing, to pressurise Washington and Moscow into continuing to support him.

The US sought to bolster the corrupt regime of Chiang Kai-shek to secure its goals. Chiang and his family were venal, and the warlords were primarily interested in feathering their own nest. All of them looked on the United States and its aid as a means to gather more fortune. Neither Chiang, nor the warlords he was in hock to, could effectively resist Japanese aggression, and in any case they were concentrating their fire on the Communists. The latter were resisting the Japanese and were gaining support because they supported land reform and were not corrupt. When US General Stilwell visited Chiang's capital he noted, 'Sympathy here was for the Nazis. Same type of government, same outlook, same gangsterism.'[4]

In conversation Chiang Kai-shek was quite open about his main priorities:

For me the big problem is not Japan but the unification of my country. I am sure that you Americans are going to beat the Japanese some day, with or without the help of the troops I am holding back for use against the Communists in the North West. On the other hand, if I let Mao Zedong push his propaganda across all of Free China, we run the risk – and so do you Americans – of winning for nothing.[5]

The reality in China was that conditions were being created which would give control to Mao Zedong's peasant armies.

As was noted earlier, at its outset the Chinese Communist Party had been concentrated in the great cities of eastern China, with 58,000 members in 1927, mostly workers and a good number of students and young intellectuals. Moscow encouraged it not simply to ally with the Guomindang (which had been founded as a progressive, radical nationalist movement) against the landlords and warlords, but to do 'coolie work' for it, offering uncritical support and even handing over its membership lists. But the Guomindang leadership was frightened by rural and urban unrest and increasingly allied itself to landowning and business interests.

In the course of 1927 the Guomindang in alliance with the Communists took Shanghai and Canton after both cities rose in revolt against the landlords. But then the Guomindang organised a massacre of the Communists. The remaining party cadre went underground. The party was itself reformed in 1935 after the Long March to the remote Shensi region in western China. Ninety thousand Red Army fighters and their followers had broken out of the Guomindang's encirclement in Jiangxi in south-east China. A year later just 20,000 reached safety near the Tibetan border. En route Mao Zedong had emerged to become leader of the Red Army and the Communist Party, ousting opponents who were acting in concert with Russian advisers. The new leadership was markedly more nationalist and centred on building support among the peasantry rather than in the cities.

The Chinese ruling class was too corrupt and weak to impose any solution but Chiang Kai-shek had inflicted a crucial defeat on the Chinese working class, which ceased to play any independent role. Into this vacuum stepped a military movement, staffed by middle-class intellectuals but peasant based, which while describing itself as Communist, looked to Soviet-style state-led industrialisation to develop China into an independent power. Resentment at Chiang's failure to resist the Japanese, at rising taxation by the landlords, and at conscription into Chiang's starving army – which did not fight but existed so that its leaders could draw off the US subsidies that paid the army's wages and supplied it with equipment – fuelled opposition to the Guomindang. Indeed, the US knew that Chiang sent his only effective units against the Communists while agreeing truces with the Japanese. A policy of surrendering territory in the hope this would eventually wear down the Japanese meant huge areas of the country were devastated by war and occupation. Chiang's army numbered 2.7 million on paper. Its primary role was to raise taxes from the peasantry. It moved across the country devastating regions as it stole food.

Most of Chiang's commanders were no more than warlords commanding private armies. Conscription, the realities of military life, and the impact of ragged, starving bands roaming the countryside produced a widespread radicalisation in areas far from Mao Zedong's forces. In addition the influx of US dollars unleashed terrible inflation. Chiang's policies led to a famine in 1942–43 in Henan province, affecting 5 million people, a majority of whom died. Chiang's armies were recruited or press-ganged from among the peasantry, but those same peasants had no wish to actually fight for their masters. His government took decisions but had no effective means of carrying them out. Various warlords controlled their own armies, landowners raised their own militias to deal with rural unrest and their own territories, while magistrates and officials bought local positions in order to line their pockets. All seized grain from the peasants, profited from the opium trade, and secured repayments for money lenders. Peasants fled the Japanese invaders, the Guomindang and the landlords.

So in one key region a dynamic was created which would act against Chiang and the Guomindang. In Hunan province during 1942–43 there was simply not enough food to feed local people and the troops, but the requisition of food by the army continued, leading to clashes with peasants. Famine led to the hoarding of supplies for profit and an immense growth of corruption.[6] A power vacuum was being created, into which stepped the one force that was consistent in opposing the Japanese and was relatively free of corruption – Mao's Communist-led armies. The Communists began to attract widespread support among the peasantry for the first time. Mao combined nationalism with peasant radicalism. The Chinese Communist Party had little or no contact with the working class concentrated along the eastern seaboard or with Moscow, which meant its leadership began to work out its own strategy, based on its experience, and building the basis for a future break with Moscow – though that was not the original intention. As Gabriel Kolko argues:

> The basic ingredient of the party was the appeal to nationalism and patriotism, to reform, and to collaboration of all nationalist classes. This required a structure of political organisation which incorporated peasant power but did

not move reform so far as to sacrifice the United Front, yet enough to win
and hold the allegiance of the masses.⁷

The Communist mobilisation against the Japanese led to its expansion and base
building in northern China and the Yangzi region, where the River Yangtze
meets the sea. In order to defend railways and communications the Japanese set
up blockhouses at intervals and sent out columns to mete out reprisals for guerrilla
attacks. Both became targets for a hit-and-run guerrilla war which tied down
Japanese forces. On the other hand, the People's Liberation Army launched its
first offensive with great success, but then could not resist the counter-offensive
the Japanese launched after they had concentrated their forces.⁸

By 1943 with the Axis on the defensive and Japanese forces beginning to
be spread thin, the Communists resumed offensive operations.⁹ American
and British missionaries repatriated in 1943 from Japanese-occupied Chinese
territory provided eye-witness accounts of the Communist-led resistance. The
US War Department published the following report:

> In regard to the border area between Shantung and Hopeh provinces one
> Catholic priest stated: the Eighth Route Army 'move from place to place
> constantly to elude Japanese watchfulness. Their influence is enough to cause
> constant worry to the Japanese, although their effectiveness remains small
> because they lack the necessary heavy arms ... Their hatred of the Japanese is
> real, and in equal combat they put up a good show. They specialise and excel
> in guerrilla fighting'...
>
> A Protestant missionary from Shantung reported: Formerly 'I just thought
> of them [the Communists] only as a nuisance but their effectiveness [in
> Shantung] is now [in 1943] an established fact. They are fighting the Japanese
> and spreading their doctrine. I do not know about their numbers but they
> must be numerous because when the Japanese start one of their expeditions to
> "mop up bandits," they have to collect from 400 to 500 soldiers before they
> start out ... The "Eighth Route Army" (Communists) are well disciplined
> and where they have control the common people enjoy a measure of security
> and of freedom from exorbitant taxes.'¹⁰

In 1944 Mao explained his strategy to an American journalist, in words designed
to please Washington, but in reality reflecting his thinking accurately enough:

> What China needs now is democracy and not socialism. To be more precise,
> China's needs at present are three: (1) to drive the Japanese out; (2) to realise
> democracy on a nationwide scale by giving the people all the forms of modern
> liberty and a system of national and local governments elected by them in
> genuinely free general elections, which we have already done in the areas
> under our control; and (3) to solve the agrarian question, so that capitalism of a
> progressive character can develop in China and improve the standard of living
> of the people through the introduction of modern methods of production.
> These, for the present, are the tasks of the Chinese revolution. To speak of

the realisation of socialism before these tasks are accomplished would merely be empty talk.[11]

The Communists lowered rents and interest repayments but did not abolish them. Land was redistributed but private ownership remained. Mao was able to win over the resistance forces on the basis of nationalist politics which stressed cross-class alliances and which pursued moderate social policies with honest government. Above all, the Communist-led forces fought the Japanese and their soldiers did not steal from the peasants. In April 1944 Mao explained to his comrades:

> What the Kuomintang has gained from looking on with folded arms for five and a half years is the loss of its fighting capacity. What the Communist Party has gained from fighting and struggling hard for five and a half years is the strengthening of its fighting capacity. This is what will decide China's destiny.[12]

The United States urged the Guomindang and the Communists to form a coalition. Both seemingly agreed while preparing for renewed civil war when Japan eventually surrendered. American diplomats on the ground warned of an incipient civil war but were ignored.[13] Stalin meanwhile backed Chiang, in large part because he saw that a Communist takeover in China would create a rival to Moscow control in the Communist camp, telling the Americans that Mao's supporters were 'margarine communists'. Russian arms were sent to the Guomindang, and would be used against Mao's forces, and Stalin volunteered a statement of support for Chiang which went into the final declaration issued at Yalta. Yet Stalin was not in a position to control events. The Chinese Communist Party was already operating independently of Moscow, and while it looked to the Soviet model of forced industrialisation it was not prepared to obey Russian diktats.

The US had slowly grasped that Chiang was a gangster and that no amount of money or aid would make him fight the Japanese. Inflation and a rigged exchange rate to the disadvantage of the dollar meant that even the Americans could not carry the cost of prosecuting a war in China. Yet there were over a million Japanese troops there.

In April 1945 Roosevelt's personal envoy to Chiang Kai-shek had met with the Russian foreign minister, Molotov, in Moscow. Chiang reported the Russian as saying: 'The Soviet Union is not supporting the Chinese Communist Party. The Soviet Union does not desire internal dissension or civil war in China. The Government of the Soviet Union wants closer and more harmonious relations in China.'[14]

In the autumn of 1945, after Japan's surrender, the Communists advanced across northern China. Chiang ordered the Japanese forces not to surrender but to fight them. As the Japanese in Manchuria laid down their arms, Guomindang and Communist forces raced to take control of territory, the former garrisoning the cities, the latter concentrating on building support in the countryside. Meanwhile the US moved 53,000 marines into Beijing and Tianjin [Tientsin] and transported Guomindang armies by air and sea into the region. The Russians advancing south into Manchuria honoured their promise to hand over territory to the Guomindang.[15]

On paper, the end of the war left Chiang Kai-shek in a very strong position. Both America and Russia loyally backed him and he was awash with arms. Russian and Japanese commanders ensured they handed territory to the Guomindang and not the Communists, who seemed marginal in the late summer of 1945. But the corruption at the heart of Chiang's regime meant all of this was thrown away. Chiang's forces were thinly spread in an attempt to control the greatest amount of territory, making them vulnerable in the civil war which re-commenced after the Japanese surrender.[16]

By the end of 1945 one of the People's Liberation Army's most successful commanders, Lin Bao, had 280,000 troops in Manchuria under his command. The Guomindang lost control of the province and Lin Bao's forces swept across northern China, winning two of the three crucial battles in the civil war which saw Chiang lose control of mainland China.[17] The Communists seized the nationalist banner and were able to win over allies across Chinese society, paving the way for their 1949 victory. Washington, denied its prize of an open door to China, would refuse to recognise the existence of the new regime for nearly three decades.

Korea

Across eastern and south-eastern Asia, the collapse of first the European imperial powers and then of the Japanese occupation led directly to a nationalist revolutionary wave. In December 1943, at the Cairo summit, the American, British and Chinese governments agreed that Korea would become 'free and independent ... in due course' after Japan's defeat. The Russians subscribed to this principle when they eventually declared war on Japan. At the Yalta conference Roosevelt and Stalin had agreed that Korea would be placed in international trusteeship after the Japanese occupation was ended, but no decision was made on how the peninsula would actually be governed.[18]

Soviet forces entered the Korean peninsula on 9 August as part of their assault on Japan. The next day the Truman administration instructed two young officers, Dean Rusk and Charles Bonesteel, to divide the peninsula, creating an American zone of occupation. The two men had to use a National Geographic map to draw a line of division, dividing Korea into two and including the capital, Seoul, in the southern US zone. No Koreans were consulted. Stalin agreed to the division of Korea at the 38th Parallel. On 18 August the Red Army carried out three amphibious landings in North Korea. Three weeks later, after the Japanese surrender, US forces landed at Incheon in the south.[19]

The Japanese occupation had bred indigenous resistance groups. The Korean Liberation Army (KLA) was formed in 1941 in China under Guomindang control. It was loyal to the Provisional Government of the Republic of Korea, formed as early as 1919. By the end of the war the KLA deployed 10,000 fighters. On 6 September the Provisional Government met in Seoul to declare Korea independent. The presence of left-wing nationalists fuelled US objections to the Provisional Government and they refused to recognise it.

Meanwhile Communist-led guerrilla groups had formed in territory controlled by the Chinese Communists. After carrying out several attacks in Korea they were eventually forced by the Japanese to seek sanctuary in the Soviet Union. One of their leaders, Kim Il-sung, became an officer in the Red Army, returning to Korea with the advancing Russian army in September 1945.

When Allied foreign ministers met on 7 December 1945, it was agreed that Korea would be placed in international trusteeship for five years, during which a Korean interim government would prepare the country for independence. A joint US-Russian commission was formed to aid the organisation of the new administration. The Korean Communists objected to this postponement of independence but quickly fell into line with Moscow. The right-wing Syngman Rhee, a US-based professor who had returned from 33 years exile and received strong US support, argued that a provisional government would be a stalking horse for Communist rule. Washington and Moscow came to no agreement on establishing a common government for the whole peninsula.[20]

Both powers moved to secure control of their zones. The US placed South Korea under military administration. Officials who had served under the Japanese colonial authorities remained in place. Many Japanese officials stayed in office until the following year. Syngman Rhee eventually became head of a southern-based government which waged war against left-wing insurgents. In 1948 it declared South Korea independent, with US forces departing.[21]

To the north, after a period of direct Russian rule, Kim Il-sung headed a North Korean Provisional People's Committee. In 1948 Russian troops left the peninsula and Kim began building an army. He was now allied with the neighbouring People's Republic of China. After several border clashes a full-scale war erupted in 1950 with northern forces crossing the 38th Parallel. US forces rushed to stop a complete victory for the North but their advance northwards led to the Chinese People's Liberation Army entering the war. Upwards of 3.5 million people died before an armistice restored the border and established a demilitarised zone near the 38th parallel.[22]

Vietnam

Vietnam had been run from 1941 onwards by a limited number of Japanese occupation troops who kept in place the pro-Vichy French colonial authorities. Neither was strong enough to police the countryside. Despite an abundance of rice, by seizing rice to feed their own troops, the Japanese engineered a famine which killed up to 2 million people in 1944–45. Peasants fled their land in search of food. Many drew the conclusion that they had to overthrow a colonial regime, whatever its stripe.[23]

The small Vietnamese Communist Party, led by Ho Chi Minh, had attempted to launch a guerrilla war, but until 1945 it was small in scale. In March 1945 the

Japanese disarmed and jailed the French colonial forces because with France now liberated they could no longer depend on forces once loyal to Vichy. In the final months of the war the Communists attempted to build a wider unity with other nationalists, launching a people's militia, the Vietminh, and issuing a call for a national rising to open up the warehouses where huge stocks of rice were stored. This allowed the Communist-led Vietminh to gain popular support.[24]

The decisive organising slogan was 'Break Open the Rice Stores to Avert Famine'. The Vietminh took control of the north virtually unopposed in June 1945. When news of the Japanese surrender came through, the Vietminh ordered a national insurrection. With crowds on the streets celebrating, it was relatively easy to engineer a takeover of the cities, towns and villages.[25] At Potsdam it had been agreed that Vietnam would be divided into two occupation zones, one, south of the 16th parallel, to be run by the British, preparing for a French return, the other, north of that line, by the Chinese forces of Chiang Kai-shek.[26]

In April 1945 Churchill sent a message to Roosevelt arguing it was 'essential not only that we support the French by all the means in our power, but also that we should associate them with our operations into their country'.[27] Roosevelt never replied, dying the day after the message was dispatched. His successor, Truman, decided to assist the French regain control of 'their' country. The British had been tasked with taking the Japanese surrender in Vietnam and in late September British forces moved in, discovering that the Vietminh were in control.

Ho Chi Minh and the Vietminh welcomed their supposed allies, who had landed by sea and moved into Saigon, ignoring the fact that they might be there to help re-establish French colonial rule. The Vietminh urged compliance with the British, taking the line from Moscow. Ho Chi Minh ordered the evacuation of Saigon and tried to negotiate, but he could not stop a rebellion in the city which then spread to the countryside as peasants opposed attempts to re-impose colonial rule.[28]

In Saigon, the Trotskyists were at the forefront of a genuine working-class rebellion which took control of the city. The workers of the Go-Vap tram depot, responding to the arguments of the Trotskyist Spark group, took the lead in forming armed workers' militias across the Saigon region. The poorer suburbs came under their control and many French colonialists were executed.[29] Lacking sufficient force, the British rearmed Japanese prisoners who then disarmed the population and put down the rebellion in Saigon, prior to adequate French forces arriving.[30]

As fighting threatened to spread the Vietminh leadership agreed a ceasefire with the British. In the meantime the Vietminh had eradicated the Trotskyists, murdering their leaders. Yet the re-imposition of full French colonial rule was eventually too much for the Vietminh, who, under pressure from below, were drawn into conflict with the restored colonial rulers.[31] The Vietnamese Trotskyist, Ngo Van, notes that in December 1946 the Vietminh gave up the cities, including Hanoi, and returned to the countryside to launch the guerrilla war, first against the French, then the Americans, which only ended in 1975.

Their failure to take control in 1945 meant the country paid a tremendous price for eventual liberation.[32]

Malaya

Japanese killings and ill-treatment of Malaya's Chinese population had led the Malayan Peoples' Anti-Japanese Army (MPAJA) to be formed under Communist leadership. It received British backing. Until mid 1943, lacking expertise and arms, its attempt at guerrilla war led to it losing a third of its number. Over the next year, it re-organised and grew fourfold.[33] The guerrillas claimed to have eliminated 5,500 Japanese troops, losing 1,000 fighters themselves. The Japanese admitted to losing 600 of their own troops and 2,000 local police, claiming MPAJA losses at 2,900.[34]

After the Japanese surrender, the British returned and attempted to re-impose the old colonial order. Malayan rubber and tin were vital dollar earners for the post-war British Labour government. Unemployment, low wages, high prices and lack of food led to a strike wave in Malaya between 1946 and 1948. The colonial authorities met labour unrest with repression.[35] The killing of three white plantation managers in June 1948 was immediately followed by emergency measures. The Malaysian Communist Party and other leftist parties were outlawed, while police were given the power to imprison without trial Communists and those accused of helping them.

The Communists, who had disarmed at the end of the war, took to the jungle and formed the Malayan National Liberation Army (MNLA). Its mainstay of support was among the Chinese population, who were denied voting rights, had few if any land rights, and were among the poorest sections of the population. The MNLA did enjoy support, to a lesser extent, among the Malay population. For 12 years the British fought a guerrilla war, coming near to defeat by 1951. Severe repression, the forcible transfer of Chinese villagers to military control, divide and rule, aerial bombing, and repression eventually overcame the resistance, though Britain was forced to grant independence in 1957.[36] British forces killed 6,700 guerrillas and captured 1,300. Some 2,000 British security forces were killed and 2,500 civilians died.[37]

The Philippines

The Philippines had been captured by the United States from Spain in 1898, and effectively run by them since. The country developed into a producer of raw materials and agricultural products for the US. This accordingly led to the land question becoming more volatile as land became concentrated in fewer hands. In the 1930s there were food shortages because of the eradication of peasant agriculture. Prior to the Japanese occupation of the Philippines, civil war had been simmering for the previous decade as resentment grew at US control and the amassing of wealth by elite landlords.

The Japanese occupation utilised the same small, corrupt and self-seeking elite that had served the Americans. Lack of occupation troops allowed the peasantry to resume their struggle for land on an even greater scale. A massive guerrilla army, the Hukbalahap (the People's Anti-Japanese Army), arose following spontaneous rural uprisings which were denounced by the Communist Party as 'extreme leftist actions'.[38]

By the war's end the Huks fielded some 100,000 fighters and held vast swathes of territory, having killing some 20,000 Japanese and occupation troops. The liberated territories were run on a co-operative basis.[39]

The story of the Philippines after the Americans returned parallels events in Greece. The Communists succeeded in disarming the Huk units and winning their acceptance of a government dominated by the old elite, but repression triggered a rebellion which launched a civil war. General Douglas MacArthur simply rehabilitated the old elite, recruiting the occupation police force into the new security forces who were quickly unleashed on the Huks. MacArthur favoured Manuel Roxas, whom the OSS described as 'an exonerated collaborationist'.[40]

The US employed indiscriminate bombing of civilian areas. The corruption, inflation and prostitution which followed US occupation inflicted massive damage on a fragile society. Throughout this conflict, the Communists were on the moderate wing of the left, urging compromise. Internal divisions on the left allowed the Americans to restore order.[41]

Indonesia

Further south, Indonesia had fallen within months of Japan declaring war. The Dutch colonial authorities had no way of defending the islands. The Japanese occupation authorities encouraged Indonesian nationalism out of self-interest, and the two nationalist leaders previously committed to a strategy of non-co-operation with the Dutch, Sukarno and Mohammed Hatta, worked with them.

In September 1944 the Japanese promised independence, which Sukarno and Hatta held up as validation of their policy of co-operation with the new occupiers. Two days after Japan surrendered, Sukarno and Hatta declared independence. The former became president, the latter vice-president. A wave of revolutionary celebration passed over the archipelago. Nationalist militias sprouted up in the absence of Dutch forces as the Japanese withdrew to barracks.[42] But the Dutch, who denounced Sukarno and Hatta as collaborators and independence as a child of Japanese fascism, received a $10 million loan from the US to help re-occupy the islands.[43]

British troops were the first to arrive in September 1945, tasked with taking the Japanese surrender, but they quickly utilised Japanese forces in order to restore 'order', clashing with nationalist militias. In October 6,000 British and Indian troops had to fight for three days to take the city of Surabaya. Fighting continued in the surrounding area. By the beginning of 1946 British forces had retreated from the interior of the main island, Java. By November 1946 the British had quit and 55,000 Dutch forces had arrived, equipped by the United States.

In three years of fighting the Dutch failed to regain control of either Java or Sumatra and at the end of 1949 were forced to recognise the Indonesian Republic. Between 45,000 and 100,000 Indonesians had died and there were 7 million refugees on Java and Sumatra. Across South East Asia, China and Korea there was bitterness over the broken promise of liberation which followed the war's end. US historian John Dower points out that this was one consequence of the US's decision to turn Japan into a key Cold War ally:

> One of the most pernicious aspects of the occupation [of Japan] was that the Asian people who had suffered most from imperial Japan's depredations – the Chinese, Koreans, Indonesians and Filipinos – had no serious role, no influential presence at all in the defeated land. They became invisible. Asian contributions to defeating the emperor's soldiers and sailors were displaced by an all-consuming focus on the American victory in the 'Pacific War.' By this process of vaporisation, the crimes that had been committed against Asian people through colonisation as well as war were easily put out of mind.[44]

CHAPTER ELEVEN

The Post-War World

The surrender ceremony in Tokyo Bay marked the formal end of the Second World War. Deaths caused by this conflict were between three and five times the figure for the First World War. They totalled between 10 and 20 per cent of the total population in the USSR, Poland and Yugoslavia; and between 4 and 6 per cent in Germany, Italy, Austria, Hungary, Japan and China. Casualties in Britain and France were far lower than in the First World War – about 1 per cent, but in the US higher.[1]

Yet despite these terrible casualties the end of the war did not mean the end of the fighting. Very quickly the old empires were battling to maintain their colonial possessions in Asia, there was civil war in Greece, and soon France was dragged into a bitter war in Algeria whose wounds still remain. Eventually the United States would intervene in Vietnam against the Communist-led liberation movement, to disastrous effect. The Cold War that developed between the US and Russia boiled over into full-scale war in Korea. The list continues. The world since 1945 has yet to enjoy peace.

The American Century is Declared

The United States was already a world power in December 1941 but its involvement in the Second World War raised it to new and dizzying heights. After the Japanese attack on Pearl Harbor, Panama, Costa Rica, the Dominican Republic, El Salvador, Haiti, Honduras, Nicaragua, Guatemala and Cuba all declared war on Japan. Roosevelt's declaration of war meant the US-controlled territories of Samoa, Guam, the Philippines, Puerto Rico, and the Virgin Islands were also at war. By the end of the war Argentina, Bolivia, Brazil, Chile, Colombia, Ecuador, Mexico, Paraguay, Peru, Uruguay and Venezuela had all joined the Allied camp.[2] While it might not have enjoyed a formal empire like Britain's, Washington had a very real imperial sway over Latin America and the Pacific.

In the course of the Second World War US gross national product almost doubled – rising from $91 billion to $166 billion.[3] Industrial output doubled. Shipbuilding grew from 1 million to 19 million tonnes a year, while agricultural production grew by 20 per cent.[4] Kolko points to how the state-directed war economy would shape US industry's post-war power: 'By Spring 1944 the United States government financed three-quarters of the $20 billion in new industrial plant constructed during the war until that time, in addition to contracting for the construction of 2,700 Liberty ships to carry goods abroad.'[5]

General Motors supplied one tenth of US war production and hired three quarters of a million new workers. The Ford motor company alone produced more military equipment than Italy.[6]

President Roosevelt and his cabinet were explicit about their plans to safeguard and capture foreign markets. Secretary of state Cordell Hull declared: 'Leadership toward a new system of international relationships in trade and other economic affairs will devolve largely upon the United States because of our great economic strength. We should assume leadership and the responsibility that goes with it, primarily for reasons of pure self-interest.'[7] Roosevelt's vice president, Henry Wallace, boasted that, 'the American businessman of tomorrow' would understand that 'the new frontier extends from Minneapolis ... all the way to Central Asia'.[8] Under their 'open door' policy the ruling class wanted to break into the other imperialists' colonial markets, smash protectionist barriers, and establish their control of the world capitalist system.[9] No other power could spare the resources that the US could deploy. The Manhattan Project that developed the atomic bomb employed 120,000 people based in 37 installations spread across 19 different states. In order to build the bomb in just three years the Federal government spent $2,000 million.[10]

The United Nations was created by the Allies as a replacement for the League of Nations, which had failed to prevent the outbreak of war. The name had been adopted by the Allies following the signing of the Atlantic Charter between the United States and Britain in January 1942. The Americans successfully pushed for the creation of a permanent Security Council in which they and the other great powers had a majority and in which any one could employ a veto on any decision it disliked. The existence of the Security Council and the veto overcame the objections raised after the First World War regarding the League of Nations limiting the US's room for manoeuvre. As secretary of state Hull explained, 'We should not forget that this veto power is chiefly for the benefit of the United States.'[11] The United States provided 70 per cent of the costs of the United Nations Relief and Rehabilitation Administration, which meant it controlled where food aid was directed – of major importance in swathes of Europe and Asia facing hunger in the wake of the war.[12] In 1945 Stalin's concerns were more limited: protecting a greater Russia, preventing a revived Germany allied with the West, and creating a bulwark in Eastern Europe protecting the USSR.

As for Britain's alliance with the United States, it was never a case of equal partners. By 1944 British exports were at a third of the 1938 level while imports were up by 50 per cent. Overseas capital assets worth £1.3 billion had been liquidated while Britain's overseas debts were five times the pre-war figure. Britain was actually in debt to parts of its Empire – Egypt, India and Iraq. Its debts were seven times greater than its currency reserves, reducing sterling to the status of a non-convertible currency (it could not be exchanged for a hard currency like the dollar).[13]

A week after Japan surrendered the US ceased the Lend-Lease scheme without warning. The new Labour government dispatched John Maynard Keynes to Washington to 'negotiate' a $3.75 billion loan at a 2 per cent rate of interest. Britain had to accept membership of the General Agreement on Tariffs and

Trade (GATT), in other words the liberalisation of global trade, and to agree to return sterling to being a convertible currency at a far lower rate than pre-war. Much of the US loan, as Keynes pointed out, was to be spent on overseas military expenditure.[14] The Labour foreign secretary, Ernest Bevin, told the House of Commons in May 1947:

> Her Majesty's Government do not accept the view ... that we have ceased to be a Great Power or the contention that we have ceased to play that role. We regard ourselves as one of the Powers most vital to the peace of the world and we still have our historic part to play. The very fact that we have fought so hard for liberty, and paid such a price, warrants our retaining this position, and indeed it places a duty upon us to continue to retain it. I am not aware of any suggestion, seriously advanced, that by a sudden stroke of fate, as it were, we have overnight ceased to be a Great Power.[15]

British leaders could talk of Britain being Greece to America's imperial Rome or boast of their 'special relationship' with Washington, but the truth was that any Anglo-American alliance was simply viewed as a matter of expediency by US political and military leaders. The economic gap between the states was yawning. In 1938 gross national product per head in the US was just 10 per cent above the British figure. By 1944 it was 50 per cent higher.[16]

Kolko points to another long-standing US objective — control of European oil supplies: 'As an oil reserve the Middle East was too distant to be reliable. Middle Eastern oil to the United States ultimately represented exports to Europe and a source of profit, and potentially an instrument to control the European economy.'[17] The United States was determined to control the oil its rivals depended on so they could be forced into line if necessary. During the war itself matters came to a head with the Americans determined to exclude the British from the immense Saudi Arabian oilfields. As the wrangle continued Churchill wrote to Roosevelt:

> Thank you very much for your assurances about no sheep eyes at our oilfields in Iran and Iraq. Let me reciprocate by giving you fullest assurances that we have no thought of trying to horn in upon your interests or property in Saudi Arabia. My position in this as in all things is that Great Britain seeks no advantage, territorial or otherwise, as a result of the war. On the other hand she will not be deprived of anything which rightly belongs to her.[18]

But in regards to Saudi Arabia, deprived Britain was. In 1943 and 1944 the US pushed the British to allow an 'open door' to Middle Eastern supplies. After difficult negotiations the British were forced to cede control of Saudi Arabia. Crucial to this was the outbidding of the British in the bribes and 'aid' given to the House of Saud, the autocratic rulers of Saudi Arabia. The Saudi king was awarded major US loans and arms, and Washington clinched the deal in late 1944.[19]

In Iran, however, the Americans failed to secure outright control. They, the British and the Russians became embroiled in a fight for control of the oilfields. After the Germans attacked Russia, Iran had become vital not only for its oil but as a supply line to the Soviet Union. Both London and Moscow were nervous at the pro-Nazi sympathies of Iran's ruler, the Shah, and in August 1941 Soviet troops invaded from the north, linking with British and Indian forces invading from the south. Two months later they forced the Shah to abdicate in favour of his son, Mohammad Reza Shah Pahlavi, who ruled until his overthrow in the Iranian revolution of 1979. American troops arrived in Iran after the US had joined the war. The British effectively controlled Iranian oilfields through the Anglo-Iranian Oil Company, the future BP. The Russians wanted control of oil development in the north and the US began courting the new Shah to break the British monopoly.[20]

All of this helped create a popular campaign for the nationalisation of Iran's oil. The Iranian parliament asserted its right in December 1944 to control the granting of oil concessions. The prime mover in this was Mohammad Mosaddeq. Anglo-Iranian Oil continued to exploit its concession but in 1951 a nationalist government led by Mosaddeq took the company into state hands, sparking a CIA/MI5-sponsored coup two years later which gave full powers to the Shah.[21] In the end Washington, fearful of the rising power of Russia, decided that it could not afford to weaken Britain too much. A deal was reached over Iranian and Iraqi oil which gave Britain the junior share in an American-controlled global oil industry.

Meanwhile Washington acted to increase its hegemony over Latin America by excluding British goods. Britain accounted for 40 per cent of Latin American imports in 1938 but ten years later this figure had fallen to 8 per cent. Washington was particularly keen to eradicate British economic influence in Argentina, part of the sterling bloc. As late as 1942 Britain controlled 60 per cent of foreign investment there, compared to the US's 20 per cent. In January 1945 the US ambassador to Mexico, who worked closely with the State Department on policy towards Latin America, stated that one aim was to 'bring about the appropriate change in Argentina and bring her back into the fold'.[22] Washington succeeded.

On 17 February 1941 an editorial entitled 'The American Century' appeared in *Life* magazine signed by its founder and publisher, Henry Luce. This Republican-supporting millionaire had been an admirer of Mussolini prior to the war and was violently opposed to Roosevelt's New Deal. He argued that the US had missed its chance in 1918 to mould the world around its economic and social model and now this renewed opportunity must not be wasted: 'We must accept whole-heartedly our duty and our opportunity as the most powerful and vital nation in the world and in consequence to exert upon the world the full impact of our influence, for such purposes as we see fit and by such means as we see fit.' He added that 'in any sort of partnership with the British Empire, America should assume the role of senior partner'.[23] The editorial was mass-produced and circulated widely, appearing in full in the *Washington Post* and *Reader's Digest*. It was a call that fell on receptive ears in US ruling circles.

This new empire would not follow the British and European model of creating an empire by open colonial conquest. Instead, the American Century would be presented, particularly in Asia and Africa, as a champion of liberty and democracy and as a supporter of an end to colonial rule. The American Century would also champion global free trade, to the benefit of the world's strongest post-war economy. Later, in 1948, the State Department planning head, George F. Kennan, wrote in a confidential internal memo: 'We have about 50% of the world's wealth but only 6.3% of its population ... Our real task in the coming period is to devise a pattern of relationships which will permit us to maintain this position of disparity without positive detriment to our national security.'[24]

The institutions for ordering world trade established at the 1944 Bretton Woods conference – the IMF, the World Bank, and the GATT agreements – swept away restrictions on trade. As the biggest single contributor the US ensured its effective domination of the IMF and the World Bank. The International Monetary Fund (IMF) was created to stabilise the world financial system after the war, while the World Bank was intended to revive the economies of the US's European allies (and its former enemies Germany and Japan).

The International Trade Organisation also stemmed from discussions at Bretton Woods. In December 1945 the US invited its wartime allies to discuss a multilateral agreement on reducing tariffs. This would become today's World Trade Organisation. In return for lowering barriers to US exports, Washington financed a massive programme of financial credits to war-torn countries. 'The United States could not passively sanction the employment of capital raised within the United States for ends contrary to our major policies or interests', said the State Department's Herbert Feis in 1944. 'Capital is a form of power.'[25] The post-war program of Marshall Plan loans and grants to countries made this explicit. 'Benefits under [the Marshall Plan] will come to an abrupt end in any country that votes Communism to power', said General George Marshall, President Truman's secretary of state and the aid program's namesake.[26]

The United States held the overwhelming majority of world central bank monetary gold reserves. The Bretton Woods Gold Exchange Standard uniquely privileged the role of the US dollar, which remains to this day the world reserve currency. In the immediate post-war years, war-torn countries from Western Europe to Japan needed dollars to buy US capital equipment, oil, foodstuffs and much more. All IMF member country currencies were to be fixed in value to the US dollar but only the US dollar would have its value fixed at a rate of $35 per ounce of gold. Foreign states and banks could only exchange dollars for gold at this fixed rate. The dollar was 'as good as gold', effectively the world's currency.[27]

To back up economic clout with military muscle, the US built military alliances spanning the globe. The most important of these, the North Atlantic Treaty Organisation (NATO), founded in 1949, served to involve the US permanently in European affairs. Ostensibly formed to present a common European front against a Soviet invasion of the West, its real aim was to keep the US in Europe, to keep Russia out, and to keep Germany tied down, to paraphrase Britain's Lord Ismay. George Kennan, the US State Department's architect of the 'containment' of Communism, nevertheless ridiculed NATO as a 'military defense against an attack no one is planning'. He added that NATO 'added depth and recalcitrance to the division of the continent and virtually forced individual countries to choose sides'.[28]

The US entered the Second World War with limited access to the world's markets and without military bases to enforce its will. It emerged with troops in 56 countries stationed at more than 400 military bases. The US economy, rejuvenated by the war, accounted for 75 per cent of invested capital in the world.[29] The US immediately solidified this new power. It rebuilt European capitalism through the Marshall Plan and set up NATO to enforce its rule over the continental powers. After defeating Japan, the US laid claim to political and economic rule in Asia. It first assisted and later replaced the French in Indochina. It partitioned Korea with Russia, and later engaged in a proxy war with Russia and China over the partition, a war that claimed more than 2 million lives.[30]

The US built its empire out of the rubble of Europe's colonies. But instead of building colonial regimes, it backed dictators such as the Shah of Iran, Suharto in Indonesia, and Mobutu in Zaire who would obey US economic and political orders. Where it did intervene directly, in Vietnam, the US killed 2 million people in order to prevent the country from achieving independence. The United States beat back anti-imperialist movements and workers' rebellions all around the world in the name of fighting Communism. It thereby turned itself into the globocop of world capitalism, the greatest foe of workers' power at home and abroad. The reality of American power still casts a dark shadow over our lives.

The Passing of the British Empire

The decision of the US to support the re-imposition of British, French and Dutch colonialism in much of Asia represented something of a U-turn, Washington having been anti-colonial, in its rhetoric at least, in regard to the European powers prior to the outbreak of war. Now the growth of left-wing liberation movements across much of Asia meant the Truman administration was fearful of a Communist takeover in the region.

A sense of imperial decline gripped the British ruling class. Both before and after the First World War, aware of its own fading fortunes, it had turned on the working class in an effort to restore international competitiveness, by driving down wages and benefits and enforcing anti-trade union laws. Churchill had been associated with much of this and his post-war career was marked by a virulent anti-communism, a refusal to grant any concessions to Indian demands for self-government, and support at the time of the 1936 abdication crisis for Edward VIII (who was pro-Nazi). Yet this arch-imperialist would preside over the key moment in the dissolution of the short history of Britain's Empire. In truth he had a weak set of cards. His triumph was to keep Britain in the war in the summer of 1940, denying Hitler complete victory. After that he would have to rely on others to achieve victory – and a victory which came at a heavy price for British ambition.

When King George VI declared war on Hitler's Germany he did so not just on behalf of the people of Britain but also of the population of the Indian subcontinent and the rest of the Empire. None were consulted. Over 2 million men from the subcontinent fought for Britain between 1939 and 1945. The Indian army successfully stopped the Japanese invading Bengal and was responsible for recapturing Burma ('Britain's' only military success in the Asian theatre).[31] The record of the Fifth Indian Division illustrates the importance of the Indian army. It fought in the Sudan against the Italians, and then in Libya against the Germans. The division was moved to Iraq to protect the oilfields, then to the Burma front, together with eight other Indian divisions, and then occupied Malaya. After this it was moved to Java to disarm the Japanese garrison there.[32]

While many imperial subjects fought loyally for the King-Emperor, growing numbers were infected with a spirit of rebellion. The example of the Irish Republicans, who had forced Britain to the negotiating table and then to quit most of the island in 1921, struck a chord across the Empire, particularly in India. In contrast, there was resistance to the war in one British dominion where the standpoint was radically different. In September 1939 prime minister general J.B.M. Hertzog stood up to address the South African parliament. He told the assembly that he could not back war against Hitler:

> I have carefully followed his actions step by step, and I have asked myself where is the proof that this man is out for world domination? ... With what justification can one ask me and South Africa to take part in a war because Hitler and the German nation will no longer suffer this humiliation? ... We are asked to plunge ourselves into this war. We have no right to do so, and if we do so the Afrikaans-speaking people outside will get such a shock that it will take them years and years to get over it.[33]

South Africa was treaty-bound to go to war with Britain. Hertzog resigned the premiership to be replaced by General Smuts. But opposition to the war continued, with over 20,000 attending anti-war rallies in late June 1940. In January of the following year there were riots. Members of the far right Ossewa Brandwag (Ox-Wagon Fire Brigade) carried out armed attacks, aided by the police, on soldiers in transit to the front in Egypt.

Hundreds of members of the Ossewa Brandwag were interned along with hundreds of their police sympathisers. One of those held was the future Apartheid premier, B.J. Vorster. Yet the former minister of defence, Oswald Pirow, who openly proclaimed his loyalty to Nazism, remained free. As head of the South African 'New Order', he would go on to co-operate with Oswald Mosley in trying to revive an international fascist organisation in the post-war years. At the end of the war the detained nationalists, still parading their Hitlerite sympathies and anti-Semitism, were released and given a warm welcome home from prison. The right-wing Nationalist Party would build on opposition to the war and to Smuts's collaboration with Churchill to become the eventual ruling party, establishing the Apartheid regime in 1948.[34]

Across the colonial world, the Second World War gave rise to an unstoppable tide of liberation. Popular movements had already begun to form prior to 1939 but the collapse of the British, French and Dutch empires when attacked by Japan now spurred on resistance. The initial reaction of the old colonial powers was not to budge an inch.

The approach of war had created fears among Britain's Tory cabinet ministers of what fate might befall the British Empire. Lord Lothian believed that Nehru was just waiting for the declaration of war 'to let loose revolution in India'. Sir Anthony Eden feared a 'race riot from Cairo to the Cape'.[35]

On 12 August 1941 Churchill and Roosevelt signed the Atlantic Charter, which stated that the two governments would 'respect the right of all people to choose the form of government under which they will live'. The following month the British prime minister asserted that this did not apply to British-ruled India. The British ruling class's real agenda was summed up by Leo Amery at the India Office, who stated in December 1942, 'After all, smashing Hitler is only a means to the essential end of preserving the British Empire and all it stands for in the world.'[36]

Churchill could not countenance any retreat from full-blooded colonialism. In 1944 he floated the idea of a Council of Asia, dominated by the colonial powers, 'to prevent trouble arising with the yellow races'. He assured the exiled Dutch prime minister that he 'was going to stand up for the Dutch Empire after the war'.[37] When the Labour leader and deputy prime minister, Clement Attlee, told students that promises of self-government would apply to colonial peoples, Churchill expressed his astonishment 'that the natives of Nigeria or East Africa could by a majority vote choose the form of government under which they live'. He expressed that bluntly to one of Roosevelt's advisers, saying in December 1942, 'We will not let the Hottentots by popular vote throw the white people into the sea.' Finally in December 1944, in words aimed at Labour and the Americans, he declared, '"Hands off the British Empire" is our maxim and it must not be weakened or smirched to please sob-stuff merchants at home or foreigners of any hue.'[38]

Ten months later the message was similar from the new Labour government, when foreign secretary Ernest Bevin stated, 'I am not prepared to sacrifice the British Empire, because I know that if the British Empire fell ... it would mean that the standard of life of my constituents would fall considerably.'[39] Later, at the Yalta Conference in February 1945, he added that talk in the summit statement about the right of nations to self-determination did not apply to any part of the British Empire.[40] At Yalta the world was divided between the victorious allies into spheres of influence. Russia got Eastern Europe, Britain much of its old Empire and the US took the lion's share, including supposedly China. Yet the truth was that British and European colonialism in Asia was doomed. The dominant reason for that was the huge surge of national liberation unleashed by the war. The secondary factor was the US, which wanted to crack open the British Empire's stranglehold on global 'free trade'. Thirdly, Britain was now too over-stretched to maintain imperial control. Fourthly, the dramatic collapse of its power in South East Asia demonstrated its weakness.

The Americans had already forced the British to give up the 'concessions' it had gained from China, such as Shanghai, but they were out to achieve much more. They were helped by the fact that imperial ties had weakened between Britain and its dominions. The inability of British forces to defend Australia and New Zealand meant that both relied on Washington for their defence and both effectively switched over into the US camp. After the fall of Singapore the Australian prime minister declared, 'Australia looks to America.' Canada too was increasingly economically linked with its southern neighbour.[41]

The Japanese attack on South East Asia came just as powerful nationalist movements were emerging there. Yet whenever the Japanese conquered a European colony they did nothing to act on their anti-colonial rhetoric. Rather, they established puppet regimes which ruled in Japan's imperial interests.

India

India was the beating heart of Britain's Empire. The nationalist Congress Party had swept into control of most of India's provinces in the elections of 1937 (central control remained in British hands). After Indians were told they were at war by the Viceroy, Lord Linlithgow, bargaining began: Congress demanded independence but Britain needed the Congress to rule India.[42]

Troops from the Indian subcontinent were key to the British war effort in the Middle East, Italy and against Japan. Yet the independence agitation could feed on grievances inside the Indian army. Until 1932 the British had refused to commission Indians as officers; by 1939 there were still only 290 Indian-born officers and even after a wartime influx just three Indians had reached the rank of brigadier by 1946.[43] As early as June 1940 a major mutiny broke out after a Sikh squadron sent overseas from Bombay was shunted into a railway siding and left there for a day and a night.[44]

Under pressure from Washington, Churchill, a violent opponent of Indian independence, was forced to reopen negotiations. As the Japanese reached India's borders, the Leader of the House of Commons, Labour's Sir Stafford Cripps, was sent to India. The offer he carried with him was that a constituent assembly should meet after the war to determine India's position and that while it was hoped it would remain in the Commonwealth it could decide either way. Cripps also proposed that areas with a Muslim majority could hold referendums to determine whether to secede from an independent India. It was made clear that in the short term Congress leaders would have no effective say over Indian participation in the war.

Both the key Congress leaders, Gandhi and Nehru, favoured the Allied cause but they could not back Britain's war effort unless it promised independence. Gandhi turned the offer down saying it was a 'post-dated cheque on a failing bank' and launched the Quit India agitation in August 1942.[45] Gandhi told his followers to 'Do or Die'.[46] His arrest on the day after the campaign's launch unleashed a rebellion that saw clashes with the police and army, mass strikes, and a peasant rebellion in Bihar and the United Provinces. The Quit India Movement lasted until March 1943 and was only defeated by massive repression. Lord Linlithgow telegrammed Churchill that it was 'by far the most serious rebellion since that of 1857, the gravity and extent of which we have so far concealed from the world for reasons of military security'.[47]

This was no exaggeration. The railway between Delhi and Calcutta, the main artery for British colonial rule, was blown up in Bihar province, which was out of British control for over two weeks. Supplies to the frontline in Burma were stopped for a time and across the subcontinent police stations were burnt down, officers killed, and telegraph wires cut. For a week or more the British authorities suppressed news of all this, fearful it would lead to a collapse in morale in both India and Britain. During those days they were doubtful they could re-assert control.[48]

One British fusilier recalled being sent to Kalyan in India and the commanding officer addressing them thus: 'Well you are now in India. Forget about your democratic ideas. This is a completely different situation here, and I'll expect you to treat these people – it was: these wogs – in the same way as the regulars have been treating them for hundreds of years.'[49]

Huge numbers of troops were used to restore control, and the RAF bombed villages to suppress popular unrest. Congress was banned. In order to appease the Indian upper classes 11 of their members were brought onto the Viceroy's 14-strong Executive Council. At this point Britain promoted Mohammad Ali Jinnah's Muslim League, which was invited to form regional governments in Sind, Assam, Bengal and the North West Frontier Province. For centuries Hindus, Muslims and Sikhs had lived together. Now the British were promoting the idea of a Muslim state in what was termed Pakistan and an essentially Hindu state in India. This, as the British authorities were aware, was likely to unleash communal violence in mixed communities across the subcontinent. The stage was set for the tragedy of partition.[50]

Some nationalists were not prepared to limit themselves to non-violence. Subhas Chandra Bose had come fourth in the British civil service exams in 1920 but resigned his subsequent post in protest at the Amritsar massacre. Bose was twice elected president of the Indian National Congress but was forced to resign from the post after a motion of no-confidence moved by supporters of Mahatma Gandhi. Bose opposed the strategy of non-violence arguing in favour of armed resistance. At the outbreak of war Bose successfully evaded British security forces to reach Afghanistan, going on to Germany where he recruited three battalions of Indian PoWs into a nationalist army with the blessing of the Germans. In February 1943 he was taken by submarine to rendezvous with a Japanese submarine which took him to Tokyo. Some 40,000 Indian PoWs in Japanese hands had already pledged to join an Indian National Army (INA). Many had been shocked from their loyalty to the Raj by the collapse of British power, reacting against the racism and indignity they suffered at the hands of British officers.[51]

Meanwhile the British Raj was adding to its catalogue of horrors. Between 3.5 and 5 million people died from starvation, malnutrition and related illnesses during the Bengal famine of 1943. The famine was not a natural catastrophe, it was man-made. The British were stockpiling food for the Indian army and rice was exported to the Middle East to feed British soldiers and to Sri Lanka where the British-run South East Asia Command was based. The loss of Burma cut rice supplies from there while a 'scorched earth' policy was implemented in the region nearest the Burmese border.

Overall there was no fall in the rice harvest in 1943, but the rural labourers, peasants and fishing families of Bengal had seen their incomes fall by two thirds since 1940 while the price of rice had soared. Bengal had enough rice and other grains to feed its population, yet millions of people were too poor to buy it.[52] The British authorities failed to implement normal peacetime famine relief measures and were more concerned with quelling the Quit India movement. The Bengal government failed to prevent rice exports, and made little attempt to import surpluses from elsewhere in India, or to buy up stocks from speculators to redistribute to the hungry. Starving people flocked into Calcutta, many dying in a city with well-stocked markets. The British authorities removed (at times forcibly) tens of thousands of destitute, starving people from Calcutta and other urban areas in late 1943. These people were relocated to die in the countryside. Churchill repeatedly opposed food for India and specifically intervened to block provision of 10,000 tons of grain offered by Canada, because he saw that as weakening British rule. The US declined to provide food aid in deference to the British government. The British government rejected the Viceroy Lord Wavell's request for 1 million tons of grain in 1944 and also rejected his request that the US and the United Nations Relief and Rehabilitation Administration (UNRRA) be approached for assistance.[53]

Elsewhere, Black Africans and Afro-Caribbeans were also radicalised. Ex-soldiers were to the fore in the militant anti-colonial campaign which developed in the Gold Coast (Ghana) after the war. Some 374,000 had enlisted from Britain's African colonies.[54] The Caribbean contributed too, with 8,500 joining the RAF.[55] West Indians were recruited to aid Britain's domestic war effort – 800 forestry workers were brought from British Honduras to work in the freezing highlands of Scotland. On their arrival some discovered that they had to build their own barracks, and all were paid less than they had been promised. Some 520 men came from the Caribbean colonies to work in Britain's war industries. Approximately 15,000 colonial merchant seamen served in the British merchant fleet, of who 5,000 perished.[56]

The Middle East

Britain had conceded formal independence to Egypt after the First World War but retained the right to maintain a considerable garrison. There was both a king and a government in Cairo, rivals often at daggers drawn, but the British also wielded considerable power. At the outbreak of war Egypt broke off diplomatic relations with Germany and ceded control of its ports to Britain. The Egyptian government refused, however, to declare war on Italy and withdrew its troops from the border with Libya when Mussolini entered the war in June 1940. The British forced the government's dismissal and the retirement of the army Chief of Staff.

In February 1942 the British were facing the prospect of losing control of Egypt. Axis forces were nearing Alexandria. King Farouk was regarded as being fickle in his loyalty and had recently appointed as prime minister a man the British regarded as pro-German. The British demanded Farouk appoint the pro-British Nahas Pasha as prime minister. Farouk refused. The British issued him with an ultimatum to comply by 6pm or face the consequences. Brian Lapping describes events:

> At 6.15pm the King delivered his reply. The ultimatum was an infringement of the Anglo-Egyptian treaty and of the rights of Egypt: the King could not assent to it. Lampson [the British ambassador] sent a message to say that he would be calling on the King at 9pm. By the time he did so, British tanks and armoured vehicles had surrounded the Abdin palace. The King prudently ordered his royal guard not to resist.[57]

Farouk gave way after this threat of forced abdication. A young Egyptian officer wrote of these events of 4 February 1942, 'What is to be done now that this has happened and we accepted it with surrender and servility? ... I believe that colonialism, if it felt that some Egyptians intended to sacrifice their lives and face force with force, would retreat like a prostitute.'[58] Lieutenant Gamal Abdel Nasser spoke for a generation of young Egyptians.

Iraq had been a British protectorate since the end of the First World War and Iraqi oil was important to Britain. In 1941, however, a coup brought a new pro-Axis government headed by Rashid Ali to power. The pro-British King Faisal II fled to the Habbaniya RAF air base and was spirited out of the country. Hitler promised weapons to be delivered from Vichy-run Syria but in the meantime Rashid Ali surrounded the RAF base to try to stop reinforcements arriving. It was surrounded by an eight-mile fence and was home to 56 tennis courts, swimming pools, stables, a polo ground and golf course. RAF bombers were called in and two relief columns marched from Jordan. German aircraft were operating from Syria and the RAF had to attack their bases before imperial troops forced Rashid Ali to flee.[59]

Iraq was the main outlet for British-controlled oilfields in neighbouring Iran. Germany had vied for influence there and with the Wehrmacht seemingly near victory in Russia in 1941, the Shah, Reza Khan Palavi, was in touch with the Germans and refused to obey British orders. At a time of serious military set backs for both countries, Russia and Britain sent in large numbers of troops, tanks and aircraft to occupy Iran and depose the Shah in favour of his son. Roosevelt had sanctioned the move at the meeting where he and Churchill announced the Atlantic Charter, promising freedom to the world.[60]

In order to remove the German presence in Syria, British and Free French forces invaded, hoping to meet no resistance, but the pro-Vichy forces fought back. The eventual occupation of the country involved a far bloodier campaign than had been planned for.[61]

In Palestine Churchill championed the creation of the future Israeli state. In June 1943 General Spears, who broached the matter with him, noted: 'He said he had formed an opinion which nothing would change. He intended to see to it there was a Jewish state. He told me not to argue with him as this would merely make him angry and would change nothing.'[62] The next month the cabinet agreed to allow Jewish immigration, but only to the limits set in a 1939 White Paper, and supported a partition policy which would have created a small Jewish state, a small Arab state attached to Syria, and a larger British mandatory territory. Churchill opposed this policy and continued to meet the Zionist leader, Chaim Weizmann, advising him to campaign against British policy when he visited the US. The prime minister also vetoed any action being taken against the growing Zionist underground forces in Palestine and the stocks of weapons they were gathering.[63]

From India to Palestine, British imperialism was fostering divisions which would burn for decades, just as it had done in Ireland years before. Neither repression nor divide and rule could staunch the desire for freedom.

The End of the French Empire

A similar story could be told of French imperialism. De Gaulle's Free French units relied on troops recruited from its colonies. Two out of the four French divisions which helped force the Gustav Line in southern Italy were Moroccan and one was Algerian. By the end of the war there were 300,000 Moroccans in the French army. Many of these Arab volunteers were dispatched home or withdrawn from the frontline as soon as de Gaulle could enlist white Frenchmen to replace them, so that the army that invaded Germany would be white. The policy was called *blanchissement* (whitening). A deep sense of bitterness developed.[64]

A West African soldier in de Gaulle's army, Yeo Kouhona, recalled how his unit was withdrawn from the frontline in eastern France to the south: 'We had started the war and it was almost over now and we were being replaced by French troops who had been afraid. We wanted the Africans to win the war.'[65]

On VE Day in 1945, 8,000 people demonstrated in Setif in Algeria under the slogan, 'For the Liberation of the People, Long Live Free and Independent Algeria'. They were also brandishing, for the first time, the green and white flag that had once been the standard of that legendary hero of resistance against the French, Abdul el-Kader, and was later to become that of the National Liberation Front, the FLN. The French sub-prefect of Satif, Butterlin, ordered his chief of police, Valère, to intervene and seize the banners. Valère warned that that might mean a fight. 'All right', replied Butterlin, 'then there'll be a fight.'[66]

The police opened fire but were overcome by the crowds. Arms were seized and demonstrators fanned out across the area attacking colonists, killing 103. The French repression that followed was fierce: 'The casualties inflicted by the armed forces were set officially (by the Tubert Commission) at 500 to 600, but the numbers of Muslim villagers killed by the more indiscriminate naval and aerial bombardments may have amounted to more.' Alistair Horne puts the number of Muslims killed at 6,000.[67]

What had changed in Algeria? Horne explains that, 'The Second World War came and with it France's crushing defeat in 1940. To Muslim minds, particularly sensitive to prestige and *baraka* [good fortune], the humiliation made a deep impression.'[68] The events at Setif helped spark the eight-year liberation war which would drive France out of Algeria. The world had been turned upside down.

Conclusion

The Second World War was not, in the minds of those who ruled the Allied powers, a war against fascism. Neither was it a war for democracy. In 1938 Britain and France refused to fight in defence of a democratically elected government in Czechoslovakia but did go to war a year later in defence of Poland, a country ruled by a military clique with pronounced anti-Semitic policies. One of Britain's allies was Greek dictator Metaxas, whose regime had many fascist traits. Britain's major concern when its forces entered Greece (after the Germans had withdrawn) was not to enforce democracy but to crush the Communist-led Resistance army, ELAS, and its civilian wing, EAM, in order to restore the old order. Regarding Italy, Churchill's secretary of state for India, Leo Amery, said in August 1941 that, 'If Italy prefers, after we have got rid of Mussolini, to retain their corporative and functional basis of government, there is no reason why she should not do so.'[1]

In 1942, at the time of the Allied landings in North Africa, President Roosevelt wrote to the Spanish dictator, Franco, describing himself as 'your sincere friend' and assuring him, 'Spain has nothing to fear' from the Allies.[2] On 24 May 1944 Churchill told the Commons that, 'the internal affairs of Spain were a matter for Spaniards alone'.[3] The former leader of the Spanish Communist Party, Fernando Claudin, points out that this position was also accepted by Stalin: 'The maintenance in power of the Fascist dictatorship in Spain after the Second World War is one of the clearest results of Stalin's policy of sharing out "areas of influence".'[4] In Portugal and Spain fascist dictatorships would survive until 1974 and 1975.

In terms of the colonial world, talk of a war for democracy must have seemed risible. There the old colonial powers were fighting to preserve their empires and the racism embedded in colonial rule. While the US might have used anti-imperialist rhetoric to undermine Britain's imperial position, when it came to its own sphere of influence it was similarly ruthless.

Towards a Marxist Interpretation of the War

The central argument of this book is that the Second World War was an imperialist war but that fascism ensured it took place in an entirely different ideological environment than did the 1914–18 conflict. Across the world millions of people yearned for the destruction of fascism and were prepared to back their country's leaders if they could achieve that.

Just two days after the outbreak of war the exiled Russian revolutionary Leon Trotsky argued, 'The struggle is going on between the imperialist slaveholders of different camps for a new division of the world ... the present war is a direct prolongation of the previous war.' He summed up the situation thus: 'The initiative for the new redivision of the world this time, as in 1914, belonged naturally to German imperialism. Caught off guard, the British government first attempted to buy its way out by concessions at the expense of others (Austria, Czechoslovakia). But this policy was short lived.'[5] Trotsky was clear that it was an imperialist war but one in which ideology played a crucial role. In particular the working classes' hatred of fascism meant revolutionaries had to adopt a somewhat different approach to that of 1914. Then, Lenin, Trotsky, Luxemburg and Liebknecht had proclaimed it was an imperialist war in which there was nothing to choose between the powers. In that situation 'the main enemy was at home'.[6]

In March 1939, after Hitler had occupied the rump Czech state and absorbed it into the Third Reich, Trotsky replied to those on the left who argued that faced with the Nazi threat, the old approach could not be taken. He pointed out that the Czech government and ruling class had offered no resistance to Hitler, and that was no accident. In the 24 hours of 'universal confusion and indignation', the Czech working class could have toppled the 'capitulatory' government, taken power and appealed for international support in its resistance to the Nazis.

In March 1939 Trotsky wrote in reply to those who argued that revolutionary defeatism was no response in a war against fascism, in reference to the absorption of the rump Czechoslovakia into the Third Reich. The exiled revolutionary issued a very clear warning:

> the Czech working class did not have the slightest right to entrust the leadership of a war 'against fascism' to Messrs Capitalists who, within a few days, so safely changed their coloration and became themselves fascists and quasi-fascists. Transformations and recolorations of this kind on the part of the ruling classes will be on the order of the day in wartime in all 'democracies'. That is why the proletariat would ruin itself if it were to determine its main line of policy by the formal and unstable labels of 'for fascism' and 'against fascism'.[7]

Yet anti-fascist ideology played a key role in September 1939 and the resulting mood of the working class had to be taken into account. Accordingly, in discussions with American Trotskyists in the early summer of 1940, just as France surrendered to Hitler, Trotsky pointed out that the Roosevelt administration had already set the process of militarisation in motion and that it had widespread support among the working class, because 'They bear a sentimental hatred against Hitler mixed with confused class sentiments.'[8] American workers hated Hitler and Mussolini but their trade union leaders, allied in the main to Roosevelt, tried to use that to justify support for the Churchill government in London. Trotsky argued for a different approach based on creating anti-fascist militias. He returned to this at the beginning of August:

> The feeling of the masses is that it is necessary to defend themselves. We must say: 'Roosevelt ... says it is necessary to defend the country; good it must be our country, not that of the Sixty Families [the mega rich] and their Wall

Street. The army must be under our own command; we must have our own officers, who will be "loyal to us".' In this way we can find an approach to the masses that will not push them away from us, and thus prepare for the second step – a more revolutionary one. We must use the example of France to the very end. We must say, 'I warn you, workers, that they (the bourgeoisie) will betray you! Look at Pétain, who is a friend of Hitler. Shall we have the same thing happen in this country? We must create our own machine, under workers' control.[9]

The reference to Pétain would have struck a chord in Britain in the summer of 1940 when there were numerous candidates for such a role in Britain. Many working people in Britain believed that if Hitler did invade then a section of the ruling class would speedily come to a deal. And despite the rhetoric of the British government and King George VI about resisting the Germans in the ruins of London, they would have fled. From his cell in Brixton prison the jailed fascist leader, Sir Oswald Mosley, was confident he would be brought to power by a German invasion.[10]

In the dark days of 1940 when Hitler seemed set to win, Trotsky argued with those who believed that all they could do was support Britain and its semi-ally the US and that revolution could only return to the agenda after Hitler's defeat. Trotsky was confident that in occupied Europe Hitler's problems had only just begun, pointing out that the Third Reich was not sufficiently strong to position a soldier over every worker and peasant in the occupied territories, and did not have the means to transform them from a foe into a friend. While Hitler boasted of a 'thousand year' Reich, Trotsky doubted it could last ten years. As resistance to Nazism grew, that would create revolutionary explosions, and the task of the left was not to trust in British or US imperialism but to prepare for those explosions. He pointed out that if the left renounced independent revolutionary politics, who would utilise a revolutionary situation which might result from Hitler's defeat?[11]

As we have seen, his question was prescient. Trotsky started from the need to maintain independent working-class organisation. He proposed building a bridge to those workers who wanted to see fascism defeated but were uneasy with their own rulers' war aims. But this meant little as the tiny Trotskyist movement was a weak vessel cast adrift in stormy seas, unable to act on Trotsky's strategic and tactical advice. In both France and the US the Trotskyists suffered damaging splits. Added to this was Trotsky's assassination and then the repression suffered by his followers during the war. More generally, the left felt the impact of the collapse of the French Popular Front government, the defeat of the Spanish Revolution, and the harmful impact of the Hitler-Stalin pact.[12]

In *Trotskyists and the Resistance in World War Two*, the Belgian Marxist Ernest Mandel argued that 'the Second World War was in reality a combination of five different wars'. He lists the wars as first, 'an inter-imperialist war' fought between the Axis and Allied powers; second, 'a just war of self-defence by the people of China, an oppressed semi-colonial country, against Japanese imperialism'; third, 'a just war of national defence of the Soviet Union, a workers' state, against an imperialist power'; fourthly, 'a just war of national liberation of the oppressed colonial peoples of Africa and Asia ... launched by the masses against British and French imperialism, sometimes against Japanese imperialism, and sometimes against both in succession, one after the other'. Mandel's fifth and last war was 'a war of liberation by the oppressed workers, peasants, and urban petty bourgeoisie against the German Nazi imperialists and their stooges', which was fought 'more especially in two countries, Yugoslavia and Greece, to a great extent in Poland, and incipiently in France and Italy'.[13]

Another Marxist, Donny Gluckstein, argues that there were 'two distinct wars', an imperialist war and a 'people's war' against fascism. This, he states, was a war fought *by* the people, '*for* the people'.[14] Yet these wars, supposedly separate, were by no means of equal weight. The inter-imperialist war between the Axis and the Allies dominated events. The sacrifice of the self-interests of the working class by the Communist Parties, which dominated the Resistance movements in Europe and Asia, to the diplomatic interests of the Kremlin meant that the potential for an 'autonomous' liberation war was never realised.

Where powerful guerrilla armies succeeded in taking state power, first in Yugoslavia and later in North Vietnam and China, they created societies which mirrored Stalin's Russia, with a state-directed drive to industrialise given total priority and with not a smidgen of proletarian democracy. Stalin himself was none too happy with Tito and Mao, whom he saw as rivals. The nationalist ideologies of these regimes led the Yugoslavs and, later, the Chinese to break with Moscow. The people did not take control of the 'People's Democracies' in Eastern Europe, not in the People's Republic of China and certainly not in the states which would be created from the post-war struggle against colonialism.

The imperialist nature of the war impacted on the Resistance movements because they were prepared to accept the strategic demands of Moscow. In Italy the forces of the Resistance grouped in the CLNs followed the Communists by accepting the authority of the government installed by the Allies, despite the deep reservations of the rank and file.[15] In Greece, Vietnam and Malaya, Communist-led Resistance forces accepted the arrival of British forces after liberation and urged co-operation at heavy cost. When, post-war, the national liberation struggle resumed in all three countries against both the imperialist powers and their ruling class allies, it was in drastically less favourable circumstances. None of this means that these movements should not have accepted material aid from those imperialist powers that were engaging the same enemy, but it did require that they maintain complete strategic and political independence. That simply did not happen.

The imperialist nature of the war shaped everything. Churchill, Roosevelt and Stalin succeeded in containing the forces of the anti-fascist resistance in Europe. In Asia they were only able to keep the lid on it for a brief time before it boiled over again.

In discussions in Britain I have often been challenged by those demanding to know 'what would you have done?' faced with the prospect of a German invasion in the summer of 1940. One response would have been to say that while Churchill may have wanted to fight the Germans for his own imperial reasons, there was a queue of top Tories ready to cut a deal with the Führer. Pointing to the debacle of the surrender in France, and the performance of the ruling class and the officer corps, the conclusion might have been that a people's militia was needed, and quick!

By 1944 the final destruction of Nazism was required for the sake of humanity, but that did not involve writing the Allied leaders a blank cheque. Rather it necessitated demanding arms for the Resistance movements in Europe and Asia, freedom for India and other colonies and, at home, immediate implementation of the welfare state and other promised reforms.

Was Revolution Possible?

The Communist Party leaders in France and Italy pointed to the Allied presence in Western Europe as the reason why revolution was not possible in 1944 and 1945. Later Thorez argued, 'With the Americans in France the revolution would have been annihilated.'[16] The reality was that in the winter of 1944–45 de Gaulle could not rely on his own armed forces to control France and the Communists had control of many regions and had arms to hand. The general was relying on the support of Moscow and, in consequence, his ability to co-opt and restrain the PCF at the price of a few minor seats in government.

De Gaulle did request, in September 1944, that two French divisions be withdrawn from the front to deal with the Communist presence in the vast Toulouse-Limousin area. Eisenhower refused because, faced with an assault on the Third Reich, he needed every possible soldier. That refusal increased de Gaulle's reliance on Stalin and Thorez to hold back the French working class and peasantry.[17]

By the second half of 1944 the British armed forces were already shrinking in size, the Canadians had used up their pool of volunteers for overseas duties, and while France was not short of men it had neither the finances nor the means to equip them. The Americans might have been less affected, but war weariness was sweeping through the ranks. US and British service personnel wanted home. Mutinies became common as demobilisation was postponed. Strike fever was also affecting the home front as the number of disputes reached a climax in 1946, the year of the US's greatest ever strike wave. In the Philippines there were repeated mass demonstrations by GIs who were not eager to be used against the left-wing Huk guerrillas and were protesting at the delay in demobilisation. The *New York Times* reported in January 1946 on one of these demonstrations: '"The Philippines are capable of handling their own internal problems", was the slogan voiced by several speakers. Many extended the same point of view to China.'[18]

In the event the old colonial powers emerged from the war too weak to maintain their hold. The demand for land reform coupled with hatred of the colonial order, built as it was on racism, and of the venal, native rich, created powerful movements that forced their leaders to abjure any compromise with the old order.

In 1946 the British Army of the Rhine numbered just two divisions and, for a while, the Americans just one. Any Allied intervention against, for example, partisan-controlled northern Italy in support of the former fascists, collaborators and monarchists in 1945 would have been difficult to sustain. Similarly in Greece, British troops were only able to win control of Athens after Moscow and the Communist Party leaders forced ELAS to accept a ceasefire. The British and their right-wing allies had nothing like the resources available had ELAS decided to retain its control of the countryside (including the second city Salonika) by force of arms.

Some evidence for the possibility of revolution comes from Yugoslavia, where the Communist-led partisans defied the Yalta conventions and took power. This was not a socialist revolution led by the working class; rather the new Tito regime replicated Russian state capitalism for nationalist ends. But Britain and America were powerless to intervene in 1945 just as Stalin felt restrained from invading when Yugoslavia broke free of Moscow's control.

Later the Western Communist leaders would cite British and American actions in Greece as proof that they could not have advanced beyond the limits set by the division of Europe agreed at Yalta. Togliatti warned the PCI's national council in April 1945 of a 'Greek outcome' where 'a violent clash, an armed conflict between the armed forces of the anti-fascist front and the forces of the old police and the army led by anti-democratic elements', could only lead to elections being suspended, the Allied occupation continuing, and a split between a 'progressive' anti-fascist north and a south 'kept against its will in pre-fascist conditions'.[19] But in Greece the left had fought back half-heartedly. Indeed the British were effectively beaten in December 1944 when the left brokered a ceasefire. Churchill was hamstrung because there were simply not enough British troops available to divert to Greece.

Thorez and Togliatti had no intention of spearheading any radical challenge. Thorez was allowed back into France precisely because de Gaulle knew he could be relied upon to restrain his comrades. Communists were allowed junior positions in de Gaulle's government and in return Thorez told the liberation committees to hand over their administration of swathes of the country to the authorities in Paris, who usually installed ex-Vichyites, ordered Communist resisters into the army, and urged increased production and a ban on strikes. In the October 1945 elections for a Constituent Assembly the Socialists and Communists won an overall majority of the votes – 302 deputies out of 586. Rather than form a government of the left the Socialists insisted that it should incorporate the MRP (Mouvement Républicain Populaire), which was broadly identified with de Gaulle.[20] Ian Birchall points to the reasoning behind the decision not to form a government of the left:

> Such a government would not (as some on the right feared) have taken France into the Russian bloc; Stalin would have made sure the Yalta bargain was kept. Circumstances would have obliged it to impose austerity on the working class in the interest of reconstruction and productivity. But a government of the

left alone would have raised expectations of the working class, and it would have had fewer excuses for failing to deliver.[21]

The Communists had played a key role in the Resistance but they had to struggle to ensure loyalty to the Allies above all else. In Italy many of those who identified with the Communist Party had little or no contact with it and believed it was a revolutionary party. The party's internal leadership, until Togliatti's return, was operating largely independently from their exiled leadership in Moscow. The dominant ideology was nationalist – looking back to the traditions of Garibaldi, the Risorgimento and republicanism. But with the king, the ruling elite and the church hierarchy so closely linked to fascism, nationalist ideology moved quickly to the left.

Nationalism was a powerful force motivating resistance to the German occupiers and their fascist allies, but it had its limitations. Togliatti brought back the message that the central goal was not socialism but a strong, democratic Italy. In April 1945 the Resistance rose and liberated Milan, Turin, Genoa, Venice and all the towns and cities still under occupation. As Kolko explains: 'The Resistance was triumphant and in power. Was Italy on the verge of revolution? ... The Allied military wasted no time in finding out. They knew it was necessary to disarm the Partisans and take over local governments. Disarmament ... the Anglo-Americans executed with astonishing success.'[22]

Across northern Italy the Allies organised parades after they arrived in Resistance-held towns and cities at the end of April and the beginning of May, where the partisans marched past, were given speeches and toasts, and were then requested to hand in their arms. Military authority was established and with the acquiescence of the Resistance forces all CLN decrees and appointees were subject to military approval. Until the end of 1945 northern Italy remained under military rule, despite the fact that the government in Rome had ruled the south and centre of the country for some time.

They could only be successful in this because the Resistance leadership and the PCI acquiesced in disarming the Resistance fighters and dissolving the CLNs.

That was not inevitable. Togliatti's ability to carry that argument relied on the absence of any coherent left challenge and his suggestion to the party membership that he was playing for time and once the situation was more favourable the party would move back to insurrection. Kolko rather simplifies the process and exaggerates the success in getting Resistance fighters to hand over their arms. The Communists had to put across a dual message in order to do so. The PCI argument for 'progressive democracy' could be understood by armed workers and peasants as the first step on the path to socialism. For Togliatti it meant the creation of a bourgeois democratic Italy – perhaps a republic, perhaps not. As Paul Ginsborg argues:

> Many of the rank and file members of the party, especially the partisans, remained perplexed about the adoption of 'progressive democracy' as their end aim. But they interpreted this as essentially a tactical move on Togliatti's part, to ensure the immediate legality of their party. They were convinced

too that once the Allied troops had left, the revolutionary goals of the PCI would once again be proclaimed. They were quite wrong, but this double think, or *doppiezza* as it came to be called, this confusion of strategy for tactics, was fundamental in reconciling class aims with the leadership's insistence on compromise.[23]

Togliatti was helped by the break in the continuity of the left imposed by two decades of fascism. The evidence points to the rank and file of the PCI wanting socialism and believing revolution was necessary to achieve it. But that did not mean they had the confidence to rise up to bring down fascism *and* the institutions of the new state being created by the parties who had formed the new coalition government, including their own. The years of fascism had not destroyed the spirit of resistance but they did ensure there was no immediate discussion of tactics and strategy.[24]

Another factor was the enormous prestige that Stalin's Russia had accrued from its overwhelming role in the defeat of Hitler. Pictures of Stalin decorated homes and factory floors across Italy. People believed that having conquered Eastern Europe, 'il Baffone' (walrus moustache) would be on the march again. But as Ginsborg notes:

> The belief in socialist revolution as something that was brought from outside deprived the Italian working class of any chance of evolving a revolutionary strategy that was based on their own resources. Under Communist leadership political action was split into three distinct spheres, the immediate day-to-day battles waged by workers against cold, hunger and penury; the struggle for progressive democracy waged by the party in parliament; and the revolution itself, an impossibility until Stalin moved.[25]

The PCI would become a cornerstone of the new Italian Republic, settling down into the parliamentary chamber. Looking back on the close of the war the former leader of the Spanish Communist Party, Fernando Claudin, writes:

> The possibility of revolutionary development in France and Italy was seriously threatened [by the line of the Communist Parties]; the position was as it would have been in Russia in the course of 1917 if Lenin's April Theses had been rejected by the Bolshevik Party. The bourgeois revolution would have consolidated itself, one way or another, but the proletarian revolution would not have taken place.[26]

Ginsborg concludes:

> In practice, national unity in the fight for liberation became for the Communists an objective to be placed not just above but to the exclusion of all others. The policy of liberation first, 'progressive democracy' second, was fatally misconceived. It meant that at the very moment when the partisan and workers' movement was at it height, when the 'wind from the North'

was blowing most strongly, the Communists accepted the postponement of all questions of a social and political nature until the end of the war ... While the Communists postponed, in the honourable name of national unity, their opponents acted, decided, manoeuvred and, not surprisingly, triumphed.[27]

The missing link was the one Trotsky had identified – the independent organisation of the working class. Ernest Mandel, interviewed in 1976, argued that the Resistance movements in Southern Europe

> possessed an inner logic that made it possible to challenge capitalism and the bourgeois state, and above all to take initiatives in the construction of a popular power from below; initiatives which could have led to the generalisation of revolutionary situations of dual power.
>
> I do not think that the immediate struggle for power was possible in countries like France as soon as the Nazi front collapsed. Nor do I think that we can treat as insignificant the presence of American troops, which has been held up as the sole, irrefutable argument by the Stalinists and which revolutionaries have tended to dismiss too lightly. The nearest we can get to a correct formulation is this: during the liberation struggles it was possible to develop factory occupations and takeovers, to form local organs of popular power, and above all to bring about the general arming of the masses, in such a way as to generalise the situations of dual power and open up the possibility of a later seizure of power.
>
> We should not forget that the presence of American troops was limited in time and that the American soldiers brought strong pressure to bear for their return. Moreover, even without any pre-existing situation of dual power, the fluctuations in the political conjuncture brought about highly explosive crises. The most important of these was in Italy in 1948, when, in response to the attempted assassination of Togliatti on 14 July, the masses went well beyond a general protest strike to occupy factories, railway stations, electric power stations, etc., thus demonstrating that they instinctively posed the question of power. If workers' councils had already existed and if a part of the proletariat had been armed then July 1948 could have opened up an extremely deep revolutionary crisis in Italy.[28]

This has the merit of breaking from the 'one fine day' approach to revolution. For Marxists revolution is not simply one day of street fighting. It is a protracted crisis in which the old clashes with the new. In tsarist Russia this only took a few months because of the weakness of the absolutist regime, of the bourgeoisie and, crucially, of a rooted 'bourgeois workers' party' committed to reforming the system. In the debates in the Communist International following the October Revolution, particularly at its Third and Fourth Congresses, a revolutionary crisis in Western Europe was seen as one lasting years rather than months, with all sorts of ups and downs for the forces of the new. This is what happened in Germany between 1918 and 1923 – when the Communist Party let what was a revolutionary moment slip away.

In January 1943 the writer Arthur Koestler, a former member of the German Communist Party who had settled in Britain, wrote:

> The nearer victory comes in sight, the clearer the character of the war reveals itself as what the Tories always said that it was – a war for national survival, a war in defence of certain conservative 19th century ideals, and not what I and my friends of the left had said that it was – a revolutionary civil war in Europe on the Spanish pattern.[29]

As Trotsky had predicted, that revolutionary civil war did briefly emerge. But his warnings of what would happen if Koestler's 'friends of the left' ensured it was safely bottled up again were vindicated.

Seventy years on capitalism still produces wars and fascism – but it also still creates the desire for revolutionary change.

Timeline

1918
11 November – The Armistice with Germany marks the end of the First World War.

1919
18 January – Opening of the Paris Peace Conference to negotiate peace treaties between the belligerents of the First World War.
28 June – Germany and the Entente powers sign the Treaty of Versailles after six months of negotiations. The German armed forces are limited in size to 100,000 personnel and Germany is ordered to pay large reparations for war damages.

1920
21 January – The Paris Peace Conference comes to an end with the inaugural General Assembly of the League of Nations.

1922
6 February – The Washington Naval Conference ends with the signing of the Washington Naval Treaty by the United Kingdom, the United States, Japan, France and Italy. The signing parties agree to limit the size of their naval forces.
29 October – Fascist leader Benito Mussolini is appointed prime minister of Italy by the king.

1927
12 April – The Chinese Civil War begins between nationalists and Communists.

1929
29 October – The Great Depression begins.

1931
19 September – Japan invades Manchuria.

1932
28 January – Fighting around Shanghai between China and Japan.
27 February – Japan takes control of Manchuria from the Republic of China.

1933
30 January – Nazi leader Adolf Hitler is appointed Chancellor of Germany by President Paul von Hindenburg.

27 February – Germany's parliament building the Reichstag is set on fire. The German government blames the Communists.
28 February – The Reichstag Fire Decree is passed, nullifying several German civil liberties.
23 March – The Reichstag passes the Enabling Act, making Hitler dictator of Germany.
27 March – Japan leaves the League of Nations.
19 October – Germany leaves the League of Nations.

1934

30 June – The Night of Long Knives occurs, during which Hitler executes the leaders of the Sturmabteilung (SA) and other rivals.
2 August – Hitler becomes Führer of Germany, becoming Head of State as well as Chancellor.
8 August – The Wehrmacht swears a personal oath of loyalty to Hitler.
18 September – The Soviet Union joins the League of Nations.
29 December – Japan renounces the Washington Naval Treaty and the London Naval Treaty.

1935

2 October – Italy invades Ethiopia, beginning the Second Italo-Abyssinian War.

1936

7 March – German forces occupy the Rhineland, established as a demilitarised zone under the Treaty of Versailles.
5 May – Italian forces occupy Addis Ababa in East Africa.
7 May – Italy annexes Ethiopia.
9 May – Chiang Kai-shek, Chinese nationalist leader, claims that Japan is waging war in China without a declaration of war.
18 July – The Spanish Civil War begins when nationalist forces led by Francisco Franco rise against the current Republican government.
25 October – Rome-Berlin Axis is formed.

1937

7 July – The Marco Polo Bridge Incident, which most historians regard as the beginning of the Second Sino-Japanese War.
13 August – The Battle of Shanghai begins between Japan and China.
26 November – The Battle of Shanghai ends in Japanese victory.
11 December – Italy leaves the League of Nations.

1938

6 March – Japanese troops reach the Yellow River in China.
13 March – Austria is annexed by Nazi Germany.
29 July – The Soviet-Japanese Border Wars begin with the Battle of Lake Khasan.
11 August – Soviet Union wins the Battle of Khasan against Japan.

24 September – Hitler issues ultimatum to Czechoslovakia that either they cede the Sudetenland to Germany or he will order an invasion.

30 September – The Munich Agreement is signed. Britain and France agree to German annexation of Sudetenland without presence of Czech government.

1939

15 March – The German Army occupies Czechoslovakia.

31 March – The United Kingdom and France offer the 'guarantee' of Polish independence.

1 April – The Spanish Civil War ends with nationalist troops winning. Spain becomes a fascist state with Franco as the head of the new government.

7 April – Italy invades Albania.

28 April – In a speech before the Reichstag, Hitler renounces the Anglo-German Naval Agreement and the German-Polish Non-Aggression Pact.

11 May – Battle of Khalkhin Gol begins with Japan and Manchukuo (Japanese satellite state in Manchuria) against the Soviet Union and Mongolia.

22 May – The Pact of Steel, known formally as the Pact of Friendship and Alliance between Germany and Italy.

10 July – Prime Minister Neville Chamberlain reaffirms support for Poland and that Britain would intervene on behalf of Poland if hostilities broke out between Germany and Poland.

23 August – The Molotov-Ribbentrop Pact is signed between Nazi Germany and the Soviet Union, with secret provisions for the division of Eastern Europe – joint occupation of Poland and Soviet occupation of the Baltic states, Finland and Bessarabia.

1 September – Hitler invades Poland.

3 September – Britain and France declare war on Germany. Mussolini declares Italy neutral but allied to Germany.

17 September – USSR invades and occupies Eastern Poland under terms of the Molotov-Ribbentrop Pact.

28 September – Warsaw surrenders.

6 October – Polish forces surrender.

4 November – The US Neutrality Act is passed: the French and British may buy arms, but on a strictly cash basis.

30 November – Russia attacks Finland to begin the 'Winter War'.

1940

12 March – Finland signs a peace treaty with the Soviet Union. The Finns are forced to give up significant territory in exchange for independence.

9 April – German forces invade Norway and Denmark. British and French forces sent to Norway but ultimately fail to prevent German occupation.

10 May – Winston Churchill replaces Neville Chamberlain as Prime Minister of Britain. Germany invades Netherlands, Belgium, Luxemburg and France.

26 May – British forces in France begin evacuation from Dunkirk.

10 June – Italy declares war on Britain and France.

13 June – German troops occupy Paris.

21 June – Russia occupies Baltic states – Estonia, Lithuania and Latvia.
25 June – France surrenders.
10 July – Battle of Britain begins with German air attacks on shipping in the English Channel.
20 August – Chinese Communists launch the Hundred Regiments Offensive against the Japanese in northern China.
2 September – US President Roosevelt agrees to hand over 50 destroyers in return for the UK granting America bases in various imperial possessions. Effectively start of US aid to the UK.
22 September – Japanese forces occupy French Indochina.
16 October – Jews in Warsaw and surrounding area ordered into Warsaw Ghetto.
28 October – Italy invades Greece.
6–9 December – British forces counter-attack after Italian army enters Egypt. Italians driven back into Libya suffering major losses.

1941

11 February – German troops of Afrika Corps arrive in Libya to combat British advance.
11 March – President Roosevelt signs Lend-Lease scheme under which US provides UK with arms and material under a loan scheme.
24 March – German-led counter-offensive in North Africa compels British retreat back to Egypt.
6 April – German, Italian, Bulgarian and Hungarian forces invade Yugoslavia and Greece.
17 April – Yugoslavia surrenders.
27 April – Greece surrenders.
22 June – Operation Barbarossa, German invasion of Russia, begins.
8 August 1941 – Siege of Leningrad begins.
28 September – German SS troops kill over 30,000 Jews at Babi Yar on the outskirts of Kiev, in the Ukraine.
2 October – German attack on Moscow begins.
5 December – Germans call off attack on Moscow, Red Army begins counter-attack.
7 December – Japanese carrier-based planes attack US Pacific naval headquarters at Pearl Harbor, Hawaii. US and Japan at war.

1942

20 January – Wannsee conference in Berlin agrees on 'Final Solution' to the 'Jewish problem'.
15 February – British forces surrender Singapore to the Japanese.
8 May – Final surrender of US troops in Philippines. Naval battle of Coral Sea sees US halt Japanese invasion of New Guinea.
20 May – Japanese complete conquest of Burma reaching border with India.
4 June – Battle of Midway begins. Ends in decisive US victory over Japan.
28 June – Beginning of German offensive which would carry them to Stalingrad.

7 August – Battle of Guadalcanal begins. First successful US offensive in the Pacific theatre.

19 November – Operation Uranus. Red Army offensive to cut off German forces in Stalingrad.

1943

18 January – The Warsaw Ghetto Uprising begins.

24 January – The Casablanca Conference attended by Churchill and Roosevelt ends with agreement that Germany must surrender unconditionally.

2 February – German surrender at Stalingrad.

9 February – Battle of Guadalcanal ends with American victory over Japan.

5 March – Mass strike in Turin begins. It will spread across northern Italy heralding the end of fascism in Italy.

13 May – German and Italian forces in Tunisia surrender. The Allies take over 250,000 prisoners. End of North Africa campaign.

16 May – The Warsaw Ghetto Uprising ends. Fourteen thousand Jews killed and about another 40,000 sent to the death camp at Treblinka.

5 July – Operation Citadel (the Battle of Kursk) begins.

10 July – Allied forces invade Sicily.

25 July – Mussolini is arrested and removed from power.

3 September – Italian government signs secret armistice with Allies. Italian Armistice is signed and Italy drops out of the war.

3 September – Allied forces invade mainland Italy.

8 September – Allies announce surrender of Italy. German forces occupy bulk of country. King and government flee Rome refusing to resist.

9 September – Allied forces land at Salerno, in southern Italy.

12 September – Mussolini rescued by German SS troops, flown to Germany where he is proclaimed as the head of the puppet 'Italian Social Republic'.

28 November – Roosevelt, Stalin and Churchill meet at the Tehran Conference and agree on June 1944 Anglo-American invasion of Europe.

1944

4 January – Red Army enters Poland.

18 January – End of siege of Leningrad.

22 January – Allied forces land at Anzio.

31 May – The Japanese retreat from Imphal ending their invasion of India.

5 June – Rome falls to the Allies.

6 June – D-Day, 155,000 Allied troops land on the beaches of Normandy in France.

19 June – The Battle of the Philippine Sea begins. It will be the largest aircraft carrier battle in history. Ends with a decisive victory for the Americans.

1 July – Opening of the Bretton Woods conference in United States, which would establish International Monetary Fund, the World Bank and the General Agreement on Tariffs and Trade (GATT).

22 June – Operation Bagration begins. Over the next two months the Red Army will advance westwards to Warsaw.

24 July – Majdanek Concentration Camp is liberated by Soviet forces, the first among many.
1 August – Polish Home Army begins Warsaw Uprising.
19 August – French Resistance begins uprising in Paris.
25 August – Paris is liberated.
1 October – Soviet troops enter Yugoslavia.
2 October – Polish independence forces in Warsaw surrender to the Red Army.
12 October – Athens is liberated by Greek Resistance forces.
16 October – The Red Army and Yugoslav partisans liberate Belgrade.
23 October – Battle of Leyte Gulf begins, the largest sea battle in history. Ends in Japanese defeat.
1 December – Heinrich Himmler orders the crematoriums and gas chambers of Auschwitz concentration camp dismantled and blown up.
16 December – The Battle of the Bulge begins as German forces attempt a breakthrough in the Ardennes region. Last German offensive in the west ends in failure.

1945

12 January – Red Army offensive in East Prussia begins.
27 January – Auschwitz concentration camp is liberated by Soviet troops.
31 January – Red Army crosses the Oder River into Germany and is now less than 50 miles from Berlin.
4 February – Roosevelt, Churchill and Stalin meet at Yalta in the Soviet Union to agree post-war spheres of influence.
13–14 February – Dresden is firebombed by Allied air forces and large parts of the historic city are destroyed. Allies claim it is strategically important.
9–10 March – US firebomb attack on Tokyo destroys 15 square miles of the city.
22–23 March – Allied forces cross the Rhine.
12 April – President Roosevelt dies, succeeded by Harry S. Truman.
13 April – Vienna falls to Red Army.
16 April – Battle of Berlin begins. Final Russian assault on German capital.
24 April – Russian forces encircle Berlin.
25 April – Italian Resistance launches insurrection, liberating northern Italy. First meeting of United Nations in San Francisco.
28 April – Mussolini captured by Resistance and executed the following day.
30 April – Hitler commits suicide.
2 May – Berlin surrenders.
8 May – End of the War in Europe with German surrender.
5 June – Allies agree to divide Germany into four occupied zones (Russian, American, British and French).
22 June – Americans capture island of Okinawa.
5 July – US declares liberation of Philippines.
10 July – 1,000-bomber raids against Japan begin.
16 July – First atomic bomb is successfully tested in the US.

17 July – Truman, Stalin and Churchill meet at Potsdam. Russia agrees to attack Japan.
26 July – Labour Party wins landslide election in Britain.
6 August – First atomic bomb dropped on Hiroshima.
8 August – USSR declares war on Japan, invading Manchuria.
9 August – Second atomic bomb is dropped on Nagasaki.
15 August – Emperor Hirohito broadcasts to the Japanese nation announcing unconditional surrender.
17 August – Nationalists declare independence of Indonesia.
2 September – Formal Japanese surrender ceremony in Tokyo Bay as President Truman declares VJ Day. Ho Chi Minh declares Vietnam independent.

1946
5 March – Winston Churchill declares that an Iron Curtain divides Eastern and Western Europe

1947
5 May – Communists removed from French government.
31 May – Italian government formed excluding Communists.
5 June – Launch of Marshall Plan, economic plan for European recovery, launched by US. Aid conditional on acceptance of economic 'freedom'.
15 August – Indian Independence.

1948
21 February – Communists assume total control of Czechoslovakia.
24 June – Russia begins economic blockade of Western-controlled Berlin.

1949
1 October – Mao Zedong proclaims establishment of the People's Republic of China.
27 December – Dutch accept Indonesian independence.

Notes

Introduction
1. Tammy Bruce, 'Neville Chamberlain's Grandchildren', FrontPageMagazine.com, 13 September 2002.
2. A. Trevor Thrall, *American Foreign Policy and The Politics of Fear: Threat Inflation Since 9/11* (Taylor and Francis, 2009), pp. 124–5.
3. Jason A. Edwards, *Navigating the Post-Cold War World: President Clinton's Foreign Policy Rhetoric* (Lexington Books, 2008), p. 86.
4. Anthony Barnett, *Iron Britannia* (Allison and Busby, 1982), p. 20.
5. Angus Calder, *The People's War* (Granada, 1982), p. 37.
6. Eric Hobsbawm, *Age of Extremes* (Michael Joseph, 1994), p. 144.

Chapter 1
1. League of Nations, *Commercial Policy in the Interwar Years* (1942).
2. Paul N. Hehn, *A Low Dishonest Decade* (Continuum, 2002), p. 14.
3. See Thomas Ferguson and Hans-Joachim Voth, 'Betting on Hitler: The Value of Political Connections in Nazi Germany', *Quarterly Journal of Economics* (February 2008), pp. 112–13.
4. Chris Harman, *Explaining the Crisis* (Bookmarks, 1984), p. 65.
5. Tim Mason, *Nazism, Fascism and the Working Class* (Cambridge University Press, 1995), p. 51.
6. Leon Trotsky, *Writings of Leon Trotsky 1933–34* (Pathfinder, 1975), p. 302.
7. Gabriel Kolko, *The Politics of War: The World and United States Foreign Policy, 1943–1945* (Pantheon, 1990), p. 251.
8. Ernest Mandel, *The Meaning of the Second World War* (Verso, 1986), p. 16.
9. Alan Clark, *Barbarossa* (Penguin, 1966), p. 43.

Chapter 2
1. John Charmley, *Churchill: The End of Glory* (Sceptre, 1993), p. 327.
2. Clive Ponting, *1940: Myth and Reality* (Cardinal, 1990), p. 19.
3. Ibid., p. 14.
4. David Williams, 'The Evolution of the Sterling System', in C.R. Whitlesey and J.S.G. Wilson (eds), *Essays in Money and Banking* (Oxford University Press, 1968), p. 268.
5. Leon Trotsky, 'Military Doctrine or Pseudo-Military Doctrinairism', *Kommunisticheskii International*, 5 December 1921.
6. James Levy, 'Ready or Not?: The Home Fleet at the Outset of World War II', *Naval War College Review* (Autumn 1999), available at http://www.usnwc.edu/NavalWarCollegeReviewArchives/1990s/1999%20Autumn%20.pdf
7. R.F. Holland, *The Pursuit of Greatness: Britain and the World Role 1900–1970* (Fontana, 1991), pp. 100–3 and Clive Ponting, *Churchill* (BCA, 1994), pp. 273–5.
8. Hehn, *A Low Dishonest Decade*, pp. 10–11.
9. Austen Morgan, *J. Ramsey MacDonald* (Manchester University Press, 1976), pp. 176–86, and W.R. Garside, *British Unemployment 1919–1939* (Cambridge University Press, 1990), pp. 130–7.

10. Adam Tooze, *The Wages of Destruction* (Penguin, 2007), pp. 50–1.
11. W.R. Garside, *British Unemployment 1919–1939* (Cambridge University Press, 1990), p. 173.
12. Alexander Anievas, 'The International Political Economy of Appeasement', *Review of International Studies* 37:2 (2010), pp. 601–29.
13. Ponting, *1940*, p. 37.
14. Holland, *The Pursuit of Greatness*, p. 180.
15. Kolko, *The Politics of War*, p. 195.
16. Graham Stewart, *Burying Caesar: Churchill, Chamberlain and the Battle for the Tory Party* (Phoenix, 2000), p. 205.
17. Ponting, *1940*, p. 35.
18. Holland, *The Pursuit of Greatness*, p. 109.
19. Ibid., p. 140.
20. Angus Calder, *The Myth of the Blitz* (Pimlico, 1991), p. 211.
21. Jasper Ridley, *Mussolini* (Constable, 1997), p. 164.
22. Martin Pugh, *Hurrah for the Blackshirts* (Jonathan Cape, 2005), p. 41.
23. Ibid., p. 49.
24. 'Cassius', *The Trial of Mussolini* (Victor Gollancz, 1943), p. 16.
25. Christopher Hibbert, *Benito Mussolini* (The Reprint Society London, 1962), p. 99.
26. Ian Kershaw, *Making Friends With Hitler* (Allen Lane, 2004), p. 74.
27. Alvin Finkel and Clement Leibovitz, *The Chamberlain–Hitler Collusion* (Merlin, 1997), p. 96.
28. Charmley, *Churchill*, p. 309.
29. Mervyn Jones, *Michael Foot* (Victor Gollancz, 1994), p. 65.
30. Kershaw, *Making Friends With Hitler*, p. 155.
31. Nigel Todd, *In Excited Times* (Bewick Press, 1995), p. 106.
32. Andrew Roberts, *Eminent Churchillians* (Phoenix, 1995), p. 6.
33. Kitty Kelley, *The Royals* (Warner Books, 1997), p. 22.
34. *Independent on Sunday*, 5 March 2000.
35. Ponting, *Churchill*, pp. 377–8.
36. Ibid., p. 393.
37. Ibid., pp. 359–60.
38. Ibid., pp. 373–4.
39. Ibid., p. 399.
40. Ibid., p. 464.
41. Ponting, *1940*, p. 30.
42. Julian Jackson, *France: The Dark Years 1940–1944* (Oxford University Press, 2001), pp. 70–1.
43. Alastair Horne, *To Lose a Battle: France 1940* (Penguin, 1979), p. 90.
44. Jackson, *France: The Dark Years*, p. 73.
45. Horne, *To Lose a Battle*, p. 117.
46. Ibid. Marc Bloch was shot as a resistant.
47. Jackson, *France: The Dark Years*, p. 79.
48. Leon Trotsky, *The History of the Russian Revolution* (Sphere Books, 1967), p. 21.
49. Ibid., pp. 21–2.
50. E.H. Carr, *Twilight of the Comintern, 1930–1935* (Pantheon, 1982), p. 4.
51. J. Stalin, *Works, July 1930–January 1934, Volume 13* (Lawrence and Wishart, 1955).
52. Alec Nove, *An Economic History of the USSR* (Penguin, 1982), p. 157.

53. Burnett Bolloten, *The Spanish Civil War: Revolution and Counter-Revolution* (University of North Carolina Press, 1991), p. 111.
54. Richard Overy, *Russia's War* (Penguin, 1999), p. 19.
55. Jeffrey Zuehlke, *Joseph Stalin* (Twentieth Century Books, 2005), p. 78.
56. John Erickson, *The Soviet High Command: A Military-Political History, 1918–1941* (Routledge, 2001), p. 500–3.
57. David M. Glantz and Jonathan House, *When Titans Clashed* (Birlinn, 2000), p. 10.
58. Hew Strachan, *European Armies and the Conduct of War* (Routledge, 1988), p. 159.
59. Carr, *Twilight of the Comintern*, p. 7.
60. M.K. Dziewanowski, *Russia in the Twentieth Century* (Prentice Hall, 2003), p. 138.
61. Carr, *Twilight of the Comintern*, p. 29.
62. Ibid., p. 52.
63. Ibid., p. 86.
64. Otto Preston Chaney, *Zhukov* (University of Oklahoma Press, 1996), pp. 62–76.
65. Thomas Guinsburg, 'The Triumph of Isolationism', in Gordon Martel (ed.), *American Foreign Relations Reconsidered 1890–1993* (Routledge, 1994), pp. 90–104.
66. William Widenor, *Henry Cabot Lodge and the Search for an American Foreign Policy* (University of California Press, 1980), p. 318.
67. Henry F. Pringle, *Theodore Roosevelt: A Biography* (Harcourt, Brace and Co, 1931), pp. 408–9.
68. House Report, no. 1385, 60th Congress, 1st session (4 April 1908), pp. 2–3.
69. Jerry Israel, *Progressivism and the Open Door: American and China 1905–1921* (University of Pittsburgh Press, 1971), pp. 4–15.
70. David Harvey, *The New Imperialism* (Oxford University Press, 2003), p. 50.
71. Richard Overy, *Why the Allies Won* (Pimlico, 1996), p. 260.
72. Hehn, *A Low Dishonest Decade*, p. 26.
73. Tooze, *The Wages of Destruction*, p. 149.
74. Hehn, *A Low Dishonest Decade*, p. 166.
75. Emily Goldman, *Power in Uncertain Times: Strategy in the Fog of Peace* (Stanford University Press, 2010), pp. 106–7.
76. Kolko, *The Politics of War*, p. 381.
77. Michael S. Bell, 'The Worldview of Franklin D. Roosevelt: France, Germany and United States Involvement in World War Two in Europe', dissertation submitted to the Faculty of the Graduate School of the University of Maryland, College Park, 2004, p. 312, available at https://drum.umd.edu/dspace/bitstream/1903/1393/1/umi-umd-1397.pdf?lpos=fromtheweb
78. Harold L. Ickes, *The Secret Diary of Harold L. Ickes, Vol 2: The Inside Struggle, 1936–1939* (Simon and Schuster, 1954), p. 469.
79. Hehn, *A Low Dishonest Decade*, p. 168.
80. Bradley F. Smith, *The Shadow Warriors* (Andre Deutsch, 1983), p. 24.
81. Henry L. Stimson and McGeorge Bundy, *On Active Service in Peace and War* (Harper & Brothers, 1947), pp. 318–19.
82. Ponting, *1940*, p. 198.
83. John Keegan, *Six Armies in Normandy* (Penguin, 1983), p. 32.
84. Smith, *The Shadow Warriors*, p. 25.

Chapter 3

1. Leon Trotsky, *Struggle Against Fascism in Germany* (Pathfinder, 1971), p. 283.
2. Hermann Levy, *Industrial Germany: A Study of its Monopoly Organisations and Their Control by the State* (Routledge, 1966), pp. 54–63.

3. Tooze, *The Wages of Destruction*, pp. 19–23.
4. Ibid., pp. 19–23.
5. Hehn, *A Low Dishonest Decade*, p. 31.
6. Peter Hayes, *Industry and Ideology: IG Farben in the Nazi Era* (Cambridge University Press, 2001), pp. 12–19.
7. Dick Geary, 'The Industrial Bourgeoisie and Labour Relations', in David Blackbourn and Richard J. Evans (eds), *The German Bourgeoisie: Essays on the Social History of the German Middle Class from the Late Eighteenth to the Early Twentieth Century* (Routledge, 1993), p. 157.
8. Ibid., pp. 158–9.
9. Martin Collier and Philip Pedley, *Hitler and the Nazi State* (Heinemann, 2005), p. 167.
10. Fabrice d'Almeida, *High Society in the Third Reich* (Polity, 2008), pp. 44–5.
11. Hayes, *Industry and Ideology*, pp. 12–19.
12. Tooze, *The Wages of Destruction*, p. 86.
13. Overy, *Russia's War*, p. 35.
14. Tooze, *Wages of Destruction*, p. 213.
15. Ian Kershaw, *The Nazi Dictatorship* (Edward Arnold, 1989), p. 56.
16. Ibid., pp. 121–2.
17. Tooze, *Wages of Destruction*, p. 198.
18. Detlev J.K. Peukert, *Inside Nazi Germany: Conformity, Opposition and Racism in Everyday Life* (Penguin, 1993), pp. 43–4.
19. Jackson, *France: The Dark Years*, p. 170.
20. MacGregor Knox, *To the Threshold of Power, 1922/33: Origins and Dynamics of the Fascist and National Socialist Dictatorships*, Vol. I (Cambridge University Press, 2007), p. 288.
21. Jurgen Forster, 'Motivation and Indoctrination in the Wehrmacht, 1933–37', in Paul Addison and Angus Calder (eds), *Time to Kill* (Pimlico, 1997), p. 265.
22. Ian Kershaw '"Working Towards the Fuhrer": Reflections on the Nature of the Hitler Dictatorship', *Contemporary European History* 2:2 (July 1992).
23. Klaus-Jurgen Muller, 'The Structure and Nature of the National Conservative Opposition in Germany up to 1940', in H. Koch (ed), *Aspects of the Third Reich* (Macmillan, 1985), pp. 175–7.
24. Knox, *To the Threshold of Power*, p. 199.
25. Tim Mason, *Social Policy in the Third Reich* (Berg, 1993), p. 29.
26. T.W. Mason, 'The Workers' Opposition in Nazi Germany', *History Workshop Journal* 11 (Spring 1981), p. 120.
27. Hehn, *A Low Dishonest Decade*, p. 32.
28. Ibid., pp. 32–3.
29. Lecture by Major-General Thomas, delivered 24 May 1939, at the German Foreign Office, available at http://www.yale.edu/lawweb/avalon/imt/document/nca_vol1/chap_08.htm
30. Hehn, *A Low Dishonest Decade*, p. 107.
31. Mason, *Social Policy in the Third Reich*, p. 206.
32. Ibid., p. 263.
33. Peukert, *Inside Nazi Germany*, p. 61.
34. Ibid., p. 63.
35. Mason, *Social Policy in the Third Reich*, p. 274.
36. P.M.H. Bell, *The Origins of the Second World War in Europe* (Longman, 1986), p. 151.

37. Mason, *Social Policy in the Third Reich*, p. 328.
38. The best accounts of Mussolini's path to power remain A. Rossi [Angelo Tasca], *The Rise of Italian Fascism 1918–1922* (Methuen, 1938), Adrian Lyttelton, *The Seizure of Power: Fascism in Italy 1919–1929* (Charles Scribner's Sons, 1973), and Knox, *To the Threshold of Power, 1922/33*. More local accounts include Frank M. Snowden's *The Fascist Revolution in Tuscany 1919–1922* (Cambridge University Press, 1989) and *Violence and the Great Estates in the South of Italy: Apulia 1900–1922* (Cambridge University Press, 2004), and Paul Corner, *Fascism in Ferrara 1915–1925* (Oxford University Press, 1975).
39. R.J.B. Bosworth, *Mussolini's Italy* (Allen Lane, 2005), pp. 380–3.
40. MacGregor Knox, *Hitler's Italian Allies* (Cambridge University Press, 2001), p. 40.
41. MacGregor Knox, *Common Destiny* (Cambridge University Press, 2000), pp. 120–1.
42. Ibid., p. 140.
43. John Gooch, *Mussolini and His Generals* (Cambridge University Press, 2007), p. 293.
44. Davide Rodogno, *Fascism's European Empire* (Cambridge University Press, 2006), p. 333.
45. For an assessment of the Italian high command's performance in Ethiopia see Gooch, *Mussolini and His Generals*, pp. 252–314.
46. Alvin Finkel and Clement Leibovitz, *The Chamberlain-Hitler Collusion* (Merlin Press, 1997), p. 61.
47. Michelle Sarfati, 'Characteristics of the Anti-Jewish Racial Laws in Fascist Italy 1938–1943', in Joshua D. Zimmerman (ed.), *Jews in Italy Under Fascist and Nazi Rule 1922–1945* (Cambridge University Press, 2005), pp. 19–34.
48. Rodogno, *Fascism's European Empire*, pp. 290–8.
49. Knox, *Hitler's Italian Allies*, p. 30.
50. See Colin Barker, *Origins and Significance of the Meiji Restoration* (1982), available at http://www.marxists.de/fareast/barker/index.htm, and Jamie C. Allinson and Alexander Anievas, 'The Uneven and Combined Development of the Meiji Restoration: A Passive Revolutionary Road to Modernity', *Capital and Class* 34:3 (October 2010), pp. 469–90.
51. Perry Anderson, *Lineages of the Absolutist State* (Verso, 1979), pp. 458–61, and Allinson and Anievas, 'The Uneven and Combined Development of the Meiji Restoration', pp. 475–9.
52. Allinson and Anievas, 'The Uneven and Combined Development of the Meiji Restoration', p. 483.
53. E. Herbert Norman, *Japan's Emergence as a Modern State: Political and Economic Problems of the Meiji Period* (UCB Press, 2000), pp. 46–7.
54. Allinson and Anievas, 'The Uneven and Combined Development of the Meiji Restoration', p. 481.
55. Eric Hobsbawm, *The Age of Empire 1875–1914* (Weidenfeld and Nicolson, 1987), pp. 281–3.
56. Michael Smitka, *Introduction to Japanese Economic History 1600–1960: Japanese Economic Ascent* (New York: Garland Publishing, 1998), pp. xvii–xviii.
57. Wolf Mendel, *Japan's Asia Policy: Regional Security and Global Interests* (London: 1995), p. 62.
58. Richard Bowring and Peter Kornicki (eds), *The Cambridge Encyclopedia of Japan* (Cambridge University Press, 1993), p. 84.

59. Timothy D. Saxon, 'Anglo-Japanese Naval Cooperation, 1914–1918', *Naval War College Review* (Winter 2000), available at http://www.nwc.navy.mil/press/Review/2000/winter/art3-w00.htm
60. Hobsbawm, *Age of Extremes*, p. 92.
61. Kenneth Douglas Brown, *Britain and Japan: A Comparative Economic and Social History Since 1900* (Manchester University Press, 1998), p. 40.
62. Ibid., p. 72.
63. Ibid., pp. 76–7.
64. Shigeru Akita and Nicholas J. White, *The International Order of Asia in the 1930s and 1950s* (Ashgate, 2010), p. 119.
65. Brown, *Britain and Japan*, p. 77.
66. Akita and White, *The International Order of Asia*, p. 120.
67. Ibid., p. 113.
68. Brown, *Britain and Japan*, p. 76.
69. Jay Taylor, *The Generalissimo: Chiang Kai Shek and the Struggle for Modern China* (Harvard University Press, 2009), p. 59.
70. Ibid., p. 107.
71. Bradford A. Lee, *Britain and the Sino-Japanese War, 1937–1939: A Study in the Dilemmas of British Decline* (Stanford University Press, 1973), pp. 8 and 9.
72. Eiko Maruko Siniawer, *Ruffians, Yakuza, Nationalists: The Violent Politics of Modern Japan, 1860–1960* (Cornell University Press, 2008), p. 135, and Sheldon N. Harris, 'Japanese Biomedical Experimentation During the World War ll Era', *Military Medical Ethics* 2 (2003), pp. 473–4.
73. Hobsbawm, *Age of Extremes*, p. 79.
74. Hu Chi-his, 'Mao, Lin Biao, and the Fifth Encirclement Campaign', *China Quarterly* 82 (June 1980), pp. 257–60.
75. Taylor, *The Generalissimo*, pp. 94–5.
76. James R. Brandon, *Kabuki's Forgotten War: 1931–1945* (University of Hawaii Press, 2009), pp. 69–73.
77. Iris Chang, *The Rape of Nanking* (Penguin, 1998), p. 6.
78. Taylor, *The Generalissimo*, p. 99.
79. Chalmers A. Johnson, *Peasant Nationalism and Communist Power* (Stanford University Press, 1962), p. 109.
80. Ibid., p. 85.
81. Kolko, *The Politics of War*, p. xii.
82. Tetsuya Kataoka, *Resistance and Revolution in China: The Communists and the Second United Front* (University of California Press, 1974), p. 145.
83. Ibid., p. 230.

Chapter 4
1. Pugh, *Hurrah for the Blackshirts*, p. 263.
2. Finkel and Leibovitz, *The Chamberlain-Hitler Collusion*, pp. 43–4.
3. Horne, *To Lose a Battle*, p. 71.
4. Ibid., p. 75.
5. Alan Bullock, *Hitler: A Study in Tyranny* (Odhams, 1952), p. 135.
6. Ian Kershaw, *Making Friends with Hitler* (Allen Lane, 2004), p. 178.
7. Antony Beevor, *The Battle for Spain* (Weidenfeld and Nicolson, 2006), p. 135.
8. Ibid., pp. 132 and 241.
9. Jackson, *France: The Dark Years*, p. 107.
10. Hugh Thomas, *The Spanish Civil War* (Penguin, 1988), p. 394.

11. Ibid., p. 943.
12. Beevor, *The Battle for Spain*, p. 138.
13. Thomas, *The Spanish Civil War*, p. 463.
14. Paul Preston, 'Italy and Spain in Civil War and World War 1936–1943', in Sebastian Balfour and Paul Preston (eds), *Spain and the Great Powers in the Twentieth Century* (Routledge, 1999), pp. 169–71.
15. Willard C. Frank, 'The Spanish Civil War and the Coming of the Second World War', *International History Review* 9:3 (August 1987), pp. 368–409.
16. Thomas, *The Spanish Civil War*, p. 941.
17. Beevor, *The Battle for Spain*, p. 290.
18. Martin S. Alexander, 'Soldiers and Socialists: The French Officer Corps and Leftist Government, 1935–1937', in Martin S. Alexander and Helen Graham (eds), *The French and Spanish Popular Fronts* (Cambridge University Press, 1989), p. 72.
19. Nicole Jordan, *The Popular Front and Central Europe* (Cambridge University Press, 1992), p. 309.
20. Finkel and Leibovitz, *The Chamberlain-Hitler Collusion*, p. 107.
21. Clement Leibovitz, *The Chamberlain-Hitler Deal* (Les Editions Duval, 1993), p. 283.
22. Andrew Roberts, *The Holy Fox: A Life of Lord Halifax* (Papermac, 1991), p. 66.
23. Ibid., p. 67.
24. Ibid., p. 68.
25. Finkel and Leibovitz, *The Chamberlain-Hitler Collusion*, p. 115.
26. Ibid., p. 115.
27. Roberts, *The Holy Fox*, p. 75.
28. David Faber, *Munich: The 1938 Appeasement Crisis* (Pocket Books, 2009), p. 83.
29. Roberts, *The Holy Fox*, p. 103.
30. Ibid., p. 91.
31. Jordan, *The Popular Front and Central Europe*, p. 316.
32. Hehn, *A Low Dishonest Decade*, p. 124.
33. Ibid., p. 125.
34. Mark Mazower, *Hitler's Empire* (Allen Lane, 2008), p. 50.
35. Dieter Wagner and Gerhard Tomkowitz, *Anschluss: The Week Hitler Seized Vienna* (St Martins Press, 1971), p. 236.
36. Eduard Kubů, Jiří Novotný and Jiří Souša, 'Under the Threat of Nazi Occupation', in Christopher Kobrak and Per H. Hansen (eds), *European Business, Dictatorship, and Political Risk, 1920–1945* (Berghahn Books, 2004), p. 210.
37. Oscar Pinkus, *The War Aims and Strategies of Adolf Hitler* (McFarland, 2005), pp. 30–2.
38. John Toland, *Hitler* (Wordsworth Editions, 1997), p. 469.
39. Jordan, *The Popular Front and Central Europe*, p. 280.
40. Jones, *Michael Foot*, p. 65. Lady Astor was one of the key figures in the pro-Nazi Cliveden Set who socialised with the German ambassador.
41. Stewart, *Burying Caesar*, p. 298.
42. Ibid., p. 299.
43. Noreen Branson, *History of the Communist Party of Great Britain 1927–1941* (Lawrence and Wishart, 1985), p. 256.
44. Stewart, *Burying Caesar*, p. 300.
45. Roberts, *The Holy Fox*, p. 110.
46. Ibid., p. 111.
47. Stewart, *Burying Caesar*, p. 302.
48. Finkel and Leibovitz, *The Chamberlain-Hitler Collusion*, p. 151.

49. Stewart, *Burying Caesar*, p. 303.
50. Finkel and Leibovitz, *The Chamberlain-Hitler Collusion*, p. 170.
51. *The Times*, 1 October 1938.
52. Ponting, *1940*, p. 38.
53. Hehn, *A Low Dishonest Decade*, p. 307.
54. Ingeborg Fleischhauer, 'Origins of the Hitler-Stalin Pact', in Bernd Wegner (ed.), *From Peace to War: Germany, Soviet Russia and the World 1939–1941* (Berghahn Books, 1997), pp. 31–3.
55. Finkel and Leibovitz, *The Chamberlain-Hitler Collusion*, p. 205.
56. Stewart, *Burying Caesar*, p. 353.
57. Ibid., p. 354.
58. Philip M. Taylor, *British Propaganda in the 20th Century: Selling Democracy* (Edinburgh University Press, 1999), p. 135.
59. Martin Gilbert, *Kristallnacht: Prelude to Destruction* (HarperCollins, 2007), p. 118.
60. Toland, *Hitler*, p. 505.
61. Finkel and Leibovitz, *The Chamberlain-Hitler Collusion*, p. 183.
62. Stewart, *Burying Caesar*, p. 358.
63. Hehn, *A Low Dishonest Decade*, p. 314.
64. Ibid., p. 313.
65. Ibid., p. 131.
66. Stewart, *Burying Caesar*, p. 370.
67. Ibid., p. 374.
68. Ibid., p. 387.
69. Hehn, *A Low Dishonest Decade*, p. 340.
70. Seppy Myllyniemi, 'Consequences of the Hitler-Stalin Pact for the Baltic Republics and Finland', in Wegner (ed.), *From Peace to War*, p. 79.
71. John Lukacs, *Five Days in London: May 1940* (Yale University Press, 1999), p. 55.
72. Ponting, *1940*, p. 39.
73. Obituary: Lord Aberconway, *Daily Telegraph*, 6 February 2003, available at http://www.telegraph.co.uk/news/obituaries/1421186/Lord-Aberconway.html
74. Jones, *Michael Foot*, p. 75.
75. Toland, *Hitler*, p. 531.
76. Roberts, *The Holy Fox*, p. 173.
77. Roberts, *Eminent Churchillians*, p. 37.
78. Anthony P. Adamthwaite, *The Making of the Second World War* (Routledge, 1989), p. 95.
79. Holland, *The Pursuit of Greatness*, p. 160.
80. Calder, *The People's War*, p. 70.
81. Horne, *To Lose a Battle*, p. 105.
82. Finkel and Leibovitz, *The Hitler-Chamberlain Collusion*, p. 44.
83. Julian Jackson, *The Fall of France: The Nazi Invasion of 1940* (Oxford University Press, 2004), p. 203.
84. Gaetano Salvemini and George La Piana, *What To Do With Italy?* (Duell, Sloan and Pearce, 1943), p. 75.
85. Roberts, *Holy Fox*, pp. 258–9.
86. A.D. Harvey, *Collision of Empires* (Phoenix, 1994), p. 512.
87. Finkel and Leibovitz, *The Chamberlain-Hitler Collusion*, pp. 256–60.
88. Jordan, *The Popular Front and Central Europe*, p. 294.
89. Patrick R. Osborn, *Operation Pike: Britain Versus the Soviet Union 1939–1941* (Greenwood Publishing Group, 2000), pp. 127–9.

90. Charmley, *Churchill*, pp. 467, 456.
91. Maurice Cowling, 'The Case Against Going to War', *Finest Hour* 70 (1991).
92. David Edgerton, *Britain's War Machine: Weapons, Resources, and Experts in the Second World War* (Oxford University Press, 2011), p. 66.

Chapter 5
1. Klaus Fischer, *Nazi Germany* (Constable, 1995), p. 439.
2. Mazower, *Hitler's Empire*, pp. 68–9.
3. Gooch, *Mussolini and His Generals*, pp. 496–7.
4. Nicholas Bethell, *The War Hitler Won, September 1939* (Allen Lane, 1972), p. 169.
5. Macgregor Knox, 'Conquest, Domestic and Foreign, in Fascist Italy and Nazi Germany', *Journal of Modern History* 56 (1984), pp. 46–57.
6. George Bruce, *The Warsaw Uprising* (Pan, 1974), p. 15.
7. Hehn, *A Low Dishonest Decade*, p. 98.
8. Ibid.
9. Tooze, *The Wages of Destruction*, p. 166.
10. Ibid.
11. Mazower, *Hitler's Empire*, p. 90.
12. Toland, *Hitler*, p. 584.
13. Mazower, *Hitler's Empire*, p. 95.
14. Cathy Porter and Mark Jones, *Moscow in World War Two* (Chatto and Windus, 1987), p. 30.
15. Ernest R. Mayer, *Strange Victory: Hitler's Conquest of France* (I.B. Tauris, 2000), pp. 279–81.
16. Ibid., pp. 281–2.
17. Jackson, *France: The Dark Years*, p. 4.
18. Ibid., p. 115.
19. Ibid., p. 114.
20. Horne, *To Lose a Battle*, p. 214.
21. David Brown, *Naval Operations of the Campaign in Norway, April–June 1940* (Routledge, 1951), pp. 19–26.
22. Elmer Belmont Potter and Henry Hitch Adams, *Sea Power: A Naval History* (Naval Institute Press, 1981), p. 246.
23. Roberts, *Eminent Churchillians*, p. 37.
24. Piers Brandon, *Winston Churchill: A Biography* (Harper and Row, 1984), p. 141.
25. Ponting, *1940*, p. 70.
26. Roberts, *The Holy Fox*, p. 202.
27. Stephen Dorril, *Blackshirt: Sir Oswald Mosley and British Fascism* (Penguin, 2007), p. 495.
28. Roberts, *The Holy Fox*, p. 164.
29. Calder, *The People's War*, p. 89.
30. Peter Tsouras, *Hitler Triumphant: Alternate Decisions of World War 2* (MBI Publishing Company, 2006), pp. 28–9.
31. Malcolm Smith, *Britain and 1940: History, Myth and Popular Memory* (Routledge, 2000), p. 37
32. Ian Ousby, *Occupation: The Ordeal of France 1940–1944* (Pimlico, 1999), p. 23.
33. Ibid., p. 36.
34. Beevor, *The Battle for Spain*, p. 386.
35. Horne, *To Lose a Battle*, pp. 538 and 561–70.
36. Ponting, *1940*, p. 89.

37. Ibid., p. 90.
38. Ibid.
39. Ibid.
40. Hugh Sebag-Montefiore, *Dunkirk: Fight to the Last Man* (Viking, 2006), p. 411.
41. Ponting, *1940*, p. 137.
42. Lukacs, *Five Days in London*, p. 17.
43. Calder, *The Myth of the Blitz*, p. 92.
44. Roberts, *Eminent Churchillians*, p. 164.
45. Charmley, *Churchill*, p. 396.
46. Lukacs, *Five Days in London*, p. 19.
47. Ponting, *1940*, pp. 145–6.
48. Lukacs, *Five Days in London*, p. 73.
49. MacGregor Knox, *Mussolini Unleashed 1939–1941* (Cambridge University Press, 1986), p. 112.
50. Lukacs, *Five Days in London*, pp. 92–109.
51. Roberts, *The Holy Fox*, p. 229.
52. Charmley, *Churchill*, p. 403.
53. Lukacs, *Five Days in London*, p. 109.
54. Philip Michael Hett Bell, *France and Britain 1900–1940* (Longman, 1996), p. 237.
55. Lukacs, *Five Days in London*, p. 113.
56. Ponting, *1940*, p. 107.
57. Stewart, *Burying Caesar*, p. 432.
58. Lukacs, *Five Days in London*, p. 181.
59. Ibid., p. 5.
60. Horne, *To Lose a Battle*, pp. 635–6.
61. Ousby, *Occupation*, pp. 39–40.
62. Jackson, *France: The Dark Years*, p. 126.
63. Smith, *The Shadow Warriors*, p. 10.
64. Jackson, *France: The Dark Years*, p. 133.
65. Julian Jackson, *The Popular Front in France* (Cambridge University Press, 1988), p. 288.
66. Mazower, *Hitler's Empire*, p. 417.
67. Paul Webster, *Pétain's Crimes* (Pan, 2001), p. 156.
68. Mazower, *Hitler's Empire*, pp. 108–9.
69. Jackson, *France: The Dark Years*, p. 192.
70. Webster, *Pétain's Crimes*, p. 112.
71. Ibid., p. 153.
72. Ousby, *Occupation*, pp. 187–8.
73. David Fraser, *The Jews of the Channel Islands and the Rule of Law, 1940–1945* (Sussex Academic Press, 2000), pp. 17–18.
74. Ponting, *1940*, p. 92.
75. Ibid., p. 92.
76. Peter Grafton, *You, You and You: The People Out of Step with World War Two* (Pluto Press, 1981), p. 15.
77. Jean-François Bergier, *Switzerland, National Socialism and the Second World War* (Berghahn Books, 2002), p. 182, and Alan S. Milward, *War, Economy and Society 1939–1945* (University of California Press, 1980), p. 87.
78. Roberts, *The Holy Fox*, p. 232.
79. Ibid., p. 232.
80. Ponting, *1940*, pp. 112–14.

81. Ibid., p. 116.
82. Ibid., p. 117.
83. Both quoted in Jones, *Michael Foot*, p. 83. Foot helped write the *Evening Standard*'s editorials.
84. Norma Denny, 'British Society During World War II: An Interview with Michael Foot', available at http://www.docstoc.com/docs/5952283/what-happened-in-world-war-2
85. Ibid.
86. 'The three authors (still concealing their identity) sold the book from barrows in Farringdon Road and recruited friends to take turns' (Jones, *Michael Foot*, p. 91). The manager of the Independent Labour Party bookshop in London was visited by the police who told him he was selling a banned book. WH Smith banned the book from its shops in the interests of 'national unity'.
87. Calder, *The People's War*, p. 100.
88. Ibid., p. 158.
89. Christopher Hill, *Cabinet Decisions on Foreign Policy: The British Experience, October 1938–June 1941* (Cambridge University Press, 2002), pp. 212–13.
90. Ponting, *1940*, p. 148.
91. Ibid.
92. Calder, *The People's War*, p. 160.
93. Jeff Hill, 'A War Imagined', in Nick Hayes and Jeff Hill (eds), *'Millions like us'?: British culture in the Second World War* (Liverpool University Press, 1999), pp. 331–2.
94. Calder, *The People's War*, p. 158.
95. Ibid., p. 160. Priestley was stopped from broadcasting at Churchill's instigation.
96. George Orwell, *A Patriot After All 1940–1941* (Secker and Warburg, 1998), p. 188.
97. Mark Donnelly, *Britain in the Second World War* (Routledge, 1999), pp. 92–3.
98. Ponting, *Churchill*, p. 461.
99. Bryan Clough, *State Secrets: The Kent-Wolkoff Affair* (Hideaway Publications, 2005), pp. 139–40.
100. Ponting, *Churchill*, p. 461.
101. Ibid., p. 460.
102. Ian Kershaw, *Hitler 1936–1945: Nemesis* (Allen Lane, 2000), p. 309.
103. Calder, *The Myth of the Blitz*, pp. 103–4.
104. Harvey, *Collision of Empires*, p. 661.
105. Ponting, *1940*, pp. 162–3.
106. Harvey, *Collision of Empires*, p. 666.
107. Ibid.
108. Calder, *The People's War*, p. 215.
109. Roberts, *Eminent Churchillians*, p. 148.
110. William Rust, *The Story of the Daily Worker* (People's Press Print Society, 1949), p. 67.
111. Holland, *The Pursuit of Greatness*, p. 170.
112. Ponting, *Churchill*, p. 291.
113. Ibid., pp. 494–5.
114. Knox, *Mussolini Unleashed*, p. 183.
115. Ibid., p. 241.
116. Gerhard Schreiber, Bernd Stegemann and Detlef Vogel, *The Mediterranean, South-east Europe, and North Africa, 1939–1941* (Oxford University Press, 1995), pp. 643–5.

117. Randolph Spencer Churchill and Martin Gilbert, *Winston S. Churchill, Volume 3* (Heinemann, 1971), p. 301.
118. John Latimer and John Laurier, *Operation Compass 1940: Wavell's Whirlwind Offensive* (Osprey Publishing, 2000), p. 21.
119. Stephen L.W. Kavanaugh, *Hitler's Malta Option* (Nimble Books, 2010), p. 7.
120. Ciro Paoletti, *A Military History of Italy* (Greenwood Publishing, 2008), p. 176, and Harvey, *Collision of Empires*, pp. 604–9.
121. Rodogno, *Fascism's European Empire*, p. 28.
122. Paul Coller and Robert O'Neill, *World War II: The Mediterranean 1940–1945* (Rosen Publishing Group, 2010), pp. 28–9.
123. Rodogno, *Fascism's European Empire*, p. 31.
124. Schreiber, Stegemann and Vogel, *The Mediterranean*, pp. 499–526.
125. Evelyn Waugh, *Officers and Gentlemen*, in *Sword Of Honour Trilogy* (Penguin Modern Classics, 2001). Whatever Waugh's politics I heartily recommend this trilogy.
126. Bosworth, *Mussolini's Italy*, p. 470.
127. H. James Burgwyn, *Empire on the Adriatic: Mussolini's Conquest of Yugoslavia 1941–1943* (Enigma Books, 2005), p. 51.
128. Rodogno, *Fascism's European Empire*, p. 333.
129. Christer Jörgensen, *Rommel's Panzers: Rommel and the Panzer Forces of the Blitzkreig 1940–1942* (Zenith, 2003), pp. 74–5.
130. Ashley Jackson, *The British Empire and the Second World War* (Continuum, 2006), pp. 146–54.
131. Ibid., pp. 156–60.
132. Holland, *The Pursuit of Greatness*, p. 631.
133. Harvey, *Collision of Empires*, p. 631. This was true after El Alamein when Rommel's Afrika Korps succeeded in withdrawing and in the failure to capture Caen after the initial D Day landings. The exception was the September 1944 attack on Arnhem when Montgomery tried to capture the Rhine Bridge by dropping paratroops on an SS Panzer division and sending an armoured column 75 miles across a single road through the flat, Dutch countryside.
134. Ponting, *1940*, p. 221.
135. John Keegan, *Intelligence in War* (Random House, 2010), pp. 193–5, and Harvey, *Collision of Empires*, pp. 593–4.
136. Harvey, *Collision of Empires*, p. 557, and William Hardy McNeill, *America, Britain and Russia: Their Cooperation and Conflict 1941–1946* (Johnson Reprint Corp, 1970), p. 231.
137. See http://news.bbc.co.uk/onthisday/hi/dates/stories/december/1/newsid_4696 000/4696207.stm
138. Calder, *The People's War*, pp. 607–9.
139. Tooze, *The Wages of Destruction*, p. 407. By 1943 the US produced 48,000 aircraft in that year.
140. Ponting, *1940*, p. 205.
141. David Reynolds, *Lord Lothian and Anglo-American Relations 1939–1940* (American Philosophical Society, 2007), pp. 18–34.
142. Britton Hadden and Henry Robinson Luce (eds), *Time*, Volume 36, Issues 15–27, p. 289, *Time*, 16 December 1940.
143. Ponting, *1940*, p. 209.
144. Alan P. Dobson, *US Wartime Aid to Britain 1940–1946* (Taylor and Francis, 1986), pp. 26–7.

145. Ponting, *1940*, pp. 210–13.
146. Samuel Eliot Morison, 'Thoughts on Naval Strategy, World War II', *Naval War College Review* (March 1968), available at http://www.nwc.navy.mil/press/Review/1998/winter/art6-w98.htm
147. Bell, 'The Worldview of Franklin D. Roosevelt', p. 332.
148. Superintendent of Documents, US Government Printing Office, US Army in World War ll: European Theatre of Operations, Cross Channel Attack, 1951, p. 96.
149. Edgerton, *Britain's War Machine*, pp. 159–60.
150. Andrew Williams, *The Battle of the Atlantic* (Random House, 2010), pp. 44–5, and Terry Hughes and John Costello, *The Battle of the Atlantic* (Dial Press, 1977), p. 170.
151. Williams, *The Battle of the Atlantic*, p. 55.
152. Harvey, *Collision of Empires*, pp. 623–4.
153. Meir Finkel and Moshe Tlamim, *On Flexibility: Recovery from Technological and Doctrinal Surprise on the Battlefield* (Stanford University Press, 2011), pp. 184–5.
154. Jack Greene and Alessandro Massignani, *Rommel's North Africa Campaign, September 1940–November 1942* (De Capo Press, 1999), p. 193.
155. Edgerton, *Britain's War Machine*, pp. 222–3.
156. G. Ward Price, *Giraud and the African Scene* (Macmillan, 1944), p. 260.
157. Anthony Verrier, *Assassination in Algiers: Churchill, Roosevelt, de Gaulle and the Murder of Admiral Darlan* (Macmillan, 1991), pp. 141–92.
158. Kolko, *The Politics of War*, pp. 64–71.
159. *Der Spiegel*, 23 May 2007.
160. Samuel W. Mitcham, *Rommel's Desert Commanders* (Greenwood Publishing Group, 2007), p. 170.
161. Harvey, *Collision of Empires*, pp. 619–21.
162. Max Hastings, *Overlord: D Day and The Battle For Normandy 1944* (Pan, 1984), p. 23.
163. David Murray Horner, Russell Hart and Stephen Hart, *The Second World War: North West Europe 1944–45* (Osprey Publishing, 2002), p. 41.

Chapter 6

1. Jane Degras (ed.), *Soviet Documents on Foreign Policy*, Volume 3 (Oxford University Press, 1953), p. 305, cited by Robin Blick, 'Review of Geoffrey Roberts, *Unholy Alliance: Stalin's Pact With Hitler*', *Revolutionary History* 3:4 (Autumn 1991), available at http://www.marxists.org/history/etol/revhist/backiss/vol3/no4/revrob.html#n7
2. Helen Rappaport, *Joseph Stalin: A Biographical Companion* (ABC-CLIO, 1999), p. 99, and Blick, 'Review of Geoffrey Roberts, *Unholy Alliance*'.
3. Isaac Deutscher, *Stalin* (Penguin, 1966), p. 435.
4. Schreiber, Stegemann and Vogel, *The Mediterranean*, pp. 451–2.
5. Tooze, *The Wages of Destruction*, p. 321.
6. Kershaw, *Hitler 1936–1945*, p. 343.
7. Overy, *Why the Allies Won*, p. 62.
8. Glantz and House, *When Titans Clashed*, p. 23.
9. John Erickson, *The Road to Stalingrad* (Panther, 1985), p. 72.
10. Robin D.S. Higham, Frederick W. Kagan, *The Military History of the Soviet Union* (Palgrave, 2002), p. 76.

11. Eugene Davidson, *The Unmaking of Adolf Hitler* (University of Missouri Press, 2004), pp. 423–9.
12. Toland, *Hitler*, p. 645.
13. Ibid., p. 644.
14. Brian Moynahan, *The Claws of the Bear* (Hutchinson, 1989), p. 79.
15. Clark, *Barbarossa*, pp. 62, 76.
16. Otto Preston Chaney, *Zhukov* (University of Oklahoma Press, 1996), p. 85.
17. Erickson gives detail after detail of reports reaching Stalin confirming German plans, including reports from the well-placed Rote Kapelle group which penetrated the German command. See Erickson, *The Road to Stalingrad*, p. 115.
18. Overy, *Russia's War*, p. 53.
19. Robert Whymant, *Stalin's Spy: Richard Sorge and the Tokyo Espionage Ring* (I.B. Tauris, 2007), p. 184.
20. Fischer, *Nazi Germany*, p. 494.
21. Mazower, *Hitler's Empire*, p. 147.
22. Erickson, *The Road to Stalingrad*, p. 72.
23. Porter and Jones, *Moscow in World War Two*, p. 48.
24. Erickson, *The Road to Stalingrad*, p. 53.
25. David M. Glantz, *Barbarossa Derailed: The Battle for Smolensk 10 July–10 September 1941* (Casemate Publishers, 2010), p. 577, and Stanley G. Payne, *Franco and Hitler: Spain, Germany and World War II* (Yale University Press, 2008), p. 152.
26. Erickson, *The Road to Stalingrad*, pp. 168–9, and Glantz, *Barbarossa Derailed*, pp. 28–9.
27. Glantz and House, *When Titans Clashed*, pp. 49–51.
28. John Erickson, *The Road to Berlin* (Panther, 1985), p. 53.
29. Clark, *Barbarossa*, p. 187.
30. Fischer, *Nazi Germany*, p. 469.
31. Clark, *Barbarossa*, p. 225.
32. Mazower, *Hitler's Empire*, p. 164.
33. Rodric Braithwaite, *Moscow 1941* (Profile Books, 2007), pp. 92–3.
34. Fischer, *Nazi Germany*, p. 471.
35. David M. Glantz, *The Siege of Leningrad, 1941–1944: 900 Days of Terror* (Zenith, 2001), p. 41.
36. Glantz and House, *When Titans Clashed*, p. 72.
37. Harvey, *Collision of Empires*, p. 567.
38. Braithwaite, *Moscow 1941*, pp. 285–6.
39. John Erickson, 'Red Army Battlefield Performance, 1941–45: The System and the Soldier', in Addison and Calder (eds), *Time to Kill*, p. 243.
40. Konstantin Pleshakov, *Stalin's Folly: The Tragic First Ten Days of World War II on the Eastern Front* (Houghton Mifflin Harcourt, 2005), p. 178.
41. Braithwaite, *Moscow 1941*, p. 258.
42. Chaney, *Zukhov*, pp. 158–71.
43. Erickson, *The Road to Stalingrad*, pp. 375–6.
44. Geoffrey Roberts, *Stalin's Wars: From World War to Cold War, 1939–1953* (Yale University Press, 2006), p. 159.
45. Toland, *Hitler*, p. 770.
46. Overy, *Russia's War*, p. 19.
47. Erickson, *The Road to Stalingrad*, p. 325.
48. Glantz and House, *When Titans Clashed*, p. 105.
49. Roberts, *Stalin's Wars*, p. 114.

50. Erickson, *The Road to Stalingrad*, pp. 331–42 and 517.
51. Ibid., p. 513.
52. Kershaw, *Hitler 1936–1945*, p. 448.
53. Clark, *Barbarossa*, p. 221.
54. Peter Antill and Peter Dennis, *Stalingrad 1942* (Osprey Publishing, 2007), p. 31.
55. Kershaw, *Hitler 1936–1945*, p. 514.
56. Erickson, *The Road to Stalingrad*, p. 517.
57. Stephen Walsh, *Stalingrad 1942–1943: The Infernal Cauldron* (Simon & Schuster, 2000), p. 55.
58. Erickson, *The Road to Stalingrad*, p. 575.
59. Chaney, *Zukhov*, pp. 215–16.
60. Erickson, *The Road to Stalingrad*, p. 616.
61. Clark, *Barbarossa*, p. 282.
62. Kershaw, *Hitler: 1936–1945*, p. 565.
63. Fischer, *Nazi Germany*, p. 475.
64. Glantz and House, *When Titans Clashed*, p. 154.
65. Tooze, *The Wages of Destruction*, p. 588.
66. Glantz and House, *When Titans Clashed*, p. 155.
67. Overy, *Russia's War*, p. 160.
68. Erickson, *The Road to Berlin*, p. 87.
69. Ibid., p. 114.
70. Glantz and House, *When Titans Clashed*, p. 163.
71. George C. Herring, *Aid To Russia 1941–1946* (Columbia University Press, 1973), p. 116.
72. Niklas Zetterling and Anders Frankson, *Kursk 1943: A Statistical Analysis* (Routledge, 2000), p. 112.
73. Omar Bartov, *The Eastern Front 1941–45* (Palgrave, 2001), pp. 12–13.
74. Ibid., p. 15.
75. Overy, *Russia's War*, p. 98.
76. Kershaw, *The Nazi Dictatorship*, p. 101.
77. Peukert, *Inside Nazi Germany*, p. 220.
78. Bartov, *The Eastern Front 1941–45*, pp. 94, 153.
79. Kershaw, *Hitler 1936–1945*, p. 358.
80. Annemarie Sammartino, *The Impossible Border: Germany and the East, 1914–1922* (Cornell University Press, 2010), p. 57.
81. Christopher R. Browning, *The Origins of the Final Solution* (University of Nebraska Press, 2007), p. 113.
82. Kershaw, *The Nazi Dictatorship*, p. 97.
83. Kershaw, *Hitler 1936–1945*, p. 462.
84. Tooze, *The Wages of Destruction*, p. 469.
85. Fischer, *Nazi Germany*, p. 503.
86. Clark, *Barbarossa*, p. 182.
87. Bartov, *The Eastern Front 1941–45*, p. 27.
88. Peukert, *Inside Nazi Germany*, p. 129.
89. Toland, *Hitler*, p. 701.
90. Kershaw, *Hitler 1936–1945*, p. 382.
91. Geoffrey P. Megargee, *War of Annihilation: Combat And Genocide on the Eastern Front, 1941* (Rowman and Littlefield, 2007), pp. 94–6.
92. Kershaw, *The Nazi Dictatorship*, pp. 101–2.
93. 'Hitler's Army Shares SS Guilt', *Guardian*, 6 April 1995.

94. Jean Ancel, 'The Opposition to the Antonescu Regime: Its Attitude to the Jews During the Holocaust', in David Bankier and Israel Gutman (eds), *Nazi Europe and the Final Solution* (Berghahn Books, 2009), pp. 345–57.
95. Peter Longerich, *Holocaust: The Nazi Persecution and Murder of the Jews* (Oxford University Press, 2010), p. 215.
96. Fischer, *Nazi Germany*, p. 504.
97. Percy Ernst Schramm, *Hitler: The Man and Military Leader* (Quadrangle Books, 1971), p. 204.
98. Laurence Rees, *Auschwitz: The Nazis and the Final Solution* (BBC Books, 2005), p. 79.
99. Peukert, *Inside Nazi Germany*, p. 220.
100. Patricia Heberer, 'The Nazi Euthanasia Programme', in Jonathan C. Friedman (ed.), *The Routledge History of the Holocaust* (Routledge, 2010), pp. 137–47.
101. Peukert, *Inside Nazi Germany*, p. 212.
102. Toland, *Hitler*, p. 704.
103. Christopher R. Browning, *The Origins of the Final Solution* (University of Nebraska Press, 2004), p. 407.
104. Toland, *Hitler*, p. 704.
105. Fischer, *Nazi Germany*, p. 505.
106. Browning, *The Origins of the Final Solution*, pp. 356–7.
107. Toland, *Hitler*, p. 713.
108. Jeremy Noakes and Geoffrey Pridham, *Nazism: A Documentary Reader*, vol. 3 (University of Exeter Press, 2001), p. 570.
109. Mazower, *Hitler's Empire*, p. 414.
110. Bartov, *The Eastern Front 1941–45*, p. 98.
111. Mason, *Nazism, Fascism and the Working Class*, p. 73.
112. R.J.B. Bosworth, *Mussolini* (Arnold, 2002), pp. 393–4.
113. Ibid.
114. Rodogno, *Fascism's European Empire*, pp. 382–4.
115. Ridley, *Mussolini: A Biography*, p. 334.
116. Mark Mazower, *Inside Hitler's Greece* (Yale University Press, 1993), pp. 243–4.
117. Toland, *Hitler*, p. 735.
118. Ibid., p. 767.
119. Tooze, *The Wages of Destruction*, p. 609.

Chapter 7
1. Overy, *Why the Allies Won*, pp. 190–8.
2. Seymour Edwin Harris, *Inflation and the American Economy* (McGraw Hill, 1945), p. 84.
3. Ed Shaffer, *The United States and the Control of World Oil* (Taylor and Francis, 1983), p. 75.
4. Overy, *Why the Allies Won*, p. 192.
5. The Marshall Cavendish Corporation, *History of World War Two* (Marshall Cavendish, 2004), pp. 588–97.
6. Hugh Rockoff, *Drastic Measures: A History of Wage and Price Controls in the United States* (Cambridge University Press, 2004), pp. 85–126.
7. Overy, *Why the Allies Won*, pp. 233–4.
8. Ibid., pp. 196–7.
9. Ian Birchall, *Bailing Out the System* (Bookmarks, 1986), p. 3.
10. Ponting, *1940*, p. 77.

11. Calder, *The People's War*, p. 456.
12. Harvey, *Collision of Empires*, pp. 537–41.
13. Mason, *Social Policy in the Third Reich*, p. 252.
14. Harvey, *Collision of Empires*, pp. 541–9.
15. Mason, *Social Policy in the Third Reich*, pp. 261–2.
16. George Fink, *Stress of War, Conflict and Disaster* (Academic Press, 2010), p. 277.
17. Peukert, *Inside Nazi Germany*, p. 70.
18. Tooze, *The Wages of Destruction*, p. 363.
19. Peukert, *Inside Nazi Germany*, p. 127.
20. Tooze, *The Wages of Destruction*, p. 623.
21. Mazower, *Hitler's Empire*, p. 261.
22. Omar Bartov, *Hitler's Army* (Oxford University Press, 1992), p. 16.
23. Overy, *Why the Allies Won*, p. 2.
24. Tooze, *The Wages of Destruction*, p. 571.
25. Ibid., p. 636.
26. Anton Kaes, *From Hitler to Heimat: The Return of History As Film* (Harvard University Press, 1992), pp. 3–4.
27. Werner Warmbrunn, *The German Occupation of Belgium 1940–1944* (Peter Lang, 1993), pp. 201–9.
28. Gabriel Kolko, *Century of War* (The New Press, 1994), p. 190.
29. Mason, *Social Policy in the Third Reich*, p. 32.
30. David Welch, *The Third Reich: Politics and Propaganda* (Routledge, 2002), pp. 131–2.
31. Walter Scott Dunn, *The Soviet Economy and the Red Army 1930–1945* (Greenwood Publishing Group, 1995), p. 7.
32. Mary Evans and David Morgan, *The Battle for Britain: Citizenship and Ideology in the Second World War* (Routledge, 2002), pp. 13–24.
33. Calder, *The Myth of the Blitz*, p. 210.
34. *Guardian*, 6 April 1995.
35. Kelley, *The Royals*, p. 33.
36. Grafton, *You, You and You*, p. 16; D.S. Lewis, *Illusions of Grandeur: Mosley, Fascism and British Society 1931–1981* (Manchester University Press, 1987), p. 90.
37. M. Beckman, *The 43 Group* (Centerprise Publications, 1990), p. 18.
38. Bosworth, *Mussolini's Italy*, p. 484.
39. Tobias Abse, 'Italian Workers and Italian Fascism', in Richard Bessel (ed.), *Fascist Italy and Nazi Germany: Comparisons and Contrasts* (Cambridge University Press, 1996), pp. 57–60.
40. Ibid., p. 60.
41. Peter Calvocoressi, Guy Wint and John Pritchard, *The Penguin History of the Second World War* (Penguin, 1999), p. 398.
42. David W. Ellwood, *Italy 1943–1945* (Leicester University Press, 1985), pp. 31–48.
43. Alessandro Portelli, *The Order Has Been Carried Out: History, Memory and Meaning of a Nazi Massacre in Rome* (Palgrave, 2003), pp. 80–4.
44. The advice came from General Giacomo Zanussi, who had served as Deputy Chief of Staff 2nd Army, Yugoslavia, and was involved in the anti-partisan war there. Peter Tompkins, *Italy Betrayed* (Simon and Schuster, 1966), p. 123.
45. Ellwood, *Italy 1943–1945*, pp. 49–98.
46. Cinzia Villani, 'The Persecution of Jews in German-Occupied Northern Italy', in Zimmerman (ed.), *Jews in Italy Under Fascist and Nazi Rule*, p. 250.

47. Rossana Rossanda, 'The Comrade from Milan', *New Left Review* 49 (January–February 2008), pp. 81–2.
48. Ponting, *Churchill*, p. 566.
49. Ibid., p. 593.
50. Ibid., p. 605.
51. Ibid.
52. Holland, *The Pursuit of Greatness*, p. 187.
53. Hastings, *Overlord*, p. 26.
54. Ibid., p. 27.
55. Keegan, *Six Armies in Normandy*, p. 55.
56. Ponting, *Churchill*, p. 612.
57. Hastings, *Overlord*, p. 23.
58. Overy, *Why the Allies Won*, p. 178.
59. Hastings, *Overlord*, p. 27.
60. Ibid., p. 43.
61. Ibid., p. 177.
62. Ponting, *Churchill*, p. 623.
63. Calvocoressi, Wint and Pritchard, *The Penguin History of the Second World War*, p. 538.
64. Hastings, *Overlord*, p. 285.
65. Terry Copp, 'First Canadian Army, February–March 1945', in Addison and Calder (eds), *Time to Kill*, pp. 148–9.
66. Mark Zuehlke, *Holding Juno: Canada's Heroic Defence of the D-Day Beaches: June 7–12, 1944* (Douglas & McIntyre, 2006), p. 360.
67. Kolko, *The Politics of War*, pp. 87–92.
68. John Nelson Rickard and Roger Cirillo, *Advance and Destroy: Patton As Commander in the Bulge* (University Press of Kentucky, 2011), p. 73.
69. Lloyd Clark, *Crossing the Rhine: Breaking Into Nazi Germany 1944 and 1945* (Atlantic Monthly Press, 2008), p. 106.
70. Calvocoressi, Wint and Pritchard, *The Penguin History of the Second World War*, pp. 549–51.
71. Dwight D. Eisenhower, *Crusade in Europe* (William Heinemann, 1948), p. 389.
72. Stanley Baldwin, House of Commons, 10 November 1932, 270 Parliamentary Debates (House of Commons), Official Report, 5th Series, c632.
73. Alan J. Levine, *The Strategic Bombing of Germany 1940–1945* (Greenwood Publishing, 1992), pp. 37–8.
74. Stephen L. McFarland and Wesley Phillips Newton, *To Command the Sky: The Battle for Air Superiority Over Germany, 1942–1944* (University of Alabama Press, 2006), pp. 39–41.
75. Overy, *Why the Allies Won*, p. 111.
76. Ibid., pp. 119–20.
77. Ibid., pp. 123–4, and Harvey, *Collision of Empires*, p. 695.
78. Ponting, *1940*, pp. 162–3.
79. Tooze, *The Wages of Destruction*, pp. 649–51, and Levine, *The Strategic Bombing of Germany*, pp. 174–80.
80. Harvey, *Collision of Empires*, pp. 659–60.
81. Martin Gilbert, *The Second World War* (Weidenfeld & Nicolson, 2000), p. 544.
82. Erickson, *The Road to Berlin*, p. 304.
83. Kolko, *The Politics of War*, pp. 156–8.

84. Arno J. Mayer, *Why Did the Heavens Not Darken: The 'Final Solution' in History* (Pantheon, 1990), p. 361.
85. Erickson, *The Road to Berlin*, p. 543.
86. Krisztián Ungváry, *The Siege of Budapest: One Hundred Days in World War Two* (Yale University Press, 2006), pp. 188–200.
87. Erickson, *The Road to Berlin*, p. 567.
88. Ibid., p. 666.
89. Kolko, *The Politics of War*, p. 371, and Overy, *Russia's War*, p. 236.
90. Kershaw, *Hitler 1936–1945*, p. 747.
91. Antony Beevor, *Berlin: The Downfall 1945* (Viking, 2002), p. 247.
92. Tony Le Tissier, *The Battle of Berlin 1945* (Jonathan Cape, 1998), pp. 6, 14, 41.
93. Jon Lewis (ed.), *The Mammoth Book of Eye-witness History* (Carrol and Graf, 2006), p. 465.
94. Tom Behan, *The Italian Resistance: Fascists, Guerrillas and the Allies* (Pluto Press, 2009), pp. 93–106.
95. Le Tissier, *The Battle of Berlin*, p. 87.
96. Ibid., p. 119.
97. John Erickson, 'Red Army Battlefield Performance, 1941–45: The System and the Soldier', in Addison and Calder (eds), *Time to Kill*, p. 248.
98. Glantz and House, *When Titans Clashed*, pp. 284–5.
99. Overy, *Why the Allies Won*, p. 3.
100. Clark, *Barbarossa*, p. 404.
101. Robert Murphy, *Diplomats Among Warriors* (Doubleday, 1964), pp. 412–13, and Andre Fontaine, *History of the Cold War* (Secker and Warburg, 1968), pp. 243–4.
102. Erickson, *The Road to Berlin*, pp. 647, 670.
103. Ibid., pp. 647, 853–4.
104. Toland, *Hitler*, p. 819.
105. Henryk Świebocki, *London Has Been Informed: Reports by Auschwitz Escapees* (Auschwitz-Birkenau State Museum, 1997), p. 65.
106. Alan J. Levine, *Captivity, Flight, and Survival in World War II* (Greenwood, 2000), pp. 198–203. For a full account by a participant in the resistance see Marek Edelman, *The Ghetto Fights* (Bookmarks, 1990).
107. Levine, *Captivity, Flight, and Survival*, pp. 203–10.
108. Hermann Langbein, *People in Auschwitz* (University of North Carolina, 2004), pp. 198–202.
109. Hermann Langbein, *Against All Hope: Resistance in the Nazi Concentration Camps 1938–1945* (Constable, 2005), p. 393.
110. Beevor, *Berlin: The Downfall 1945*, p. 189.
111. Ibid., pp. 122, 191–2.
112. Toland, *Hitler*, pp. 844–5.
113. Ernst Nolte, 'Between Myth and Revisionism? The Third Reich in the Perspective of the 1980s', in Koch (ed), *Aspects of the Third Reich*, p. 36.
114. Andreas Hillgruber, 'No Questions are Forbidden to Research', in J. Knowlton and T. Cates (eds), *Forever in the Shadow of Hitler? Original Documents of the Historikerstreit, The Controversy Concerning the Singularity of the Holocaust* (Atlantic Highlands, 1993), p. 159.
115. Harvey, *Collision of Empires*, p. 723.
116. Roberts, *Stalin's Wars*, p. 45.
117. Mazower, *Inside Hitler's Greece*, p. 98.
118. Renzo de Felice, *Mussolini l'alleato 2: La Guerra civile* (Einaudi, 1997), p. 72.

119. Liliana Picciotto, 'The Shoah in Italy: Its History and Characteristics', in Zimmerman (ed.), *Jews in Italy Under Fascist and Nazi Rule*, pp. 209–23.
120. Peukert, *Inside Nazi Germany*, p. 63.
121. Ibid., p. 164.
122. Joachim Kramarz, *Stauffenberg: The Life and Death of an Officer* (Deutsch, 1967), p. 152.

Chapter 8

1. Fernando Claudin, *The Communist Movement: From Comintern to Cominform* (Monthly Review Press, 1975), pp. 311–12.
2. John Lukacs, *The Last European War: September 1939–December 1941* (Yale University Press, 2001), p. 303.
3. Hobsbawm, *Age of Extremes*, p. 167.
4. The French Popular Front assembly of 1936 voted full powers to Marshal Pétain with three quarters of the Socialist deputies voting their approval (Birchall, *Bailing Out the System*, p. 29). Another prominent collaborator was Hendrik de Man of the Parti Ouvrier Belge (see Harvey, *Collision of Empires*, p. 504), while in Denmark the Social Democrats were in government for the first two years of the Nazi occupation.
5. Hobsbawm, *Age of Extremes*, pp. 166–7, and David Caute, *Communism and the French Intellectuals 1910–1960* (Macmillan, 1964), p. 181.
6. Birchall, *Bailing Out the System*, p. 32.
7. Kolko, *The Politics of War*, p. 455.
8. Ibid., pp. 34–6.
9. Thomas, *The Spanish Civil War*, pp. 954–5.
10. Smith, *The Shadow Warriors*, p. 158.
11. Ibid., p. 305.
12. George Bruce, *The Warsaw Rising* (Pan, 1974), p. 81.
13. Kolko, *The Politics of War*, pp. 115–20.
14. Ibid.
15. Bruce, *The Warsaw Rising*, p. 247.
16. Kolko, *The Politics of War*, pp. 115–20.
17. Ibid., pp. 507–8.
18. Behan, *The Italian Resistance*, p. 211.
19. Ellwood, *Italy 1943–1945*, p. 163.
20. Kolko, *The Politics of War*, p. 437.
21. Behan, *The Italian Resistance*, pp. 40–4.
22. Ponting, *Churchill*, p. 666.
23. See the chapter on the Naples insurrection in Maria de Blasio Wilhelm, *The Other Italy* (W.W. Norton, 1988) and Behan, *The Italian Resistance*, pp. 32–9.
24. Kolko, *Century of War*, pp. 251–2.
25. James Holland, *Italy's Sorrow: A Year of War, 1944–45* (HarperCollins, 2008), p. 221.
26. Ibid., p. 265.
27. Ibid., p. 290.
28. Ibid., p. 445.
29. Ibid., p. 303.
30. Ibid., p. 388.
31. Behan, *The Italian Resistance*, pp. 49–52.
32. Aldo Agosti, *Palmiro Togliatti: A Biography* (I.B. Tauris, 2008), p. 148.

33. Ibid.
34. Frank Rosengarten, *The Italian Anti-Fascist Press (1919–1945): From the Legal Opposition Press to the Underground Newspapers of World War II* (Case Western Reserve University Press, 1968), p. 198.
35. Agosti, *Palmiro Togliatti*, pp. 151–2.
36. Behan, *The Italian Resistance*, pp. 125–6.
37. Holland, *Italy's Sorrow*, p. 448.
38. Behan, *The Italian Resistance*, pp. 52–3.
39. Charles T. O'Reilly, *Forgotten Battles: Italy's War of Liberation 1943–45* (Lexington Books, 2001), pp. 288–9.
40. Behan, *The Italian Resistance*, pp. 114–15.
41. Agosti, *Palmiro Togliatti*, p. 170.
42. Bosworth, *Mussolini's Italy*, p. 502.
43. Laurence Lewis, *Echoes of Resistance: British Involvement with the Italian Partisans* (Costello, 1985), p. 114.
44. Jackson, *France: The Dark Years*, p. 288.
45. Ibid., pp. 292–3.
46. Jackson, *France: The Dark Years*, pp. 216–19.
47. Ibid., p. 1.
48. Kolko, *Century of War*, p. 256.
49. Jackson, *France: The Dark Years*, p. 423.
50. Ousby, *Occupation*, p. 268.
51. James Shields, *The Extreme Right in France From Pétain to Le Pen* (Routledge, 2007), p. 38.
52. Kolko, *Century of War*, p. 259.
53. Ian Birchall, 'With the Masses, Against the Stream: French Trotskyism in the Second World War', *Revolutionary History* 1:4 (Winter 1988–89), available at http://www.ucc.ie/acad/appsoc/tmp_store/mia/Library/history/etol/revhist/backiss/Vol1/No4/France.html
54. Ibid.
55. Alain Rouvez, Michael Coco and Jean-Paul Paddack, *Disconsolate Empires: French, British and Belgian Military Involvement in Post-colonial Sub-Saharan Africa* (University Press of America, 1994), pp. 18–19.
56. Kolko, *The Politics of War*, p. 82.
57. Ousby, *Occupation*, p. 242.
58. Blake Ehrlich, *Resistance: 1940–1945* (Little Brown and Company, 1965), p. 166.
59. Frida Knight, *The French Resistance 1940–1944* (Lawrence and Wishart, 1975), p. 154.
60. Max Hastings, *Das Reich* (Pan, 1981), pp. 181–202.
61. Kolko, *Century of War*, p. 288.
62. M.S. Alexander, 'Soldiers And Socialists: The French officer Corps and Leftist Government', in Alexander and Graham (eds), *The French and Spanish Popular Fronts*, p. 70.
63. Antony Beevor and Artemis Cooper, *Paris After The Liberation: 1944–1949* (Penguin 1995), p. 391.
64. Kolko, *The Politics of War*, p. 283.
65. Ibid.
66. Paul Preston, *The Spanish Civil War: Reaction, Revolution and Revenge* (Harper Perennial, 2006), p. 202
67. Andy Durgan, *The Spanish Civil War* (Palgrave, 2007), pp. 80–1, 105–6.

68. Pieter Lagrou, 'Belgium', in Bob Moore (ed.), *Resistance in Western Europe* (Berg, 2000), pp. 25–64.
69. Martin Conway, *The Sorrows of Belgium: Liberation and Political Reconstruction 1944–1947* (Oxford University Press, 2012), pp. 105–10.
70. Martin van Creveld, 'Prelude to Disaster: The British Decision to Aid Greece 1940–41', *Journal of Contemporary History* 9:3 (1974), pp. 65–92.
71. Kolko, *Century of War*, p. 270.
72. Mazower, *Inside Hitler's Greece*, p. 24.
73. Ibid., p. 82.
74. Ibid., p. 137.
75. Charmley, *Churchill*, p. 586.
76. Marion Sarafis (ed.), *Greece, From Resistance to Civil War* (Spokesman, 1980), p. 93.
77. Mazower, *Inside Hitler's Greece*, p. 329.
78. Kolko, *Century of War*, p. 299.
79. Erickson, *The Road to Berlin*, p. 451.
80. Kolko, *Century of War*, pp. 274–5.
81. Holland, *The Pursuit of Greatness*, p. 192.
82. Thanasis D. Sfikas, *The British Labour Government and the Greek Civil War 1945–1949* (Ryburn, 1994), pp. 34–5.
83. Ponting, *Churchill*, pp. 672–3.
84. John Louis Hondros, *Occupation and Resistance: The Greek Agony 1941–1944* (Pellas Publishers, 1983), pp. 247–8.
85. Kolko, *The Politics of War*, p. 189.
86. Dominique Eudes, *The Kapetanios: Partisans and Civil War in Greece 1943–1949* (New Left Books, 1972), p. 216.
87. Holland, *The Pursuit of Greatness*, p. 192.
88. Ponting, *Churchill*, pp. 674–5.
89. Erickson, *The Road to Berlin*, pp. 647, 670.
90. Kolko, *The Politics of War*, p. 431.
91. Erickson, *The Road to Berlin*, pp. 450–1.
92. Charmley, *Churchill*, p. 607.
93. Kolko, *The Politics of War*, p. 584.
94. Ibid., p. 585.
95. Mazower, *Inside Hitler's Greece*, p. 296.
96. Ibid., p. 360.
97. Kolko, *Century of War*, p. 272.
98. Ibid., p. 272
99. Erickson, *The Road to Berlin*, p. 497.
100. Robert R. King, *A History of the Romanian Communist Party* (Hoover Institution Press, 1980), p. 71.
101. Hehn, *A Low Dishonest Decade*, pp. 368–93.
102. Mazower, *Hitler's Empire*, p. 240.
103. Paul Mojze, *Balkan Genocides: Holocaust and Ethnic Cleansing in the Twentieth Century* (Rowman & Littlefield, 2011), pp. 87–9.
104. Burgwyn, *Empire on the Adriatic*, p. 176.
105. Misha Glenny, *The Balkans 1844–1999: Nationalism, War and the Great Powers* (Granta Books, 2000), pp. 493–4.
106. Jozo Tomasevich, 'Yugoslavia During the Second World War', in Wayne S. Vucinich and Jozo Tomasevich (eds), *Contemporary Yugoslavia: Twenty Years of Socialist Experiment* (Stanford University Press, 1969), p. 99.

107. Ibid., pp. 101–2.
108. Sean M. McAteer, *500 Days: The War In Eastern Europe 1944–1945* (Dorrance Publishing, 2009), pp. 233–4.
109. Kolko, *The Politics of War*, p. 135.
110. Stevan K. Pavlowitch, *Hitler's New Disorder: The Second World War in Yugoslavia* (Columbia University Press, 2008), pp. 215–16.
111. *Time*, 8 February 1943, available at http://www.time.com/time/magazine/article/0,9171,774177,00.html
112. Ibid.
113. Pavlowitch, *Hitler's New Disorder*, pp. 215–38.
114. Barbara Jancar-Webster, *Women and Revolution in Yugoslavia, 1941–1945* (Arden Press, 1990), pp. 46–9.
115. McAteer, *500 Days*, p. 234.
116. G. Bruce Strang, *On the Fiery March: Mussolini Prepares For War* (Greenwood Publishing, 2003), pp. 242–4.
117. Bernd J. Fischer, *Albania at War 1939–1945* (Hurst and Co, 1999), p. 124.
118. Ibid., pp. 195–6.
119. Owen Pearson, *Albania in the Twentieth Century, A History, Volume Two, Albania in Occupation and War 1939–1945* (I.B. Tauris, 2006), p. 271.
120. Jozo Tomasevich, *War and Revolution in Yugoslavia 1941–1945, Occupation and Collaboration* (Stanford University Press, 2001), p. 154.
121. Fischer, *Albania at War*, p. 200.
122. Ibid., p. 267.

Chapter 9

1. Mira Wilkins, *The History of Foreign Investment in the United States, 1914–1945* (Harvard University Press, 2004), p. 422.
2. Ken Kotani, *Japanese Intelligence in World War II* (Osprey Publishing, 2009), p. 45.
3. See http://ibiblio.org/hyperwar/USA/USA-P-Strategy/Strategy-2.html#fn30#fn30
4. *Foreign Relations of the United States: Japan, 1931–1941*, Vol. II (US Department of State, 1943), pp. 173–81.
5. Gerhard L. Weinberg, *Germany and the Soviet Union 1939–1941* (Brill Archive, 1954), p. 159.
6. Kotani, *Japanese Intelligence*, p. 127.
7. Ibid., p. 117.
8. Ibid.
9. Ibid., pp. 150–1.
10. Ibid.
11. John W. Dower, *Embracing Defeat: Japan in the Wake of World War Two* (Penguin, 2000), p. 468.
12. Michael Barnhart, *Japan Prepares for Total War* (Cornell University Press, 1968), p. 20.
13. Toland, *Hitler*, p. 691.
14. Samuel Eliot Morison, *Breaking the Bismarck's Barrier: 22 July 1942–1 May 1944* (Little, Brown and Company, 1950), pp. 15–22.
15. Kotani, *Japanese Intelligence*, p. 158.
16. Ibid., p. 118.
17. Ibid., p. 119.
18. Ibid., pp. 48–9.

19. Ibid., p. 15.
20. Ibid., p. 112.
21. Ibid., p. 114.
22. Ibid., p. 114.
23. David Fraser, *Alanbrooke* (Harper Collins, 1982), p. 227.
24. James Leasor, *Singapore: The Battle That Changed the World* (House of Stratus, 2001), p. 247.
25. See http://www.4to40.com/history/index.asp?p=Subhas_Chandra_Bose_To_Delhi_To_Delhi&sc=India
26. Harvey, *Collision of Empires*, p. 580.
27. Naoko Sajima and Kyochi Tachikawa, *Japanese Sea Power: A Maritime Nation's Struggle for Identity* (Sea Power Centre Australia, 2009), p. 118.
28. Calvocoressi, Wint and Pritchard, *The Penguin History of the Second World War* (Penguin, 1999), p. 966.
29. Dower, *Embracing Defeat*, p. 23.
30. Calvocoressi, Wint and Pritchard, *The Penguin History of the Second World War*, p. 967.
31. Harvey, *Collision of Empires*, p. 624.
32. Overy, *Why the Allies Won*, p. 210.
33. Dallas Woodbury Isom, *Midway Inquest: Why the Japanese Lost the Battle of Midway* (Indiana University Press, 2007), p. 1.
34. Sajima and Tachikawa, *Japanese Sea Power*, p. 49.
35. David M. Kennedy, *Freedom from Fear: The American people in World War II* (Oxford University Press, 2003), p. 127.
36. Eric M. Bergerud, *Fire in the Sky: The Air War in the Pacific* (Westview Press, 2000), p. 86, and Kotani, *Japanese Intelligence*, p. 57.
37. Kennedy, *Freedom from Fear*, p. 127.
38. Kotani, *Japanese Intelligence*, p. 105.
39. Ponting, *Churchill*, p. 635.
40. Gordon Daniels, 'The Great Tokyo Air Raid, 9–10 March 1945', in William G. Beasley (ed.), *Modern Japan: Aspects of History, Literature and Society* (University of California Press, 1975), pp. 116–17.
41. Ibid., p. 119
42. Ibid., p. 129.
43. Dower, *Embracing Defeat*, p. 45.
44. Harvey, *Collision of Empires*, p. 582.
45. Kolko, *The Politics of War*, pp. 550–1.
46. Ibid., p. 544.
47. Ibid., p. 561.
48. Ibid., pp. 555–6.
49. William Leahy, *I Was There* (McGraw Hill, 1950), p. 441.
50. 'Ike on Ike', *Time*, 11 November 1963.
51. Leon V. Sigal, *Fighting to a Finish: The Politics of War Termination in the United States and Japan* (Cornell University Press, 1988), p. 178.
52. Overy, *Why the Allies Won*, p. 301.
53. Kolko, *The Politics of War*, pp. 540–1.
54. Ibid., p. 540.
55. See http://news.bbc.co.uk/onthisday/hi/dates/stories/august/15/newsid_35810 00/3581971.stm
56. Holland, *The Pursuit of Greatness*, p. 180.

57. Gerhard L. Weinberg, *A World at Arms: A Global History of World War II* (Cambridge University Press, 2005), p. 894, and Dower, *Embracing Defeat*, p. 22.
58. Shigeru Akita and Nicholas J. White, *The International Order of Asia in the 1930s and 1950s* (Ashgate Publishing, 2010), p. 109.
59. Dower, *Embracing Defeat*, p. 27.
60. Ibid., p. 26.

Chapter 10

1. John W. Graver, 'China's Wartime Diplomacy', in James Chieh Hshing and Steven I. Levine (eds), *China's Bitter Victory: The War with Japan 1937–1945* (East Gate Books, 1992), p. 3.
2. Ibid., pp. 6–7.
3. Ibid., p. 14.
4. Harvey, *Collision of Empires*, p. 491.
5. Kolko, *The Politics of War*, p. 205.
6. John King Fairbanks and Merle Goldman, *China: A New History* (Harvard University Press, 2006), p. 314.
7. Kolko, *The Politics of War*, p. 238.
8. Fairbanks and Goldman, *China: A New History*, pp. 319–20.
9. Ibid., pp. 326–7.
10. Lyman P. Van Slyke, *The Chinese Communist Movement: A Report to the United States War Department, July 1945* (Stanford University Press, 1968), pp. 106–7.
11. Mao's Interview with an American Journalist, Gunther Stien, 1944, available at http://www.marxists.org/reference/archive/mao/selected-works/volume-6/mswv6_38.htm
12. Mao, 'The Current Situation', in *Selected Works of Mao Tse-tung, Vol. III* (Foreign Languages Press, 1967), p. 171.
13. Fairbanks and Goldman, *China: A New History*, p. 328.
14. Robert Carver North, *Moscow and Chinese Communists* (Stanford University Press, 1963), p. 208.
15. Fairbanks and Goldman, *China: A New History*, p. 329.
16. Kolko, *The Politics of War*, p. 616.
17. Barbara Barnouin and Yu Changgen, *Zhou Enlai: A Political Life* (Chinese University of Hong Kong, 2006), pp. 103–16.
18. Kolko, *The Politics of War*, p. 602.
19. Michael J. Seth, *A Concise History of Korea: From the Late Nineteenth Century to the Present* (Rowman & Littlefield, 2010), p. 84.
20. Hugh Deane, *The Korean War 1945–1953* (China Books, 1999), p. 45.
21. Seth, *A Concise History of Korea*, pp. 95–7.
22. Kolko, *Century of War*, pp. 399–408.
23. Ibid., p. 341.
24. Ibid., p. 346.
25. Gabriel Kolko, *Vietnam: Anatomy of War: 1940–1975* (Unwin, 1987), pp. 36–7.
26. William Warbey, *Ho Chi Minh and the Struggle for an Independent Vietnam* (Merlin, 1972), p. 52.
27. Smith, *The Shadow Warriors*, p. 325.
28. Warbey, *Ho Chi Minh*, p. 49.
29. Ian Birchall, *Workers Against the Monolith* (Pluto Press, 1974), p. 35.
30. John Saville, *The Politics of Continuity: British Foreign Policy and the Labour Government 1945–1946* (Verso, 1993), pp. 199–204.

31. Ellen Joy Hammer, *The Struggle for Indochina, 1940–1945* (Stanford University Press, 1966), pp. 115–21.
32. N. Van, *Revolutionaries They Could Not Break* (Index Books, 1995), p. 117.
33. Cheah Boon Kheng, *Red Star Over Malaya* (Singapore University Press, 1983), pp. 56–60.
34. Ibid., p. 64.
35. Lennox Algernon Mills, *Malaya: A Political and Economic Appraisal* (University of Minnesota Press, 1958), pp. 44–7.
36. John Springhall, *Decolonization Since 1945: The Collapse of European Overseas Empires* (Palgrave, 2001), pp. 54–60.
37. Jeff Goodwin, *No Other Way Out: States and Revolutionary Movements, 1945–1991* (Cambridge University Press, 2001), p. 116.
38. Kolko, *Century of War*, p. 360.
39. Ibid., p. 357.
40. Kolko, *The Politics of War*, p. 606.
41. Kolko, *Century of War*, pp. 389–95.
42. Nicholas Tarling, *A Sudden Rampage: The Japanese Occupation of South East Asia 1941–1945* (C. Hurst & Co, 2001), pp. 174–92.
43. Benedict Richard O'Gorman Anderson, *Java In A Time of Revolution, Occupation and Resistance 1944–1946* (Equinox, 2005), p. 117.
44. Dower, *Embracing Defeat*, p. 27.

Chapter 11

1. Hobsbawm, *Age of Extremes*, p. 43.
2. Craig Shirley, *December 1941: 31 Days That Changed America and Saved the World* (Thomas Nelson, 2011), pp. 286–7.
3. Overy, *Why the Allies Won*, p. 192.
4. Milward, *War, Economy and Society, 1939–1945*, pp. 63–5.
5. Kolko, *The Politics of War*, p. 252.
6. Overy, *Why the Allies Won*, p. 195.
7. Kolko, *The Politics of War*, p. 251.
8. Ibid., p. 540.
9. Bartov, *Hitler's Army*, p. 253.
10. Harvey, *Collision of Empires*, p. 564.
11. Ponting, *1940*, pp. 233–4.
12. Kolko, *The Politics of War*, p. 259, and Scott Newton, 'Keynesianism 1940–1952', in R.C. Michie and Philip Williamson (eds), *The British Government and the City of London in the Twentieth Century* (Cambridge University Press, 2004), p. 260.
13. Kolko, *The Politics of War*, p. 490, and Alan P. Dobson, *US Economic Statecraft for Survival, 1933–1991: Of Sanctions, Embargoes, and Economic Warfare* (Routledge, 2002), p. 68.
14. Ponting, *1940*, p. 233.
15. Andrew J. Pierre, *Nuclear Politics: The British Experience With An Independent Strategic Force 1939–1970* (Oxford University Press, 1972), p. 68.
16. A.J. Brown, *Applied Economics: Aspects of the World Economy in War and Peace, Volume 1* (Routledge, 2003), p. 60.
17. Kolko, *The Politics of War*, p. 295.
18. Quoted in *Time*, 22 October 1984, available at http://www.time.com/time/magazine/article/0,9171,951370-4,00.html
19. Kolko, *The Politics of War*, pp. 303–12.

20. Jackson, *The British Empire and the Second World War*, pp. 156–9.
21. Joyce Kolko and Gabriel Kolko, *The Limits of Power: The World and United States Foreign Policy 1945–1954* (Harper and Row, 1972), pp. 417–18.
22. Kolko, *The Politics of War*, p. 460.
23. *Life*, 17 February 1941, p. 61.
24. F. William Engdahl, 'The Financial Tsunami: The Financial Foundations of the American Century', *Global Research*, 16 January 2008, available at http://globalresearch.ca/index.php?context=va&aid=7813
25. David M. Andrews, *Orderly Change: International Monetary Relations Since Bretton Woods* (Cornell University Press, 2008), p. 51.
26. John Rees, *Imperialism and Resistance* (Routledge, 2006), p. 41.
27. Ibid.
28. David Horowitz, *Containment and Revolution* (Beacon Press, 1967), pp. 11–14.
29. Rees, *Imperialism and Resistance*, p. 42.
30. Maurice Isserman and John Stewart Bowman, *The Korean War* (Infobase, 2003), p. 120.
31. *Survey of British Commonwealth Affairs* (Oxford University Press, 1958), p. 3.
32. Alan Jeffreys, Kevin Lyles and Jeff Vanelle, *British Infantryman in the Far East 1941–1945* (Osprey, 2003), p. 62.
33. Harvey, *Collision of Empires*, pp. 507–8.
34. Christoph Marx, *Oxwagon Sentinel: Radical Afrikaner Nationalism and the History of the 'Ossewabrandwag'* (LIT Verlag Münster, 2009), pp. 434–49, and Richard C. Thurlow, *Fascism in Britain: From Oswald Mosley's Blackshirts to the National Front* (I.B. Tauris, 1998), p. 225.
35. Hehn, *A Low Dishonest Decade*, p. 167.
36. Brian Lapping, *End of Empire* (Granada, 1985), p. 527.
37. Ponting, *Churchill*, p. 677.
38. Ibid., pp. 689–91.
39. Birchall, *Bailing Out the System*, p. 46.
40. Kolko, *The Politics of War*, p. 361.
41. Deryck Marshall Schreuder and Stuart Ward, *Australia's Empire* (Oxford University Press, 2008), p. 249.
42. Lapping, *End of Empire*, p. 51.
43. Gerard Douds, 'Indian Troops in the North African and Italian Theatres', in Addison and Calder (eds), *Time to Kill*, p. 117.
44. Ibid., p. 120.
45. Mazhar Kibriya, *Gandhi and Indian Freedom Struggle* (APH Publishing, 1999), p. 326.
46. Rajmohan Gandhi, *Gandhi: The Man, His People and the Empire* (University of California Press, 2006), p. 471.
47. Sumit Sarkar, *Modern India 1885–1947* (Macmillan, 1983), p. 391. The powerful Indian Communist Party opposed the Quit India campaign as disrupting the Anglo-Russian war effort.
48. Lapping, *End of Empire*, p. 56.
49. Grafton, *You, You and You*, p. 89.
50. Claude Markovits, *A History of Modern India 1480–1950* (Anthem Press, 2004), p. 472.
51. Joyce C. Lebra and Joyce Lebra-Chapman, *The Indian National Army and Japan* (Institute of Southeast Asian Studies, 2008), pp. 114–15.

52. Amartya Sen, *Poverty and Famines: An Essay on Entitlement and Deprivation* (Oxford University Press, 1981), pp. 70–8.
53. Madhusree Mukerjee, *Churchill's Secret War: The British Empire and the Ravaging of India During World War II* (Basic Books, 2011), p. 220.
54. *West Africa*, Issues 4031–4055 (West Africa Publishing Company Limited, 1995), p. 304.
55. Humphrey Metzgen and John Graham, *Caribbean Wars Untold: A Salute to the British West Indies* (University of West Indies Press, 2007), p. 145.
56. *West Africa*, Issues 4031–4055, p. 304.
57. Lapping, *End of Empire*, p. 242.
58. Ibid., p. 243.
59. Jackson, *The British Empire and the Second World War*, pp. 146–54.
60. Ibid., pp. 156–61.
61. Ibid., pp. 154–6.
62. Norman Rose, 'Churchill and Zionism', in Robert Blake and William Roger Louis (eds), *Churchill* (Oxford University Press, 1996), p. 162.
63. Ponting, *Churchill*, pp. 700–1.
64. Alan Rice, *Creating Memorials, Building Identities: The Politics of Memory in the Black Atlantic* (Liverpool University Press, 2010), pp. 157–9.
65. David Killingray, 'African Soldiers in the Mediterranean and European Campaigns, 1939–45', in Addison and Calder (eds), *Time to Kill*, p. 101.
66. Alistair Horne, *A Savage War of Peace: Algeria 1954–1962* (Peregrine, 1979), p. 25.
67. Ibid., p. 27.
68. Ibid., pp. 25–41.

Conclusion

1. Harvey, *Collision of Empires*, p. 511.
2. See http://www.jewishvirtuallibrary.org/jsource/ww2/fdrfranco.html
3. Claudin, *The Communist Movement*, pp. 409–10.
4. Ibid., p. 410.
5. Leon Trotsky, *Writings of Leon Trotsky 1939–1940* (Pathfinder Press, 1973), p. 85.
6. Rees, *Imperialism and Resistance*, p. 230.
7. Leon Trotsky, *Writings of Leon Trotsky 1938–1939* (Pathfinder Press, 1974), pp. 209–10.
8. Ibid., p. 253.
9. Trotsky, *Writings 1939–1940*, p. 334. Wilkie was the Republican presidential candidate opposing Roosevelt, and 'the Sixty families' refers to a book detailing the tight circle which controlled much of corporate America.
10. Dorril, *Blackshirt: Sir Oswald Mosley and British Fascism*, pp. 507–8.
11. Trotsky, *Writings 1938–1939*, p. 297.
12. Alex Callinicos, *Trotskyism* (Open University Press, 1990), p. 23.
13. Ernest Mandel, *Trotskyists and the Resistance in World War Two* (1976), available at http://www.marxists.org/archive/mandel/1976/xx/trots-ww2.htm
14. Donny Gluckstein, *A People's History of the Second World War* (Pluto Press, 2012), pp. 11–12.
15. Behan, *The Italian Resistance*, p. 125.
16. Kolko, *The Politics of War*, p. 95.
17. Kolko, *Century of War*, pp. 289–90.
18. *New York Times*, 8 January 1946.
19. Agosti, *Palmiro Togliatti*, p. 163.

20. Maxwell Adereth, *The French Communist Party: A Critical History (1920–1984)* (Manchester University Press, 1984), p. 137.
21. Birchall, *Bailing Out the System*, pp. 40–1.
22. Kolko, *The Politics of War*, p. 437.
23. Paul Ginsborg, *A History of Contemporary Italy* (Penguin, 1990), p. 54.
24. Tom Behan, *The Long Awaited Moment: The Working Class and the Italian Communist Party in Milan 1943–1948* (Peter Lang, 1997), p. 136.
25. Ginsborg, *A History of Contemporary Italy*, p. 88.
26. Claudin, *The Communist Movement*, p. 440.
27. Ginsborg, *A History of Contemporary Italy*, p. 47.
28. Ernest Mandel, 'Revolutionary Strategy in Europe', *New Left Review* 100 (November 1976–January 1977).
29. Arthur Koestler, quoted in Calder, *The People's War*, p. 605.

Index

Abse, Tobias, 148
Action Party, 175–6
AEG (Allgemeine Elektricitäts-Gesellschaft Aktiengesellschaft), 38
Afghanistan, 1, 234
Akita, Shigeru, 57
Alamein, 112
Albania, 105, 171, 191–2
Alexander, Field Marshal Alexander, 90, 173, 176, 184
Algeria, 100, 112–13, 179, 225, 237–8
Allied Bombing Campaign of Germany, 21, 23, 85, 102, 104, 107, 153, 156–9, 160, 168
Allinson, Jamie C., 54
d'Almeida, Fabrice, 40
Amery, Leo, 2, 232, 239
Andorra Star, 147
Anglo-German Naval Agreement, 17, 75
Anglo-Iranian Oil Company, 228
Anievas Alex, 54
Anschluss, 66–8
Antonov, General Aleksei, 160
Anti-Comintern Pact, 60
Anti-Semitism, 11, 36, 43, 45–6, 52–3, 63, 67–8, 73, 82–3, 85, 95–7, 106, 113, 117, 166, 231
Antonescu, General Ion, 135, 187
Anzio, 149
Ardennes, 88, 91, 155, 161
Argentina, 1, 15, 109, 225, 228
Aritomo, Count Yamagata, 55
Arnhem, 155
Arnold, Lord Sydney, 78
Astor, Lady Nancy, 31, 69
Asturias Uprising, 10, 62
Atlantic Charter, 226, 232, 236
Attlee, Clement, 87–8, 93, 142, 232
Auschwitz, 133, 136, 161, 164–7
Australia, 6, 56, 147, 194, 199, 200–1, 205, 233
Axis, 8, 31, 33, 35, 63, 105–7, 110–13, 123, 141, 188–9, 190, 193–4, 217, 236, 241–2

Badoglio, Marshal Pietro, 149, 173–5
Bagration, 160
Baldwin, Stanley, 14–21, 28, 42, 52, 61, 65–6, 87, 99, 156
Ball, Sir Joseph, 73
Bank of England, 14, 18, 21, 42, 92
Barbarossa, 118, 121, 123, 126, 132–3, 136, 139
Bastianini, Giuseppe, 92
Beaton, Cecil, 103
Beaverbrook, Lord 'Max', 18, 98–9, 104
Beck, Jósef, 69
Belgium, 35, 77, 88–9, 90, 92–3, 97, 145, 161, 169, 181–2
Belsen, 2
Belzec, 138, 161
Benes, Edvard, 69
Bengal Famine, 235
Bennett, General Gordon, 201
Beria, Lavrenti, 127
Berle, Adolph, 33
Berlin, Battle of, 161–3
Bermuda, 108
Beveridge, Lord William 108
Bevin, Ernest, 88, 142, 227
Birchall, Ian, 179
Biennio Rosso, 51
Birkenau, 136–7, 161, 165
Bloch, Marc, 23, 65
von Blomberg, General Field Marshal Werner, 40–1, 45
Blum, Léon, 2, 23, 63–4, 67
BMW, 144
Bohlen, Charles, 163
Bonesteel, Charles, 219
Bosch, Carl, 38
Bose, Subhas Chandra, 201, 234
Bouhler, Philip, 138
Brack, Victor, 137
Bretton Woods Conference, 229
Bridge on the River Kwai, 205
Britain, 1–4, 9, 10–11, 22–3, 25, 27–8, 31, 37, 41–2, 46, 50–3, 58, 115, 117, 124–5, 127, 129, 130, 136, 146,

156–9, 160, 163, 169, 170, 173, 179, 183, 189, 244, 249
  Alliance with Japan, 54–7
  Appeasement, 16–19, 20, 61–9, 70–9, 80
  Battle of Britain, 101–2, 119, 160
  Domestic wartime policy, 107–8, 141–3, 147
  Economy, 5–8, 15–16, 20–1
  End of Empire, 230–6
  Intervention in Greece, 183–6
  Invasion of Europe, 151–6
  Relations with USA, 31–4, 108–9, 110–11, 208–9, 214, 225–9, 230, 239
  Poland and, 81–2, 187
  Threat of invasion, 86–9, 90–9, 100–4, 241–2
  War in North Africa, 104–7, 111–14
  War in the Far East, 193–6, 199, 204, 207, 222
British Empire, 3–5, 8, 13–16 , 21, 31, 33, 42, 56, 80, 90–2, 104, 113, 118, 154, 201, 226, 228, 230–7
British Union of Fascists, 147
Brassilach, Robert, 23
Brazil, 16, 225
Brooke, Field Marshal Alan, 111, 152–3
Brooke-Popham, Air Marshal Robert, 200
Brown, Kenneth Douglas, 56
Bruce Lockhart, Robert, 18
Brüning, Heinrich, 28, 38–9
Buchenwald, 144, 147
Bulgaria, 74, 105, 118, 121, 138, 160, 183, 187–8
Burma, 194, 199, 201, 204, 207–8, 231, 234–5
Butler, R.A.B., 16, 67, 77, 87–8, 92, 97–8, 100, 146

Cadogan, Sir Alexander, 74, 79, 91, 111
Cagoule, 65, 96
Calder, Angus, 99
Canada, 6, 90–2, 109, 113–14, 147, 151, 154, 233, 235, 243
Candide, 23
du Cann, Edward, 2
Caporetto, 51
Carboni, General Giacomo, 82

Carr, E.H., 25
Cavallero, General Ugo, 82
Cazalet, Victor, 103
CGT, 65, 178
Chamberlain, Sir Austen, 17
Chamberlain, Neville, 1–2, 14–19, 20–1, 28, 30–1, 42, 52, 65–9, 70–9, 80, 85–8, 91–4, 98–9, 103, 108, 156
Channel Islands, 96
Channon, 'Chips', 18, 61, 77, 87–8, 100
Channon, Paul, 100
Charmley, John, 79
Chatfield, Lord Admiral, 12
Chetniks, 188–9
Chiang Kai-Shek, 57–9, 60, 194–5, 207–8, 210, 214–16, 218–9, 221
China, 4, 8, 16, 20, 30–1, 54–9, 60–1, 110, 193–9, 207–8, 210–13, 214–19, 220, 224–5, 230, 232–3, 241–3
  People's Liberation Army (China), 217, 219, 220
  Red Army 59–60
Chouffet, Armand, 63
Christian Democrats, 175–6, 213
Chuikov, General Vasily, 127–8
Churchill, Randolph, 104
Churchill, Winston, 2, 4, 18, 21, 23, 72, 79, 102–3, 132, 156, 172–3, 181, 189, 190–1, 194, 197, 200–1, 207, 209, 210, 221, 232–7, 239, 240, 242, 244
  Alliance with United States, 91–2, 104, 108–9, 110, 114, 208, 227–8
  Conduct of War, 89, 90, 104–7, 113–14, 151–3, 155
  Determination to fight on in 1940, 91–4, 97–9, 100
  Domestic policies, 108, 142, 145–7
  Intervention in Greece, 182–6
  Japan and, 16
  Mussolini and, 17
  Premiership, 86–8
  Pre-war career, 3, 14, 19–20, 67, 73, 230
  Yalta conference, 187
Ciano, Count Galeazzo, 76, 106, 134
City of London, 13–14, 22, 42, 102
Clark, Alan, 122, 127, 129
Clark, General Mark, 113
Class, Heinrich, 46

INDEX   287

Claudin, Fernando, 239, 246
Clerk, Sir George, 103
CLN (Comitato di Liberazione Nazionale), 176, 242, 245
Colville, Jock, 87
Comites des forges, 63
Communist International, 170, 247
Communist Parties, 4, 10, 19, 28, 116, 169, 170, 192, 242–4
　Albania, 191–2
　Belgium, 181–2
　Britain, 73, 103, 147
　Bulgaria, 160
　China, 4, 57, 59, 60, 194–5, 214–19
　France, 2, 22–5, 67, 86, 94, 169, 170, 176–9, 180–1, 243–4
　Germany, 10, 36, 38–9, 40, 75, 116, 168–9, 173, 239, 247
　Greece, 169, 182–7, 242
　Italy, 169, 170, 173, 175–6, 187, 242, 244–6
　Korea, 219–20
　Malaya, 222, 242
　Philippines, 223
　Poland, 171
　Romania, 160, 187
　Soviet Union, 8, 25–6, 115, 121–2, 161
　Spain, 20, 25, 62, 239
　Vietnam, 220–1, 225, 242
　Yugoslavia, 169, 188–9, 1990–1991
Conservative Party (Tories), 2, 14–16, 18, 22–3, 70, 87–8, 91, 99, 146–7, 243–8
Coral Sea, Battle of, 205
Corvignolles, 64
Coulondre, Robert, 78
Courtaulds, 109
Cowling, Maurice, 80
Cripps, Sir Stafford, 121, 233
Croatia, 53, 106, 145, 183, 188–9, 190
Croix de Feu, 22, 86
Cruati, Robert, 179
Czechoslovakia, 31, 38, 49, 62–3, 65–6, 68, 70–4, 115, 145, 162, 230, 240

Dachau, 144
Daily Express, 1
Daily Herald, 70
Daily Mail, 16–17

Daily Telegraph, 75, 85
Daily Worker, 103
Daimler Benz, 144
Daladier, Edouard, 24, 71, 76
Dalherus, Birger, 76
Dalton, Hugh, 88, 94
Darlan, Admiral Jean Francois, 112–13
Darnand, Joseph, 178
Darre, Richard, 44
Davidson, Basil, 173
Davies, Ralph K., 142
Dawson, Geoffrey, 18, 31, 69
Deat, Marcel, 95
D-Day, 107, 114, 149, 152, 161, 153, 180
Delbas, Yvon, 67
Dempsey, General Miles, 154
Denmark, 87, 97, 169
Dill, Field Marshal Sir John, 17, 12
Doenitz, Admiral Karl, 164, 168
Dolfuss, Englebert, 67
Doriot, Jacques, 95
Donskoi, Dmitri, 124
Dormoy, Marx, 96
Douhet, Giulio, 156
Doumerge, Gaston, 22
Dowlin, Air Chief Marshal Hugh, 156
Dower, John, 196, 212, 224
Duke of Buccleuch, 78, 88
Duff Cooper, Alfred, 100
Duff Cooper, Diana, 103
Duke of Westminster, 78
Dunkirk, 89, 93, 97, 104, 123, 147, 156
Dupont, 63

EAM (Ethnikón Apeleftherotikón Métopon), 182–6, 204, 239
Edelweiss Pirates, 168
Eden, Anthony, 21, 52, 62–3, 65–7, 71–3, 86, 90, 94, 98, 126, 151, 171, 182–3, 185, 186, 232
Edward, Duke of Windsor, 18–19
Ehrenburg, Ilya, 163
Eichmann, Adolf, 68, 138, 164
Eighth Route Army, 60, 194, 197
Einsatzgruppen, 135–6, 164
Eisenhower, General Dwight D., 112–13, 149, 153, 155, 164, 181, 190, 211, 243
ELAS (Ethnikós Laïkós Apeleftherotikós Strátos), 182–5, 239, 244

Elizabeth, Princess (Queen Elizabeth ll), 147
Elizabeth, The Queen Mother, 19, 88
Erickson, John, 121–2, 126, 128, 163, 183, 185, 187
Eritrea, 104
Estonia, 75, 116
Ethiopia, 20, 52–3, 104, 149, 173
Evening Standard, 65, 98–9

Fabien, Colonel, 171, 178
Faisal II, King of Iraq, 236
Falkland Islands (Malvinas), 1–2
Farben, I.G., 38, 41, 43, 182
Farouk, King of Egypt, 236
Fascist Party (Italy), 50–3, 139, 148
Faure, Paul, 63
Feis, Herbert, 229
Le Figaro, 63
Finland, 9, 75, 79, 116–18, 160
First World War, 2–3, 5, 9, 12–13, 15, 19, 21, 27, 30, 46, 50, 53, 56, 68, 74, 87, 107–8, 111, 129, 133, 135, 153, 168, 170, 179, 188, 191, 225–6, 230, 235–6
Fischer, Bernd J., 192
Foot, Michael, 1–2
Ford, 63, 141, 226
Ford, Henry, 142
France, 2, 4–6, 8, 9, 13, 16–17, 21–5, 27–8, 31–3, 35, 37–8, 41–2, 50–4, 61–4, 67–9, 70, 72–9, 80–1, 83, 85–6, 97–9, 101–3, 105, 110, 112–19, 132, 134, 143–6, 148, 150, 170, 194, 199, 207, 221, 225, 237–9, 240–4, 247
  Defeat, 86–9, 90–6, 151–6, 161, 164
  Popular Front government, 64–5
  Resistance, 169, 177–9, 180–1
Franco, Francisco, 10, 18, 20, 54, 62–4, 78
Franc-Tireurs et Partisans (FTP), 170, 178, 180
Frank, Hans, 83, 85, 133, 137–8
Friedeberg, Admiral Hans-Georg, 164
Fromm, General Friedrich, 43
Fuller, General John, 18

Gamelin, General Maurice, 61, 77–9, 82, 89

Gandhi, Mahatma, 233–4
Garibaldi, Giuseppe , 98, 174, 189, 245
GATT Agreements, 229
de Gaulle, General Charles, 78, 112–13, 155, 178–9, 180–1, 237, 243–4
General Motors, 63, 141, 226
Geneva Convention, 122
George VI, King of Britain, 19, 71, 77, 87, 147, 231, 241
George II, King of Greece, 182
German Psychiatric Institute, 46
Germany, 1–4, 12–15, 17–19, 20–4, 27–8, 30–4, 53, 56, 60, 63–4, 77–9, 80, 96–9, 105–6, 107–8, 110–11, 142, 147, 169, 172, 177, 182–3, 188–9, 193–5, 199, 207, 210, 212, 214, 225–6, 229, 231, 234, 236–7
  Anschluss, 67–8
  Air attacks on Britain, 102–3
  Atrocities, 81–4, 126, 174–5, 180, 188
  Bombing of, 104, 107, 156–9, 160
  Killing of Jews, 82–5, 132–9, 140, 164–7
  Nazi Dictatorship, 7–9, 10–11, 40–9, 50
  North Africa campaign, 111–14
  Relations with Britain, 65–9, 70–7
  Relations with Soviet Union, 115–19, 120–1
  Revolution 1918–1919, 35–6, 142, 247
  Rhineland, 61–2
  Weimar Republic, 5–7, 36–9, 40
  War and the domestic front, 143–6
  War in Italy, 147–9, 150
  War in Poland, 81–3
  War in Russia, 121–9, 130–2, 160–4
  War in the West 1940, 85–9, 90–5
  War in the West 1944–1945, 151–6
  Working class, 167–8
Gestapo, 49, 68, 73, 116, 136, 168, 170, 179
Ginsborg, Paul, 245–6
Giraud, General Henri, 112–13
Glanz, David M., 27, 123, 126
Gluckstein, Donny, 242
Goebbels, Joseph, 73, 88, 96, 137, 140, 145, 162
Goethe, 98
Gollancz, Victor, 99

Göring, Hermann, 7, 18, 41, 43, 73, 75–7, 81, 102, 120, 134, 138, 145
Gort, Lord Edmund, 79, 89, 90
Gramsci, Antonio, 10, 192
Grandi, Dino, 52, 66
Graver, John W., 214
Great Depression, 5–9, 14, 51, 56–7, 191
Greece, 9, 74, 105–6, 118, 139, 145, 148–9, 151, 169–70, 182–8, 191, 223, 225, 227, 239, 242, 244
Greenland, 34, 111
Greenwood, Arthur, 2, 87–8
Greiser, Arthur, 133
Grew, Joseph C., 210
Le Gringoire, 23
Grynszpan, Herschel, 96
Guadalcanal, Battle of, 205–6
Guderian, General Heinz, 130
Guilty Men, 1, 99–100
Gulag, 25, 124, 166–7
Guomindang, 53–5, 57–9, 60, 214–19
Gulf War, 1

Halder, General Franz, 120, 128, 134
Halifax, Lord Edward, 12, 19, 31, 62, 65–9, 70–1, 76–9, 87–8, 92–4, 97–9, 100, 103, 109
Harmsworth, Vere, 100
Harris, air Chief Marshal Arthur, 156
Harvey, A.D., 124, 166, 201, 209
Harvey, David, 30
Harvey, Oliver, 67, 91
Hatta, Mohammad, 223
Hehn, Paul N., 38, 47
Heidenreich, Richard, 135
Heinkel, 144
Henderson, Sir Neville, 65–9, 70
Henry V., 144
Hertzog, J.B.M., 231
Heydrich, Reinhardt, 49, 68, 73, 82, 85, 134, 138
Hilferding, Rudolf, 96
Hillgruber, Andreas, 166
Himmler, Heinrich, 49, 133–4, 136–9, 140, 164
von Hindenburg, Field Marshal Paul, 36, 39, 40–1, 49
Hirohito, Emperor, 210, 213
Hiroshima, 210–11

Hitler, Adolf, 1–4, 9, 10, 29, 30, 79, 80, 92–4, 98, 100–4, 107, 110, 142, 154–5, 161, 169, 170, 172–4, 178, 182, 190, 193, 195, 230–2, 236, 240–1, 246
  Anschluss, 67–8
  British policy towards, 15–19, 20–1, 65–7
  Churchill's attitude, 20
  Decision to go to war, 48–9, 50, 61, 74–8
  Defeat and suicide, 161–3
  French attitude, 22–5
  Great Depression and, 7–8, 9–11
  Jewish policy, 45–6, 113, 122, 132–9, 140, 164–7
  Invasion of France, 85–9, 90, 95–7
  Invasion of Poland, 81–5
  Invasion of Russia, 104, 115–19, 121–7
  Mussolini and, 50, 53, 105–6
  Occupation of Czechoslovakia, 68–9, 70–8
  Occupation of the Rhineland, 61–2
  Pre-war domestic policy, 41–8
  Rise to power, 35–9, 40
  Roosevelt's attitude, 31–4
  Spanish Civil War, 62–5, 115–19, 120
  Stalin's attitude, 28, 116, 119, 120–1
  Stalingrad, 127–8
  War in Russia, 129, 130–2
  Wartime domestic and economic policy, 142–6, 167–8
Hitler Youth, 139, 162, 168
Hitler-Stalin Pact, 82, 85–6, 116, 118–19, 168–9, 195, 241
Hoare, Samuel, 31, 52, 70, 91, 99
Hobsbawm, Eric 2, 178
Ho Chi Minh, 220–1
von Hohenlone, Prince Max, 98
Holland, 8, 35, 90, 97, 155, 169, 199, 207, 212
Holland, Robert
Holocaust, 1, 4, 132–9, 140, 164–7
  Croatia, 106
  Italy, 149–50
  Origins, 122, 124, 132–8
Home, Sir Alex Douglas (Lord Dunglass), 87, 91
Home Army (Poland), 171–2
Home Guard, 101, 162

Hoover, Herbert, 6
Höss, Rudolf, 133–4, 138
Horne, Alastair, 22, 61, 86, 238
House, Jonathan, 27, 123, 126
Hoxha, Enver, 191–2
Hukbalahap, 223, 243
Hull, Cordell, 9, 31, 97, 226
L'Humanite, 86
Hungary, 37, 118, 74, 121, 135, 138, 160–1, 183, 187–8, 225

Ickes, Harold I., 141–2
Imphal-Kohima, Battle of, 204, 208
India, 3, 13–14, 16, 21, 54–6, 58, 74, 87, 106, 109, 113, 117, 194, 199, 200–1, 204, 207–8, 226, 230–5, 237, 239, 243
Indonesia, 199, 201, 223–4, 230
International Monetary Fund, 229
International Trade Organisation, 229
Ioannou, Giorgos, 139
Iran, 15, 79, 107, 132, 192, 227–8, 230, 236
Iraq, 1, 13, 15, 79, 106, 226–8, 231, 236
Ironside, General Edmund, 101
Ismay, Lord Hastings, 92
Israel, 138, 237
Italy, 6, 12–13, 16–17, 20–2, 31–2, 61, 63, 66, 74, 92–3, 98, 106, 113, 118, 132, 146, 148–9, 150–1, 153, 156, 162–3, 167, 169, 170–1, 181, 183, 184, 187–9, 190–1, 193, 194–5, 213, 225–6, 233, 236–7, 239, 242–7
   Anti Jewish laws and violence, 52–3
   Axis, 60, 67
   Fascism, 9, 50–3
   Invasion, 113, 148–9, 173
   Resistance, 173–7
   Spanish Civil War, 63–4
   Strikes, 148, 167, 173
ITMA, 146–7

Jackson, Julian, 22–3, 86, 95, 177
Japan
   Atrocities, 212
Je suis partout, 23, 86, 95
Jinnah, Mohammad Ali, 234
Jodl, General Alfred, 102, 136, 164
Johnson, Chalmers, 59
Jones, Thomas, 18

Jowitt, William, 88
J.P. Morgan Bank, 15
Junkers, 144
Jutland, Battle of, 111

Kataoka, Tetsuya, 60
Kehrl, Hans 43
Kennan, George F., 229
Kennedy, Joseph, 75–6, 91
Keppler, Wilhelm, 43
Kershaw, Ian, 43, 117, 133
Kesselring, Field Marshal Albert, 174–6
Kim Il-sung, 220
King, Admiral Ernest, 184
Kingsley Wood, Sir Howard, 73, 77
Kirdof, Emil, 46
Kirov, Sergei, 26
Knox, Frank, 34
Knudsen, William, 141
Koch, Erich, 133
Koestler, Arthur, 248
Kolko, Gabriel, 170, 172–4, 181, 187, 211, 216, 225, 227, 245
Konoye, Prince, 194, 209
Konev, Marshal Ivan, 162
Korea, 55, 57–8, 194, 207, 211–13, 219, 220, 224–5, 230
Kouhona, Yeo, 237
Krauch, Carl, 43
Kristallnacht, 46, 73, 96
Krupp von Bohlen und Halbach, Alfried, 44
Krupps, 77, 144, 182
Kulmhof, 138
Kursk, 130–2
Kutusov, Mikhail, 124

Labour Party, 1–2, 14–15, 19, 66, 70, 72–3, 87–8, 93–4, 98–9, 101, 103, 108, 110, 121, 142, 146–7, 169, 222, 226–7, 232–3, 235
Langhein, Hermann, 165
Lapping. Brian, 236
de La Rocque, Francois, 22
Latvia, 75, 116
Laval, Pierre, 45, 52, 96
League of Nations, 20, 28–9, 41, 52, 58, 74, 76, 83, 226
Lebensraum, 38, 43–4, 66, 76, 104
Lemay, General Curtis, 209, 211

INDEX

Lend-Lease, 109, 129, 130, 226
Lenin, Vladimir, 25, 28,179, 240, 246
Levy, James, 13
Leyte Gulf, Battle of, 207–8
Libya, 51, 53, 104–7, 111, 231, 236
Lin Biao, 59
Linlithgow, Lord Victor, 233–4
Lithuania, 25, 75, 116, 136
The Life and Times of Colonel Blimp, 146
Lloyd George, David, 9, 13–14, 16, 18
Lloyd, Lord George, 78
Locarno Treaty, 61
Lodge, Henry Cabot, 29–30
Londonderry, Lord Charles, 17–18
Longo, Luigi, 171
Lothian, Lord Philip Kerr, 18, 31, 61, 91, 98, 109, 232
Louisville courier, 108
Loustaunau-Lacau, Major Georges, 64
Luce, Henry, 228
Lublin-Majdanek, 136, 160
von Ludendorff, General Erich, 36
Luftwaffe, 41, 44, 47, 81–2, 85, 89, 90, 101–2, 107, 112, 119, 121, 129, 144, 156, 159
Luxemburg, Rosa, 38, 240, 35

MacArthur, Douglas, 201–2, 206–8, 212–13, 223
MacDonald, Ramsey, 14–15, 18, 87
Mackenzie King, William, 92
Macmillan, Harold, 73
Maginot Line, 68, 77, 82, 93, 120
Magowan, Lord, 18
Malaya, 194, 197, 199, 200, 222, 231, 242
Malayan National Liberation Army, 222
Malta, 93, 105, 146
Manchester Guardian, 76
Manchuria, 8, 16, 20, 28, 55, 57–9, 60, 195, 207, 209, 210–12, 218–19
Mandel, Ernest, 241–2, 247
Mandel, George, 94
von Manstein, Field Marshal Erich, 130
Mao ZeDong, 59, 60, 215–18, 242
Maquis, 178
Margaret, Princess, 147
Margesson, David, 99
Marshall, General George, 230
Marshall Plan, 229–30
Mason, Tim, 46–7, 50, 139, 143

Mass Observation, 101
Matsuoka, Yosuke, 194
Mazower, Mark, 166–7, 183, 186
Mauriac, François, 63
Mazower, Mark, 166–7, 183, 186
Meiji Resoration, 53–4
Mekhlis, Lev, 26
Messerschmitt, 144
Metaxas, General Ioannis, 182, 186, 239
Mexico, 31, 54, 225, 228
MI5, 73, 228
Midway, Battle of, 205
Milch, Erhard, 41
Milice française, 178
Minin, Kuzina, 124
Michell, General William, 156
Mihailovic, General Dragoljub, 189, 190
Mitsubishi, 54–5, 57, 202
Mitsui, 55, 57–8
Mobutu, Sese Seko, 230
Molotov, Vyacheslav, 75, 115–18, 125–6, 186, 218
Monte Cassino, 149
Montgomery, Field Marshal Bernard, 107, 112, 154–5, 164
Morgenthau, Henry, 31, 109
Morocco, 62, 112–13
Morrison, Herbert, 88, 103
Mosley, Sir Oswald, 86, 94, 147, 231, 241
Mosaddeq, Mohammad, 228
Mottistone, Lord John Seely, 78
Mountbatten, Lord Louis, 100
Mount Temple, Lord, 18
Mouvement Réublicain Populaire, 244
Muslim League, 234
Mussolini, Benito, 10, 15, 31, 36, 49, 61, 67, 71, 73, 76, 78–9, 82, 92–3, 139, 167–8, 170, 182, 187, 191–2, 228, 236, 239, 240
  Alliance with Hitler, 53
  British admirers 16–17, 19, 20
  Dictatorship, 51–2
  Execution, 163
  Invasion of Ethiopia, 52
  Italian Resistance, 173–6, 179, 189
  Military leadership, 105–6, 146, 148–9, 150
  Path to Power, 50–1
  Spanish Civil War, 62–4
Ustashi, 188

Müller, Hermann, 38
Müller, Klaus-Jürgen, 45
Munich
  Putsch, 36
  Summit, 45, 63–5, 69, 71–6, 80, 92, 115

Nagasaki, 210–11
Nagy, Kosta, 190
Nahas Pasha, 236
Nasser, Gamal Abdel, 186, 236
NATO, 1, 229–0
Nazis, 1–4, 7, 17, 19, 33, 143, 61, 66, 68, 70, 79, 81, 83, 85, 96, 98, 124, 126, 142, 145, 163, 166, 168–9, 174, 188, 192, 215, 231, 240–1, 243
  Dictatorship, 41–9, 50
  Genocide, 117, 122, 125, 132, 134–6
  Rise to Power, 10–11, 28, 39, 40–1
Nehru, Jawaharlal, 232–3
Neutrality Act, 31, 63
Nevsky, Alexander, 124
New Deal, 7, 228
New York Times, 196, 243
New Zealand, 56, 194, 199, 205, 233
Ngo Van, 221
NKVD, 26, 125, 127
Nicolson, Harold, 64, 98
Night of the Long Knives, 41–2
Nimitz, Admiral, Admiral Chester, 206–7, 212
Nolte, Ernst, 166
Norman Montagu, 42
Norway, 79, 86–7, 97
Norwich, John Julius, 100

October Revolution, 9, 24–5, 51, 166, 124, 247
Office of Strategic Services, 171, 176, 190, 223
Oil
  Germany, 8, 14, 38, 43, 48, 116, 119, 157
  Hungary, 161
  Japan, 56, 195–7, 207, 229
  Iran, 228
  Iraq, 231, 236
  Latin America, 15
  Middle East, 8, 15, 21, 106, 214, 227
  Romania, 48, 97, 116, 123, 145, 160

  South East Asia, 193, 201, 208
  Soviet Union, 79, 116, 119, 127
  Spain, 63
  United States, 141–2, 196
Olivier, Laurence, 146
Operation Overlord, 114, 152–3
Oranienburg, 144
Orwell, George, 101
Ossewa Brandwag, 231
Overy, Richard, 26, 117, 163
OVRA, 170

Pahlavi, Shah Mohammad Reza, 107, 228, 230
Pahlavi, Shah Reza, 107, 236
Palestine, 106, 237
von Papen, Franz, 7, 28, 39, 40, 42, 47
Patton, General George S., 154–5
Paul, Prince of Yugoslavia, 188
Von Paulus, Field Marshal Friedrich, 128–9
Pavelic, Ante, 106, 188
Pearl Harbor, 30, 34, 110, 125, 141, 196, 198–9, 200–2, 204, 212, 225
Percival, General Arthur, 200–1
Perry, Commandant Matthew C., 53
Pesce, Giovanni, 171
Pétain, Marshal Philippe, 22, 64, 89, 94–6, 98, 112, 117, 179, 241
Peter II, King of Yugoslavia, 188
Le Petit Parisien, 86
Peukert, Detlev J.K., 44, 143, 168
Philippines, 8, 29, 30, 193–4, 197, 199, 201, 206–8, 222–3, 225, 243
Phillips, Sir Frederick, 15
Phoney war, 79, 85–6
Piratin, Phil, 103
Pirelli, Alberto, 52, 139
Pirow, Oswald, 231
Pleiger, Paul, 43
Poland, 2–4, 9, 28, 48, 69, 72, 74–8, 81–6, 89, 107, 115–19, 132–4, 136–40, 145, 148, 160, 163, 166, 168, 171–2, 185, 225, 239, 242
Ponting, Clive, 19, 90, 151
Pope, James S., 108
Popular Front, 15
  Communist Strategy, 170
  France, 2, 23–4, 42, 63–5, 79, 241
  Spain, 9–10, 42, 79, 62, 95–6, 241

Portugal, 31, 63, 79, 114, 239
Potemkin, Vladimir, 72
Pozharski, Dimitri, 124
Pravda, 26, 28
Priestley, J.B., 100, 147
Prytz, Björn, 97

Ranfurly Plunkett-Ernle-Erle-Drax, Sir Reginald Aylmer, 75
Rape of Nanjing, *Rassemblement du Peuple Français*, 181
Rashid Ali, 236
Rassemblement du Peuple Français, 181
Readers Digest, 228
Red Army, 9, 12, 27–9, 82, 116–18, 120–2, 125–7, 137, 152, 155, 160, 161, 166–7, 183, 191, 195, 211, 219–20
  Berlin, 163–4
  German invasion, 121
  Killing of Red Army prisoners, 138, 164–5
  Kursk, 130–2
  Losses, 123, 163
  Purges, 26–7
  Soviet-Finnish War, 117
  Stalingrad, 127, 129
  Warsaw Uprising, 171–2
Reichsbank, 7, 37, 42
Rex Party, 181
Rhineland
  French Occupation, 27, 137
  German Occupation, 61–2
  von Ribbentrop, Joachim, 18, 62, 67, 75, 115–16, 118, 126
Roberts, Andrew, 77
Rodogno, David, 106
Rokossovsky, Marshal Konstantin, 124
Rol-Tanguy, Colonel, 171
Roma, 46, 132, 138, 167
Romania, 37–8, 48, 75, 97, 116, 118, 121, 123, 128, 135–6, 145, 151, 160, 187
Rommel Field Marshal Erwin, 95, 106–7, 111–13
Roosevelt Franklin, 7, 9, 16, 30–4, 63, 91–2, 100, 104, 108–9, 110, 112–13, 132, 141, 145, 151–2, 155, 162–3, 172–3, 190, 193, 195–7, 207–8, 210, 218–19, 221, 225–8, 232, 236, 239, 240, 242
Roosevelt, Theodore, 30
Roosevelt, Theodore, 30
Rosenberg, Alfred, 122, 138
Rossanda, Rossana, 150
Rothermere, Lord Harold, 16–18, 100
Roussin, Rene, 147
Roxas, Manuel, 223
Royal Air Force, 21, 23, 77
  RAF Bomber Command, 156, 111
Royal Navy, 13, 17, 23, 32, 35, 62, 71, 81, 90, 101, 106, 111, 200
Russo Japanese War (1905), 196, 55
Rusk, Dean, 219

SA (Sturmabteilung), 39, 41
Sachsenhausen, 144
Saddam Hussein, 1–2
Salazar, Antonio, 79
Salerno, 149
Salisbury, Lord Robert Gascoyne-Cecil, 87
Sato, Major General Kenryo, 197
Saudi Arabia, 15, 227
Saxon, Timothy D., 56
Schacht, Hjalmar, 7, 40–2, 46
Schmidt, Paul, 66, 71
von Schleicher, Kurt, 28, 39, 40–1
Schuschnigg, Kurt, 67
Serbia, 1, 184, 188–9, 191
Shang-K'un, Yang, 60
Shehu, Mehmet, 171
Sidi el Barrani, 105
Siemens, 38, 144
Simon, Sir John, 70
Sinclair, Sir Archibald, 73, 93
Singapore, 56, 111, 199, 200–1, 208–9, 212, 233
Skoda, 68, 70
Smuts, Jan, 231–2
Sobibor, 138, 161, 164
South Africa, 109, 231
Spain, 10, 18, 27, 29, 43, 52, 61–4, 67, 69, 77–9, 80, 89, 91, 181, 222, 239
Spanish Civil War, 2, 10, 27, 72, 171, 178
Spears, General Edward, 23, 237
Special Operations Executive, 171, 176, 183, 192

Speer, Albert, 140, 144–6, 187
Sri Lanka, 3, 235
SS (Schutzstaffel), 41–4, 46, 49, 96, 106,
    113, 132–9, 140, 145, 155, 161,
    164–9, 172, 178, 180–1, 192
Stalin, Josef, 4, 8, 10, 21, 25–6, 72, 74,
    77–9, 80,-82, 85–5, 103, 119, 124,
    125–7, 130, 132, 146, 150, 152, 155,
    160, 162–4, 170–3, 175, 184,-187,
    189, 192, 195, 207, 210–12, 214,
    218–19, 226, 239, 242–4, 246–7
  Invasion June 1941, 120–2
  Purges, 26–7, 118, 124
  Hitler, 28, 75, 104, 115, 117, 119, 12
  Terror, 166–7
  Yalta, 163–4
  Yugoslavia, 190–1
Stalingrad, 46, 127,-129, 132, 140, 163,
    169, 191
Standard Oil, 43, 63, 142
Von Stauffenberg, Colonel Claus, 168
Stavka, 121, 128, 251
Stella Rossa Brigade,, 174
Sterling Bloc, 6, 8, 109, 228
Stilwell, General Joseph, 208, 215
Stimson, Henry, 33–4, 151, 211
Stinnes, Edmund, 37
Strasser Gregor, 40, 42
Stresemann, Gustav, 27, 37–8
Studebaker, 63
von Stulpnagel, Lieutenant Colonel
    Joachim, 45
Stutthof, 161, 165
Sudetenland, 63, 68–9, 70, 72, 168
Suez Canal, 52, 74, 104–5, 186
Sugiyama, Marshal Hajime, 196
Suharto, Haji Muhammad, 230
Sumitomo, 55
Sun Yat-Sen, 54
Suvarov, Alexander, 124
Sweden, 86, 98, 124, 209
Switzerland, 97–8, 176
Syria, 79, 89, 106, 236–7

Taiwan, 55, 57, 206–7
Taylor, Jay, 58
Teschen, 69, 72
Texaco, 63
Thälmann, Ernst, 75
Thatcher, Margaret, 87, 100

Thierack, Otto Georg, 138
Thomas, Major-General George 48, 64
Thomas, Hugh, 64, 170
Thorez, Maurice, 86, 94, 170, 180–1,
    243–4
Thyssen, Fritz, 7, 37, 40–1, 44
Tiarks, F.C., 18
Time, 7, 190, 211
The Times, 17, 18, 69, 70–1
Tito, Joseph Broz, 171, 188–9, 190–2,
    242, 244
Tobruk, 111, 113
Togliatti, Palmiro, 170, 175–6, 245–7
Tojo, General Hideki, 194, 196–7, 202,
    209
Tonypandy, 3
Tooze, Adam, 42, 143, 144, 146
Treaty of Rapallo, 27–8
Treblinka, 138, 161, 164
Trenchard, Viscount Hugh, 21, 156
Tripartite Pact, 60, 116, 118, 195
Trotsky, Leon, 8, 10, 12, 24–5, 35,
    239–41, 247–8
Trotsky, Leon, 8, 10, 12, 24–5, 35,
    239–41, 247–8
Trotskyists, 179, 221
Truman, Harry, 32, 163, 210–11, 219,
    221, 229–30
Tsuyoshi, Inukai, 58
Tukhachevsky, Mikhail, 26–8, 46
Tunisia, 113
Turkey, 9, 13, 15, 51, 79, 118
Turner, General Harald, 188

United Nations, 226
United Nations Relief and Rehabilitation
    Administration, 235
United Steel Trust, 37
USA, 1, 4–5, 11, 16, 22, 27, 42, 60, 63,
    100, 104, 112, 115, 124–5, 129, 146,
    224, 225
  Britain and, 13–16, 67, 74, 91–2, 104,
    107–9, 110, 142, 151, 184, 232–3
  Imperialism, 8–9, 29, 30–1, 225–9, 230
  Invasion of Europe, 150–5, 160
  China and, 55, 57, 214–15, 218
  Division of Europe, 187–8
  France and, 179–80
  Germany and, 32–4, 37, 104, 110
  Japan and, 43–4, 56, 195–7

Korea and, 218–19
Middle East oil, 227–8
Philippines, 222–3
Pacific War, 199, 200–9, 210–13
Russia and, 130–2, 163–4, 170, 172
USAAF, 158–9, 172, 209
  Bombing of Japan, 202, 208–9, 211
  USAAF Bomber Command, 209
USSR, 4, 9, 10, 11, 13, 17–18, 32, 35, 43, 45, 48, 51, 63–4, 68–9, 77, 79, 80–1, 103, 107, 112, 134–9, 143, 148, 155, 220, 225, 228–9, 230, 236, 246
  Anglo-American alliance, 150–2
  Battle of Kursk, 130–2
  Battle of Moscow, 125–6
  Capture of Berlin, 160–4
  China and, 195, 214–15, 218–19, 242
  Foreign policy, 27–8, 170, 187, 226
  German alliance, 72–3, 74–5, 82, 85, 115–19
  Invasion of, 104–5, 119, 120–3
  Japan and, 28–9, 54–6, 58, 60–1, 193, 196, 207, 210–12
  Policy towards Poland, 171–2
  Stalin dictatorship, 8–9, 24–7, 123–4, 126–9, 130, 144, 166–7
  Soviet-Finnish war, 79, 117
  Stalingrad, 127–8
  Yugoslavia and, 189, 190–1, 242, 244
Ustashi, 53, 106, 145, 188

Vanderberg, Senator Arthur, 169
Vasilevskii General Aleksandr, 128
Vatican, 139, 176
Veloukhiotis, Aris, 185
Vereinigte Glanzstoff-Fabriken, 38
Vereinigte Stahlwerke, 37–9, 41
Versailles Treaty, 5, 7, 28, 36, 45, 61, 66, 82, 139, 191
Vestag, 144
Vichy, 86, 95–6, 100, 106, 112–13, 169, 177–9, 181, 195, 220–1, 236–7, 244
Victor Emmanuel, King of Italy, 51, 148, 175
Vidussoni, Aldo, 139
Vienna Uprising, 9–10, 67
Vietnam, 220–2, 225, 230, 242
Vietminh, 221
Vlaams Nationaal Verbond (VNV), 181

Voegler, Dr Albert, 41
Volkssturm, 162, 165
Voroshilov, Marshal Kliment, 115, 152
Vorster, B.J., 231

Wall Street, 14, 30
  Crash, 5–6, 8, 14, 27, 37
Warsaw Ghetto Uprising, 164
Warsaw Uprising, 171–3
Washington Post, 228
Waugh, Evelyn, 106
Wedemeyer, Lieutenant General Albert C., 33–4, 151, 211
The Week, 103
Wehrmacht, 43, 61, 76, 82, 88–9, 105–6, 118, 121, 123, 125, 127, 130, 133–6, 139, 148, 151, 160–1, 165, 168, 172, 174, 182, 236
Weimar Republic, 27–8, 36, 37, 40, 44, 46
Weinberg, Gerhard L., 212
Weizmann, Chaim, 237
Weygand, General Maxine, 64, 89, 94
White, Nicholas J., 57
Widelin, Paul, 179
Wilson, Sir Horace, 17, 75
Wilson, Woodrow, 29–30
Wintringham, Tom, 100
Wisliceny, Dieter, 138
Wolff, Otto, 37
Wohltat, Dr Helmut, 75
World Bank, 229
World trade Organisation, 229

Yalta, 163, 185, 191, 218–19, 232, 244
Yamamoto, Admiral Isoroku, 197, 205
Yasuda, 55
Yoshida, Zengo, 194
Young Plan, 27, 37
Yugoslavia, 9, 37–8, 51, 105–6, 118, 149, 169, 185, 188–9, 190–2, 225, 242, 244

Zachariadis, Nikos, 170
Zaibatsu, 55, 57–8, 202
Zaire, 230
Zedong, Mao, 59–60, 215–18, 242
Zhukov, Field Marshal Georgi, 28–9, 119, 125, 127–9, 132, 160, 162
Zog, King Ahmet, 191
Zoreetti, Ludovic, 63

Lightning Source UK Ltd.
Milton Keynes UK
UKHW010628180820
368416UK00001B/19